MILTON'S BRIEF EPIC

A BROWN UNIVERSITY
BICENTENNIAL PUBLICATION

MILTON'S BRIEF EPIC

THE GENRE, MEANING, AND ART OF
Paradise Regained

BARBARA KIEFER LEWALSKI

PROVIDENCE, RHODE ISLAND
BROWN UNIVERSITY PRESS
LONDON
METHUEN & CO LTD
1966

First published in Great Britain, 1966
by Methuen & Co Ltd
11 New Fetter Lane, London EC4

Printed in the United States of America

This book was designed by David Ford.
It was set in 12 point Linotype Granjon type,
printed, and bound by Kingsport Press, Inc.

FOR KEN

PREFACE

*T*HIS BOOK is something of a hybrid, a combination of basic research and criticism. Its fundamental aim is critical: to attempt a just interpretation and evaluation of Milton's most perplexing and least appreciated major poem. But the reader may well feel that the path to this goal winds through "mazes intricate/ Eccentric, intervolv'd" of recondite literary and theological lore. This is so because much of the material necessary to illuminate important aspects of *Paradise Regained* has not yet been investigated, and the reader must judge whether the study of it provides, as I believe it does, a more adequate basis for understanding the poem.

The starting point is the vexed question of genre. Most Miltonists agree that the conventions of genre are of first importance in analyzing a Miltonic poem, but we have no history of the genre to which *Paradise Regained* apparently belongs, the biblical "brief" epic, and no comprehensive study of the tradition behind Milton's designation of the Book of Job as a model of that form. The first part of this book surveys these areas. The account of the biblical epic and its characteristic features, and of the theory of Job as an epic, will have some independent interest for the literary historian, but they appear here as an indispensable preliminary to the discussion (centered in chapter v) of how Milton has used and reworked the conventions of genre in this poem.

The analysis of theme and action, the concern of Part Two, also builds upon an investigation of some important background materials. A reconsideration of Milton's Christology and its sources helps to determine the scope of action and the kind of character development possible to the hero of *Paradise Regained*. An investigation of the typological interpretations traditionally accorded to the Old Testament and classical heroes mentioned in the poem reveals Milton's special use of typology both to extend the epic scope and to intensify the dramatic action of the poem. A study of the traditional biblical exegesis of Christ's temptation in the wilderness helps to explain the meaning and ramifications of this episode as Milton has adapted it. Finally, an examination of some Renaissance rhetorical figures which occur frequently in the poem sheds light upon its style and texture. The central argument of this book, which I believe to be substantiated by these investigations, is that *Paradise Regained* is conceived as Milton's brief epic, and merits that designation in all its aspects.

My debts are great, as is my gratitude for the help so generously proffered from so many sources. Milton students will be aware, as I am, of how much this study owes to earlier scholarship and criticism of *Paradise Regained,* and of Milton generally, which cannot be acknowledged here. I owe a particular debt to Professor Ernest Sirluck who taught me much of what I know of Milton and who criticized the manuscript with his customary combination of rigor and kindness. Special thanks are also due to Professor Irene Samuel whose perceptive and painstaking criticism has made this a better book than it would otherwise have been, both by calling attention to errors and by stimulating me to argue more closely those points upon which we disagree. I want to thank many colleagues at Brown who responded generously to calls upon their various special competencies, especially Professor Leicester Bradner who brought his wide knowledge of the Renaissance and of neo-Latin literature to bear upon several of my difficulties and who also criticized the manuscript. Professor Wendell Dietrich read chapter vi and offered helpful suggestions from a theologian's special vantage point, and Professor John Workman and Dr. Laura Durand checked several of my translations.

An AAUW postdoctoral fellowship in 1961–62 and two Brown University summer stipends made possible the research for this study at the British Museum, and an additional grant from Brown helped to defray the cost of preparing the manuscript for publication. The library staffs of the British Museum, the Bibliothèque Nationale, the Houghton Library, and the Brown University libraries offered much assistance in the search for materials. Grant Dugdale and Anne Joseph, of the Brown University Press, gave the manuscript painstaking editorial care; Toni Beckwith prepared the index. The editors of *Studies in Philology* permitted me to include some of the material which appeared in my article, "Theme and Structure in *Paradise Regained*" (*SP*, LVII, 1960). Such errors as remain after so much kind assistance are entirely my own responsibility.

My greatest debt—for interest and encouragement, for generous help with many historical problems, and especially for that constant "solace and satisfaction of the mind" which Milton knew to be of the essence of marriage—is recognized where it ought to be, in the dedication.

CONTENTS

Part Three · The Art of the Poem

PART ONE · THE GENRE

ILTON's *Paradise Regained* presents in four books, 2,070 blank verse lines, the story of Christ's temptation in the wilderness, narrated by the Synoptic Gospels in a few short verses (Matt. iv:1–11, Mark i:12–13, Luke iv:1–13). Since the poem presents Christ's three major temptations according to the sequence in Luke rather than that in Matthew, and since Luke provides some warrant for conceiving of additional temptations as well, it is evident that Luke's version is the poem's principal biblical source. The narrative in Luke reads:

And Jesus being full of the holy Ghost, returned from Jordane, and was led by the Spirit into the wildernesse,

Being fourty dayes tempted of the devill, and in those daies he did eat nothing: and when they were ended, hee afterward hungred.

And the devill said unto him, If thou be the Sonne of God, command this stone that it be made bread.

And Jesus answered him, saying, It is written, that man shall not live by bread alone but by every word of God.

And the devil taking him up into an hie mountaine, shewed unto him all the kingdomes of the world in a moment of time.

And the devill said unto him, All this power will I give thee, and the glory of them: for that is delivered unto me, and to whomsoever I will, I give it.

If thou therefore wilt worship me, all shall be thine.

And Jesus answered and said unto him, Get thee behind me, Satan: for it is written, Thou shalt worship the Lord thy God, and him onely shalt thou serve.

And he brought him to Hierusalem, and set him on a pinacle of the Temple, and said unto him, If thou be the Son of God, cast thy selfe downe from hence.

For it is written, Hee shall give his Angels charge over thee, to keepe thee.

And in their hands they shall beare thee up, lest at any time thou
dash thy foote against a stone.

And Jesus answering, said unto him, It is said, Thou shalt not tempt
the Lord thy God.

And when the devill had ended all the temptation, he departed
from him for a season.[1]

But Milton's narrative is very much more than an expansion
of the Gospel story by means of additional incidents and
temptations: it is designed to include and evaluate, through
the brilliant, complex arguments of Christ and Satan about
the meaning and implications of the temptations offered, the
fundamental values, heroic ideals, conceptions of duty, and
standards of personal excellence which derive from the
Classical-Judaeo-Christian heritage.

The design has not evoked widespread critical enthusi-
asm. Many readers complain about the static plot, about
the lack of tension resulting from the perfection and passivity of the hero, and especially about the "cold and negative" renunciations whereby Christ appears to consign to
the Devil the chief blessings of this world, including, rather
surprisingly, classical learning and poetry.[2] Such complaints
are often based upon invidious comparisons which take the
poem as a manifestly inferior sequel to the great epic, or
in W. B. C. Watkins' terms, as "more a postscript to *Paradise
Lost* than a sequel."[3] The comparative approach finds some
sanction in Milton's apparent invitation to comparison in
the opening lines of *Paradise Regained,* in Thomas Ellwood's
probably apocryphal story about suggesting the subject
"Paradise Found" to Milton as a necessary complement to
his *Paradise Lost,* and in Edward Phillips' report that Milton's contemporaries, to the author's great annoyance, compared *Paradise Regained* unfavorably to his long epic.[4]

However, the difficulties attending such comparisons point
directly to the unresolved question about the poem's genre,

for with classical writers such as Milton the established conventions of genre go far to control our approaches to and our expectations from a literary work. Such generic conventions were usually respected by Milton: he is the kind of artist who does not discard old wineskins but stretches them somehow, making them fit to contain his heady new wine. His Pegasus does not display the romantic tendency to kick over the generic traces, but on the other hand it does not trot tamely in beaten paths. *Lycidas* achieves a profundity unmatched in any other pastoral elegy, *Comus* has much more dramatic action, characterization, and dialogue than any other masque, *Paradise Lost* develops an epic subject of quite unprecedented universality and scope, and much of the art of these poems inheres precisely in the tension between the new matter and the old forms. Characteristically, Milton's tremendous creative energy modifies and transforms the genres he uses, making them adequate to sustain new demands, while his profound respect for order and discipline in art as in life preserves most of the formal traditions appropriate to each kind.

The importance of approaching a Miltonic poem in terms of its generic tradition is widely recognized, but the category into which Milton appears to place *Paradise Regained* has seemed to many readers wildly inappropriate. It seems obvious enough that the work is set forth as an epic. Many of its formal elements—proposition, invocation, infernal and supernal councils, military pageants—are standard epic features. The epic proposition suggests not only that the poem is a sequel to *Paradise Lost,* but even that it treats a vastly more noble and heroic subject:

> I who erewhile the happy Garden sung,
> By one man's disobedience lost, now sing
> Recover'd Paradise to all mankind,

By one man's firm obedience fully tried
Through all temptation, and the Tempter foil'd
In all his wiles, defeated and repuls't,
And *Eden* rais'd in the waste Wilderness. (I.1–7) [5]

Moreover, in diction and form these lines echo the verses, now widely accepted as genuine, which introduce the *Aeneid* in most Renaissance editions, supposedly announcing Virgil's movement from pastoral and georgic to epic subject:

I am he who once piped a song on a slender reed,
And then, quitting the woods, compelled the nearby fields
To provide amply for the greedy tiller of the soil—a work
Welcome to farmers: But now of Mars' bristling.
Arms and the man I sing . . . [6]

By this echo of Virgil's lines and by the allusion to *Paradise Lost* as a poem about a "happy Garden," Milton seems to imply that he also has now graduated from pastoral apprentice work to the true epic subject, the warfare and victory of Christ.

But despite such evidences of Miltonic intention, most readers have felt with E. M. W. Tillyard that the poem "is not an epic, it does not try to be an epic, and it must not be judged by any kind of epic standard." [7] Accordingly, it has been variously regarded as moral allegory, as ecclesiastical allegory, as "closet drama with a prologue and stage directions," as psychological drama staged in the hero's mind, as rhetorical argument "nearer in genre to Dryden's *Religio Laici* than . . . to *Paradise Lost,*" and, most recently, as a formal meditation on the Gospel account of Christ's temptation. [8]

This radical disagreement about the kind of poem Milton has written invites the supposition that it may be a kind now virtually unknown to the modern reader, and the supposition is supported by the puzzling comment on brief epic and the Book of Job in Milton's *Reason of Church Government* (1642). In that work Milton cites biblical as well as classical models of the great literary kinds as he considers whether he should attempt

that Epick form whereof the two poems of *Homer,* and those other two of *Virgil* and *Tasso* are a diffuse, and the book of *Job* a brief model . . . Or whether those Dramatick constitutions, wherein *Sophocles* and *Euripides* raigne shall be found more doctrinal and exemplary to a Nation, the Scripture also affords us a divine pastoral Drama in the Song of *Salomon* consisting of two persons and a double *Chorus,* as *Origen* rightly judges. And the Apocalyps of Saint *John* is the majestick image of a high and stately Tragedy, shutting up and intermingling her solemn Scenes and Acts with a sevenfold *Chorus* of halleluja's and harping symphonies: and this my opinion the grave autority of *Pareus* commenting that booke is sufficient to confirm. Or if occasion shall lead to imitat those magnifick Odes and Hymns wherein *Pindarus* and *Callimachus* are in most things worthy, some others in their frame judicious, in their matter most an end faulty: But those frequent songs throughout the law and prophets beyond all these, not in their divine argument alone, but in the very critical art of composition may be easily made appear over all the kinds of Lyrick poesy, to be incomparable.[9]

There is some justice in W. R. Parker's observation that these early, tentative speculations more than twenty-five years prior to the publication of the great poems can hardly be regarded as definite predictions of them,[10] yet neither can the passage be dismissed as irrelevant to Milton's later work, for its terms are repeated in his subsequent references to the great forms and their models. In *Paradise Regained* itself Christ offers a similar derogatory comparison of the lyric poetry of Greece to that of the Bible, and the preface to *Samson Agonistes* again links together the Greek tragedians and the Book of Revelation as examples of tragedy.

The inference is that throughout his life Milton thought of the genres much as he did in 1642. So it may not be unreasonable to chase further a hare that has often been started, the hypothesis that *Paradise Regained* is Milton's effort to write a "brief epic" on the Jobean model.

Investigation of the poem in terms of this Miltonic comment leads to two lines of inquiry: (1) What criteria and what traditions of interpretation have led Milton to regard Job as a brief epic and as a model for other attempts in this kind? (2) What evidence is there to support the designation of the biblical brief epic as a special literary category with distinctive characteristics? An attempt to answer these questions through a study of traditional ideas about biblical epic must naturally avoid the use of rigid criteria to define epic, whether neoclassical standards for the form derived from Virgilian structure and style, or qualities of the so-called epic spirit such as Tillyard's five touchstones—high quality and high seriousness, amplitude, control, heroic impression, and choric quality.[11] Rather, a study of the conception of the genre must consider a large and representative body of shorter biblical poems, however wretchedly executed, which lay claim to epic status.

No effort will be made to demonstrate Milton's probable or possible acquaintance with all the Jobean commentaries, the treatises on biblical style, or the would-be epics mentioned here, although it is a fair enough assumption that his astonishing range of learning encompassed many of them. What is important is not specific indebtedness to this or that text, but rather the existence and pervasiveness of certain literary and exegetical traditions which Milton, like other educated men of his time, could not help encountering in one form or another. This line of investigation points to a long tradition of Jobean exegesis and comment, and also to a long tradition of theory and practice relating to the brief biblical epic, both of which furnished assumptions, materials, and methods to Milton's hand. But, characteristically, he has produced from them something unique, the crowning achievement of the kind.

CHAPTER II · JOB AS EPIC: THE
EXEGETICAL AND LITERARY TRADITION

*M*ILTON's reference to Job as an epic, and specifically as the model for a brief epic, stems from a tradition which flourished from patristic times through the seventeenth century.[1] The chief sources of this tradition are the harmonistics which sought to relate biblical and classical literature, and the heroic cast of much Jobean exegesis. The literary products of this tradition are a number of poems with epic features on the subject of Job, and several epic-like poems on other subjects obviously imitating the structure of the Book of Job.

BIBLICAL POETICS AND THE "EPIC" OF JOB

In the first Christian centuries the often recurring problem of how to relate, compare, or harmonize the highly respected but pagan tradition of classical letters with the literature of the Bible and its true revelation gave rise to a "biblical poetics," by means of which classically educated Hebrew and Christian writers demonstrated the Bible's beauty and worth by presenting it as an analogue, and sometimes even as the source, of classical learning and literature. Josephus, Clement of Alexandria, and later Isidore of Seville were among those who asserted that the Greeks had derived much of their ethical and political theory as well as their other disciplines from Moses and the Hebrews, and Jerome spoke of the biblical books as compendiums of all knowledge.[2] In the Greek church especially, several of the Fathers noted resemblances between the subject matter of classical and biblical literature —the fallen angels and the giants, Samson and Hercules,

Noah's flood and Deucalion's flood—and argued that the classical myths must therefore have derived originally from the Scripture record.[3] Moreover, the Bible was said to contain, and even to have been the source of, the technical elements of classical poetry. Philo cited the song of Moses and Miriam in Exodus xv to illustrate that the Hebrews anticipated the Greeks in the use of classical meters, and Josephus, Jerome, and Eusebius of Caesarea found other such examples.[4] In addition, Jerome identified several examples of poetic texture in the Bible, Cassiodorus discovered over one hundred and twenty rhetorical figures in the Psalms alone, and both he and the Venerable Bede claimed the prior appearance in Scripture of all the figures of language and thought.[5] This biblical poetics treats Job as an analogue of the classical epic.[6]

The comparison was no doubt reinforced by the idea of the great antiquity of the Book of Job, which was thought to be among the first literary productions of mankind, its remote origins shrouded in mystery. Though modern exegesis places the work with the Hebrew Wisdom Literature in the fifth or fourth century B.C., the Syriac Bible, Jerome, and many later Christian writers located it between the Pentateuch and Joshua because of its supposed great antiquity.[7] Most commentators agreed that Job himself lived in patriarchal times before the Mosaic law was delivered, since he offered sacrifices and lived righteously without any reference to that law. Jewish tradition identified him as a Hebrew, the third in descent from Nachor, brother of Abraham; the Babylonian Talmud suggested that he was of the time of Moses but recorded some opinion that he was contemporaneous with Isaac or Jacob or Joseph.[8] Most of the Church Fathers were agreed on the matter of Job's antiquity—Origen declaring that Job was "even earlier than Moses," and Eusebius of Caesarea that he was "older than Moses himself" by two generations [9]—and some Christian commentators early and late transmitted the Hebrew theory of his descent.[10] But the dominant Christian tradition asserted, on the basis of an addition to the Greek text of the Book of Job, that Job was a gentile, and that he was identical with Jobab, king of Edom, who was five generations from Abraham in the line of Esau (Gen. xxxvi:33).[11] In the sixteenth and seventeenth centuries commentators often cited both traditions without endeavoring to decide the issue, insisting that the important fact was the very great antiquity of Job.[12]

Not only the antiquity of hero and book but also the idea of uncertain authorship and possible oral transmission served to link the Book of Job to the early folk epics of other nations. Most of the rabbinical commentators in the Babylonian Talmud ascribed the Book to Moses, and most insisted on the historicity of the story, but one rabbi described it as fiction or parable, an opinion later reiterated by Maimonides and with some modification by Luther.[13] Several Christian commentators early and late reiterated the ascription to Moses,[14] some thought Job himself wrote it,[15] and a few attributed it variously to Job's friend Elihu, to Solomon, or to a prophet.[16] But the most common theory was that ascribed to Origen, that Moses while wandering in the land of the Midianites either heard the story of Job or more probably encountered a book written by Job in Syrian, which he then translated into Hebrew to console the Israelites suffering in Egyptian captivity.[17] Many sixteenth- and seventeenth-century commentators emphasized the uncertainty of authorship by their refusal to decide among the rival traditions.[18] In the words of the Congregational minister Joseph Caryl, one of Milton's contemporaries, "Some say it was one of the Prophets, but they know not who, some ascribe it to *Solomon,* some to *Elihu,* not a few to *Job* himselfe; but most give it to *Moses* ... Onely take this, that it is conceived to be the first piece of scripture that was written." [19] J. F. Senault asserted the work's mysterious antiquity even more forcefully, terming it "the first Booke in the World." [20]

But the biblical poetics case for Job as epic turned principally upon its supposed hexameter verse form. Jerome was primarily responsible for this metrical mistake which was perpetuated for centuries after him. Jerome's preface to the *Chronicle of Eusebius* contains a reference to the Jobean hexameters in a passage comparing the meters of classical and biblical verse:

What can be more musical than the Psalter? Like the writing of our own Flaccus [Horace], and the Grecian Pindar, it now runs along in iambics, now flows in sonorous Alcaics, now swells in Sapphics, now marches in half-foot meter. What can be more lovely than the strains of Deuteronomy and Isaiah? What more elevated than Solomon? What more perfect than Job? All these were composed in hexameters and pentameters, as Josephus and Origen tell us, and so circulated among their own people. [21]

More specifically, the preface to Jerome's translation of the Book of Job calls attention to the work's "slippery" figurative language, and certifies that from chapter iii to chapter xlii, verse 6, "there are hexameter verses running in dactyl and spondee." Jerome explains, however, that this scansion is not based upon a strict syllable count: "owing to the idiom of the language other feet are frequently introduced not containing the same number of syllables but the same quantities." [22] In translating Job from the Hebrew, Jerome rendered these chapters as poetry. [23]

Arator (sixth century), Aldhelm (seventh century), and Albertus Magnus (thirteenth century) contain early paraphrases and restatements of Jerome's theory regarding the Jobean hexameters. [24] Later, some of the famous Renaissance defenses of poetry cite the Jobean hexameters among the several scriptural precedents justifying the writing of poetry.

In a rather surprising extension of Jerome's statement Barnabe Googe (1553) insisted that "the prophecies of Esay, the Lamentations of Jeremie, the Songs and Ballades of Solomon, the Psalter of David, and the Book of Hiob were written by the first authors in perfect and pleasaunt hexameter verses." [25] And Thomas Lodge (1579) answered the Puritan Stephen Gosson's attacks on poetry by invoking the usual patristic authorities on the subject of biblical meters:

Among the precise Jewes you shall find poetes...Beroaldus can witness with me that David was a poet, and that his vayne was in imitating (as S. Ierom witnesseth) Horace, Flaccus, and Pindarus; somtimes his verse runneth in an Iambus foote, anone he hath recourse to a Saphic vaine, and *aliquando semipede ingreditur.* Ask Josephus, and he wil tel you that Esay, Job, and Solomon voutsafed poetical practises, for (if Origen and he fault not) theyre verse was Hexameter and Pentameter.[26]

Among sixteenth- and seventeenth-century biblical commentators, Catholics such as Augustinus Steuchius and Franciscus Titelmann and Protestants such as Joannes Quistorpius, Edward Leigh, and John Trapp cited Jerome's description of the Jobean hexameters with full approval.[27] More than this, in his highly influential commentary on Job the Spanish Jesuit Joannes de Pineda cited a long list of additional authorities substantiating Jerome's opinion:

Genebrardus affirms that Moses rendered in spondaic verses the history of Job...Marius Victor...has found by experiment that the verses of the Book of Job are hexameters composed of spondees, dactyls, and other feet—trochees, iambs, and proceleumatics—running in these by the constituted rules not so much of syllable as of measure...Certainly that there is poetry in sacred Scriptures and the cultivation of song and meter by the Hebrews is agreed upon by all the holy doctors...In truth Andraeas Masius skillfully collects the poetry and knowledge of heroic song that was not wholly lost in Jerome's time...Others also have attempted with the greatest labor to recover and teach [this poetry]. See the treatise of R. David Jahaia *Of the meters of the Hebrews,* which Gilbert Genebrardus translated into Latin.[28]

Even more remarkable is the testimony of Joannes Mercerus, celebrated Calvinist commentator and Regius Professor of Hebrew at the Collège de France, to the effect that his own efforts to arrange and to scan the verses of Job confirm Jerome's statements: "I have undertaken (according to Jerome's teaching) to restore many verses to metrical measure. Indeed, I have discovered that the measures are in the greatest part hexameter: truly there with dactyls and spondees, other feet run indiscriminately, according to the idiom of the language as Jerome said." [29]

This assumption about the Jobean hexameters provided support for yet more sweeping statements about the Book's epic character. Drepanius Florus (sixth century), observing that "Job ... has sung his battles in heroic measure," implied that the Book has a heroic subject.[30] Isidore of Seville (seventh century) offered a religious definition of the term "heroic" and a defense of the epic hexameter in shorter poems, both serving to accommodate Job:

A poem is called heroic because the deeds and affairs of brave men are narrated. For men are called heroes who because of their wisdom and bravery are deemed lofty and worthy of heaven. This meter takes precedence in authority over other meters, for with its pleasantness and sweetness it is suitable for works great and small ... It is the oldest of the meters. Moses is known to have used it first in his song in Deuteronomy, long before Pherecydes and Homer.... From this also it appears that the practice of poetry was more ancient among the Hebrews than among the Gentiles, since Job, of the same period as Moses, runs in hexameter verses with dactyls and spondees.[31]

The Venerable Bede (eighth century) explicitly identified Job as the biblical counterpart of classical epic both in form and matter. Citing Job as an example of dactylic hexameter, he explained that this meter is called heroic verse because it sings "of greatest heroes, that is, of the bravest men," and may be used "both in prolix and brief works." Also, after supplying definitions and classical examples of the various poetic genres drawn from Plato and the grammarian Diomede, Bede appended biblical illustrations of each category: the dramatic kind he exemplified by Virgil's *Eclogue IX* and the Song of Songs; the narrative kind by the *Georgics,* the poems of Lucretius, the parables of Solomon, the Book of Ecclesiastes, and the Psalter; and the "mixed" or epic kind by "the *Iliad* and *Odyssey* of Homer, and the *Aeneid* of Virgil; and among us the history of blessed Job." [32] The influential commentator Rabanus Maurus (ninth century) repeated these definitions and biblical examples almost verbatim.[33] Advancing beyond the simple comparison of Job to classical epic the Greek theologian Suidas (tenth century) asserted the vast superiority of the Jobean heroic subject over that of other epics, intimating that the work is a philosophical epic uniting and surpassing the excellencies of Homer and Plato:

Job. You have here the riches of this philosopher. You have his [Job's] book, singing more sweetly than the Homeric and Platonic Muses. It neither sets forth a narration of the fabulous tales nor of the absurd calamities of boldest Achilles or most cunning Ulysses for whom slaughters are a triumph and pollutions of women are illustrious crimes; but it describes Satan conquered by one who was naked and unarmed.[34]

The Renaissance and the seventeenth century are heirs to the tradition of the heroic subject matter of Job and its resemblance to classical epic. Giovanni Battista Spagnuoli (Mantuan) cited the heroic verse of Job as precedent for his own *Parthenice Mariana* and Guillaume Du Bartas' very popular poem *Uranie* linked together the poets who sing of war with those who sing of suffering, implying that both are epic, "So *Debora* and *Judith* in the Camp;/ So *Job* and *Jeremy,* in cares oppressed." [35] Among the biblical commentators, Victorinus Strigelius elaborated upon Suidas' view of Job as philosophical epic; Gasparus Sanctius compared Job to classical epic in that the hero is a pattern of virtue, and the plot is based on true history with an admixture of fiction; Christianus Chemnitius cited Jerome and Mercerus on the Jobean hexameter and found many parallels between the opening lines of Job and those of the *Aeneid;* and Steuchius suggested an additional parallel between God's sending Satan to tempt Job and Juno's employment of Allecto.[36] Thus, some fifteen Christian centuries viewed the Book of Job as epic-like on the grounds of ancient and uncertain origin, classical epic meter, heroic subject, and certain aspects of narrative technique.

HEROIC ACTION AND EPIC DIMENSION IN JOBEAN COMMENTARY

The apparently bizarre assumption of the biblical poetics commentators that the Book of Job has a heroic subject can readily be understood in relation to an exegetical tradition beginning in patristic times and continuing through the seventeenth century, according to which Job's encounter with Satan is a heroic combat of cosmic significance involving an unparalleled hero. Modern exegesis has virtually lost contact with this tradition. Denying the textual integrity of the work, most modern commentators regard the "frame story" (chapters i, ii, and the last portion of chapter xlii) as the remnant of a very ancient folk tale, and the intervening dialogue section as a later and much more sophisticated addition. The modern interest is almost wholly in the dialogue portion where, according to Ernest Renan, Job appears "arrogant, bold, almost blasphemous." [37] Because of the dialogue form, the work is often regarded as philosophical discourse exploring various attitudes to the problem of evil and suffering, and

even more often as tragic drama.[38] Speaking to the latter
point, S. R. Driver observes:

In structure, the Book of Job is of the nature of a drama, and may
be termed a dramatic poem. Its principal parts are constructed in
the form of a dialogue; and the action which it represents passes
through successive stages of entanglement, development, and solution. The action is, however, for the most part internal and mental,
the successive scenes exhibiting the varying moods of a great soul
struggling with the mysteries of fate, rather than trying external
situations.[39]

Only those few modern writers who emphasize the frame
tale with its suggestion of a cosmic contest discern in the
work some affinities with epic.[40]

   Several features of the modern conception of Job stem from
Reformation biblical commentary, which in its turn was influenced by Hebrew exegesis. Protestant theology, emphasizing the sin and corruption of all mankind and the importance
of the spiritual struggle of the individual soul, prepared naturally enough for the focus on the Jobean dialogues as revealing Job's human frailty and the imperfections to which
even the saints are subject. The standard Protestant exegesis
of the story, appearing with minor differences in the writings
of Luther, Calvin, Beza, and many others,[41] may be summarized as follows: In chapters i and ii, Job, sustained by
the grace of God, patiently and gloriously overcomes all the
trials to which Satan has subjected him—loss of goods and
children, tormenting ulcers in his own flesh, the temptation
to blasphemy and despair posed by his wife. However, Job's
curse on the day of his birth (chap. iii), and his subsequent
rash and sinful though not actually blasphemous complaints
against God's justice throughout his dialogues with Eliphaz,
Bildad, and Zophar, constitute a fall from his former uprightness: at this time he manifests what the Geneva Bible

calls "his great imperfections in this battel between ye spirit & the flesh," or what John Trapp calls the weakness of the soul temporarily deserted by God. Job does, however, speak the truth with regard to his former uprightness and the mysterious ways of God's providence in dealing with man, while his friends, though well-meaning toward Job and pious toward God, are wrong in their opinion that God's favors and punishments in this world are exactly squared to man's deserts, and wrong also in deducing from this false premise that Job's apparent virtue must be hypocrisy. Chapter xxxii begins the resolution of the situation in the young Elihu's just estimation of Job's case: he acquits Job of earlier hypocrisy but convicts him of sin in his present questionings of God's dispensations. God, speaking from the whirlwind, confirms Elihu's argument with further demonstrations of the incomprehensibility of his ways. He forgives the repentant Job, restoring his former blessings in double measure, and he harshly censures Job's friends for their wrong doctrine, though he offers to forgive them if Job will offer sacrifice for them.

In this reading, the Job story records a fall from great material prosperity and moral righteousness, and the dialogues exhibit much dramatic tension and agonizing questioning of the universal order. However, only a few of the Protestants carried out the obvious implications of this reading and labeled the work drama or tragedy. The Anabaptists reputedly thought it tragicomedy.[42] Luther likened its form to that of Terentian comedy in that the various characters one after another dispute and argue about what is in their hearts, but he also intimated its epic quality by comparing Job and Aeneas with regard to the range of their experiences: "That Hebrew poet and master of this book, let him be who he will, has had similar *Temptations* and tribulations, has seen, experienced, and also described them. In the same way Virgil describes his dear hero Aeneas, and leads him through all waters, seas,

and shelters, making of him a fine statesman and soldier."⁴⁸
Beza, calling attention to the dialogue form of Job, developed
a structural analysis of it as a five-act drama and observed that
it might be called tragedy "both for the matter (than which
nothing can be thought or imagined more grave and weightie),
and also for the exceeding worthinesse of the persons, that
here talke and reason together." But his uneasiness with the
tragic label is revealed by his prefatory disclaimer to this passage, "if it were not that it is shut up with a joyfull and wished
ende." ⁴⁴ Despite the ending, Aquace D'Albiac, Joannes Oecolampadius, and Mercerus treat Job as a tragedy in three acts,
the first act showing Job's trials and actions, the second his
discourses and lamentations with his friends, and the third
God's judgments and assignment of the palm of victory to
Job. The Lutheran Joannes Brentius also terms it a tragedy
because of the great personages, fears, lamentations, slaughters, and blasphemies involved, explaining that the tragedies
of the pious unlike those of the Greeks have, as here, a glorious
and happy end.⁴⁵

The dominant tradition, however, which was initiated by
the Greek and Latin Fathers, preserved intact in Catholic
commentary throughout the Middle Ages, Renaissance, and
seventeenth century, and taken over by many Protestant exegetes,⁴⁶ makes something very different of the story. This
tradition emphasizes chapters i and ii, scanting or sometimes
entirely omitting treatment of the dialogues. Accordingly, the
chief elements of the story are the two "councils in heaven"
in which Job is singled out to be God's champion in the contest with Satan, and the trials and miseries which Satan in-
flicts upon Job. If discussed at all, the dialogues are regarded
simply as a continuation of the trial: Job's friends, signifying
heretics, are seen as Satan's agents endeavoring to lead Job
to the spiritual pitfalls of false belief and despair. In this reading God's commendation of Job in chapter i as "a perfect and

an upright man" unparalleled on earth, and the authorial observation in chapter ii that "In all this did not Job sinne with his lips" define the terms for the entire contest. Job's later outcries are simply pious lamentations like those of Jeremiah and of Christ on the cross, or else they are prophetic and typological utterances. Some commentators will concede that Job commits slight venial sins of ignorance and rashness in his outcries, but others deny that he exhibits any imperfections whatever. Gregory the Great's lengthy and influential commentary strongly defends the latter position:

> Whoever then maintains that the holy man, when in the midst of the strokes, committed sin by the words which he uttered, what else doth he than reproach God, Who had pledged Himself for him, with having been the loser? For the same God was pleased to take upon Himself the cause of the Saint under his trial, Who both extolled him before his afflictions, and on thus extolling allowed him to undergo the trial of those scourges. If then Job is said to have gone wrong, his advocate is made out to have been foiled: though the gifts vouchsafed him alone testify, that he did not transgress at all: for who does not know that what is due to faults is not reward but chastisement? [47]

This interpretation views Elihu as a proud and arrogant teacher or else a faithless gentile; he rather than Job is the object of God's first words from the whirlwind, "Who is this that darkeneth counsell by words without knowledge?" (Job xxxviii:2). God's subsequent address to Job is not a rebuke but an instruction of his ignorance or an exercise in humility, after which God declares Job victor in all his combats and gives him due reward.

This exegesis provides two important bases for the assumption that the work is an epic: the conception of the plot as a rising action in which an amazing hero overcomes ever more difficult trials and at length achieves complete victory; and the provision for supernatural machinery in the involvement

of God and Satan in the hero's affairs. The epic view of Job
was also forwarded by the constant use of martial idiom and
imagery to describe Job's spiritual battles. The Greek Fathers
frequently invoked the metaphor of Job as wrestler or fighter
in an athletic contest. Origen terms him "most strong athlete"
and paraphrases Job's complaint, "I cry aloud, but there is
no judgment" (xix:7), as the speech of a wrestler: "As an
athlete in the stadium I cried, yet judgment by no means
came; still I keep wrestling." [48] Chrysostom describes the assembly in heaven visited by Satan in terms of the same metaphor: "The day came, in which the theater was opened, and
the athlete descended into the arena. . . . Here we see God permitting Job to be tried, just as a nobly born athlete: and for
this cause he [God] speaks with the Devil, in order that he
might furnish to him the opportunity of wrestling." [49] Similarly, Olympiodorus portrays Job's trial as God's occasion for
displaying his athlete: "Because Job was a great athlete, because even the Devil, Prince of Apostate Powers, had come
down into contention against him, God who honors his ath-
letes worthy of a laudation with a crown allowed that just
man to endure all things and to bear all his blows, lest any
pretext be left to the adversary." [50]

For the Latin Fathers Job is sometimes wrestler and sometimes warrior on the battlefield. For Prosper and Methodius
he is a combatant engaged in struggles and agones; for Tertullian he is a warrior whose temptations blunt themselves
against the "corselet and shield" of his patience; for Cassiodorus he is "exercitatissimus miles Christi," a most strong and
experienced soldier of Christ whose story gives inspiration to
the young recruits. [51] In Prudentius' *Psychomachia* Job appears on the battlefield as the companion of Patience: "Job
had clung close to the side of his invincible mistress throughout the hard battle, hitherto grave of look and panting from
the slaughter of many a foe, but now with a smile on his stern

face as he thought of his healed sores and, by the number of his scars, recounted his thousands of hard won fights, his own glory and his foes' dishonour." [52] Gregory the Great used both varieties of martial imagery, appealing to the "wrestler" metaphor to describe Job at the outset of his contest and to the "embattled warrior" imagery to describe the course of Job's trial:

It is the custom of narrators, when a wrestling match is woven into the story, first to describe the limbs of the combatants, how broad and strong the chest, how sound, how full their muscles swelled, how the belly below neither clogged by its weight, nor weakened by its shrunken size, that when they have first shewn the limbs to be fit for the combat, they may then at length describe their bold and mighty strokes. Thus because our athlcte was about to combat the devil, the writer of the sacred story, recounting as it were before the exhibition in the arena the spiritual merits in this athlete, describes the members of the soul, saying, *And that man was perfect and upright, and one that feared God, and eschewed evil;* that when the powerful setting of the limbs is known, from this very strength we may already prognosticate also the victory to follow.

Job, therefore, being caught in the warfare of this conflict, received the losses which befel him like foes in his front; he took the words of his comforters like enemies on his flank, and in all turning round the shield of his stedfastness, he stood defended at all points, and ever on the watch, parried on all sides the swords directed against him.[53]

The martial metaphor persisted in Renaissance and seventeenth-century Catholic exegesis: Didacus á Stunica describes Job as stripping nude to wrestle with Satan, Pineda depicts God as mocking Satan with the words, "Now, O most strong, who before the battle sang of victory and triumph, who then is master at the end of the battle?" and Corderius affirms that "Job is as worthy to be sung as a thousand warriors." [54]

This heroic exegesis of Job was predominant not only in
Catholic but in Protestant, and especially Calvinist, commentary, despite the apparent conflict with what has been termed
the characteristic Protestant position. Noting that Job's admitted faults were slight indeed in comparison with his many
virtues, and utilizing the familiar martial metaphors, many
Protestants presented Job as the prototype of the embattled
soul struggling against powerful enemies, enduring some defeats, but at length winning a glorious victory. The Geneva
Bible depicts Job as one who finds in himself Paul's "battel
betweene ye spirit & the flesh, Rom. 7:18, and after a maner
yeeldeth, yet in the end he getteth victorie, though he was
in the meane time greatly wounded." Beza, terming Job a
"stout champion of God" who in the end "getteth the upper
hand and victoriously triumpheth over Satan," cites the commendation of Job's patience in James v:11 as evidence that
in judging Job we should not regard "that which was done
while the combat lasted, but the end of the fight it selfe." [55]
Similarly, Henry Holland, invoking the familiar wrestling
metaphor, compares the progress of Job's combats with the
flesh and the Devil to that of "wrastlers in the world: for
among them we shall see often, some one neere cast downe,
and yet in the ende gives his adversarie the foyle." [56] Milton's
contemporary Joseph Caryl, whose commentary on Job is even
longer and more detailed than Gregory's, worked out a Protestant version of the heroic Job using the characteristic warrior
imagery:

A man is a conquerour, though in the battell he suffers many foiles
and receiveth many wounds. . . . *Job* was in a great battell, in a sore
fight of afflictions, though it be granted that he received some
wounds, and had some foyles, and sometimes lookes as if he had
been beaten, and speakes as if he had been overcome, yet in the
close, in the evening, in the making up of all, he went away a

conquerour: the conclusion was victory and glory, *Job* had the victory and God had the glory.[57]

It would seem that the Calvinist commentary, despite occasional reference to the tragic or dramatic qualities of the work, did little to undercut the traditional view of Job as an epic hero comparable to the great classical epic heroes and of his temptation as an epic combat.

In addition to providing the basis for viewing the subject and the protagonist as heroic, the dominant tradition of Jobean commentary extends the scope and significance of the Book so as to give it a kind of epic dimension. First, hero and book are set forth as compendiums of moral virtue. Origen finds in Job all the merits of all the other Old Testament heroes: "So admirable was that Job ... that he resembled Abraham in loving faith in God, and followed Isaac in truest chastity, and approached Israel in bright purity of heart, & Melchisedec in the sacrificing of his sons, and Joseph in chastity, and Moses in mildness, and Samuel in justice, and Lazarus in the passion for judgment ... Therefore indeed blessed Job was made sharer in the sanctity of all the saints." [58] Elsewhere, Origen employs the martial metaphor to develop the proposition that Job underwent every species and variety of human trial and and temptation:

And just as a noble soldier, who knows how to fight in the night, on the walls, among footsoldiers, among fighting soldiers on shipboard, to send arrows in an arc, to draw the sword, in the depths and in the valleys and in all kinds of fighting to overcome his adversaries and finally to win: so truly that most noble man endured all temptation with great fortitude, temptation of poverty, famine, death, sorrow, the burial of sons: temptation from friends, from adversaries, from his wife, from the household. There was no human calamity which he did not bear in his body. Nevertheless, in truth, he overcame all.[59]

Chrysostom, Tertullian, Ambrose, and Protestants John Diodati and Joannes Cocceius also made the point that Job was conqueror over every variety of human temptation.[60]

Second, the Book of Job is often described as a compendium of all knowledge—even as the *Aeneid* was said to be in much medieval and Renaissance criticism.[61] The source of that concept is probably to be found in rabbinical commentary and especially in Jerome's observation that the Book of Job has "all the laws of dialectic, proposition, assumption, confirmation, conclusion." [62] Among later Catholic writers, Pineda found in Job all dialectic and also much natural history, the whole range of domestic and political ethics, and all the fundamentals of theology.[63] J. F. Senault still more emphatically declared that "revelation or study" had taught the author of Job

all that a man can know; sometimes he reasons like an Excellent Philosopher, and serves himself with all the secrets of Retorick and Morality, to perswade or move; sometimes he Speakes like a sage Politician, and describes all the Maximes which States men hold for the conduct of the people: sometimes he treats like a curious Naturalist, and discovers the most hidden Beauties of Nature; oftentimes he discourseth like a profound Divine, and describes to us those adorable Perfections, which seperate [sic] God so nobly from his works.[64]

Among Protestants, Chemnitius found all theology and metaphysics in Job as well as many humane sciences, and Joseph Caryl asserted that the work "is a *Summary, a Compendium* of all knowledg, both humane and divine, both concerning ourselves, and concerning God." [65]

Another element contributing to the epic dimension of the Book of Job is the extended scope and significance its subject acquired by the customary typological exegesis of Scripture, which interpreted Job's words and actions as foreshadowing future events in the life of Christ or the experience of the

church. Such a reading sets up historical reverberations not
too unlike the effects Virgil achieves by suggesting in the
episode of Dido and Aeneas the continuing historical animos-
ity of Carthage and Rome, and in Aeneas' successful exploits
the greatness of the Augustan empire. In the first place, by a
kind of reverse typology, Job's experience is treated as a re-
enactment of the first great event in man's history, the temptation of Adam. Gregory's statement is typical:

For he [Satan] has recourse again to his arts of ancient contrivance,
and because he knows by what means Adam is prone to be deceived,
he has recourse to Eve.... But he could do nothing by this artifice.
For the holy man minded that the woman was set under and not
over him, and by speaking aright, he instructed her, whom the
serpent set on to speak wrongly.... And so the old enemy was
beaten by Adam on a dunghill, he that conquered Adam in
Paradise.[66]

Then, in virtually every aspect of his experience Job is seen
as foreshadowing Christ, and that more completely, declares
Gregory, than any other Old Testament type since he prophesies Christ's sufferings "not merely with his lips but also by
suffering." [67] In addition, Job's conflict with his friends is
often seen as foreshadowing the experience of the Christian
church embattled against heretics throughout history, and
Job's restoration is taken as a figure of the church's final
glorification.[68] A large number of Catholic exegetes throughout the centuries [69] and many Protestants also,[70] despite their
emphasis on the literal interpretation of Scripture and their
scorn of medieval allegorizing, retain the principal features
of this patristic typological reading—the parallels between Job
and Adam, between Job's passion and Christ's, and even between Job's trials and those of the church.

The tradition of biblical exegesis thus supports the conception of the Book of Job as an epic by a heroic interpretation
of its chief character and its action, by an extension of its

meaning and scope through typological interpretation, and by exaltation of the Book as a compendium of ethics and of knowledge.

Although the Book of Job is more dramatic in form than any other biblical book, it has until recently inspired few dramas—a paradox no doubt partially explicable by the epic view of the subject transmitted by the commentaries. From the period before 1650 we have record of only one neo-Latin Job play, three in English (all lost), and a very few in French, German, and Italian; by comparison there are in Latin alone a dozen plays on the subject of Joseph.[71] On the other hand, several poetic treatments of the Job story incorporate epic elements, and even the straightforward poetic paraphrases of Job which follow the text chapter by chapter often claim some association with the epic form by a title, a preface, an epic proposition, or the use of epic diction and meter.

To take some examples: Thomas Manley (1652) was like most other seventeenth-century English paraphrasers of Job in using heroic couplets for this purpose, but in addition he explicitly justified this "English Heroicall Verse" as wholly appropriate to the matter of Job.[72] Francis Quarles suggested the epic quality of his subject by titling his paraphrase *Job Militant* (1624).[73] Joshua Sylvester's paraphrase (1621) bears the descriptive label "A Divine & True Tragi-Comedy," but its title and subtitle, *Job Triumphant in His Triall: Or the Historie of His Heroicall Patience,* together with its prefatory epigram terming Job "more Heroik and more *HOLY* True/ ...Past all the Patterns of Old Rome & Greece,*" as well as its epic proposition pronouncing Job a worthier hero than Odysseus, indicates that the epic conception predominates.[74] Sylvester's proposition is followed by the typical epic invocation and question about the causes of the action:

Twere labour lost, to fable (Homer-like)
The strange long Voyage of a wily Greek;
The Paines, the Perills, and extream Disease
That he endured, both by Land and Seas;
Sith Sacred Truth's *Heav'n-prompted Books present*
In Constant JOB *a worthier Argument.*
Thou then, Urania, *to whom right belongs*
The sacred Consort of Celestiall *Songs,*
Tune Thou my Voyce, Thou teach me to record
Who did incite, what did invite the Lord,
With Miseries so rewfull and so rife
So to disturb his quiet happy life;
What haynous Sin, what horrid high Offence,
The Almightie's Vengeance mought so deep incense:
Or else what Cause, what Object else might stir-it.[75]

Among the French paraphrases, that of Julien-Gatien de Morillon (1668) makes frequent references to Job as great prince and hero, but presses the poem's epic claims chiefly through the preface, which terms Job "Heros intrepide," "brave Combattant," and "brave vainqueur" who "par ses combats & ses victoires, s'est rendu la figure de JESUS-CHRIST." Moreover, the preface presents Job's combat with the forces of hell as more remarkable even than the battle in heaven when the good angels confronted Lucifer:

The Holy Scripture teaches us, that at the birth of the world there was a great combat in the Heavens; but I dare to say that a greater one occurred on earth, when that dreadful army attacked the invincible Job. The first did not seem at all surprising, there was much consonance and equality therein; spirits fought against spirits, and the number of combatants on the one side and on the other was approximately the same: But what can be seen so prodigious as the second? a single man, a mortal man is exposed to the fury of all the infernal spirits...If the faithful servant, after assiduous labor, has the right to expect a reward from his master, and if the crown is due the victor who has valiantly fought, who could contend

with Job for the glory of being crowned after so many victories and
triumphs. He has no more enemies, all Hell is vanquished, and the
Demons will no longer dare to appear before so formidable a
Hero.[76]

Helie Le Cordier's incomplete paraphrase (1667) dealing with
the first fourteen chapters of Job formally lays claim in its
preface to epic honors: the author declares that he has followed classical epic practice in his use of a narrator and in
the simple designation "Poeme" for his piece, but that he has
eschewed any epic rules not appropriate to his biblical subject, such as the *in medias res* beginning. The poem begins
with a formal epic proposition renouncing the old heroic subjects of history or legend in favor of the worthier hero of
patience:

> Let us abandon these great Heroes, to whom ancient History
> Offers incense in the Temple of Memory;
> These immortal Caesars, whose valiant exploits
> Are displayed in the heavens as brilliant stars;
>
> .   .   .   .
>
> Let us leave to great Virgil to raise up an Aeneas
> Even to defying Juno, in spite of Destiny,
> As we leave to famous Ovid to adorn everywhere
> The arrows of Cupid with the thunderbolts of Mars.
>
> .   .   .   .
>
> But let us sing one Man, to whom patience
> Gave more to celebrate of valor, and of spirit,
> Of Knowledge, of Courage, of Ardor, of Strength,
> Than all those that History could have numbered to me.[77]

Other epic elements in the poem include an invocation to God
and to Job, an Olympian council in heaven, and some suggestion of an interlocking epic struggle on two planes—Satan and
God in heaven, Satan and Job on earth.

The Latin metaphrase of Abraham Aurelius (1632) relies
chiefly on epic stylistic devices to provide epic quality: Latin

hexameter, epic diction such as "Rex magnus Olympus," and imitations such as the description of the council in heaven as an Olympian council.[78] The same devices coupled with almost cento-like borrowings from Homer and Virgil appear in Jacobus Du Port's parallel poetic versions of Job in Greek and in Latin (1653).[79] Joannes Mellius de Sousa's paraphrase (1615) also uses these stylistic devices and in addition expands and gives epic embellishment to those events of the frame story which resemble situations in classical epic, for example, the banquet of Job's children, the sacrifices of Job for his children and for his friends, the challenges exchanged between God and Satan, the rewards heaped upon Job as victor.[80]

But of all the Jobean poems Henry Oxenden's *Jobus Triumphans* (1656) comes closest to being an epic treatment of the subject.[81] The prefatory material includes several dedicatory poems ranking Job above Caesar or Pompey or Aeneas or Achilles, and also Oxenden's own affirmation that the Job story offers the greatest and most heroic subject. The poem employs the customary epic proposition and invocation as well as the customary epic diction; in addition, it augments the "heroic" elements of the biblical book such as the speeches, taunts, and challenges beteen God and Satan, and eliminates the "unheroic" dialogues. The wealth, stature, and deeds of the hero are presented in heroic terms, as this comment illustrates:

> Job still remained unconquered, the bravest man
> On earth, and steadily bore the wrath
> Of prodigious Spirits turned toward him, and hostile words,
> And afterwards desolation of spirit; he overcame all,
> And cast down the ruler heretofore unconquered,
> The King of Hell himself—a prodigy grave and marvelous—
> For this the Father omnipotent rendered him the rewards
> of victory.[82]

The last section of the poem is given over to extensive comparisons between Job and Hercules and Job and Christ, with further encomiums on Job's heroism:

> He despoils the plunderers, repels Satan
> With unconquerable spirit, and turns back the weapons
> Hurled against him. He confounds the enemy with sharp
> Arguments, and opposing Orcus with all his forces
> He presses into slavery and dominates all Avernus.
> Great praise be to thee, Job, thus journeying toward the stars
> Through thy sufferings, and through all thy torments
> Striving toward heaven, a difficult path but a sure one, a bloody
>   path
> But clear; appearing foolish perhaps, but glorious.
> Job's invincible spirit, which he bore deep in his breast
> Being not affrighted, conquered by the same way
> As Christ, and like him, ascended this path to heaven.[83]

Even more significant as background for Milton's comment in *The Reason of Church Government* than these epic-like conceptions or treatments of the Job story are the brief biblical epics on other subjects which use Job as structural model. The most interesting example is Robert Aylett's *Joseph, or Pharoah's Favourite* (1623), a poem of approximately 2,950 lines, in five books.[84] Aylett, an English Calvinist poet and master of the High Court of Chancery, might possibly have been known to Milton. Recasting his subject to fit the Jobean mold Aylett makes Jacob rather than Joseph his central character, presenting him as a Job-like hero hated by Satan because Christ is to come of his seed. The poem begins with a description of Jacob's happiness and prosperity, imitating Job i:1–5, and then presents a dialogue between Satan and God about Jacob which is modeled closely upon the following passage in Job:

> Now there was a day, when the sonnes of God came to present themselves before the LORD, and Satan came also among them.
>   And the LORD saide unto Satan, Whence commest thou? Then

Satan answered the Lord, and said, From going to and fro in the earth, and from walking up and downe in it.

And the Lord saide unto Satan, Hast thou considered my servant Job, that there is none like him in the earth? a perfect and an upright man, one that feareth God, and escheweth evill?

Then Satan answered the Lord, and said, Doth Job feare God for nought?

Hast not thou made an hedge about him, and about his house, and about all that he hath, on every side? thou hast blessed the worke of his hands, and his substance is increased in the land.

But put foorth thine hand now, and touch all that he hath, and hee will curse thee to thy face.

And the Lord sayd unto Satan, Behold, all that he hath is in thy power, onely upon himselfe put not foorth thine hand.

(Job i:6–12)

Compare Aylett:

> One day amongst the sonnes of God [Satan] appeard
> Before the Lord, desiring to be heard:
> And thus began: Dread *Thunderer:* be just,
>
> . . . .
>
> *Jacob* in *Isaacks* Tents doth quiet live,
>
> . . . .
>
> How hast thou blessed him on ev'ry side?
> His Children many, his Possessions wide;
> His stocks abound and cover all the Land,
> So thou dost blesse all workes that passe his hand:
> Well may he serve thee for so great reward,
> But touch him, thou shalt see his slight regard,
> Vexe thou but him, or any of his race,
> And he will thee blaspheme unto thy face:
> When thus, th'*Almightie;* say thou what thou can,
> *Jacob's* a matchlesse, just and perfect man,
> Who feareth God, doth good, escheweth ill,
> Try him or his, so thou no bloud dost spill.[85]

Jacob is then shown enduring the Jobean temptations—the loss of his children Joseph and Benjamin, and the famine which causes pain in his own flesh. The poem concludes with a close paraphrase of Job xix:25–26, the lines commonly interpreted as Job's prophecy of Christ, "For I know that my Redeemer liveth, and that hee shall stand at the latter day, upon the earth./ And though after my skin, wormes destroy this body, yet in my flesh shall I see God." Jacob makes the same prophecy, "I know that my *Redeemer* true and just/ Lives, and shall raise us at the last from dust,/ And though the wormes my skin and flesh destroy,/ I God shall in my body see with joy,/ Ev'n with mine owne; and with no other eyes." [86]

Joseph Beaumont's *Psyche* (1648), though neither a "brief" nor wholly a biblical epic but rather a long allegorical poem combining a *psychomachia* with an epic recital of Christ's life, uses the Jobean model in presenting the final temptations of the heroine, Psyche. Satan again comes to a council in heaven, engages in dialogue about his activities on earth, and sets forth his proposal to tempt. When he is discerned among the heavenly host Christ charges him to "relate from whence he came," and he replies with a Jobean echo, "Whence can I come, but from beneath?/ ... From visiting the Earth I come, where I/ Have far more Subjects than your Deitie." To Christ's commendation of Psyche as a notable example of piety,[87] Satan again echoes his comments on Job:

> Is not your mighty *Providential* Arm
> Become that simple *Maidens* hedge, said he,
> Infallibly to shut out *Fear* and *Harm,*
> And make her Pris'ner to *Securitie?*
>
> .   .   .   .
>
> But as for *Her,* if I had leave to trie,
> I soon would shew you of what kind of *Clay*
> She moulded is.
>
> .   .   .   .

> That *Tongue* which now your praises doth professe
> (For to the Task 'tis hir'd full dear,)
> Would change its Tune, & on your Face would spit
> More Curses than *my Selfe* e'r did on it.[88]

Christ then gives permission for the test, and Psyche endures Job-like temptations occasioned by religious persecution: loss of all her goods, the martyrdom of her friends, a contagious malady like Job's boils which she contracts in prison, and at length the visits of her parents and friends in the role of Jobean comforters pleading with her to save herself.

Postdating Milton's poem but testifying to the continued use of Job as a structural model in religious epic is Nicolas Courtin's *Charlesmagne Penitent* (Paris, 1687), which presents Charlemagne as enduring Job-like temptations and trials in his later life. First the Devil solicits God not to interfere with the proposed test; then Charlemagne receives successive reports of the loss of one after another of his children; and at length he endures Job like physical sufferings and temptations to despair.

From all of this it is obvious that Milton had weighty precedent not only for the conception of Job as an epic, but also for the actual use of that Book as a model for an epic poem. A final evidence of the perseverance, intact, of the epic view of Job through the seventeenth century may be found in the prefatory comments to Richard Blackmore's paraphrase of Job (1700). Blackmore argues that the biblical book is itself an epic, on the grounds that it is *"writ in* Metre"; that *"the* Narration, *the* Allusions, *the* Similies, *and the* Diction, *are such as are proper only to Poems";* that it is *"founded on a* true History, *as those* [poems] *of* Homer *probably were";* and that it uses supernatural machinery, for *"the* chief Apostate Angel, *and even the* Divine Being himself, *are both introduced in the most proper manner that can be."* [89] Blackmore also declares, echoing the centuries-old tradition which we have been

tracing, that the nature of the hero and the end or design of
the work are wholly suitable to epic poetry:

The Hero *is indeed a* passive *one, and this perhaps will be made
a great* Objection ... *because* Homer's *and* Virgil's Heroes *are very
active Persons. For the* Criticks *forming their* Model *of an* Heroick
Poem *intirely upon the Example of these* two famous Writers, *make*
great *and* illustrious *Actions necessary to the* Hero *of the* Poem,
which conforming *my self to their Precepts, I have formerly* asserted.
But upon what Authority is this imposed on the World? *What*
Commission *had these two* Poets *to* settle *the* limits *and* extent *of*
Epick Poetry, *or who can prove they ever intended to do so?...
It may be urged that the* Book *of* Job *was written before* Homer
and Virgil, *and the* World *has as much reason to be governed by this
Example, as by that of the* Pagan Writers. *And if we look into the
Reason of the* Matter, *and reflect on the End and Design of an
Epick* Poem, *which is to instruct the World in some important*
Moral Truth, *by the* Narration *of some great and illustrious* Subject-
Matter, *there is no question but the* relation *of the Sufferings, as
well as the* Actions *of* great Persons, *are very conducive to that end;
and indeed what else is the* Subject *of the* Odysses?... Job *then is a*
Hero *proper for an* Epick Poem ... *He is by the* Instigation of Satan
brought into miserable Streights *and unparallell'd* Sufferings, *to try
his* Constancy *and* Integrity. *He appears brave in* Distress, *and*
valiant *in* Affliction, *maintains his* Vertue, *and with that his* Character, *under the most powerful* Temptations, *and exasperating* Prov-
ocations *that the Malice of* Hell *could invent, and thereby gives
a most noble Example of* passive Fortitude, *a* Character *no way*
inferiour *to that of the* active Hero.[90]

CHAPTER III · THE BRIEF BIBLICAL EPIC: MEDIEVAL AND HUMANIST FORMS

*M*ILTON's description of the poetic kinds in *The Reason of Church Government* not only classifies the Book of Job as a brief epic, but also assumes the existence of a literary category of brief epics resembling Job in length and perhaps in certain other attributes. Literary theory and practice in classical times offers some warrant for such a category. As Allan Gilbert notes, Aristotle's differentiation between an epic of normal length containing material for several tragedies, and an epic which uses "what is really a single story" and which accordingly "seems curt when briefly told" is a possible source for Milton's distinction between "diffuse" and "brief" epics.[1] Also, the standard classical definitions of the poetic kinds according to the meters employed bring together in the epic category various sorts of poems using the dactylic hexameter—long heroic poems such as the *Iliad,* the *Odyssey,* and the *Aeneid;* certain brief heroic sequels, now lost, to the Homeric poems;[2] many comparatively brief didactic poems such as the *Works and Days* (828 lines) of Hesiod and the *Georgics* (4 books, 2,188 lines) of Virgil;[3] and even the very short epyllia (100–600 hexameters) such as Theocritus' *Infant Herakles.*[4] However, the fact that Milton offers a classical as well as a biblical or Christian example for all the other poetic kinds he mentions, but illustrates the brief epic only by the reference to Job, suggests that despite the general classical precedents for such a form, classical literature actually contained no example squaring with the Miltonic conception of the brief epic. The most likely classical example might seem to be the *Georgics,* which Louis L. Martz has suggested as an important model for *Paradise Regained* on the basis of resemblances in length, didactic subject, and style.[5] But the *Georgics* is not mentioned in this passage, and its expository form, didactic manner, and explicit abnegation of heroic subject and tone [6] seem to contrast sharply with the narrative/dramatic form and the heroic claims of Milton's poem.

Instead, the important literary ancestry for *Paradise Regained* is the considerable body of poetic narrative on biblical subjects which flourished in Europe from the fourth through the seventeenth centuries. Milton's acquaintance with some parts of this tradition can be demonstrated. His *Commonplace Book* cites Prudentius' *Peristephanon,*[7] a fourth-century collection of martyrs' tales, some of them epic-like in quality; this reference also argues his familiarity with Juvencus, Sedulius, and Avitus, other famous and often edited patristic poets whose biblical epics were studied in the schools during the Middle Ages and the Renaissance as Christian classics, sacred parallels to Virgil.[8] His cognizance of later biblical epic writers is displayed by the reference in *Mansus* to the Italian poet Marino and by various echoes throughout his verse of Mantuan, Sannazaro, Giles Fletcher, and Sylvester's translation of Du Bartas.[9] Moreover, in his abortive poem, *The Passion,* he praises M. H. Vida, a native of Cremona, for celebrating the epic aspects of Christ's life in his *Christiad,* perhaps the most famous of all the Renaissance biblical epics, better than others had done, "Loud o'er the rest *Cremona's* Trump doth sound" (ll. 24–26). The comparative judgment itself implies Milton's familiarity with several poems of this kind.

However, the point here is not the probable, or possible, influence of this or that particular poem on Milton, but rather the impact of this generic tradition as a whole upon the conception and execution of *Paradise Regained*. The tradition demands to be approached as a European development, rather than in narrowly national terms, and Milton could have been acquainted with the principal varieties of the kind—patristic, medieval, neo-Latin, Italian, French, and English.[10] A study conducted in this manner indicates the following: (1) A very considerable number of biblical epics and a majority of those on New Testament subjects are "brief" epics (*ca.* 1,500–4,000 lines), very much shorter than the nearly ten thousand lines of the *Aeneid,* and in many cases approximating the dimensions of *Paradise Regained* (2,070 lines). (2) A significant body of critical opinion in all eras has recognized and defended the epic character of the brief as well as the long biblical poems. (3) The brief as well as the long biblical epics utilize many of the narrative, structural, and stylistic devices of classical epic and of the various types of contemporary secular epic as a means of asserting their epic claims and enhancing their epic character. (4) The brief epics constitute a distinct subspecies of the biblical epic category, with characteristic features which were developed partly as a response to the common problems inherent in writing poems both "brief" and "epic," and partly because later writers were disposed to follow the famous patristic and humanist precedents. Accordingly, a proper assessment of Milton's assumptions about, and debts to, the generic tradition behind *Paradise Regained* must consider the outstanding brief epics on New Testament subjects in the literary eras prior to Milton, in the context of general developments in epic and biblical epic theory and practice.

THE PATRISTIC PERIOD

Whether, as E. R. Curtius suggests, the whole venture of biblical epic from Juvencus to Klopstock was doomed by its very nature to failure because of the incompatibility of biblical subject and epic form,[11] certainly it was attended from the start with very great artistic difficulties. The Christian poet faced the problem of adapting the classical epic conventions,

developed originally to present human heroic action and physical courage, to the biblical ideals of obedience, righteousness,
and dependence on Providence, and to the New Testament
donnée of a divine suffering hero. In addition, the poet's sense
of the sanctity of his material, especially when he dealt with
the New Testament, often made him uneasy about possible
conflicts between art and truth when he undertook on aesthetic
grounds to alter, excise, ornament, or add to his text.

The patristic period produced no comprehensive critical
theory addressing such problems, but it did outline some important concepts repeated for centuries thereafter in discussions of biblical epic. The early Christian era was one in which
all the elegance and beauty of classical antiquity seemed to shore
up the falsehoods of paganism, while the truths of Christianity
stood bare and unadorned. Accordingly, the early Christian
poets constantly affirmed their obligation to renounce the false
pagan heroes and wars and gods and Muses, substituting for
them a new Christian poetry modeled upon the Bible and inspired by the Spirit. This sentiment informs the opening passages of almost every patristic biblical epic, usually accompanied by praises of the biblical subject matter as far surpassing
the pagan heroic stories in truth and real nobility. Such comparisons imply that the new biblical poems were regarded as
epics, though one finds no direct discussion of genre as such.
Gaius Juvencus (*ca.* 330) offers the earliest and one of the
most eloquent formulations of these principles—a rather mourn-
ful prediction of the obliteration which must inevitably over-
take the false pagan heroic tales, accompanied by a joyful
prophecy of the immortality to be enjoyed by the biblical
poems which treat of "the living deeds of Christ":

> Nothing in the world will remain conjoined forever,
> Not the world, nor kingdoms of men, nor golden Rome
> Nor the sea, nor earth, nor the fiery stars of heaven,
> For the father of all things is irrevocable Time

Who hastens to burn everything in flames at the end of
the world.
But the noble deeds and the honor of bravery attending
upon innumerable men,
Poets for a long time can preserve their fame and their
praise.
These lofty songs, flowing from the fountains of Smyrna,
Those others of Mincius the sweetness of Virgil celebrates.
And not less indeed runs the glory of the poets themselves
Which endures a like eternity while the ages ordain,
While the revolution of the poles, and the sea around the
earth,
And the starry heavens by governing command will roll on.
But if so long have endured the famous songs
And deeds of ancestors compact of falsehood
Our true faith deserves the honor of eternal praise
For immortal ages, and will recompense merit.
My song is of the living deeds of Christ,
A Divine sacrifice for man without falseness or fault.
No fear that the fires will destroy with the world
This work; this truly perhaps will withdraw me from
the fire.
At that time, when with flames issuing forth, on a trembling
cloud
Christ the judge will descend, the glory of the Father
most high.[12]

Caelius Sedulius (*ca.* 430) denounced in much harsher terms
both the pagan heroic subjects and the pagan poetic manner,
while pointing to the biblical poet David as a better inspiration
for the Christian poet's more glorious poetic endeavors.[13] Reinforcing such statements by the patristic poets are the numerous commentaries identifying the Book of Job and some other
portions of the Bible as epic, and also the various patristic,
medieval, and Renaissance interpretations of the *Aeneid* as an
allegory of a saintly philosophical hero, for both assertions

suggest that the classical epic subject matter is closely analogous to the biblical stories.[14]

The patristic poets also raised the question of poetic license
in relation to the true subject and affirmed that truth must
take priority over art. Sedulius felt the need to speak to the
evidently widespread belief that a poetic form might debase
sacred truth: he defended his own poem and Christian poetry
in general on the ground that it made Christian truth palatable
to those nourished on the classics.[15] Claudius Marius Victor
(*ca.* 426) displayed even greater uneasiness, praying that his
poem would in no way injure truth by its alteration of the
order of events or of the sense of certain words from aesthetic
considerations.[16] But of all these patristic poets, Alcimus
Avitus (*ca.* 551), bishop of Vienne, showed the keenest awareness of the difficulties of adjusting the claims of sacred text
and artistic impulse:

That license of lying, which has been accorded to painters and
poets, must be banned from a serious work. Indeed in composing
works of profane verse one is called much more able and more
elegant, yea we say truly, if one will ineptly use falsehoods. I say
nothing here of those names [the pagan mythological names] which
to us it is not permitted to read frequently in the works of others,
much less to write in our own, which are among the resources of
the poet when he wishes to signify one thing by another. Thus the
judgment of the world considers us unskilled or ignorant, attacking
our work as more arduous than delightful for not using poetic
license. But we have distinguished for a long time divine censure
from human opinion....For a priest it will be safer that pomp
rather than the rule be unfulfilled, and that the poetic foot be
lamed rather than the footsteps of Truth. Nor is it excusable to
commit sins in order to achieve freedom of eloquence: if account
must be given even for the careless words which men speak (Matt.
xii:36), it is manifest that it is yet more dangerous when treating
or meditating upon the laws of life to injure them by presuming
to place above them the laws of language.[17]

All the patristic biblical poems with epic pretensions have a similar format, one which reappears frequently in subsequent eras. All are panoramic in scope, dealing with the entire Bible or with the complete Gospel story, or with the principal events of Genesis and Exodus. All are, however, comparatively brief, being about 1,500–3,000 hexameter lines, and are organized usually into three or four books; Sedulius suggests that his four-book division is an imitation of the four evangelists.[18] Also, despite the variety of subject and scope all focus primary attention upon Christ. All follow biblical chronology closely and are innocent of classical structural devices such as the *in medias res* beginning.

Moreover, the patristic epics bequeathed to subsequent practitioners of the form many of the enduring formulas for the organization of biblical poems. The *Evangeliorum* of Juvencus (*ca.* 330, 4 books, 3,226 hexameters) offers an example of the close paraphrase (in this case of Matthew's Gospel) dignified by Virgilian language. The *Cento* of Faltonia Proba (*ca.* 400, *ca.* 700 hexameters)[19] is a brief summary of Old and New Testament events with each hexameter constructed patchwork-like out of fragments of Virgilian verse—an artistic monstrosity with a surprisingly numerous progeny among later biblical poems. The *Carmen Paschale* of Sedulius (*ca.* 430, 4 books, 1,769 hexameters) develops what comes to be the most commonly employed formula for Christiads, a treatment of the Fall and its aftermath, then of the Old Testament personages and incidents which foreshadow Christ typologically, and finally of the Gospel story in its entirety. Blossius Aemilius Dracontius' *Carmen de Laudibus Dei* (*ca.* 440, 3 books, 2,234 hexameters),[20] Victor's *Alethias* (*ca.* 426, 3 books, 2,020 hexameters), and Avitus' *De Spiritalis Historiae Gestis* (*ca.* 494, 5 books, *ca.* 2,552 lines)[21] all treat significant events of Genesis and Exodus but have, like many later Old Testament poems, a strong typological emphasis relating these events to

Christ. The *De Actibus Apostolorum* by Arator (sixth century, 2 books, *ca.* 2,350 hexameters) is organized to some degree around individual human heroes, in that the two books focus, respectively, on Peter and Paul.[22] Also, though they are not biblical epics, Prudentius' *Psychomachia* and *Peristephanon*[23] contributed formulas later assimilated to that kind—the former treats the warfare of personified vices and virtues, and the latter displays the single hero, the martyr saint, whose sufferings are conceived as a militant and aggressive battle against tormenters, false gods, and the Devil himself.

These works claim epic status chiefly by their incorporation of Virgilian stylistic features—the close imitation of the Virgilian hexameter, the use of some kind of epic proposition and invocation, the imitation or echo of Virgilian diction or incident. The Virgilian names and epithets are pervasive: God is "Rector Olympi" or "Summus tonans" or "Altithronus," Christ is "heros," hell is "Avernus," "Erebus," "Tartarus"; these mythological names and allusions function simply as epic diction or as allegories of the Christian supernatural or of moral qualities, but nevertheless they give a curiously pagan flavor to these poems which have so consciously abjured the pagan supernatural for the Christian. Also there are numerous classical allusions or echoes. In Avitus' poem God's blessing of the marriage of Adam and Eve echoes Jupiter's promise to Venus of unending empire for Aeneas' race,[24] and Gabriel giving directions about the ark assumes the role of classical *nuntius*. Another classical epic device, taken over especially by the Old Testament poems, is the exploitation of potentially dramatic or spectacular scenes. In Avitus the memorable dramatic scenes are Satan's jealous soliloquy as he plots the temptation of Adam and Eve, the temptation itself, and Adam's vehement denunciation of Eve after the Fall.[25] Victor creates an intensely dramatic, moving exchange between Adam and Eve as they encounter the barren world after their expulsion from Eden, and he also

presents the Flood, Sodom, and the Red Sea crossing as awesome, epic-like spectacles.

Most important of all, the major patristic epic poets developed a new epic device by using for aesthetic as well as inter-
pretive purposes the typological symbolism endemic to the
Christian tradition. In the strict sense, typological exegesis interpreted persons and events in the Old Testament as foreshadowing Christ and his church; a common extension of such
typological reading allowed persons and events in the New
Testament to foreshadow other New Testament events and
also to prefigure the role of the church in history. At the level
of anagoge, the New Testament events shadow forth the Last
Judgment and heavenly glory. As an aesthetic device, typology
provided a means of unifying and structuring these vast narratives, and also a means of enhancing their epic dimension
by extending the significance and the ramifications of particular episodes. For example, Victor wedded typological symbolism to the classical device of the prophetic dream and vision
of the future by having Abraham learn through a dream of
his future posterity, including Christ, and then view the destruction of Sodom, type of the final holocaust.[26] Avitus' poem
is unified through typology, with the first three books treating,
respectively, the creation, fall, and sentencing of man, while
the last two treat the Flood and the Red Sea crossing as types
of Christ's deliverance of man through baptism.[27] Even Juvencus' rather pedestrian paraphrase suggests, through the
emphasis on Christ's calling, instructing, and finally sending
forth his apostles, that the Gospel story looks toward and
somehow prefigures the subsequent history of the church. At
the very outset of the biblical epic tradition, then, precedent
is established for the use of typology to allude to the experience of the church in history, a feature common to New
Testament biblical epic in all eras.

Sedulius' *Carmen Paschale,* the most frequently edited and

most constantly cited of the patristic biblical poems, is also
the one which makes the most ambitious and imaginative use
of these "epic" devices. Eschewing the simple biblical language
of Juvencus' poem, it adopts a grandiloquent rhetorical style
complete with Virgilian diction, similes, epithets, apostrophes,
and echoes of Virgilian passages, such as the use of phrases
from Virgil's account of the captured Cassandra to describe
the good thief on the cross.[28] Though less impressive than
the Old Testament epics as regards drama and spectacle, Sedulius' poem develops these features to some extent by emphasizing Christ's miraculous deeds and the glories of the
heavenly kingdom. But the poem is especially interesting because of its use of typological symbolism. The theme suggested
by the title and the opening passage—"The wondrous works
of Christ...the paschal gifts" (ll. 26, 36–37)—seems to promise, despite the broad scope of the work, that the whole will
be ordered in relation to Christ's paschal redemptive sacrifice,
and through the device of typology the promise is largely redeemed: Christ's redemptive act (passion, death, and resurrection) is made to appear as the focal point of history, reflected in a myriad of types. The first book emphasizes the
Old Testament miracles foreshadowing the paschal events,
notably the assumption of Enoch and Elias, the sacrifice of
Isaac, the passing of the Israelites through the Red Sea and
their nourishment in the desert, the deliverance of Jonah from
the whale and Daniel from the lions. The second book recalls
the Fall and its aftermath, showing thereby the need for a
redeemer, and then narrates Christ's life up to the time of
his first miracle. The third book treats his miracles, emphasizing those which foreshadow the paschal story, such as the
changing of water into wine at Cana, the feeding of the multitudes, the transfiguration, the triumphal entry into Jerusalem,
and the raising of Lazarus. The final book shows the fulfillment
of all these types in Christ's passion, death, resurrection, and

ascension. All the books conclude with intimations of the last day, and the first book explicitly invites an anagogical reading of the paschal story as itself a symbol of the pilgrim's attainment of the heavenly city. Among patristic poets, Sedulius made the most impressive and complex use of typology as a means of structuring the narrative and enhancing its epic dimension, and this example set a precedent for the ubiquity and importance of this device in subsequent New Testament epic.

THE LATER MIDDLE AGES

Later medieval poems with epic pretensions fall into three categories—Latin, Anglo-Saxon or Germanic, and Romance— according to the theories and the epic models by which they are primarily influenced. They range in format from massive paraphrases of the entire Bible to brief, dramatic accounts of a single incident. Among the best known and most influential of them are several "brief epics" about particular episodes or sequences in Christ's life, using typological symbolism as a dominant aesthetic method.

The poets in the Latin tradition are the self-avowed heirs of the patristic biblical poets and they reiterate the patristic poetic theories—that the Bible contains examples of the various poetic genres including epic, that the classical poems are themselves allegories or contain typological foreshadowings of Christ, that the Christian poet ought to provide substitutes for the profane pagan poems, and that the Bible offers subject matter far superior to the pagan heroic tales.[29] These Latin poems claim relation to the epic tradition only by the use of dactylic hexameter and by verbal echoes from Virgil, Juvencus, Sedulius, and Prudentius. Like Odo of Cluny's *Occupatio* (*ca.* 900, 7 books, *ca.* 5,560 hexameters), which treats events from creation to doomsday, most of the massive panoramic poems are so heavily laden with explicit typological references and didactic moral commentary that the narrative thrust is destroyed; and like the brief *Maria* (*ca.* 965, 859 lines) by the German nun Roswitha, many of the shorter narratives employ a naïve and colloquial rather than an elevated heroic tone.[30] The most impressive of the Latin poems is the comparatively brief *Josephina* (*ca.* 1400, 12 books, *ca.* 4,000 lines) [31] by the famous chancellor of Paris Jean Gerson, which imitates patristic epic in the use of classical epithet and phrase but also looks forward to Renaissance and post-Renaissance concern with classical structure and unity: it begins *in medias res* with the most exciting event in Joseph's life, the flight into Egypt, then presents earlier events through Joseph's stream-of-consciousness recollections as he searches for Jesus lost in the Temple, and concludes with Joseph's death just as Christ emerges into public life at the Baptism.

The second and by far the most interesting category of medieval biblical epics comprises those influenced by the Saxon and Anglo-Saxon heroic poems. These poems contain no explicit commentary on the nature of Christian epic or the duties of Christian poets; they omit classical epic thematic statements and invocations; they employ very little Virgilian diction and little typology; and they seem to retreat somewhat from the panoramic subject, although the fragmentary state of many of these poems disguises their intended scope. This category includes the so-called Cædmonian poems just possibly known to Milton in the Junius manuscript: [32] the two-part *Genesis* fragment (*Genesis A, ca.* 700; *Genesis B,* ninth century—together comprising 2,935 lines), which relates events from the fall of the angels to the sacrifice of Isaac; the *Exodus* fragment (*ca.* 700 or earlier, 589 lines), which treats a single, unified action, the march of the Israelites through the Red Sea to Sinai; and the so-called *Christ and Satan* (ninth century, 733 lines), whose three sections, at one time thought to be separate poems, deal with, respectively, Christ's battle with

Satan in heaven, his harrowing of hell, and his temptation by
Satan.[33] Other such poems are the Anglo-Saxon *Judith* (ninth-
tenth century, 3 books, 350 lines, incomplete), which presents
a unified, martial action with a single heroine; and the massive Old Saxon *Heliand* (*ca.* 830, *ca.* 6,000 lines), which treats
the entire Gospel story including sermons and parables.[34]

All of these poems employ the four-beat alliterative line,
the epic formulas, the sea similes, the kennings, and especially
the epithets characteristic of Anglo-Saxon secular epic: God
in the *Genesis* is "prince among his thanes," the Old Testament patriarchs are "folkleaders," the "joy of their warriors,"
the "dispensers of treasure." These poems also assume the
Saxon and Anglo-Saxon heroic institutions and manners, notably the comitatus relationship: in *Genesis B* Satan, chained
in hell because of disloyalty to his overlord, God, must in a
kind of infernal council invoke the comitatus bond to appeal
to his own thanes to undertake his revenge in Eden.[35] In the
Heliand Christ is incongruously portrayed as a folklord pledg-
ing thanes to his allegiance, distributing arm bands along with
the more durable joys of heaven, and inspiring followers to
spiritual combat through his Sermon on the Mount;[36] by the
same token the marriage feast at Cana and Herod's birthday
feast are described as drinking bouts in a Saxon hall, as is
also the banquet of Holofernes in *Judith*. In addition, all of
these poems attempt to evoke a martial atmosphere. The device is sometimes absurd, as in the sustained presentation of
the Gospel Christ as a warrior hero in the *Heliand,* but it is
effective when warranted: in *Judith* the descriptions of flashing
armor and gleaming casques, crows awaiting cadavers, and
eagles chanting hymns of combat are quite appropriate to the
martial subject; and in the *Exodus,* though the only real struggle is that of the Egyptians with the waves, such descriptions
create the illusion of an epic battle. But in addition to such
obvious debts to the Anglo-Saxon epic, these poems also owe

something to the patristic Latin tradition for verbal echoes and for the manner of using typology. The *Exodus* links the story of the Israelites' preservation in the Red Sea with Noah's salvation from the Flood and with the baptismal ritual,[37] thereby extending the significance of the incident treated. And the New Testament *Christ and Satan* uses typology to achieve structural cohesion, unifying by this means the apparently discrete events which comprise the poems.[38]

Christ and Satan because of its brevity, its New Testament subject, its creative fusion of patristic and Anglo-Saxon techniques, and also because it might have been known to Milton, is most significant for the present discussion. It begins with a slight variation on an Anglo-Saxon epic formula [39] and contains a few examples of Anglo-Saxon epic diction, but for the most part the poem's heroic atmosphere is created by the resounding and pervasive reiteration of certain biblical epithets for Christ—"Lord of Hosts," "King of Glory." This is a poem based upon the so-called celestial cycle; [40] it presents three typologically related phases of the warfare between Christ and Satan, in each of which Christ is manifested as King of Glory conquering Satan. The first part recounts the creation and fall of the angels, Christ's great victory over Satan in heaven, and Satan's bitter lamentations in hell over his loss of light and joy "because I said of old that I was King of Glory and Lord of all." [41] The second section describes the Harrowing of Hell, drawing details from the widely known fourth-century apocryphal Gospel of Nicodemus. It describes the terror of the fallen angels, the epic victory over Satan, Christ's dialogue with the patriarchs, the triumphal procession of the saints to heaven, and concludes with an account of Christ's final conquest over hell at doomsday. Only a fragment remains of the third part dealing with Christ's temptation, but here again Christ is the conquering King of Glory manifesting to Satan, in words somewhat reminiscent of Job xxxviii, the overwhelming power of God:

Know, accursed fiend, how measureless and wide and dreary is the pit of hell! Measure it with thy hands, take hold upon its bottom. Go, then, until thou knowest all the circle of it; measure it first from above even unto the abyss. Measure how broad the black mist stretches. Then shalt thou know more clearly that thou strivest against God, when thou hast measured with thy hands how high and deep is hell, the grim grave-house within.[42]

A third variety of medieval biblical poem was modeled upon the romances and was popular from the tenth to the fourteenth centuries. Most of the biblical poems in this period were close paraphrases, heavily freighted with conventional, unimaginative typological references and innocent of concern with literary theory except for declarations of didactic intention. A few Old Testament poems imitate earlier vernacular epic models such as the French *chanson de geste* and the Anglo-Saxon epics.[43] But the contemporary romances were a more significant literary influence for the New Testament poems—both for those dealing with the entire Gospel story and also for the very popular shorter *Passions* treating the suffering, death, and resurrection of Christ. Some of these poems testify to the romance relation only through the use of the characteristic octosyllabic couplet or metrical stanza and of some terms drawn from chivalric usages.[44] Others sound the characteristically light, almost whimsical romance tone in the opening lines, and also employ romance literary modes such as the dream vision. For example, the *Northern Passion* (fourteenth century, *ca.* 1,972 lines in the original version, later 3,575 lines) begins lightly, "Herknith alle, ihc wolle you telle/ Of muche pitie in mi spelle,"[45] and incorporates the matter of the Book of Revelation into the Passion story as a vision seen by John when he reclined on Christ's bosom at the Last Supper.[46] These *Passions* manifest the romance concern with the marvelous, the miraculous, the picturesque, in their emphasis upon the wonders and horrors attending Christ's crucifixion and upon various marvelous legends, such as that of Adam's tree preserved through the ages to become the wood of Christ's cross. Many also reflect the romance interest in and display of courteous sentiment toward women.[47]

The several poems based upon the Gospel of Nicodemus are of most interest for the development of biblical epic.[48] Among such poems are André de Coutances' thirteenth-century French paraphrase of the entire Gospel (2,040 lines), a thirteenth-century English *Harrowing of Hell* (*ca.* 250 lines), and a fourteenth-century English paraphrase (*ca.* 1,812 lines).[49] These poems use romance diction and exploit the romance-like marvels of the first part of the Gospel, such as the awesome events at the Crucifixion, the marvelous deliverance of Joseph of Arimathea from prison, and the miraculous return of Simeon's two sons from Hades to give an eyewitness account of the Harrowing. But they especially develop the epic possibilities of the second part of the Gospel, the Harrowing scene itself. Accordingly, they expand those passages from Nicodemus which present the epic-like challenges and confrontations of Christ and Satan as heroic warriors, and they cause the ringing heroic terms of Psalm xxiv:7 used in the Gospel of Nicodemus—"Lift up your hands, O ye gates ... and the King of glory shall come in"—to resound throughout the poems. Moreover, they amplify the account in Nicodemus of a violent altercation between Satan and Hades over who is responsible for the Harrowing and how to prevent it, thereby developing the council in hell *topos* much beyond its classical beginnings in Virgil's councils of the gods and Claudian's councils in Hades.[50]

The fifteenth-century *Develis Perlament, or Parlamentum of Feendis* (504 lines) [51] makes especially interesting use of these biblical epic devices. The poem takes as a subject a sequence of related incidents in hell's various machinations against Christ, restricts the narrative angle of vision to the devils, and uses the dialogues and speeches of the councils in hell as the vehicle for presenting nearly all of Christ's life. An initial parliament in hell at Jesus' birth discusses his parentage, role, and relation to Adam, and at length dispatches Satan to tempt him. The later parliament called to meet the impending threat of the Harrowing reviews Christ's miraculous deeds and hell's hitherto unsuccessful plots against him in the massacre of the Innocents and the Crucifixion. Then follows a highly dramatic account of the Harrowing itself—still from the devils' perspective—emphasizing Christ's peremptory demand for entrance, the mutual recriminations between Satan and Hades, Christ's lengthy argument proving his rightful claim to Adam and his progeny, and Satan's pathetic plea to Christ for his own salvation. The poem concludes with a brief résumé of the Resurrection, the Ascension, and the founding of the church, an ending in keeping with the ecclesiastical emphasis so common in New Testament biblical epic.

THE HUMANIST IMPULSE

Like the patristic poets, the humanists of the late *quattrocento* and the *cinquecento* faced the problem of producing Christian epic in an atmosphere rife with the claims and counterclaims of Christian and classical culture. Humanists such as Petrarch and Boccaccio undertook to defend classical poetry as allegory presenting moral truth and even as typology pointing, like the Old Testament, to the Christian mysteries.[52] Yet the tension persisted, as Petrarch clearly reveals in his explanation to his brother Gherardo, a priest,[53] of the allegorical meaning of his first pastoral eclogue: Silvius (Petrarch), who has been wandering in the mountains striving to follow after two sweet singing shepherds (Homer and Virgil), is invited by Monicus (his brother) to visit his cave where he will hear even sweeter singing (David's Psalms) beside the river Jordan. Silvius says he has heard of this river: a certain youth clad in hairy raiment (John the Baptist) bathes Apollo (Christ) in it. But he speaks slightingly of the cave poet's voice (David's), and when Monicus objects, heaping praise upon his singing, Silvius declares that he will return some-time to test the sweetness of his songs but that now he is engaged upon another task (his *Africa,* a classically inspired epic about Scipio Africanus). Exhibiting this tension in quite a different way, Pico della Mirandola the Younger flatly de-nounced classical poetry on the Christian-Platonic grounds that it corrupts youth, teaches falsehood, and blasphemes God.[54] This atmosphere stimulated great interest in the production of a new Christian poetry fusing biblical subject and classical form, which would prove that the Renaissance artist could be both a good Christian and a good classicist. One special impetus to the writing of biblical epic at the turn of the sixteenth cen-tury was the publication by the famous humanist, editor, and publisher Aldus Manutius of an important collection of pa-tristic poetry, limited, interestingly enough, to books dealing with New Testament subjects; the collection was intended in part, by Aldus' own testimony, to present models for contem-porary imitation.[55]

The humanists claimed or assumed epic status for their biblical poems on the basis of several arguments, most of which had originated in patristic times: (1) the theory that parts of the Bible are already epic poetry and so can supply proper epic subject matter; (2) the definition of a hero as one whose life merits eternal fame in heaven; (3) the stock comparisons of biblical and classical heroes; (4) the assertion of the greater nobility and excellence of biblical subjects over pagan, coupled usually with a denunciation of the classical Muses.[56] The following introductory passage from Jacobus Bonus, recalling Juvencus in its attitudes and imagery, is typical:

Singing of the great deeds of the Lord, this work
Drives me to the right, the holy place, which has no
  conflagrations,
No raging Floods, nor any misfortune from the perishable
  air,
Or terrors of thunder or rages of flashing lightning.
Because it stands in the light of God, because it is
  comprehended
In the great structure of the heavens,
And the eternal laurels are blooming for it on the eternal
  heights.
Not here does "arms and the man" astonish—a fiction of
  Apollo,
Nor do we vaunt the harsh wrath of deadly Achilles,
Nor do we toss about a wandering Ulysses in the vain wind,
Nor treat the many false things which the poets in Helicon
  present.[57]

The humanist biblical poems have a characteristic format: almost all are on New Testament subjects;[58] most are comparatively brief, often in three books; most eschew the patristic or medieval panoramic subject for a limited subject deriving from a single episode or a sequence of related events. However, most of these poems retain the panoramic effect by using recitals, prophecies, and constant typological allusion to extend the significance of the particular episode. Most also retain the traditional ecclesiastical emphasis.

The humanist poets adopted and extended several of the older methods of enhancing the epic quality of the biblical narratives—the employment of mythological references and epithets such as "Regnator Olympus," "Tonans," "Jupiter"; the use of the epic proposition and invocation to the Spirit, usually more classically regular here than in the patristic poems; the use of mythological figures as allegories for natural or moral qualities (Neptune for the Sea, Astraea for Justice). However, unlike the patristic writers, the Renaissance poets were not hampered by the sanctity of the biblical text: they re-ordered, expanded, and even created incidents without hesitation or apology, and they constantly altered the chronology of events through the use of recitals, prophecies, and dreams. In this period certain episodes and *topoi* derived from classical and medieval precedent became stock features of the biblical brief epic: (1) the council in hell at which Satan prepares to cope with some impending threat to his kingdom (evolving from the classical councils in heaven and hell, the medieval *decensus* material, and the infernal council in Boccaccio's *Filocolo*); [59] (2) the council in heaven at which God prophesies the outcome of the central action (often contrived after the pattern of the medieval parliament of heaven, wherein Justice and Truth debate with Mercy and Peace over the fate of mankind after the Fall); (3) a council of the Fathers in Limbo awaiting salvation by Christ and reiterating their typological prophecies (also deriving from the *decensus* material); (4) an Allecto passage in which that Fury or some Christian allegorical equivalent stirs up evil passions by the methods used on Turnus and Amata in Book VII of the *Aeneid;* [60] (5) a heavenly-messenger passage based upon Book IV of the *Aeneid* (ll. 238–55), with Gabriel replacing Mercury as messenger; (6) geographical catalogues of worldly kingdoms and detailed descriptions of particular cities; (7) iconographical portrayals of scenes and symbols, nearly always of typological significance, deriving ultimately from the scenes carved on Achilles' and Aeneas' shields and on the Carthaginian temple in Book I of the *Aeneid;* (8) passages describing the education and reading of the hero or heroine, a ubiquitous Renaissance *topos* perhaps inspired by Achilles' account of his education by Chiron in Statius' *Achilleid.*[61]

Characteristically the humanist poems take a subject from the life of Christ or Mary. Except for a few massive, panoramic works such as Alvarus Gomcz de Ciudad Real's *Thalichristia* (1522, 25 books, *ca.* 16,400 hexameters) and Jacobus Bonus' *De Vita & Gestis Christi* (1526, 16 books, *ca.* 10,000 hexameters), which treat sequentially the Fall, the Old Testament types of Christ, the life and death of Christ, and the founding of the church,[62] most are brief epics with some flexibility of structure. Usually they seize upon a single episode or unified sequence in Christ's life and then extend its significance and scope by introducing related matter through prophecies and recitals grounded upon established typological symbolism. Jerome Valle's *Jhesuida* (1473, 1 book, *ca.* 500 hexameters) is basically a summary of John's Gospel, but its focus is Christ's passion and death. It begins with a dramatic council in hell in which Pluto rages about the threat posed by Christ to the kingdom of Hades, recites Christ's previous life and miracles, presents a plan to test Christ's divinity by subjecting him to death, and dispatches Allecto to incite the scribes, the Pharisees, and Judas to that end.[63] *De Triumpho Christi* (1499, 1 book, 317 hexameters) by Macarius Mutius announces its epic claims by its subtitle, *Carmine cum Maiestate Heroica;* it deals with a strictly limited, martial subject, the Harrowing of Hell, and rejects all use of or allusion to pagan mythology.[64] Jacobus Bonus' *Sub Figura Herculis Christi Praeludium* (1526, 3 books, *ca.* 1,040 hexameters) treats the same subject under the figure of Hercules' descent to Avernus, portrayed as a classical-Dantesque landscape inhabited by classical figures such as Pluto, Vulcan, Erebus, Medusa, Charon, Cerberus, Allecto, Centaurs, and Harpies, along with Satan. In this place Hercules encounters and promises to save Hylas (Adam) and Proserpine (Eve), he takes part in a general battle reminiscent of the medieval "Harrowing" poems, and at length he ascends in the Sun's chariot to the "arboris antiquae" or earthly paradise. The subject of Ilarione da Verona's *La Crisias* (fifteenth century, 3 books, 937

hexameters) is doomsday: the poem begins with the signs of
the last day; then it recites Antichrist's deeds throughout
history and the opposition offered to him by certain classical types of Christ, the Curii, the Fabritii, Socrates, Hercules;
it concludes with an epic-like description of the final battle
between Christ and Antichrist.[65]

The character of the humanist biblical epic and the range
of its experimentation with structure, epic devices, adaptation
of episodes from classical epic, use of the supernatural, and
typological symbolism, can best be suggested by a more detailed examination of the most famous of these poems.[66] The
first, *Mariana* (1481, 3 books, *ca.* 1,500 hexameters) by the
Carmelite monk Giovanni Battista Spagnuoli, called Mantuan,
is in many respects the most conservative.[67] In his prefatory
"Apologeticon" Mantuan displays some defensiveness about
the use of verse and poetic ornament for sacred subjects, appealing for support to the biblical examples of David, Moses,
and Job, to the testimony of the Fathers, and to the examples
of the patristic poets Juvencus and Prudentius. In the same
preface he explains and undertakes to justify his rather conservative way of using the classical supernatural: he has
placed the entire classical theogony in Hades, conflating the
gods with the Christian devils, and presenting them as the
active antagonists of the true God whom he situates on Olympus; beyond this, he makes only occasional, figurative use of
the classical mythological names to elevate the diction. Interestingly, however, like several other humanist poets who conflate pagan deities with the devils, he recognized Hercules,
the Sibyls, and certain other classical figures as types and
prophets of Christ.

Mantuan's conception and treatment of his subject is also
conservative. He presents the entire life of Mary from conception to assumption—"Sancta Palestinae repetens exordia
nymphae"—in a straightforward sequential narration begin-

ning *ab ovo.*[68] But he achieves something of the characteristic Renaissance structural sophistication as well as a considerable extension of epic significance and dimension by using every possible occasion for recital, prophecy, and casual typological allusion, though Mantuan's emphasis is usually upon the contrasts rather than the resemblances between Christ and his types. In Book I the sterility of Ann is made the occasion for a résumé of famous Old Testament children—Abel, Isaac, Joseph, Samson—who are types of Christ; a tapestry at the childhood home of Mary depicts Old Testament history from Adam through Judas Maccabaeus; the young Mary at the Temple studies all learning, and in good Renaissance fashion contemplates especially Christ's classical types, Alexander, Hercules, Perseus, and Oedipus, eschewing the evil and retaining the good. The book concludes with a council in heaven at which God reviews the fall of the angels and man and predicts the Virgin's role in the forthcoming salvation. Book II presents a council in hell which undertakes to subvert the plans for the Virgin's marriage to Joseph; then the marriage ceremony at which an Orpheus-like harper sings of the deeds of Gideon, David, and Moses as Old Testament types of the Redemption; then the wedding night during which Mary and Joseph discourse about God's creation of the world. The Incarnation occurs during one of Mary's nocturnal meditations on the messianic prophecies of Isaiah, and Gabriel as *nuntius* delivers his message to Mary by quoting part of Virgil's *Eclogue IV.* Joseph's suspicions of Mary, aroused by Ate, are dispelled by the angel's recital of various classical types of the Incarnation in the stories of mortals who bore sons to Jove: Latona (Hercules), Maia (Hermes), Semele (Bacchus). Book III begins with a geographical catalogue and a description of the cities of the Roman world subject to the Augustan census; then it treats the events of Christ's infancy including the annunciation of his birth to Caesar by the Tiburtine Sibyl; then from the perspective of the Virgin it presents an account of Christ's passion, death, and resurrection; finally it narrates Mary's assumption and triumphal reception into heaven.

Jacopo Sannazaro's *De Partu Virginis* (1526, 3 books, *ca.* 1,450 hexameters) [69] uses an alternative strategy and structure for the brief epic: the narration of a single sequence, the incarnation and birth of Christ, with all history related to it by means of recitals, prophecies, and iconographical scenes based on typology. Sannazaro's creative ingenuity in adapting the classical form to the needs of his particular subject is shown by his subtle fusion of styles—epic elevation, pastoral simplicity, and lyric praise. It is also displayed in the Virgilian purity of his language, and in his subtle use of Virgilian borrowings so that the new contexts transform but do not obliterate the old associations: for example, the phrase "Fortunati ambo" descriptive of Nisus and Euryalus linked in death is applied to the kneeling ox and ass at Christ's nativity.[70] Sannazaro is alone among the humanists in his exuberant, positive use of the classical supernatural. He does not merely allude to the classical personages as mythic figures or types, nor does he conflate them with demons acting against God, but he uses them—or more precisely he uses the minor pagan theogony—as actors on the same plane as the biblical personages: the river-god Jordan, Proteus, the Sibyls, the Nymphs, and the Graces all join consciously and gladly in predicting and celebrating Christ. Moreover, though he is like Valle and Bonus in invoking rather than denouncing the classical Muses, Sannazaro alone praises them enthusiastically, welcoming them back formally, as it were, into Christian poetry on the ground that they are themselves virgins, virtually sisters of the Sibyls, and thus worthy to sing in the Virgin's honor.[71]

As the poem opens, God, looking down upon the exiled Fathers in Avernus, holds a kind of council in heaven with himself, and determines upon man's redemption through woman. He sends Gabriel as *nuntius* to Mary, who is discovered reading the Sibylline prophecies. After the Incarnation—delicately rendered through the imagery of light penetrating glass—Fame spreads the news everywhere; when the Fathers in Limbo hear it, David sings of the entire life of Christ, the Harrowing of Hell, the defeat of Pluto, and the triumphal procession of the saints to heaven. Book II opens with a lovely pastoral description of Nature bursting into flower as Mary journeys to visit Elizabeth, a visit which provides the occasion for Zachary to point out to her many scriptural prophecies of Christ. The incident of the Augustan census offers Sannazaro an opportunity for a catalogue and an elaborate description of the nations under the Roman aegis, culminating in Joseph's apostrophe to Bethlehem as the greatest of all cities. The birth itself is described, again delicately, under the image of dew insensibly falling. A formal council in heaven opens Book III, in which God, wearing a garb upon which is depicted the creation story, reviews the fall of the angels and man, and then prophesies the restoration of all things through the mission of Christ. At length he dispatches to Bethlehem a Virgilian/medieval allegorical entourage including Joy, Harmony, Faith, Dance, Play, the Graces, and Peace. At Bethlehem the shepherds Lycidas and Aegon from Theocritus' *Idylls* chant Virgil's *Eclogue IV*, while angels carry overhead the symbols of the coming Passion—thorns, cross, lance. At the conclusion of the poem the river-god Jordan, carrying his familiar vase on which is depicted the baptism of Christ, recounts to the nymphs a prophecy by Proteus of the miracles of Christ. Appropriately, the account emphasizes the miracles relating to water—the miracle at Cana, the multiplication of the fishes, the calming of the tempest, and the feeding of the multitude by the banks of the sea.

Marcus Hieronymus Vida's *Christiad* (1535, 6 books, *ca.* 6,000 hexameters),[72] commissioned by Pope Leo X but not published until 1535, presents the third possibility—a creative imitation of Virgilian epic structure as well as style, presenting an action and a theme which, in their centrality and significance, are the appropriate Christian analogues to the action and theme of the *Aeneid*.[73] The poem is hardly a brief epic of the scope with which we have hitherto been concerned for it is about three times the length of *Paradise Regained*. It was, however, a most important influence upon subsequent Christian epics of all sorts—Old Testament poems, lengthy Christiads, and especially brief Christiads. To the last mentioned kind it afforded the example of a fully developed Virgilian epic structure in a poem considerably shorter than the *Aeneid*, with six rather than the canonical twelve books, with a non-military, New Testament subject, a flexible application of the neoclassical rules, a continuation of the medieval/Renaissance use of typology as a means of incorporating all biblical history in the specific action, and a continuation of the traditional ecclesiastical emphasis.

The subject of the *Christiad* meets the neoclassical requirement for unified action: its subject, Christ's redemptive sacrifice which founded the Christian church, offers a suitable parallel to Aeneas' founding of the Roman Empire. The poem observes the unities of time and place, although with some flexibility: the action takes place in Jerusalem during the last week of Christ's life, but at the end of the poem that time limit is extended to permit a treatment of the formal establishment of the church at Pentecost. The Virgilian structure is imitated closely: the poem begins *in medias res* just before Christ's entry into Jerusalem, with his speech commissioning his apostles to teach all nations; the previous action is related through long epic recitals, and the future is foretold by prophecy. Vida's conservatism in the use of the classical supernatural looks forward to later neoclassical diatribes against the mixture of classical and Christian references, but Vida retains some flexibility here: the supernatural agents are all from Christian story, but the classical atmosphere and furniture of

Hell-Avernus is retained, as are such Virgilian allegorical figures as Fame.

In several respects, however, the Virgilian imitation is not an unqualified success. In terms of language and diction, the conventional epithets and phrases which Vida borrows from Virgil are usually adequate to his purposes, and the specific echoes and allusions often enhance and deepen the meaning of the poem. But the use of a single standard of elevated, Virgilian diction has made for some curious incongruities, for example, the description of Mary's cottage at Nazareth and the upper room of Christ's Last Supper as palatial dwellings. Another weakness is Vida's conspicuous failure, except with Judas and Pilate, to develop character or even to present it consistently throughout the poem.

A brief résumé will reveal Vida's use and codification of the now standard biblical epic episodes, devices, and *topoi*. The introductory epic question as to the cause of Christ's fate receives a partial answer in a council in hell wherein Satan expounds upon the danger to his kingdom, reviews his previous unsuccessful attacks upon the Son of God in the battle in heaven and in the temptation, and then sends forth his demons to incite the Jews and Judas against Christ. Entering Jerusalem Christ sees carved on the Temple the Old Testament occasions for and types of himself and his mission—the Creation, the Fall, the Flood, Abraham and Isaac, Joseph, Moses and the serpent, and the pelican. The book ends with the Transfiguration and the Father's prophecy in a heavenly council of Christ's future glorious kingdom centered in Rome. Book II presents an epic council of war wherein the Jewish priests debate the threat posed by Christ; a geographical catalogue of the twelve tribes and their homelands occasioned by the crowds pouring into Jerusalem at Passover; an account of the Last Supper at which a song is sung celebrating the manna in the desert as a Eucharistic type; and a description of the capture and subsequent arraignment of Christ before a sympathetic and complexly conceived Pilate. Books III and IV comprise two separate recitals delivered successively by Joseph and John the Evangelist who, having heard from Fame the news of Christ's capture, come to Pilate to plead for him. Joseph describes in detail Christ's infancy and childhood while John offers a summary of his own Gospel, including Christ's relation to the Godhead, the fall of the angels and man, Christ's public life, teachings, and miracles, and the coming Last Judgment. Book V presents the successful attack of the allegorical figures Fear and Sloth against Pilate, followed by a warlike scene in heaven wherein the angels mobilize to go to Jerusalem to save Christ, being inspired to this action by the scenes depicted on heaven's portals of their valiant deeds in the battle against Lucifer in heaven. They are restrained, and the Passion and Crucifixion follow. Book VI utilizes material from the *decensus* tradition, summarizing the Harrowing of Hell, the liberation of the Fathers in Limbo, the Resurrection, Ascension, and Pentecost.

Latin biblical poems during the remainder of the sixteenth century draw heavily upon these early humanist poems as regards both the theory and the practice of biblical epic. Most are brief. Most have New Testament subjects, restricted rather than panoramic in scope. Most employ the familiar structural pattern of an *ab ovo* beginning and a straightforward chronological narrative, varied by numerous recitals, prophecies, and iconographical scenes. Most incorporate the familiar episodes and *topoi*—denunciation of the Muses, council in hell, parliament of heaven, Gabriel as *nuntius*. Most use the classical epithets and diction—"Jupiter," "Olympus," "Tonans," "Avernus"—but show increasing circumspection about alluding to or using classical figures as characters or as types. Most however employ biblical typology as a central device extending the scope and significance of the limited subjects.

One of the most important of these later poems is Girolamo Fracastoro's *Joseph* (1555, 2 books, *ca.* 1,280 hexameters, unfinished),[74] the first brief epic to apply to an Old Testament subject the apparatus of humanist biblical epic, and the first to attempt much characterization of biblical personages. The poem relates itself at every possible point to the *Aeneid:* Joseph is portrayed as an ancestor of Christ and savior of the holy people from which Christ sprang, as Aeneas is ancestor of Augustus and founder of the Roman people; Egypt and Palestine correspond to Carthage and Latinum; Pluto presides over a classical hell and plots against Jacob's tribe as Juno did against the Trojans; Potiphar's wife is presented as a love-maddened Dido incited by Allecto, in language recalling Book IV of the *Aeneid*. Typology also remains important in this brief Old Testament epic. Joseph is specifically identified as a type of Christ when he is betrayed by his brother Judah, when his bloody cloak is shown to his father, when he saves his brothers from death by famine, when he endures a three-day temptation by Potiphar's wife, and when Gabriel as *nuntius* reveals to him his future progeny, including Christ. Some other brief Old Testament epics include the *Jonas Propheta* of Christianus Pierius, Coloniensis (1555, 1 book, *ca.* 550 hexameters), and the *Judith Viduae Historia* of Abbé Charles Godran (1569, 1 book, *ca.* 650 hexameters), both of which are paraphrases ornamented with some epic diction and elaboration of incident.[75] The more imaginative *Monomachia Davidis et Goliae* of Rudolph Walther (n.d., 3 books, *ca.* 2,450 hexameters) treats the single combat of David and Goliath against the background of the martial preparations and battles of the Philistines and Israelites.[76]

Among the later Latin New Testament poems are Teofilo Folengo's *L'Agiomachia* (sixteenth century), a collection of the lives of three saints, of which the first, the "Passion of St. Andrew" (920 lines), has some relation to biblical material and uses a few epic elements, and Abbé Godran's *Historia Crucis Dominicae* (1565, 3 books, *ca.* 400 hexameters), which presents the Passion, Crucifixion, and Harrowing in terms of a close paraphrase of John xviii—xix.[77] But the most interesting of the later New Testament brief epics are two companion poems written by Jacobus Strasburgus.[78] The *Oratio Secunda* (1565, 1 book, *ca.* 806 hexameters) presents a parliament in heaven in which Justice and Truth indict fallen man and Mercy and Peace defend him, the impasse being resolved by the Son who undertakes man's salvation. The *Oratio Prima* (1565, 1 book, *ca.* 800 hexameters) is the only brief epic I have found which, like *Paradise Regained,* takes Christ's temptation as its subject. The temptation is described in the epic proposition as "the duel between the victorious Christ and Satan,/ A duel waged in dialogue and with weapons divine,/ In the desolate mountains among the trackless haunts of wild animals," [79] and the conception and imagery of the duel of words is retained throughout the poem. Christ is a "young warrior," learning by the easy contests of the temptation the rudiments (*rudimentum*) of his forthcoming grand warfare at the Harrowing.[80] The temptation sequence itself is presented by the allegorical method of the *psychomachia* whereby, after each temptation is voiced, the Furies of hell in combination with certain personified vices—Avarice, Glory, Ambition, and so forth—attack Christ, while his virtues resist and ultimately defeat them. The opportunity is accordingly provided for the epic apparatus of swords, arrows, and general warfare.

The poem makes subtle rather than explicit use of typology: Isaiah and Hezekiah, who had resisted the blasphemous Assyrian Sennacherib and his delegate Rab-shakeh, and who had caused by their prayers the annihilation of the entire Assyrian army (II Kings xviii:17), are displayed as types of Christ in the third temptation when they lead forth a cohort of celestial powers to resist the attack of Blasphemy. Also, a simile relates Christ's temptation as a whole to the battle of David and Goliath, and the concluding episode wherein Christ dashes the Furies upon the rocks foreshadows the Harrowing.

The development of medieval and humanist biblical epic provides therefore a firm basis for Milton's conception of a literary category of brief epic, as well as for some of his artistic strategy in *Paradise Regained*. Throughout the long period here discussed, the overwhelming preponderance of biblical epic-like poems were of brief rather than grand proportions. Though this was probably due less to conscious choice than to the difficulty of executing a long epic poem, nevertheless the three-book format (inspired by the Trinity) and the four-book format (inspired by the four Gospels) had considerable popularity. At any rate, the precedent is firmly established for brief epics on biblical subjects, incorporating whatever traditional epic apparatus can be made relevant to the particular subject. Throughout this period, the overwhelming preponderance of brief biblical epics have Christ or Mary as subject. They are contrived according to three basic formulas: the standard patristic format of the panoramic subject presented sequentially, the often used medieval pattern of a sequence of episodes or scenes linked together typologically, and the dominant Renaissance pattern of a single action or episode expanded by the use of prophecy, recitals, and other devices. Nearly all of these poems employ typological symbolism as a most important aesthetic device to achieve unity in a vast subject, or to extend the significance and scope of a limited subject. This typological symbolism forms the basis and substance of most of the casual allusions, recitals, prophecies, and iconographical representations so prevalent in these works, thereby providing a means for the organic integration of these classical epic devices into the biblical epic.

CHAPTER IV · THE BRIEF BIBLICAL EPIC: NEOCLASSICAL INFLUENCES

*D*URING the period 1550–1650 criticism of "pagan" secular poetry intensified and recommendations for Christian or specifically biblical poetry grew more urgent. The French poet Joachim Du Bellay in *La Lyre Chrestienne* (1552) urged Christians to imitate Plato's expulsion of the poets by refusing to admit "la Lyre ethnique/ En la republique de Dieu," and to find a precedent in the Israelites' theft of gold from the Egyptians to repossess the classical poetic wealth for God.[1] The Italian critics Frosino Lapini (1567) and Lorenzo Gambara (1576) revived the old Platonic arguments regarding poetry's falseness, immorality, and blasphemy, arguing that pagan poetry should be banished and all pagan ornament eliminated from Christian poetry.[2] The Frankfurt Franciscan Henricus Petreus Herdesianus (1578) flatly denied the patristic-humanist assumptions that pagan poetry is allegorical, or that pagan learning derives from Moses, declaring that poets should take their subjects only from Christian theology and philosophy and especially from Scripture—such subjects as the patience of Job, the wisdom of Joseph, the fortitude of Judas Maccabaeus, the piety of David, the life and death of Christ.[3] Challenges like these, posed by Catholics and Protestants alike, continued for a century, and they were met by a great increase in the number and kinds of biblical poems. Most of these poems, with the significant exceptions of the celestial cycle poems and the brief epics on New Testament subjects, were strongly affected by neoclassical precepts and influences.

NEW DIRECTIONS IN BIBLICAL EPIC THEORY AND PRACTICE

As the humanist impetus declined toward the end of the sixteenth century, the most important new theoretical basis for the production of biblical epic was supplied by Guillaume Du Bartas' *Uranie* (1574), a short, dream-vision poem which consecrated a new muse for Christian poetry.[4] The poem recounts the visit to Bartas of the celestial Urania, Muse of Astronomy, and so by extension of other heavenly things such as divine poetry. Denouncing the false and licentious poetry inspired by her sisters, Urania urges Bartas to reclaim for God that noble gift, poetry, which originated in the Bible for God's praise but then was perverted by Satan to idolatrous and immoral uses:

> The chain of *Verse* was at the first invented
> To handle onely sacred Mysteries
> With more respect: and nothing else was chanted
> For long time after in such *Poësies.*

> So did my *David* on the trembling strings
> Of his divine *Harp* onely sound his *God:*
> So milde-soul'd *Moses* to *Jehova* sings
> *Jacob's* deliverance from th'*Egyptians* Rod.

> So *Debora* and *Judith,* in the Camp;
> So *Job* and *Jeremy,* in cares oppressed;
> In tune-full *Verses* of a various stamp,
> Their joyes and sighes divinely-sweet expressed.[5]

Pointing out that only heavenly inspiration can make a true poet, she promises that Bartas will attain the heights of poetic achievement and even immortality if he will take her as his guide and make the Spirit his Pegasus. She also suggests various biblical stories as offering far more promising poetical material than their classical counterparts: better Noah's flood than

Deucalion's, better Lazarus' resurrection than that of Hippoly-
tus; better the Tower of Babel than the revolt of the Titans.
Significantly, in this argument the often cited classical analogues of biblical events receive wholly negative connotations:
they are not reflections but satanic perversions of biblical truth.

For at least the next seventy-five years critics and practitioners of Christian poetry allude to or reiterate the *Uranie*
argument in treatises or prefaces or in the opening lines of
poems, most often in connection with recommendations or
defenses of New Testament poetic subjects. Urania's chief
propositions—that poetry originated in the Bible, that it subsequently degenerated in the celebration of Venus, that the
Christian poet has a pressing duty to reclaim it to God's service—are repeated by the Italian poet Erasmo di Valvasone
in a prefatory statement to his *Angeleida* (1590), and by the
French poet Antoine La Pujade in a poetic account of a new
visit of Urania, *La Muse Chrestienne* (1604).[6] In England,
Du Bartas' *Uranie* appeared in two distinguished translations:
James I's version in heroic couplets (1585) gave it royal approval, and Joshua Sylvester's somewhat shorter stanzaic
translation (1605) gave it wide currency, for Sylvester included it in his several extremely popular collections of Du
Bartas' poems.[7] Moreover, Robert Southwell gave a prose recension of the *Uranie* argument in the preface to his *Saint
Peters Complaynt* (1595); Sir John Stradling paraphrased
several stanzas of the poem and summarized its entire argument in his long Christiad (1625); Joseph Fletcher in the
opening stanzas of *Christes Bloodie Sweat* (1613) recounted
a *Uranie*-like dream vision in which Christ urged him to undertake that subject; and Robert Aylett wrote a free paraphrase
of the entire poem called *Urania, or the Heavenly Muse*
(1654), in which Urania especially recommended as poetic
subjects Christ's sacrifice for man and the love between the

Heavenly Bridegroom and his Bride, the church.[8] Interestingly enough the *Uranie* argument usually appeared in connection with New Testament poems or proposals for them.

A second theoretical current profoundly affecting biblical epic toward the end of the sixteenth century was the Italian neoclassical criticism which developed throughout that century. Much of this criticism implicitly challenged the epic claims of many if not all biblical poems, but some treatises— commentaries on Dante, on the Italian romances, on Plato, and even some on Aristotle's *Poetics*—offered formulations which could accommodate the biblical epic kind. In any event, from this time forward neoclassical precepts were seldom wholly ignored, though they might be deliberately rejected, by the writers and critics of biblical epics.

The omnipresent definition in this body of criticism of the end of poetry as moral instruction was obviously hospitable to the claims of biblical epic, and critics sometimes formulated the dictum in distinctly Christian terms: G. G. Trissino declared (1529, 1562) that the end of poetry is to teach men to live well so as to achieve peace in this life and felicity in the next, and the Jesuit Antonio Possevino (1593) observed that poetry must demonstrate its utility by glorifying Christianity.[9] Also, the widespread critical belief that the epic hero should be superlatively virtuous, possessing all the moral and theological virtues and combining the concerns of the active and contemplative lives, was readily applicable to certain Old Testament figures and especially to Christ.[10] Filippo Sassetti's defense (*ca.* 1573) of the heroic claims of Dante's protagonist, based upon a "modern" redefinition of heroic virtue suitable to an age which does not particularly need or value tremendous physical strength, is especially relevant for the theory of biblical epic as well as for Milton's own conception of the higher heroism:

If heroic virtue is virtue, generally considered, which in perfection exceeds that which is commonly found, we must believe that, just as extraordinary strength is a heroic virtue, so also is extraordinary prudence; and the same for every other disposition of the mind ... so that today in the place of the heroes we should not put those of illustrious lineage who are renowned in war, but, wishing to take cognizance of the change [in social attitudes], generally those who through their virtue ... whatever it may be, are greatly admired by other virtuous men.[11]

Giason Denores' argument (1586) that the epic hero should be morally perfect and Spenser's proposal (1589) to frame a hero "perfected in the twelve private morall vertues" testify to the influence of such thinking on the poets. The specific application of this precept to biblical epic is evident in the French poet Nicolas Frénicle's declaration (1636) that he has found in Christ an epic hero displaying "les vertus heroïques en leur plus haut degré." [12]

On the other hand, the fact that most of the Italian treatises accepted Horace's definition of the epic subject—"res gestae regumque ducumque et tristia bella"—threatened to eliminate from the epic category biblical poems based upon the New Testament or upon "peaceful" Old Testament stories. An example of the impact of this precept on the choice and conception of the biblical epic subject may be found in Bartolommeo Tortoletti's comparison (1628) of his heroine Judith to the warrior heroes Aeneas and Achilles.[13] However, certain critics challenged this concept and offered justifications for "peaceful" epic subjects which could apply to the biblical subject matter. Bernardino Daniello (1536), Trissino (1547), Benedetto Varchi (wr. 1554), and G. P. Capriano (1555) argued that the epic might properly comprehend everything in the world, or might treat specifically peaceful concerns.[14] Others gave indirect support to this concept through their defenses of Dante's *Commedia* as epic: for example, Francesco Bonciani declared (*ca.* 1589) that the *Commedia's* subject is "glorious above every other one, because through it a mortal man becomes in a certain way a participant in the glory of the blessed, than which perhaps no other can be imagined so illustrious, nor consequently better suited to the heroic poem."[15] Moreover, the Italian poet Marino's lengthy, sensuous, and wholly unheroic poem *L'Adone* (1623) was widely accepted as an epic and was defended by the French critic Jean Chapelain as an example of a legitimate variety of epic poem whose subject is peace and love rather than war and heroism.[16]

The concept of verisimilitude, which provided that the historian should deal with the true subject but the poet with a verisimilar or probable subject offering scope for poetic invention, threatened yet more severely the biblical poet's status not only as an epic poet but as any kind of poet, for he was committed to a true, indeed a sacrosanct, subject. However, some sixteenth-century Italian critics and also later writers defended the true subject as proper to poetry: Julius Caesar Scaliger (1561) conflated poetry and history by admitting Lucan to the ranks of the epic poets; the English critics Puttenham (1589) and Francis Meres (1598) followed suit, applying the epic label to certain contemporary historical poems.[17] The Latin poet Joannes Klockus (1601) not only conflated but identified the two disciplines, declaring, "History is unfettered poetry, and poetry is history reduced to number," and Tommaso Campanella (*ca.* 1596) went so far as to affirm that the true poetic subject was innately more credible and more moving for the audience than the fictional story.[18] Francesco Robortello (1548) and Jacopo Mazzoni (1587) found scope for invention in a true subject with a predetermined plot through the addition of episodes and ornaments, and later the biblical poets Nicolas Frénicle, Louis Le Laboureur, and Michael Drayton claimed to have invented in just this way, adding figures, allegories, descriptions, and new episodes as "Jems and exterior ornaments" which did not affect the substance of the true story.[19]

Also, the precept of verisimilitude greatly restricted the use of the supernatural in biblical epic, for it dictated that classical mythology be banished as incredible in modern poems, and the mixture of pagan and Christian allusions be avoided as indecorous and impious unless the pagan mythological terms are confined to the speech of the pagan characters.[20] Trissino in his epic *La Italia Liberata da Gothi* (1547) offered a novel but patently artificial solution to the problem by transforming each of the ancient gods into an angel with the same properties and functions, for example, "L'angel Nettunio col tridente in mano." But most critics simply recommended using the Christian supernatural supplemented perhaps by romance magic or by allegorical personifications of virtues, vices, and natural phenomena.[21] However, there was also some feeling that the poetic use of the Christian God as a character might be indecorous and impious, and that the use of the supernatural generally should be restrained in the interests of credibility.[22]

In the matter of epic structure, Robortello, Daniello, Trissino, and A. Sebastiano Minturno (1563) along with many other Italian critics insisted upon the observance of such neoclassical rules as the *in medias res* beginning and the unities of action, time, and place.[23] Unity of action, most critics agreed, demanded a single, unified subject, and this precept rendered inadmissible two of the traditionally popular formulas for biblical epic, the panoramic subject presented sequentially and the episodic subject comprised of related episodes linked by typological symbolism. The neoclassical unities and structural rules were specifically applied to biblical epic by poets such as Tortoletti, who prided himself upon having adhered to strict unity of action and the *in medias res* beginning, and Joannes Klockus, who praised Vida above all other writers as one who anticipated "our rules." [24] At the same time, however, the pluralistic principle developed by critics Giovanni Battista Pigna (1552) and Cinthio (1554), whereby they justified the romances on the ground that their subject matter required an organization different from that of the Homeric or Virgilian epic, provided a basis for the biblical poet to depart from the neoclassical rules and still consider his poem epic. Philippe Le Noir later (1638) appealed to such a principle when he argued that human epic rules are not appropriate to the divine story. [25]

A third major influence shaping the biblical epic of the period is the epic theory and practice of Du Bartas, and like the Italian criticism this influence leads both toward and away from neoclassicism. Du Bartas' immensely popular and often edited *Sepmaine* (1578, 7 books, *ca.* 6,500 hexameters) treating the seven days of creation, and his unfinished *Seconde Sepmaine* (1584–1608, 4 books) [26] intended to present the seven ages of man's restoration, are flagrantly antineoclassical; these celestial cycle poems are in the tradition of the panoramic patristic-medieval poems which treat sequentially the entire span of biblical history. Du Bartas' poems differ from these predecessors by their greater length—incorporating much description, didactic material, and recondite lore—and by their Old Testament emphasis, but resemble these forerunners in using typological symbolism as a principal source of unity and cohesion. These poems employ many epic devices common to humanist and neoclassical poems—classical proposition and invocation, classical diction and epithets, councils in hell and heaven. But their mixture of classical mythological references with the Christian supernatural defies strict neoclassical principles, as does their notably loose and irregular structure, defended by Du Bartas on the ground that the novelty of the subject demands a "new and unaccustomed method." [27]

However, Du Bartas' first epic, *Judit* (1574, 6 books, *ca.*

2,000 lines, translated into English by Thomas Hudson in 1584 and by Sylvester in 1614),[28] is strictly neoclassical, setting thereby an influential precedent for later brief Old Testament epics. In his preface Du Bartas openly declares his neoclassical aims: *"I have not so much aimed to follow the phrase or text of the Bible, as I have preased* [sic] *(without wandring from the verity of the History) to imitate* Homer *in his* Iliades *and* Virgil *in his* Æneidos, *and others who hath left to us works of such like matter."* He also excuses any errors which might offend the critics with the plea, *"I am the first in* France *who in a just* [i.e., neoclassically regular] Poëme *hath treated in our tongue of sacred things."* [29] As with many of the humanist poems the subject of *Judit* is a single episode, but unlike them it follows the neoclassical unities strictly: the action is the siege and deliverance of Bethulia, the places are Bethulia and Holofernes' camp, the time span is a few days. *Judit* also departs from customary humanist epic practice and moves toward a stricter neoclassicism by its *in medias res* beginning (with Bethulia under siege) and by its use of epic recitals and iconographical descriptions as history and prophecy and analogy rather than for typological extension of significance. The recitals in this poem present previous Jewish history from Abraham to Joachim, the early life of Judith as virgin, wife, and widow, and the previous battles of Holofernes. The scenes depicted in Judith's embroidery work contain biblical analogues to the deliverance wrought by Judith—the stories of Lot's wife, Susanna, Joseph, and Jephthah's daughter. The tapestries in Holofernes' tent present the stories of Cyrus and Sardanapalus as analogues to Holofernes' conquests. The poem also displays all the classical apparatus which had become standard in the humanist biblical epics: regular proposition and invocation, councils on both sides debating various proposals for war and peace, martial trappings, extended similes, classical epithets, and supernatural agents, but in accordance with strict neoclassical rules only the pagans refer without qualification to the classical supernatural. Significantly, the poem displays new strength in character development, achieving a subtlety and particularization far beyond what had seemed to be possible earlier with the New Testament or the celestial cycle poems: Judith is shown wavering and agonizing over the action she is called upon to perform, and Holofernes is displayed most humanly as a victim of vanity and self-delusion.

Still another important influence for biblical epic is Tasso, who challenged that form by defining a competing formula for Christian epic poetry. This alternative formula was set forth in his highly influential epic *Gerusalemme Liberata* (1581, reissued in extensively revised form as *Di Gerusalemme Conquistata,* 1593), and in his theoretical discussions in the "Allegoria" to the *Liberata* (1581), the *Discorsi dell'Arte Poetica* (1587), and the *Discorsi del Poema Heroico* (1594).[30] Anticipated in certain respects by Ariosto's *Orlando Furioso* (1532), Trissino's *La Italia Liberata da Gothi* (1547), and Pierre de Ronsard's unfinished *Franciade* (1572),[31] the new formula was devised according to neoclassical precepts. Tasso rejects biblical subject matter for epic because it is true, known, and sacrosanct, and so leaves no scope for necessary poetic invention; he also rejects subjects drawn from pagan history because the pagan supernatural machinery called for by such subjects is incredible to a Christian audience. Instead he recommends the great martial stories from Christian profane history—neither too ancient lest the manners recounted be disagreeable to the modern audience, nor too recent lest the stories be too well known to admit poetic alteration. Tasso's formula also calls for heroes who display lofty moral virtue and true piety as well as military prowess; for a wholly Christian supernatural machinery consisting of God, angels, devils, and Satan along with magicians and soothsayers from the romance tradition; and for a unified action with an *in medias res* beginning, although the unity provision does not preclude the mingling of numerous episodes with the principal action. Tasso's *Gerusalemme* exemplifies these features and also sets a precedent for the explication of such stories from Christian history as moral allegories of the combat and victory of the understanding (Godfrey) over the rebellious, ireful, and concupiscent parts of the soul (Rinaldo, Tancred), as well as over the temptations and vices which assault it from without (the Saracen forces). But although Tasso's precepts seem to exclude biblical epic entirely, his position on this point is not unambiguous, for he himself is author of a biblical hexameral poem modeled on Du Bartas.[32] Also, his *Discorso della Virtù Heroica, et della Charità* (1582) offers some support for biblical epic by emphasizing resemblances between the active, martial ideal of heroic virtue or magnanimity and the religious, contemplative ideal of *caritas,* and by pointing to certain biblical and classical heroes—Esther, Elijah, Curtius, and Scipio—who fused the two ideals, being at once exemplars of heroism or love of country and also types of the perfect heroism and *caritas* of Christ.[33]

BIBLICAL EPICS, 1550–1650

Throughout these hundred years the kind of development given to a particular biblical poem depends less on the nationality and religion of its author than on the literary traditions of its kind. The neoclassical influence made itself felt especially in the very considerable increase in the number of long biblical poems of the dimensions of the *Iliad* or the *Aeneid;* in the large number of poems, brief and long, with limited, unified subjects and regular neoclassical structure; and also in the large number which use martial subjects from the Old Testament and the Apocrypha. A new feature of this period was the production of several brief poems on Old Testament subjects, often classically regular and using such epic devices as recitals, dreams, and iconographical scenes to produce epic dimension within the confines of a limited, unified subject. Significantly, the production of such brief poems under the aegis of emerging neoclassicism gave increased authority to the epic claims of the brief form.

However, despite the increased number of Old Testament poems, the poems on New Testament subjects continued to equal or perhaps even to outnumber them, and these New Testament epics were generally less influenced by the new standards than by the patristic-humanist tradition,[34] especially as regards structure, use of mythological allusions, and use of typology as an epic device. Indeed, several writers of brief and longer Christiads during this period gave forthright testimony to their important debts to the earlier models: Valvasone (1590) referred to Sannazaro, Vida, and the Tasso of *Il Mondo Creato* as his literary forebears; Joannes Klockus (1601) praised Vida's *Christiad* as the best model for biblical epic; Michel Foucqué (1574) cited Mantuan, Vida, and Juvencus as his predecessors in writing sacred poetry; and Nicolas Frénicle (1636) cited as his authorities "Hierosme Vida" and "Sannazare qui égale les meilleurs Poëtes de toute l'antiquité, & dont la renommée sera venerable à tous les siecles."[35] Michael Drayton (1604) mentioned among those "that have accompanied us in this kinde...that Reverende *Hieronymus Vida* his *Christeis,* conteyning the life and miracles of *Christ,* that hath beene, and is, generally received through Christendome (and verie worthily)...and *Bartas* his *Judeth*."[36] Giles Fletcher (1610), whose work Milton certainly knew, mentioned as his models Juvencus, Prosper, "sedulous *Prudentius,*" and "prudent *Sedulius,*" as well as "*Sanazar,* the late-living Image, and happy imatatour of *Virgil,*" and "thricehonoured *Bartas*."[37] A further evidence of patristic-medieval influence may be seen in the fact that during this hundred-

year period, just as in the past, the best and best known of
the New Testament poems were brief rather than long.

   In the period 1550–1650 the great majority of Old Testament
poems were brief epics about a single hero: the warrior heroes
David and Judith were most popular, closely followed by the
peaceful Joseph, Susanna, Esther, and Job. Those poems which
predate Du Bartas or are for other reasons wholly unaffected
by the example of his *Judit* seem simply to recount the particular tale or episode in straightforward, sequential fashion,
making little effort to extend the perspective through the use
of recitals or typological references. This category includes
several close paraphrases which treat an entire biblical story
or book rather than a single unified action and which claim
epic status solely by the use of classical diction, formulaic
opening lines, and some expansion of dramatic scenes.[38] It
also includes the Italian *La Vita di Giuseppe* by Lodovico
Dolce (1561, 3 books, *ca.* 1,900 lines in ottava rima), which
moves only slightly beyond paraphrase: this work follows
Fracastoro's poem closely to the point where his narrative
breaks off, and thereafter paraphrases the text of the Bible,
but it does rework this material to some degree, deleting Fracastoro's classical epithets and mythological references and
substituting Invidia for his Allecto, Satan for his Pluto.[39] Also
unaffected by Du Bartas are several French Pléiade poems
on the subject of David—Joachim Du Bellay's *La Monomachie
de David et de Goliath* (1560, 1 book, *ca.* 300 alexandrines),
Pierre de Brach's poem of the same name (1576, 1 book, *ca.*
388 alexandrines), and Remy Belleau's *Les Amours de David
et de Bersabee* (1572, 1 book, *ca.* 380 alexandrines).[40] All of
these are of epyllion length and all deal with a single episode,
but they make no effort to extend the perspective by recitals,
prophecies, or typology. All incorporate classical epic diction
and mythological references as well as the stock episodes such
as challenges, duels, battles, infernal tempters, parliaments in

heaven, and angelic *nuntii,* but do not follow the neoclassical unities or the Virgilian structure.

Of the brief Old Testament poems which postdate Du Bartas' *Judit* some few managed to escape its influence almost entirely. One of these is Gabrielle de Coignard's *Imitation de la Victoire de Judith* (1595, 1 book, *ca.* 2,400 alexandrines). It is probably indebted to Du Bartas for choice of subject but shows little other influence, being a straightforward account of the heroine's life from birth to death.[41] The several poems of the English poet Michael Drayton are also sequential narratives depending for their epic effect not upon Du Bartas' neoclassical structure but rather upon a profusion of mythological references and some rather striking spectacles and dramatic scenes: *Moyses in a Map of His Miracles* (1604, 3 books, *ca.* 2,165 lines in heroic couplets) presents the horrors of the Egyptian plagues and the awesome passage through the Red Sea; *Noahs Floud* (1630, 1 book, *ca.* 1,025 lines in heroic couplets) includes a striking description of the earth's lushness and the giants' perversity; *David and Goliath* (1630, 1 book, *ca.* 850 lines in heroic couplets) creates a heroic atmosphere of challenges and battle.[42] Thomas Fuller's *Davids Hainous Sinne, Heartie Repentance, Heavie Punishment* (1631, 3 books, *ca.* 1,000 lines in 7-line stanzas) is also organized sequentially, presenting a series of discrete scenes casually linked together: it begins with an allegorical battle between the flesh and the spirit which culminates in David's sin with Bathsheba and the murder of Uriah, then presents a parliament in heaven at which Christ wins mercy for David, and concludes with an account of David's punishment through Absalom's revolt and death.[43]

However, most of the brief Old Testament poems make considerable use of Du Bartas' formula. Among these are several French works on the popular apocryphal subject, Susanna—Didier Oriet's *La Susanne* (1581, 3 books, *ca.* 4,320 alexandrines), Anne D'Urfé's *Hymne de Saincte Susanne* (1608, 1 book, *ca.* 1,000 alexandrines), and Antoine de Montchrestien's *Susane, ou la Chasteté* (1601, 4 books, *ca.* 1,800 alexandrines).[44] All of these use some variety of epic proposition, invocation, and diction. All contain, unlike Du Bartas' *Judit,* considerable mythological allusion, but all of them follow Du Bartas in treating a single unified action—the temptation and trial of Susanna—and in using recitals and iconographical scenes to recount the heroine's earlier life or to introduce analogous incidents. The closest imitator of Du Bartas is the English poet Robert Aylett. His *Susanna* (1622, 4 books, *ca.* 1,470 lines in heroic couplets) treats the unified, restricted action of Susanna's temptation and trial; presents her early youth, education, and study of the Bible by means of recitals; and introduces analogous Old Testament stories through a series of scenes which Susanna (in imitation of the similar episode in *Judit*) embroiders on her husband's headband. Aylett's *Joseph, or Pharoah's Favourite* (1623, 5 books, *ca.* 2,950 lines in heroic couplets) finds its unified subject in the temptation of Jacob through the supposed loss of his children and is a direct imitation of the Book of Job. Epic recital and iconographical scenes are very important devices here. Joseph en route to Egypt tells his captors the story of Jacob and Rachel. The Egyptian wise man Trismegistus tells Joseph's brothers the story of the slave (Joseph) who became viceroy after interpreting Pharaoh's dream. Joseph narrates to his father, Jacob, the story of his temptation by Potiphar's wife. And an arras (modeled upon that in Fracastoro) adorns Joseph's banquet hall, portraying Old Testament history from the Flood to Joseph's own time. Aylett's *David's Troubles Remembred* (1638, 6 books, 3,410 lines in heroic couplets) sets forth the single, unified story of Absalom's rebellion, beginning with its cause in the death of Ammon and ending with David's restoration after Absalom's defeat in battle; the underlying cause of the troubles, David's sin with Bathsheba and the murder of Uriah, is told through an epic recital by Joab.[45] Several of these poems, and especially those of Aylett, depart from Du Bartas' formula by presenting the Old Testament hero as a type of Christ. The device serves here, as usual, to relate the episode treated to the entire providential sweep of history, but typology is never so organic or so central in the Old Testament poems as in the celestial cycle poems or the Christiads.

The few long epics about individual Old Testament heroes were also neoclassical, simply blowing up to more massive dimensions the familiar *Judit* formula—*in medias res* structure with previous history related through recitals and iconographical scenes, and also the familiar apparatus of proposition and invocation, classical diction, mythological references, infernal councils, and angelic *nuntii*. *La Reina Esther* by the Italian poet Ansaldo Ceba (1615, 21 cantos, *ca.* 25,000 lines in ottava rima) fuses with the above formula a romance profusion of love episodes peripheral to the main action and a baroque reduplication of incident. Two Latin examples—Bartolommeo Tortoletti's *Juditha Vindex et Vindicata* (1628, 6 books, *ca.* 4,725 hexameters) and Antonius Millieus' *Moyses Viator* (1636, 28 books, *ca.* 13,728 hexameters)—add to the formula a prominent typological focus: Judith's conquest of Holofernes typifies the Virgin's conquest of Satan, and the Israelites wandering the desert typify the true church wandering in the world.[46]

A second category of epics in this period consists of those which treat the whole or a great part of the three-phase celestial cycle—the battle in heaven, the creation of the world and fall of man, and the redemption by Christ. Characteristically, these poems use epic proposition and invocation, classical diction, many mythological references, and stock epic episodes such as councils and messengers and spectacular events.

They show the influence of Du Bartas and of neoclassicism
in the disposition to focus on Old Testament events, but they
display closer affinities with their patristic-humanist forerunners and with contemporary Christiads in their *ab ovo* structure, and in their employment of profuse typological symbolism. The massive panoramic poems use typology as a means
of unifying the vast subject by suggesting relations between
the parts of the entire cycle. Among them are several Italian
hexameral poems inspired by Du Bartas' *Sepmaine:* Tasso's *Il
Mondo Creato* (1607, 7 books, *ca.* 8,500 lines); Gasparo Murtola's *Della Creatione del Mondo* (1607, 16 cantos, 12,200 lines
in ottava rima); and Felice Passero's *L'Essamerone, overo
l'Opra de'Sei Giorni* (1608, 6 parts, 11,200 lines). French
hexameral poems include Christofle de Gamon's *La Semaine,
ou Créatione du Monde* (1599, 7 books, *ca.* 18,600 alexandrines), undertaken to refute some of Du Bartas' theological
and cosmological views from a more extreme Calvinist viewpoint; Théodore Agrippa D'Aubigné's *La Creation* (wr. 1620–
30, 15 books, *ca.* 3,500 alexandrines); and Sieur du Saint-
Martin's *La Nature Naissante* (1667, 1 book, *ca.* 700
alexandrines, unfinished).[47] Resembling the hexamera in their
massiveness, inclusiveness, sequential narrative, and diffuseness
of style, and yet achieving greater epic quality by reason of
their heroic battle scenes and grand spectacles are the Latin
Daemonomachie of Odoricus Valmarana (1627, 25 books, *ca.*
22,500 hexameters), which begins with the battle of the angels
and treats the warfare of Christ and Satan throughout history;
the English *Glasse of Time* by Thomas Peyton (1620, 2 books,
ca. 6,360 lines in heroic couplets), which is evidently modeled
on Du Bartas' *Seconde Sepmaine;* and a massive English
Doomsday by William Alexander (1637, 12 books, *ca.* 10,520
lines in 8-line stanzas).[48]

Characteristically, the brief poems in this category take as
subject one segment or part of the celestial cycle; they use

typology in the humanist manner as a means of relating the specific story or episode to the entire cycle; and they eschew the neoclassical rules and structure. Two of the most interesting of these poems concern the war in heaven—Erasmo di Valvasone's Italian poem *Angeleida* (1590, 3 books, *ca.* 3,000 lines), and Fredericus Taubmannus' Latin *Bellum Angelicum* (1604, 3 books, *ca.* 1,225 hexameters).[49] Both emphasize martial elements such as councils of war, visits of *nuntii,* epic taunts, challenges, addresses to troops, general battles, and single combats, and Valvasone also makes impressive use of epic recitals laden with typology.

Other brief poems take the fall of man as subject, linking it to the entire Fall-Redemption sequence through recitals and typological association. The *Microcosme* of the French poet Maurice Scève (1562, 3 books, *ca.* 3,000 alexandrines) presents Adam's fall and subsequent distress; then a dream vision (resembling that in *Paradise Lost* XI–XII) wherein Adam sees the encroachment of sin upon the world, the advancements of civilization, and the Old Testament and classical types of Christ; and finally Adam's prophetic song celebrating Christ's forthcoming redemption.[50] Jacobus Masenius' *Sarcotis* (1654, 5 books, *ca.* 2,500 hexameters) treats the same material as an allegory in which Sarcothea (Man) is seduced by Antitheos (Satan), eats the forbidden fruit, and thereafter becomes a battlefield for a *psychomachia* of virtues and vices.[51] Joseph Fletcher's English poem *Historie of the Perfect-Cursed-Blessed Man* (1629, 4 books, *ca.* 1,518 lines in heroic couplets) and Andrew Ramsay's Latin *Poemata Sacra* (1633, 4 books, 1,660 hexameters) [52] are organized in much the same way, but Ramsay's poem deserves special comment as perhaps the most artful of all the celestial cycle poems. It uses the epic apparatus of proposition, invocation, classical diction, and classical mythology; it creates rounded, dramatic characters; and it achieves a tight structural unity by taking as subject the

single, unified action of the Fall, relating the other parts of
the celestial cycle to that episode by means of typological recitals and prophecies. The opening description of the creation
of the world and of Adam and Eve's prelapsarian bliss is followed by a series of intensely dramatic scenes—Satan plotting
man's destruction in a council in hell, Satan deluding Eve by
flattery and crafty rhetoric, the invasion of the earth by the
allegorized vices, Themis and Clementia quarreling in a parliament in heaven over Adam's fate. This quarrel occasions a
long recital by Sapientia of the whole course of Christ's life,
death, and harrowing of hell, by means of which the Second
Adam will restore the first Adam and his progeny. Then, as
in *Paradise Lost,* the concluding scene of the poem shifts the
perspective from this vision of the ultimate resolution of
Adam's story to the immediate conclusion of the Fall sequence
—the banishment from the Garden.

Among New Testament poems the impact of the new clas-
sicism is evident from the great increase in the number of
long Christiads, often imitating the twelve-book format of the
Aeneid or the thirteen-book *Aeneid* with Vegius' addition. The
New Testament poems, brief and long, utilize the now standard epic apparatus—classical proposition and invocation, classical diction and epithets, councils in hell and heaven, angelic
nuntii, a hell peopled with classical monsters, and Virgilian
allegorical figures such as Despair, Rumor, and Fame. But like
the Old Testament celestial cycle poems just considered, and
in contrast to those about a single Old Testament hero, the
New Testament poems show close affinities to the patristic-
humanist tradition in their very considerable use of classical
mythological references, their recognition of classical figures
such as Hercules, Pan, and Oedipus as types of Christ, and
their prominent use of typological symbolism. This affinity is
not surprising since the poems about Christ are a variety—
indeed the oldest variety—of celestial cycle poem, placing the

emphasis on the redemption rather than the fall of man. Like
their patristic and medieval ancestors the new Christiads also
endeavor to incorporate the entire range of biblical history—
the Fall, the Old Testament (and classical) types of Christ,
the life, teachings, passion, death, and resurrection of Christ.
In addition, they retain the ecclesiastical focus customary in
the older New Testament poems, and so include material relating to the establishment and development of the Christian
church.

Many of the massive Christiads follow the pattern developed in patristic times by Sedulius, in which Gospel events
are presented in more or less sequential order, prefaced by a
comparatively brief summary of the Fall and the Old Testament types of Christ. One early example of a vernacular poem
employing this format is the Italian *La Humanità del Figliuolo
di Dio* (1533, 10 books, *ca.* 5,220 lines in ottava rima) by
Teofilo Folengo.[53] Among the Latin poems are Joannes Mellius de Sousa's *De Reparatione Humana* (1615, 8 books, *ca.*
8,600 hexameters) and also several centos in the tradition of
Proba, of which the most interesting is the *Virgilii Evangelisantis Christiados* by the Scottish Presbyterian Alexander Ross
(1638, 13 books, *ca.* 10,850 hexameters).[54] This category also
includes a number of French poems: Michel Foucqué's *La
Vie, Faictz, Passion, Mort, Résurrection, et Ascension de Nostre Seigneur Jésus Christ* (1574, 8 books, *ca.* 16,400 decasyl
labic lines); Nicolas de Montreulx's *Jésus Christ en l'Authel
et en la Croix* (1607, 1 book, *ca.* 19,200 alexandrines); Jean
D'Escorbiac's *La Christiade* (1613, 5 books, *ca.* 20,000 alexandrines). Abel D'Argent's *La Sepmaine* (1629, 7 books, *ca.*
8,000 alexandrines) gives the usual summary of Old Testament
events and then treats the week of man's restoration by
Christ (Passion Week), ending with the Last Judgment and
the Eternal Sabbath. And Estiene de Sanguinet's *La Dodécade
de l'Evangile* (1614, 12 books, *ca.* 18,150 alexandrines) treats

in the first six books the entire span of biblical history with emphasis on the life of Christ, and in the last six describes the church throughout history, beginning with its formal establishment at Pentecost.[55] Much the same formula is followed in Sir John Stradling's English work *Divine Poemes in Seven Severall Classes* (1625, 7 books, *ca.* 8,600 lines in 6-line stanzas), though with a show of humility the poet eschews the "heroicke" for the pastoral tone as being more suited to his powers.

A second variety of massive Christiad uses a similar technique but begins with the New Testament material—the birth of Christ or John the Baptist—treating this material sequentially except for the use of flashback or recital to present the story of the Fall and the Old Testament types. This format is followed by two Latin poems: Klockus' *Christiados Priscae et Novae Libri XII* (1601, 12 books, *ca.* 16,000 hexameters), which narrates the Old Testament background as a flashback on the occasion of Christ's baptism; and Natalis Donadeus' *De Bello Christi* (1614, 12 books, *ca.* 8,085 hexameters), a martial poem which presents the Old Testament material through a series of recitals by the Fathers in Limbo occasioned by Gabriel's annunciation of the birth of Christ to them.[56] It is used also in the French *La Christiade* of Antoine La Pujade (1604, 3 books, unfinished), a projected long epic which includes the Fall and the Old Testament types by means of a recital by the shepherds at the time of Christ's nativity.[57]

Among the brief Christiads a few such as the English *Countesse of Pembrokes Emanuel* by Abraham Fraunce (1591, 2 books, *ca.* 900 lines in rhyming hexameters) and the French *Poème sur la Vie de Jésus-Christ* by Robert Arnauld d'Andilly (1634, 1 book, *ca.* 940 alexandrines in 10-line stanzas) [58] are merely straightforward narrations of the Gospel story with minimal epic apparatus. But most use what has come to be the standard formula for brief epics of whatever kind in this period—a plot derived from a single episode or related sequence of actions, incorporating additional material by means of recitals and prophecies. However, the brief Christiads do not employ the neoclassical unities or the *in medias res* structure often found in Old Testament brief epics. Instead they follow medieval and humanist precedent, using typological symbolism in prophecies, flashbacks, and recitals to incorporate into the particular episode Christ's entire mission, or all of biblical history and the history of the church.

Perhaps influenced by Sannazaro, Giovanni Battista Marino's *La Strage de gli Innocenti* (1610, 4 books, *ca.* 3,230 lines in ottava rima) [59] takes as subject a single episode from Christ's infancy, the massacre of the Innocents. The poem employs all the expected devices: formal thematic statement, invocation to the Muse and to the Innocents themselves, an infernal council in a classico-medieval hell with Satan tormenting himself over the mystery of Christ's nature, a visit to the underworld caverns of the allegorical personage Cruelty, an incident in which Cruelty (disguised Allecto-fashion as Herod's brother Joseph) incites Herod to the massacre, a council of state with an argument between a wise counselor and a base flatterer (from Tasso), and an angelic *nuntius* bringing the allegorical figure Vision from the Cave of Morpheus to inspire Joseph's flight to Egypt. In addition, Marino strives to make the massacre itself resemble bloody epic warfare by showing the mothers trying feebly to resist the attacking troops. The massacre is projected against all history by means of a recital in which God answers the pleas of Mercy for the rescue of the Innocents by recounting man's fall and need for redemption, the forthcoming mission of Christ, and the glorious salvation awaiting the Innocents through Christ. Also, in the final scene, David welcomes the Innocents to Limbo with words anticipating Christ's forthcoming harrowing of hell.

Alexander More's brief Latin epic *Laus Christi Nascentis* (1655, 1 book, *ca.* 1,600 hexameters) [60] is much more obviously and more deeply indebted to Sannazaro—for its subject; for its lyric quality; for its ready use of classical typology (Christ as "Verus Apollo," the Sibyls as true prophets); for its use of casual typological associations as well as flashbacks, recitals, and prophecies; for its omission of the usual denunciations of classical subjects and Muses; and for its concluding lyrical song by the shepherds at the manger echoing Virgil's *Eclogue IV*.

The best known of the French biblical poems, Nicolas Frénicle's *Jésus Crucifié* (1636, 5 books, *ca.* 4,700 alexandrines) is somewhat longer than the usual brief Christiad, but is not on the massive scale: it is especially indebted to Vida. The subject, if not a unified action in the strictest neoclassical sense, is a narrowly limited sequence—Christ's passion, death, and triumphant harrowing of hell. The last event is briefly treated but is alluded to throughout the poem as the ultimate martial victory of Christ, the culmination of his epic duel with Satan. The entire biblical panorama is related to this sequence by recitals grounded in typology: at an opening council in hell Satan reviews past history (the battle in heaven, the Fall, the promised redeemer) and plans to incite the Jews against Christ. The story of Christ's earlier life and a prophecy of his forthcoming victories are presented in a Vida-like recital delivered by the allegorical Daughter of God, Vérité, who replaces the usual angelic *nuntius* in this poem. She comes in the guise of a shepherd to console Christ's followers after his apprehension, and to answer the Jews' false charges against Christ. Classical references abound, sometimes functioning typologically (the Sibyls are true prophets of Christ), sometimes as allegorical personifications—Crainte attacks Peter, Neptune is horrified at the Crucifixion, Sommeil sends a dream to Pilate's wife.[61]

A somewhat different formula is employed in the best-known English biblical poem of the period, Giles Fletcher's *Christs Victorie, and Triumph* (1610, 4 books, *ca.* 2,120 lines in 8-line stanzas). Combining Spenserian allegory with biblical narrative, the poem achieves unity through a medieval type of organization—the linking together of certain discrete but typologically related battles and victories of Christ's redemptive mission. The first two books are heavily indebted to the Spenserian allegorical method. The first presents the parliament in heaven at which Justice together with her militant allegorical retinue demands vengeance on fallen man, and Mercy counters with a recital of Christ's redemptive role, especially the events of his nativity and childhood. The second book describes Christ's temptation in the wilderness, where he encounters not only Satan but also the allegorical figures Famine, Despair, Presumption, Pangloretta—the last presiding over a Spenserian "Bowre of Bliss" which incorporates all worldly pleasures and honors. The third book deals with the Passion and Crucifixion, and the fourth with the Resurrection, Harrowing, Ascension, and triumphal procession of the patriarchs to heaven. These last two books largely eschew allegory for the more usual biblical epic style of narrative presentation of scriptural events, though the final scene, the marriage of the Heavenly Bridegroom and "Faire Egliset" based upon the mystical passages in Revelation, owes something to both techniques.

The Latin *De Messiae Pugna, Victoria, Triumpho* of François Du Port (1621, 3 books, *ca.* 4,700 hexameters) [62] is something of a structural hybrid, presenting a sequential account of biblical history, yet organized so as to focus upon various typologically related battles of Christ. Book I presents the temptation and fall of Adam as the occasion of the battle between the Serpent and the Seed, then briefly reviews the Old Testament prophecies and types as well as the early life of Christ as preparation for the battle, and finally presents Christ's crucifixion as the long awaited conflict. Book II relates the Harrowing of Hell as an epic-like battle and triumph, reviewing as well the typological predictions of the Fathers in Limbo. Book III records Christ's ascension, Pentecost, and the preaching and martyrdom of the apostles as episodes in Christ's final battle with and triumph over Satan by humility.

Two other kinds of poems, not always clearly differentiated, the "complaint" and the "Magdaliad," may claim some relation to the New Testament biblical epic in that many of them incorporate narrations of Gospel events couched in epic terms and using epic devices. As a genre the complaint is essentially a lyrical treatment of the tears and laments of a repentant sinner or a witness to Christ's passion. However, the first and most influential of these poems, Luigi Tansillo da Nola's *Le Lagrime di S. Pietro* (1560, 13 pianti, *ca.* 9,600 lines in ottava rima) [63] is subtitled in the 1600 edition, *Poema Sacro et Heroico,* and supports the latter claim by such devices as a formal epic proposition and invocation, several lively narrative recitals of Christ's life by Peter, an iconographical representation of the entire history of Christ's church carved on the Temple walls, and finally Peter's Dantesque journey through a Christian hell and heaven. Two other Italian complaints are Valvasone's *LaGrime di Santa Maria Maddelena* (1588, 1 book, *ca.* 600 lines), which has a lively description of Mary's possession by the fiend Allecto, and Ridolfo Campeggi's *Le Lagrime di Maria Vergine* (1617, 16 pianti, *ca.* 13,000 lines), which treats the Harrowing as a triumphal epic battle in a classical hell peopled by centaurs, chimeras, and other monsters.[64] Several French poems unite the complaint and romance forms: César de Nostradame's *Les Perles, ou les Larmes de la Saincte Magdeleine* (1606, 1 book, *ca.* 750 alexandrines), which compares Mary Magdalen with Ariosto's Angelica; and Thomas Robinson's *Life and Death of Mary Magdalen* (*ca.*

1620, 2 books, *ca.* 1,630 lines in 8-line stanzas), which presents Mary's life as a Spenserian allegory—a sojourn in a bower of bliss, then a persecution by the personifications Melancholy and Despair, and finally a course of instruction in the Castle of Wisdom.[65] Two French Magdaliads, Remi de Beauvais' *La Magdeleine* (1617, 20 books, *ca.* 20,000 alexandrines) and the brief *La Magdalaine Pénitente* of Louis Le Laboureur (1643, 5 books, *ca.* 1,300 alexandrines in 6-line stanzas), are noteworthy in that they have much more epic apparatus than the foregoing—recitals, prophecies, allegorical personifications, *psychomachias, Odyssey*-like voyages among classical monsters—but their epic quality is dissipated by a baroque profusion of ornament and a cloying spirituality.[66]

THE NEOCLASSICAL ASCENDANCY, 1650–75

By 1650, strict neoclassical principles had gained complete ascendancy in French epic theory and practice and had won a great deal of ground in England. Responding to this influence, most writers concerned with Christian epic in France now abandoned biblical subjects as unavailable to poetic invention, and instead followed Tasso in producing full-scale epics drawn from Christian profane history. Some of these were Georges de Scudéry's *Alaric, ou Rome Vaincue, Poëme Héroïque* (Paris, 1654), Jean Chapelain's *La Pucelle, ou la France Delivrée, Poëme Héroïque* (Paris, 1656), Jean Desmarets de Saint-Sorlin's *Clovis* (Paris, 1657), Louis Le Laboureur's *Charlesmagne, Poëme Héroïque* (Paris, 1664), and Pierre Le Moyne's *Saint Louys, ou la Sainte Couronne Reconquise* (Paris, 1658), all of them with prefaces explaining and defending the subjects and the treatment according to Tasso's principles. The epic recipe employed by all of these poems includes: a formulaic proposition beginning *Je chante;* frequent invocations to the Muses or their Christian equivalents; an *in medias res* structure with recitals, related episodes, and prophecies; a Christian *merveilleuse* restricting pagan allusions to the pagan characters and making much use of allegorical personifications; observance of the unities of action and of time (a one-year limit for epic); and the imposition of a Tasso-like moral allegory upon the plot. The ubiquity of certain common epic devices and episodes in these poems is underscored by Michel de Marolles' plea for some originality:

Thus we find it [the Christian epic] among the French, among the Italians, and among the modern Latins with the same thoughts, the same comparisons, and the same inventions. I see the gods assembled in council almost everywhere even as in Sannazaro's *De Partu Virginis.* I see everywhere the Sibyls agitated, prophecies of a long and illustrious posterity, Cerberuses, Furies, Elysian Fields. Iris or Mercury are never absent. Neptune is always inconstant and Juno spiteful. Apollo and the Muses are incessantly invoked for inspiration; and although these do not always appear under the same names, nevertheless they appear only to say the same thing, with the sole difference that most often it is not said so agreeably.[67]

More important, the mid-century French neoclassicists strongly affirmed the Horatian dictum that the proper epic subject is *res gestae,* though they usually added a stipulation permitting the interweaving of love episodes into the martial tale. Occasionally discussions of epic theory allowed for the possibility of a peaceful subject or a suffering hero, but almost without exception the nonbiblical Christian epics produced after 1650 have martial subjects and warrior heroes.[68] This perhaps accounts for the fact that in sharp contrast to the previous fifty years, very few Christiads were produced in the third decade of the seventeenth century, and those few were made to conform as nearly as possible to the neoclassical standards. Among the French, Perachon produced a free adaptation of More's Latin poem, titling it *Poëme sur la Naissance de Jésus-Christ* (1665, 2 books, *ca.* 3,600 alexandrines), but he explicitly rejected the heroic label on the ground that the

poem does not meet the neoclassical standards for epic subject and structure.[69] Similarly, Antoine Godeau, despite his
use of epic elements such as councils, Allecto figures, and classical references in the speech of the pagan characters, explained that he avoided the epic title for his *Saint Paul* (1654,
5 books, *ca.* 5,100 alexandrines) because of the truncated form
of the work (only five books), because the material—Paul's
martyrdom by beheading—is not marvelous, and because epic
ornament is omitted out of a desire to be faithful to the
Bible.[70] On the other hand, Robert Clarke's Latin *Christiados,
sive de Passione Domini & Salvatoris Nostri Jesu Christi Libri
17* (1670, 17 books, *ca.* 14,000 hexameters) [71] endeavored to meet
the neoclassical challenge directly by producing a Christiad
obviously modeled upon but outdoing Vida in neoclassical conception and structure. Like Vida, Clarke takes as his subject
Christ's passion and triumph, beginning the action at a point
just prior to the commencement of Christ's passion. However,
Clarke's conclusion, with Christ's ascension, respects the unities
more strictly than does Vida's projection forward to Pentecost,
and Clarke endeavors, moreover, the full-scale Virgilian epic.
Like Vida, Clarke presents the events of Christ's early life—
birth, flight to Egypt, baptism, temptation, miracles—through
a recital to Pilate, in this case given by Lazarus. Again like
Vida he incorporates the standard Old Testament résumé into
his opening scene by means of an epic recital in which Christ
at the Garden of Gethsemane tells his apostles of the war in
heaven, the fall of man, and the Old Testament types and
prophets. He also follows Vida in including a Harrowing
scene, harking back to the medieval *decensus* material, in
which Adam, Daniel, Moses, David, Judas Maccabaeus, Samson, and other Fathers in Limbo reiterate their prophecies
and witness Christ's glorious victory. However, the poem devi-
ates sharply from neoclassical precept and from Vida's example in the almost Renaissance abundance of its mythological

references and classical typological allusions, aligning itself in this regard with the older medieval-humanist formula for New Testament poems.

The Old Testament poems after 1650 are nearly all long, and they include some new or infrequently used subjects—Moses, Elias, Jonas, Joshua, Samson, St. Paul—in addition to the usual Judiths, Davids, Susannas, and Mary Magdalens. They may be classified most usefully according to their ways of responding to the neoclassical challenge. The first category of poems includes a few paraphrases whose epic qualities are limited to a proposition and invocation, some epic diction, and the expansion of spectacular incidents: these works are innocent or contemptuous of the new critical mandates, but assert a forthright epic claim in title or preface solely on the basis of lofty subject matter. Examples are the very long *David, Poëme Heroïque* of Bernard LesFargues (1660, 8 books, *ca.* 10,200 alexandrines), the *Hélie, Poëme Héroïque* attributed to Jacquelin (1661, 6 books, *ca.* 6,500 alexandrines), and several Jobean paraphrases.[72]

Much the largest group of biblical poets of the period are those who explicitly defend the biblical subjects as suitable epic material and as susceptible of poetic invention through ornamentation. They use the complete neoclassical epic apparatus—proposition, invocation, *in medias res* structure, recitals, prophecies, unities of action and time, councils in hell, angelic *nuntii,* allegorical personifications, Allecto figures, pastoral or romantic episodes—but are nevertheless so strongly influenced by the demand for a warrior hero that they eschew the label *héroique* for all poems lacking this feature. Significantly, the typological emphasis traditional in biblical epic is if anything intensified in these poems, which underscore the hero's role as a type of Christ not only in the recitals but often in the added analogous episodes as well. Marc-Antoine de Gérard Saint-Amant set forth his *Moyse Sauvé* (1653, 12 books, *ca.* 6,000 alexandrines) with full epic apparatus and even a Tasso-like moral allegory, but explained that he sub-titled it *Idyle Heroïque* because the pastoral connotations of "Idyl" are suitable for this poem which does "not have a chief hero active, nor grand battles, nor sieges of cities to produce" and which "extends merely for one entire day whereas a year or thereabouts is required for epic." [73] Marie de Pech de Calages declared of her *Judith, ou la Déliverance de Béthulie, Poëme Saint* (1660, 9 books, *ca.* 5,000 alexan-drines), which is filled with all the usual epic features, "I have wished rather to give it the title of *Saint* than of *Heroïque,* because I do not have combats to describe, and because my Heroine is only that in the last action of my work, who is the principal subject of it; everywhere else she appears only as an afflicted widow, pious and holy, who dreams of quite other things than warlike exploits." [74] So also Jacques de Coras, the most prolific biblical epic writer of the period, classified his poems according to the presence or absence of a military hero, but contrived all of them in conformity to the neoclassical epic formula. The subject of his *Jonas, ou Ninive Penitente, Poëme Sacré* (1663, 12 books, *ca.* 5,880 alexandrines) is Jonah's conquest of Nineveh, said to be a greater conquest than that over Troy; yet the epic label is omitted because Jonah conquered as prophet rather than as warrior, and with God's word rather than a sword. [75] By contrast, *Josué, ou la Conqueste de Canaan, Poëme Sacré* (1665, 6 books, *ca.* 3,725 alexandrines) and *Samson, Poëme Sacré* (1665, 5 books, *ca.* 2,470 alexandrines), since they have martial heroes, are pre-sented as minor efforts in the heroic style, practice work for Coras' self-styled heroic masterpiece, *David, ou la Vertu Couro-née, Poëme Sacré* (1665, 7 books, *ca.* 5,520 alexandrines). [76] Interestingly, in *Josué* Coras prides himself also on his original-ity in undertaking to use the brief epic format in deliberate opposition to the trend of the age toward long poems—"I have preferred a brevity strong and vigorous to a length weary and languishing." [77]

A third category of biblical epic vigorously asserts the claims of biblical subjects of whatever sort, martial and nonmartial alike, to epic glory, on the ground that they can fulfill all the necessary neoclassical rules. Jean Desmarets de Saint-Sorlin is the chief, and most shrill, defender of this position. His argument rests upon the following often reiterated assertions: since the biblical subjects are true, they must be verisimilar; since the biblical *merveilleuse* is guaranteed by God it must be credible as the pagan is not; since the biblical stories far surpass secular and pagan material in dignity and worth they are clearly suited to epic treatment; since the biblical poet can add fictitious elements and episodes without altering the biblical story itself he can meet the requirement of poetic invention. On these grounds Desmarets vehemently insists on the epic status of his own poems, *Marie-Madeleine, ou la Triomphe de la Grace* (1669, 10 books, *ca.* 1,960 lines in 10-line stanzas) and *Esther: Poëme Heroïque* (1670, 4 books, *ca.* 2,000 alexandrines; 1673, 7 books), and gives them many epic features.[78] Abbé Charles Cotin's preface to his *Poësies Chrestiennes,* which contains his *La Magdeleine au Sepulchre de Jesus-Christ, Poëme* (1668, 1 book, *ca.* 615 alexandrines), repeats Desmarets' arguments.[79]

In flat contradiction to all the foregoing positions regarding Christian subject and Christian *merveilleuse* are the views of Nicolas Boileau-Despréaux in *L'Art Poetique* (1674), and René Le Bossu in *Traité du Poëme Epique* (1675). Both of these French critics denounce the biblical subjects treated by Saint-Amant, Coras, and Desmarets as trivial, absurd, and lacking in epic dignity. And both defend classical mythology as alone suited to epic poetry, on the ground that the use of Christian supernatural figures is an impious degradation of holy things, and that the classical myths have now taken on wholly al-

legorical connotations and so are perfectly innocuous for the
Christian to use.[80] The way is thus prepared for the classical
epic diction of the eighteenth century, in which classical allusions become stock poetic terms, personifications devoid of
religious significance.

In England the last significant biblical epic before Milton's
is Abraham Cowley's *Davideis* (1656, 4 books, unfinished),
and it represents a very serious attempt, rather in the manner
of Jacques de Coras, to come to terms with and to apply the
neoclassical standards to the biblical subject.[81] The important critical preface was in many respects a response to William Davenant's preface to *Gondibert* (1650), and to Thomas
Hobbes' *Answer to Davenant's Preface to Gondibert* (1650),
which had reiterated and in some ways extended the arguments of Tasso and the strict French neoclassicists.[82] Like
Tasso, Davenant disparaged biblical epic, declared that the
Christian profane constitutes the only subject matter suitable
for epic, and excluded Du Bartas, Dante, and Marino from
the epic category on the ground that invention is not possible
with true and sacrosanct material. He virtually equated tragedy and epic by applying the Aristotelian rules for tragedy
to the epic form and also by casting his poem into five books
in imitation of the drama's five-act structure. And he totally
eliminated the supernatural element in obvious extension of
the neoclassical curbs on the *merveilleuse* in the interests of
verisimilitude.

Cowley's preface defended biblical epic against this challenge by reiterating the argument of Du Bartas and the humanists for the biblical origin of poetry, its present perversion,
and the need to reclaim it for God: "Amongst all holy and
consecrated things which the *Devil* ever stole and alienated
from the service of the *Deity* ... there is none that he so universally and so long usurpt as *Poetry*. It is time to recover
it out of the *Tyrants* hands, and to restore it to the *Kingdom*

of *God* who is the *Father* of it. It is time to *Baptize* it in
Jordan, for it will never become clean by bathing it in the
Waters of Damascus." [83] He also argued the poetic potential
of the true subject: "There is not so great a *Lye* to be found
in any *Poet,* as the vulgar conceit of men, that *Lying* is *Essential* to good *Poetry.*" [84] In addition, he asserted the superiority of the biblical subjects over their classical analogues,
both as regards their truth, and their heroic character: better
Noah's flood than Deucalion's, better Samson than Hercules,
better Jephthah's daughter than Iphigenia, better Christ's miracles than the metamorphoses of the gods. From this argument he concluded that "All the *Books* of the *Bible* are either
already most admirable, and exalted pieces of *Poesie,* or are
the best *Materials* in the world for it." [85]

However, Cowley was deeply concerned to satisfy the neoclassical rules, and his preface and notes continually appeal
to classical precedent for his every practice. He chose perhaps
the most martial of Old Testament stories and designed it
"into *Twelve Books;* not for the *Tribes* sake, but after the
Patern of our Master *Virgil.*" Also, he carefully observed
the criterion of unity of action: "I had no mind to carry
him [David] quite on to his *Anointing* at *Hebron,* because it is the custom of *Heroick Poets* (as we see by the
examples of *Homer* and *Virgil,* whom we should do ill to
forsake to imitate others) never to come to the full end of
their *Story;* but onely so near that every one may see it." [86]
Similarly his claim that "though some in other Languages have
attempted the writing a *Divine Poem;* yet none, that I know
of, hath in English," [87] seems to equate the terms "divine
poem" and "biblical epic" much as the French were equating
"poëme sacré" and "poëme héroïque," with the clear implication that the earlier English biblical poems did not meet the
neoclassical standards for the epic form. Cowley's poem is
an omnium-gatherum of devices by now traditional in biblical

epic: a council in hell from which Satan sends Envy (an Allecto figure) to put a worm in the breast of Saul; a learning passage occasioned by David's flight to the college at Rama; an epic recital wherein David reviews for Moab the history of the warlike judges; a prophecy wherein David in a dream vision sees all his progeny, including Christ; an iconographical representation of the history of Abraham depicted in tapestry. And Cowley's remark, "I meant to interweave [this story of David]...with most of the illustrious *Stories* of the *Old Testament,* and to embellish with the most remarkable *Antiquities* of the *Jews,* and of other Nations before or at that *Age,*" [88] demonstrates his affinity with the several neoclassical writers on Old Testament themes who used the traditional recitals and historical surveys to gain epic dimension but conceived these stories as analogous or even as unrelated episodes, rather than as types or antitypes of the principal action.

The probabilities are strong that Milton would have known Cowley's much discussed and highly touted experiment in English biblical epic, and that this poem may have helped to review for him, just prior to his own endeavors in the genre, the traditional assumptions about biblical epic, the devices it customarily employed, and the new neoclassical standards for and challenges to the kind.

*M*ILTON's *Paradise Regained* is obviously indebted to the biblical "brief epic" tradition in
regard to conception, structure, epic devices, and
even verbal echoes. Clearly it is also indebted to the "epic"
exegetical and literary tradition of the Book of Job for some
aspects of the hero and the structure. When, however, we examine Milton's use of these generic traditions we get a measure
of the distance between noble intention and distinguished
achievement, and we see how tremendous are the transforma-
tions wrought by the true artist.

It is now evident that Milton's statement about the brief
epic does refer to traditions important for the understanding
of *Paradise Regained*. His distinction between the "diffuse"
and the "brief" epic does point to two separate categories of
biblical epic, and we have seen that until the mid-seventeenth
century the brief epic category contained a preponderance of
the biblical poems. It seems likely also that Milton's four-book
format derives from the precedent supplied by many of the
best-known and most influential brief epics—Juvencus' *Evangeliorum*, Sedulius' *Carmen Paschale*, Ramsay's *Poemata
Sacra*, Marino's *Strage*, Sylvester's *Job Triumphant in His
Triall*, Joseph Fletcher's *Historie of the Perfect-Cursed-Blessed
Man*, Montchrestien's *Susane*, Aylett's *Susanna*, Giles Fletcher's *Christs Victorie, and Triumph*. Moreover, it is clear that
Milton's reference to Job as the model of a brief epic has its
sanction in the fact that the Book of Job itself was often
described as an epic, that the Jobean theme was often given
"epic" literary treatment, and that the structure of the Book

of Job had already been imitated in other biblical and Christian epics, most notably in Aylett's *Joseph,* and Beaumont's *Psyche.* Milton could readily adopt the "epic" view of the Book of Job since, as the Job references in his prose tracts indicate, he seems to have accepted the "heroic" interpretation of Job as a sinless, perfect hero overcoming all temptation. Job is "most modest and patient of men," his outcries are evidence that "sensibility to pain, and even lamentations, are not inconsistent with true patience," and he is an example, with Christ and various Old Testament personages, of magnanimity or proper self-regard.[1] I would not be understood to limit the bases for Milton's decisions about various aspects of the poem solely to considerations of genre, but at the same time his art in the poem derives in no small measure from his conscious manipulation of this generic tradition.

As regards the epic conception of *Paradise Regained,* Milton is in the mainstream of the patristic and humanist tradition by reason of his unembarrassed choice and flexible treatment of a "peaceful" New Testament subject, as well as by his intimation, through the epithet "Above Heroic," that such a subject is vastly superior to the old heroic themes. Also, like most of the other contemporary New Testament poems *Paradise Regained* ignores for the most part the neoclassical standards and challenges which strongly influenced the Old Testament poems from the time of Du Bartas' *Judit* (1574) and which intensified their impact after 1650—insistence upon an active, military hero, adherence to strict rules regarding structure and the unities, de-emphasis on typology and the supernatural, whether classical or Christian. Instead, Milton follows the general humanist formula, selecting as a subject a particular, limited episode from Christ's life and relating all previous and subsequent history to it by means of typological allusion. He does, however, observe the neoclassical unities: the single, unified action presents Christ's temptation and victory in the desert, the time is about forty-two days, and the place is the desert, and Jerusalem adjacent to it. Also, like Vida, he uses the neoclassical structure: *Paradise Regained* begins *in medias res* with a summary of Christ's baptism as the incident which commences the hero's public life; then Jesus and Mary in their soliloquies (I.196–289; II.66–104) recapitulate, each from his own perspective, Jesus' previous life.

Milton's genius is especially apparent in his choice of the episode to constitute his subject. As has been seen, precedents for a brief epic on the subject of the temptation of Christ are almost nonexistent. The temptation episode suggests itself to Milton, obviously, as a complement to *Paradise Lost,* but beyond this it is the one episode in Christ's life (except for the Harrowing of Hell which Milton's mortalism kept him from using) that is peculiarly suited to presentation as a brief epic, in that it could be treated as a transmutation of the single combat of hero and antagonist, the event which is traditionally the epitome and climax of an epic. The subject of *Paradise Regained,* Christ's encounter with Satan in the temptation, is the epitome and the symbol of the perpetual battle of the Son and Satan throughout all time—the battle which is displayed in its full extent in *Paradise Lost* through the councils in hell and heaven, the battle in heaven, Adam's fall, and the final prophecy of Christ's redemption. Milton's choice and treatment of his subject in *Paradise Regained* indicates that for him, as for Sannazaro, the brief epic is not merely any narration told in briefer compass than the full-scale epic, but that it is rather a significant condensation and epitome of the vast span of history treated *in extenso* in the "diffuse" epic.

Also, Milton meets the growing demand for a martial hero by a brilliant stroke. He is responsive to this expectation to the extent of using suggestive martial imagery to present the permutations of the argument between Christ and Satan as the thrust and parry of a great duel, an epic single combat. He has precedent in the "heroic" exegesis of Job for such use of martial imagery to transform the patient hero's temptations and verbal conflicts into a kind of heroic battle: for the Greek and Latin Fathers Job was the *Athletorum strenuissimus,* a wrestler stripped for his contest with Satan, or else he was a warrior on the battlefield enduring blows from all sides.[2] Milton describes Christ in similar terms: he is brought "Into the Desert, his Victorious Field/ Against the Spiritual Foe" (I.9–10); his deeds there are "Above Heroic" (I.15); he will there overcome Satan "and drive him back to Hell,/ Winning by Conquest what the first man lost" (I.153–54); he will in the wilderness "lay down the rudiments/ Of his great warfare" (I.157–58); he will there enter "his great duel, not of arms,/ But to vanquish by wisdom hellish wiles" (I.174–75); he is at length proclaimed "Queller of Satan" (IV.634). However, this suggestive but unobtrusive imagery represents Milton's only concession to the demand for martial action or a warrior hero. He does not, like Strasburgus treating the same temptation episode, import the machinery of the *psychomachia* to give the episode the external apparatus of epic battle.[3] Neither does he, like Giles Fletcher, have Christ encounter and withstand various allegorical personifications of the vices involved in the temptation.[4] Rather he sets himself the task of displaying without compromise the moral battles involved in the higher heroism, the conquest of hellish wiles by wisdom. He assumes that his "fit audience though few" will be more interested in the excitement, and the heroism, involved in the inordinately subtle and complex mental combat between Christ and Satan than in that provided by physical combat, and he uses—successfully, I think—the exposed predicament of the hero and the tremendous import of the battle for all mankind to supply the necessary tension.

Milton is also indebted to the biblical epic and to the Jobean tradition for the technique of using biblical and classical allusion to extend the historical perspective and to develop further ranges of meaning through typological symbolism. Again Milton does not simply copy the humanist-neoclassical use of epic recitals or scenes on arras to recapitulate biblical history, but instead he incorporates into the debate between Christ and Satan brief allusions (similar to those found in Sedulius, Mantuan, Sannazaro, and Frénicle) to the standard Old Testament and classical types of Christ—Gideon, Jephthah, Moses, Elias, David, Judas Maccabaeus, Daniel, Job, and also Alexander, Scipio, Curius, Regulus, Socrates, Hercules, and Oedipus. The temptation episode is thereby presented against a panorama of all previous history and Christ is made the epitome and fulfillment of all the earlier pattern heroes. Moreover, Milton achieves this not by superimposing historical reference and typological symbolism upon the narrative, as was usually done, but by making the references to the types function dramatically in the poem, as part of the temptation dialogue.

Related to this extension of historical perspective through typology and allusion is the projection forward in time which the New Testament poems usually achieved through reference to the Christian church: from Juvencus onward such poems characteristically ended with the sending forth of the apostles to convert all nations, or with the founding of the church at Pentecost, or with the mystical marriage of Christ and Ecclesia, or with the historical experience of the church in the early Christian centuries or in the writer's own age. Milton retains this ecclesiastical focus and with it the foreshadowing of the time to come, but again he dramatizes. Christ undergoes the temptation chiefly in his role as head of and mediator for his church, so that his experience is an archetype of what the church will continually experience. Much of the debate between Christ and Satan is about Christ's kingdom (the church), and the temptations of Parthia and Rome especially contain allusions to the continuing problems of the church in its relations with temporal power and the Roman Antichrist.

Though the concept of Christ as the fulfillment of the ancient types and as the archetype whose experiences are continually reflected in his church is so universal that it is unquestionably the chief influence dictating Milton's practice here, yet for this aspect of the poem also the traditional Jobean exegesis provided reinforcement. Job was also understood to be a kind of epitome, reflecting the past and projecting the future. His temptation repeated and counterbalanced that of Adam in that he remained steadfast on his dunghill while Adam fell in Paradise, and rejected the instigations of his wife and the Devil whereas Adam listened to Eve. Moreover, he was described by Origen as an epitome of all the Old Testament patriarchs and saints and was constantly referred to as the type and foreshadowing of Christ both in his temptation and in his passion.[5]

As with epic conception and subject so with his hero Milton starts with a commonplace of the biblical epic tradition. Although martial imagery is used to describe Christ, and although he is engaged in a transformed epic duel, he belongs in the category of the patient or suffering heroes—Christs, Magdalens, Adams, Susannas, Josephs, Jobs. Some theorists, it will be recalled, defended such heroes as appropriate to epic on the ground that their achievement of self-conquest through enduring temptation or suffering is a higher heroism than that manifested by "active" conquerors or rulers. This is the moral which Francis Quarles draws in his comparison of Job to Alexander the Great:

> The proudest pitch of that victorious spirit [Alexander]
> Was but to win the World, whereby t'inherit

The ayrie purchase of a transitory,
And glozing Title of an ages Glory;

.   .   .   .

But would'st thou conquer, have thy Conquest crown'd
By hands of Seraphins, tryumph'd with the sound
Of Heavens lowd Trumpet, warbled by the shrill
Celestiall Quire, recorded with a Quill,
Pluck't from the Pinion of an Angels wing,
Confirm'd with Joy, by heavens Eternall King?
Conquer thy selfe . . .[6]

Milton's definition of the higher heroism as self-conquest, and
his reference to Job as the most notable hero by reason of his
wisdom and patient endurance, manifests his debt to these
traditions (*PR* II.466–67; III.88–95). Shortly after the reference to Job, Christ specifically identifies himself with the
Jobean heroic pattern by portraying his own condition in
terms equally suitable to Job and often employed by the commentators to describe him:

What if he [God] hath decreed that I shall first
Be tried in humble state, and things adverse,
By tribulations, injuries, insults,
Contempts, and scorns, and snares, and violence,
Suffering, abstaining, quietly expecting
Without distrust or doubt, that he may know
What I can suffer, how obey? (III.188–94)

Throughout the poem Christ is presented in the Jobean mold
—alone, seemingly abandoned by God, forced to endure a
relentless barrage of temptations many of which take the form,
as in Job, of subtle intellectual arguments.

But though he uses a patient, suffering hero Milton manages to avoid the dullness, the static quality, the oppressive
didacticism which often characterized biblical epics about
such heroes, and especially those about the divine Christ
whose presentation as a fully human character would have

seemed to most writers sacrilegious. Though Milton accepts the *donnée* of the story that Christ is "perfect" and though he shows Christ as a theological symbol fulfilling the types and exemplifying his mediatorial role, he nevertheless manages to give to Christ's character much of the psychological interest and progressive development previously found only in Old Testament heroes subject to doubts and human frailties, such as Du Bartas' Judith or Aylett's David. By avoiding either the broad panoramic treatment of Christ's life, or the choice of such particular episodes as the Birth or the Passion and Death which virtually demand ritualistic rather than dramatic treatment, Milton has seized upon a subject which he can develop as a genuine adventure. Also, by presenting his hero in terms dictated by his anti-Trinitarian theology he is able to create a Christ subject to doubts and fears, and undergoing a genuine adventure of testing and self-discovery.

Milton was also indebted to the biblical epic tradition for several now standard biblical epic devices, but he avoided the simple repetition or imitation of them which characterized the work of most of his predecessors. There are no formal recitals or arras summarizing biblical history or the hero's early life, no analogous episodes paralleling the main plot, no Allecto figures, angelic *nuntii,* or Virgilian personifications. But many of the expected devices do appear, as well as modifications of some of those just mentioned. *Paradise Regained* has an epic proposition and invocation; a declaration of intention to deal with a subject more heroic than the usual heroic theme; two "infernal" councils now held in mid-air rather than in hell; a council in heaven wherein God addresses Gabriel, making reference to his earlier employment as angelic *nuntius* at the Annunciation (I.138–40); a prophecy of Christ's immediate and ultimate victory over Satan spoken by God before the encounter. It has also a transformed recital—Christ's meditation about his youthful experiences and aspirations—which presents relevant information about the hero's earlier life; an "analogous episode" parodying the temptation episode in the discourse about women wherein Satan plays Christ to Belial's Satan; an epic catalogue of the kingdoms of the world; a detailed description of a great city (Rome); an epic-like, martial pageant of the Parthian warriors; and a passage dealing with the education or learning of the hero (the learning temptation).

For the over-all structure of *Paradise Regained* the Book of Job in itself and as interpreted by the commentators is the chief model, as it had been for Aylett and Beaumont.[7] Throughout *Paradise Regained* a tissue of references and allusions to Job makes explicit the link between the two works: the character Job is named on six occasions (I.147, 369, 425; III.64, 67, 95), the Book is quoted twice (I.33, 368), and either the Book itself or the tradition of commentary explaining it is alluded to on at least ten other occasions. Especially at the beginning of the poem the Jobean model is placed under heavy contribution in order to establish at once the terms in which the subsequent action should be viewed. The initial action in chapter i of the Book of Job is described as follows:

> Now there was a day, when the sonnes of God came to present themselves before the LORD, and Satan came also among them.
> And the LORD saide unto Satan, Whence commest thou? Then Satan answered the LORD, and said, From going to and fro in the earth, and from walking up and downe in it.
> And the LORD saide unto Satan, Hast thou considered my servant Job, that there is none like him in the earth? a perfect and an upright man, one that feareth God, and escheweth evill?
>
> (Job i:6–8)

In an obvious echo of this passage, the action in *Paradise Regained* begins when Satan, still in his character as "Adversary," comes to another "assembly," Christ's baptism, where

he again hears God's high commendation of a hero—the proclamation of Christ as Son of God:

> That heard the Adversary, who roving still
> About the world, at that assembly fam'd
> Would not be last, and with the voice divine
> Nigh Thunderstruck, th'exalted man, to whom
> Such high attest was giv'n, a while survey'd. (I.33-37)

In both cases God's acclaim provokes Satan's determination
to tempt the hero: he proposes the test of Job to God in the
heavenly assembly and develops the plan for tempting Christ
in his own council in mid-air, but this plan also is immediately
ratified by God in a heavenly council.

Moreover, God's comment indicates that Christ's trial will
be of the same order as Job's, and will serve (in part) the
same purpose—to display Christ as Job had been displayed,
for "a spectacle to angels and to men":

> this man born and now upgrown,
> To show him worthy of his birth divine
> And high prediction, henceforth I expose
> To Satan; let him tempt and now assay
> His utmost subtlety, because he boasts
> And vaunts of his great cunning to the throng
> Of his Apostasy; he might have learnt
> Less overweening, since he fail'd in *Job,*
> Whose constant perserverance overcame
> Whate'er his cruel malice could invent.
> He now shall know I can produce a man
> Of female Seed, far abler to resist
> All his solicitations, and at length
> All his vast force, and drive him back to Hell,
>
> .   .   .   .
>
> That all the Angels and Ethereal Powers,
> They now, and men hereafter, may discern
> From what consummate virtue I have chose

This perfect Man, by merit call'd my Son,
To earn Salvation for the Sons of men. (I.140–53, 163–67)

Gregory the Great affords a precedent for relating Job and
Christ in this way as heroes exhibited by God: "God's saying
to Satan in figure, *Hast thou considered My servant Job,* is
His exhibiting in his despite the Only-Begotten Son as an
object of wonder in the form of a servant." [8] Moreover, just
as God according to the patristic commentators was fully confident of Job's continuing sinlessness and ultimate victory when
he exposed him to Satan, so in *Paradise Regained* the angelic
choir acclaims God's confidence in Christ's victory:

> The Father knows the Son; therefore secure
> Ventures his filial Virtue, though untried,
> Against whate'er may tempt, whate'er seduce,
> Allure, or terrify, or undermine.
> Be frustrate, all ye stratagems of Hell,
> And devilish machinations come to nought. (I.176–81)

Subsequent action in the temptation sequences of *Paradise
Regained* also follows the Jobean model, though of course with
due adaptation to the requirements of the different subject.
In his first temptations Job suffers the loss of servants, goods,
and children, while Christ in the desert is first invited by
Satan to see himself as abandoned, desolate, deprived of all
worldly goods and comforts, and even of the sustenance he
will need for life. In Job the failure of the first attempt leads
to a second council in heaven at which Satan wins permission to afflict Job's flesh with boils; in relation to this temptation, according to the commentators, Satan also instigated
Job's wife to subvert him (Job ii:9) as Eve did Adam, but
unlike Adam, Job was properly scornful of the woman's suggestions. In *Paradise Regained* also a second council is held,
in mid-air, to plan further strategy, and a suggestion for a
temptation by women is rejected on the ground that the no-

blest men "have with a smile made small account/ Of beauty and her lures" (II.193–94). Satan's second attempt on Christ, the banquet temptation, is designed to aggravate Christ's newly experienced hunger—a pain in the flesh paralleling in some degree Job's boils. There is even some faint reflection of Job's lamentations (chap. iii) in Christ's manifestation of uneasiness at the experience of hunger:

> Where will this end? four times ten days I have pass'd,
> Wand'ring this woody maze, and human food
> Nor tasted, nor had appetite
>
> . . . .
>
> But now I feel I hunger, which declares
> Nature hath need of what she asks. (II.245–53)

Reduced to utter misery by the losses and physical pains of the initial temptations, Job then encounters what the commentators describe as his most arduous trial, the steady, remorseless arguments of his three friends set on by Satan to lead him to false beliefs and despair. Many note also that these discourses are in large part concerned with the substance of Job's virtue: his temperance in respect to women and wealth (chap. xxxi), his right use of magisterial power (chap. xxix), and his wisdom (chap. xxviii).[9] Similarly in *Paradise Regained,* after Christ is shorn of all material support and assailed by hunger, Satan attacks him relentlessly with a steady stream of arguments intended to subvert his beliefs and attitudes regarding wealth, power, glory, and wisdom.

God's address to Job from the whirlwind (chaps. xxxviii–xlii) was often interpreted as an apparent rather than a real rebuke, as simply a further test of Job's faith and humility. So in *Paradise Regained,* Christ endures a fearsome storm which Satan interprets to him as a possible portent of God's displeasure (IV.460–66). The Jobean commentators construed

God's last remarks to Job as a proclamation of his complete triumph over all temptation and described the twofold multiplication of all his former goods as the heroic victor's fit reward.[10] Similarly, in *Paradise Regained,* Christ's victory is proclaimed and celebrated by the angelic host, and, as if in reward, all the goods which he refused to receive at Satan's hand are given or promised to him in a more exalted form— instead of diabolic agents disguised as ministrants of Nature he has angelic ministrants, instead of a carnal banquet a heavenly one, instead of satanic recognition of his divinity an affirmation by God's angelic choir of his divine sonship and mediatorial role, instead of a false earthly kingdom an assurance of a true and immortal kingdom.

With respect to the epic supernatural and the use of the mythological references and epithets to simulate classical epic diction, Milton again achieves an original synthesis which is more effective than the practice of most of his forerunners or contemporaries. Sharply rejecting the neoclassical prescription to restrict the supernatural in the interests of verisimilitude, to avoid the direct presentation of God in the interests of decorum, and to substitute allegorical personifications for supernatural personages, he presents two infernal councils and one heavenly council with angels and demons in full attendance and introduces God the Father directly in a lengthy colloquy with Gabriel. He does observe the caveat followed by some humanists but much more rigidly by the neoclassicists against mixing pagan and Christian supernatural elements: the acting characters are all from the Christian supernatural, and most allusions to pagan myths are covered by the accepted excuses—either they are labeled explicitly as false or feigned, or they are explained as deriving from Satan and his crew. Satan has been the real source of the Delphic and other Greek oracles (I.457–59); Belial has been the true agent of the amorous scapes laid to the charge of Apollo, Neptune, Jupiter, or

Pan (II.189–91); the Nymphs, Naiades, and Ladies of the Hesperides who serve the satanic banquet are "Fairer than feign'd of old, or fabl'd since" (II.354–58); the erstwhile conquerors who claim to be sons of Jove or Mars are merely absurdly proud mortals seeking false glory (III.84–85). In this respect Milton seems at first to have surpassed even the neoclassicists in his restrictions on the pagan supernatural, for he also avoids using such terms as Olympus and Avernus as allegories for the Christian supernatural regions, and such Virgilian personifications as Fama, Rumour, Aeolus, and Clementia—terms which as a mere technique of epic diction were almost universally employed and defended. Yet despite his avoidance of both pagan supernatural references and the usual epic diction, Milton alludes to two commonly accepted classical types of Christ—Hercules and Oedipus (IV.563–76)—not as false myths but as genuine foreshadowings of Christ's conquest over Satan, thereby placing himself in the tradition of such Renaissance poets as Ilarione da Verona, Bonus, Sannazaro, Mantuan, Abel d'Argent, D'Escorbiac, Sanguinet, Frénicle, and Giles Fletcher. It would seem that, in abandoning the classical references, Milton had decided to eschew what had come to be merely repetitive, meaningless, formal poetic diction in favor of an attempt to create a genuine "biblical" epic language suited to his subject. But his incorporation of the accepted classical types without hesitation or apology indicates that his approach to the classical supernatural is within the humanist rather than the later neoclassical tradition, and that he is ready to call upon the humanist classical allusions where they serve his purposes.

In addition to these general influences upon the conception and structure of the poem, certain passages in *Paradise Regained* contain parallels in thought and language to various biblical epics, especially to certain Christiads and works on Job. I am not concerned here to try to establish sources—

though in a few instances the parallels seem conclusive—but only to show by citing some of these parallels how profoundly Milton was influenced by traditional ways of treating even the specifics of his subject, in the matter of common *topoi,* episodes, and diction.

Milton's echo of the pseudo-Virgilian opening of the *Aeneid,* by means of which Milton suggests his own shift from the "pastoral" *Paradise Lost* to the higher heroic subject, closely resembles in form the similar use of the Virgilian opening in several Christiad centos:

> I who erewhile the happy Garden sung,
> By one man's disobedience lost, now sing
> Recover'd Paradise to all mankind,
> By one man's firm obedience fully tried
> Through all temptation, and the Tempter foil'd
> In all his wiles, defeated and repuls't,
> And *Eden* rais'd in the waste Wilderness. (*PR* I.1–7)

Othon Gryphius' *Virgilii Centones* begins,

> I who, onetime, following a not inferior example,
> As the first rudiments and shows built by my hands
> Piped a light thing on a slender reed,
> I now set forth a greater work. Now with a loud voice,
> I trumpet the power and the coming of God.[11]

Stephen Pleurreus, assuming the person of Virgil, asserts that the *Aeneis Sacra* or Christiad that he is about to sing surpasses the *Aeneid:*

> I who once piped a song on a slender reed
> Then, leaving the woods for rural flowers,
> Sang until now the cultivation of fields and cattle,
> And the wars so famous throughout the world
> Of great Aeneas: (a very long series of deeds
> Leading back through so many generations to the ancient
>   beginning of a people).
> A greater work I now set forth.[12]

And Alexander Ross's *Christiados Libri XIII* begins,

I who once piped a song on a slender reed,
And led forth the Israelites going out from Egypt through
    hostile reefs,
And through the desert home and empty Kingdom of Arabia
Now I sing about the awesome deeds of Christ, and about
    God.[13]

The induction to Milton's poem also contains close verbal parallels to other Christiads. In *Paradise Regained* the Father speaks of Christ as a young warrior whom he will "exercise ... in the Wilderness," the place where "he shall first lay down the rudiments/ Of his great warfare, ere I send him forth/ To conquer Sin and Death the two grand foes,/ By Humiliation and strong Sufferance" (I.155-60). Interestingly enough Strasburgus, in the only other brief epic I have seen which takes the temptation of Christ as its subject, represents the temptation in much the same terms and uses the same word, "rudiments" (*rudimentum*), to describe what Christ will learn from it:

Behold, by the holy breath moving through the swift
    breezes
He [Christ] is raised, and through a journey long and
    circuitous,
Borne by the air he is carried into empty groves of the
    forests,
And dens of wild beasts, that he might frequent the great
    ridges
Of the waste desert. And being one day
To conquer the Stygian plunder from despoiled Avernus,
The young warrior should first learn here the rudiments,
    in easy contests,
And prepare himself for great deeds of daring.[14]

The imagery of the temptation as duel has its sources in Job commentary as has been seen, but it appears also in the tempta-

tion scenes of several Christiads such as that of Estiene de Sanguinet, "There Christ is borne to bring down by arms/ The
arms of Satan, and to strike off his horns,/ Body against body
in duel." [15]

The Christiads and the biblical epic tradition generally also
provide close conceptual and verbal parallels to Milton's presentation of the temptations themselves. In Milton, Satan appears first as an "aged man in Rural weeds,/ Following, as
seem'd, the quest of some stray Ewe" (I.314–15)—symbolically
a false shepherd, false pastor. He claims that he is himself
suffering hunger and misery along with other desert inhabitants, and accordingly couches his temptation in part as an
appeal for charity:

> we here
> Live on tough roots and stubs, to thirst inur'd
> More than the Camel, and to drink go far,
> Men to much misery and hardship born;
> But if thou be the Son of God, Command
> That out of these hard stones be made thee bread;
> So shalt thou save thyself and us relieve
> With Food, whereof we wretched seldom taste. (I.338–45)

Giles Fletcher gives the only other version I have seen in
poetry or in prose commentary in which Satan presents himself as an aged, pious, but deprived desert dweller—"A good
old Hermit.../ That for devotion had the world forsaken."
Lamenting that he is unable to offer food to Christ, he declares,

> The heav'ns, alas, too envious are growne,
> Because our fields thy presence from them keepe;
> For stones doe growe, where corne was lately sowne:
> (So stooping downe, he gather'd up a stone)
> But thou with corne canst make this stone to eare. [16]

Also the passage in which Milton's Satan insists upon Christ's
lonely and abandoned state—

> Sir, what ill chance hath brought thee to this place
> So far from path or road of men, who pass
> In Troop or Caravan, for single none
> Durst ever, who return'd, and dropt not here
> His Carcass, pin'd with hunger and with drought? (I.321–25)

—rather closely resembles a passage in La Pujade's temptation scene,

> I feel pity, seeing you in danger of perishing,
> And no one can succor you here.
> This is a horrible desert where we are now,
> Very far from and beyond any place inhabited by men.[17]

There is little foundation in the Christiads for Milton's banquet sequence, but Sedulius' reference in the *Carmen Paschale* to the tempter's presentation of "deceitful feasts" may have been suggestive,[18] as may also John Bale's inclusion in his drama, *The Temptacyon of Our Lord,* of an offer to Christ of "fayre women, of countenaunce ameable,/ With all kyndes of meates, to the body dylectable" [19] as part of the kingdoms temptation. Closer analogues are Giles Fletcher's inclusion of wine and delectable ladies in the first part of Pangloretta's estate offered to Christ,[20] and Joseph Beaumont's representation, in his *Psyche,* of Satan as a wealthy monarch with a long train of followers offering aid and food to the hungry Christ if he will but prove his divine status by miracle.[21] The disappearance of the fraudulent banquet "With sound of Harpies' wings and Talons heard" (II.403) recalls the passage in the *Aeneid* wherein the Harpies foul the banquet of Aeneas and his men; [22] the passage in the *Tempest* wherein Ariel disguised as a Harpy snatches away the banquet from the three "men of sin" Alonzo, Antonio, and Sebastian; [23] and the description in Beaumont's *Psyche* of the melting of the globe which held the entire pageant of the kingdoms offered to Christ, leaving only "Ashes, which so strongly smelt/ That other Stincks compar'd with this, might seem/ Perfumes." [24]

In the temptation of the kingdoms Milton's arrangement of
the lures—first the banquet containing elegant sensual delights,
then wealth, then ambition, then glory—follows precisely the
order found in Fletcher's allegorical presentation of the kingdoms temptation as the House of Pangloretta, wherein Christ
is tempted first by Bacchus and Luxurie, then by Avarice,
then by Ambitious Honor, and finally by Pangloretta (Glory)
herself. And Milton's statement of the interrelation and progression of these temptations—"Thou neither dost persuade me
to seek wealth/ For Empire's sake, nor Empire to affect/ For
glory's sake" (III.44–45)—has a close parallel in Fletcher, "The
poore man would be rich, the rich man great,/ The great man
King, the King, in Gods own seat." [25] Milton's addition of a
yet higher lure, classical learning, as the climax of this sequence finds a parallel in Quarles' *Job Militant,* in a meditation upon the varieties of false felicity which seduce other
men but not Job:

> One digs to *Pluto's* Throane, thinkes there to find
> Her Grace, rak't up in Gold: Anothers mind
> Mounts to the Courts of Kings, with Plumes of Honour,
> And feather'd Hopes, hopes, there, to seize upon her;
> A third, unlocks the painted Gates of Pleasure,
> And ransacks there, to find this peerlesse Treasure.
> A fourth, more sage, more wisely melancholy,
> Perswades himselfe, her Deity's too holy,
> For common hands to touch, he rather chuses,
> To make a long dayes journey to the Muses:
> To *Athens* (gown'd) he goes, and from that Schoole
> Returnes unsped, a more instructed foole.[26]

Also, Milton's description of particular cities as a part of
the temptation of the kingdoms has some precedent in earlier
Christiads: in Bonus' poem, for example, Satan also offers
Christ the cities of Rome and Athens.[27] But Milton's descriptions are further indebted to a common *topos* in biblical epic,

the detailed description of a pagan metropolis. The nearest
analogue to Milton's use of this *topos* in the Parthia episode
is the passage in Fracastoro's *Joseph* describing the hero's
prospect, as he nears Egypt, of the city of Memphis and of
the Egyptian troops exercising on the green:

> Now, having past *Judaea's* confines quite,
> From a steepe Hill, they have anon the sight
> Of stately *Memphis* lofty Towers and Walles,
> With glittering roofes of high & sumptuous Halls.
>
> . . . .
>
> And, neere the Citie, on a spacious Greene,
> They might behold, as in some Martiall Muster,
> Thousands of Youth in severall Troops to cluster;
> Attending all, Some, manly Exercise;
> Some, light and speedy, running for a prize:
> Some, strongly active, wrastling for a fall,
> Some, hurling Sledges, till they sweat withall:
> Some, on swift Horse-backe to out-swim the winde;
> Some, to shoot backward at their foes behind:
> Some with their Launces ready coucht in Rest,
> Wheeling about, to charge in Flanke or Brest:
> Some, at the Tilt, in strong and steddy course,
> To breake their Staves, or beare down man & horse.[28]

In *Paradise Regained* Christ's view of the Parthian warriors
exercising outside the city walls is pretty clearly a reworking
of this *topos:*

> He look't and saw what numbers numberless
> The City gates outpour'd, light armed Troops
> In coats of Mail and military pride;
> In Mail thir horses clad, yet fleet and strong,
> Prancing their riders bore,
>
> . . . .
>
> He saw them in thir forms of battle rang'd,
> How quick they wheel'd, and flying behind them shot
> Sharp sleet of arrowy showers against the face

Of thir pursuers, and overcame by flight;
The field all iron cast a gleaming brown,
Nor wanted clouds of foot, nor on each horn,
Cuirassiers all in steel for standing fight.

(III.310–14, 322–28)

Several Protestant Christiads identified Rome as the principal kingdom offered to Christ, and, like Milton, suggested by
means of that symbol the Roman church. Le Noir's version
of Satan's offer, "Do you see clearly, he said, the empire of
the Romans?/ Know that I dispose of it, and that it is in my
hands./ I can give you that scepter and that Empire/ Under
which the whole world at present sighs," [29] resembles the
description of Rome by Milton's Satan as "Queen of the Earth/
So far renown'd, and with the spoils enricht/ Of Nations.../
All Nations now to *Rome* obedience pay" (IV.45–47, 80). A
very close parallel indeed is the pageant in Beaumont's *Psyche,*
in which Satan calls forth Tiberius from the globe wherein
he is displaying all the kingdoms to Christ, upbraids him for
his wanton mismanagement of the Empire, and offers Christ
his place:

> By him [Tiberius] I see how Princes love to slide
> Down the glib way of wretched Luxury:
> And what should silly People doe, whose Guide
> Leads them the way to Ruine? Have not I
> Just cause to choose some sober Man, whose Care
> May stop that desperate vicious Carrier?
>
> Now whether Thou bee'st *Son to God,* or no,
> Surely Thou spring'st from some Heroick Race,
> I see the noblest Sparks of Virtue so
> Full writ in thy, though pin'd yet, princely Face.
>
> . . . .
>
> And such a Prince, and none but such, can cure
> The wide Contagion which rank Vice hath spred
> On this poor Age.[30]

Milton's Satan in remarkably similar terms also denounces the vices of Tiberius and acclaims the regal virtues of Christ as urgently needed to save the Empire:

> This Emperor hath no Son, and now is old,
> Old, and lascivious, and from *Rome* retir'd
> To *Capreae,* an Island small but strong
> On the *Campanian* shore, with purpose there
> His horrid lusts in private to enjoy,
> Committing to a wicked Favorite
> All public cares, and yet of him suspicious,
> Hated of all, and hating. With what ease,
> Endu'd with Regal Virtues as thou art,
> Appearing, and beginning noble deeds,
> Might'st thou expel this monster from his Throne
> Now made a sty, and in his place ascending
> A victor people free from servile yoke? (IV.90–102)

The learning temptation also has precedents in earlier biblical epics. A passage concerning the education, reading habits, or wisdom of the hero is a common *topos* in the biblical poems, and customarily it dealt with the relation of pagan and religious learning. In a typical humanist example, Mantuan's *Mariana,* Mary in the Temple studies biblical history and also classical history and myth, from all of which she extracts only what is good:

> She learned the songs and poems of the holy King
> Who sang with solemn harps to the Holy Ark
> And played on them with prophetic song for the festivals.
> Whatever the divine books of the Sacred Law held,
> Whatever was contained in the Books of the Arabs, she
>   examined,
> And all the annals of the Greeks; and the triumphs of the
>   Romans,
> And how great was the pouring out of Latin Blood
> By the Punic arms: how the surface of the sea
> Reddened in naval battles: What leaders

> Attacked Troy: By means of what soldier
> The King of the Macedonians conquered the Parthians,
>   Trucians, and Indians.
> [She read of] the monsters that Hercules conquered, by
>   what wings
> Dedalus fleeing Crete flew away to the frozen Arctic,
> And by what wings the winged horse, supported in the
>   air,
> Flew forward, disturbing the gentle waves with the soles
>   of his feet.
>
> .   .   .   .
>
> Whatever in this mixture is exaggerated, whatever is
>   crude and tasteless
> And whatever by any means offended by not attesting to
>   pious manners,
> These she condemned. Through reading she imitated the
>   best.[31]

The *topos* also appears in Du Bartas' *Judit,* but with the typical Reformation emphasis on biblical studies and the accompanying disparagement of other learning as vain and foolish:

> For, look how soon her childish tongue could chat,
> As children do, of this thing or of that;
> He taught her not to reade inventions vaine,
> As fathers daily do that are profaine:
> But in the holy Scriptures made her read;
> That with her milke she might even suck the dread
> Of the most high.
>
> .   .   .   .
>
> (Her travell done) her lute she then assayes,
> And unto God she sings immortall prayes:
> Not following those that plyes their thriftless paine
> In wanton verse and wastefull ditties vaine.[32]

A learning passage of a somewhat different kind, but resembling Milton's in its disparagement of all the schools of pagan philosophy and its specific mention of Socrates' famous disclaimer as evidence of the comparative lack of substance in pagan learning, occurs in Alexander More's *Laus Christi Nascentis,* where Bethlehem's wisdom is extolled over that of Athens:

> More than your Garden, Epicurus, more than the gloomy
> porches of the Stoic school,
> More than the entire Lyceum of Aristotle,
> This poor house knows, and is ignorant of nothing,
> Having been deemed worthy of a teacher from heaven.
> Yield to the village of Bethlehem,
> Yield, glorious name, Athenians, descendants of Pallas Athena
> Behold the unknown God to whom you placed an empty
> altar.
>
> . . . .
>
> In which [place] I read wonders unknown to venerable Plato,
> Or you, O wise Stagirite, who were his best student,
> Or you also Samos, or your neighboring Hymettus,
> For the only one to know himself professed to know nothing:
> The King from Heaven has now led Wisdom down from the
> stars.[33]

Moreover, the meditation on wisdom in Quarles' *Job Militant* referring to Job as a most notable example of heavenly wisdom, offers an even closer parallel to Milton:

> The Morall sayes, All Wisedome that is given
> To hood-wink't mortals, first, proceeds from heaven:
> Truth's errour, Wisedom's, but wise insolence,
> And light's but darknesse, not deriv'd from thence;
> Wisdom's a straine transcends Morality,
> No Vertu's absent, Wisedome being by.
> Vertue, by constant practice, is acquir'd,
> This (this by sweat unpurchas't) is inspir'd.
>
> . . . .
>
> Wisdom's the Card of Knowledge, which, without
> That Guide, at random's wreckt on every doubt:

Knowledge, when Wisedome is too weak to guide her,
Is like a head-strong Horse, that throwes the Rider:
Which made that great Philosopher avow,
He knew so much, that he did nothing know.[34]

In Milton's poem, Satan adapts the familiar *topos* of the
hero's learning to suggest that Christ is not properly educated
for his role and function, that he requires, in addition to the
biblical learning which he admittedly possesses, a broad classical education, both to extend his own wisdom, and also to
enable him to converse with the pagans whom he means to
convert. Christ's answer reflects the humanist uses of the
learning *topos* in claiming and demonstrating acquaintance
with the learning Satan offers, but is especially related to the
Protestant variations on this *topos,* such as those of Du Bartas
and Quarles, which disparage all pagan learning in comparison with the light from above, or the Scriptures:

Think not but that I know these things; or think
I know them not; not therefore am I short
Of knowing what I ought: he who receives
Light from above, from the fountain of light,
No other doctrine needs, though granted true;
But these are false, or little else but dreams,
Conjectures, fancies, built on nothing firm.
The first and wisest of them all profess'd
To know this only, that he nothing knew;

. . . .
                              Who therefore seeks in these
True wisdom, finds her not, or by delusion
Far worse, her false resemblance only meets,
An empty cloud. However, many books
Wise men have said are wearisome; who reads
Incessantly, and to his reading brings not
A spirit and judgment equal or superior
(And what he brings, what needs he elsewhere seek)

Uncertain and unsettl'd still remains,
Deep verst in books and shallow in himself,
Crude or intoxicate, collecting toys,
And trifles for choice matters, worth a sponge;
As Children gathering pebbles on the shore.

(IV.286–94, 318–30)

The resemblance of Milton's perplexing learning passage in
diction and attitude to the other "learning passages" quoted
above indicates that it may be understood from one perspective at least as a *donnée* of the biblical epic tradition.

There is also some precedent in the earlier Christiads for
Milton's storm scene followed by a glorious dawn:

                    either Tropic now
'Gan thunder, and both ends of Heav'n; the Clouds
From many a horrid rift abortive pour'd
Fierce rain with lightning mixt, water with fire
In ruin reconcil'd: nor slept the winds
Within thir stony caves, but rush'd abroad
From the four hinges of the world,

. . . .

                            while thou
Satt'st unappall'd in calm and sinless peace.
Thus pass'd the night so foul till morning fair
Came forth with Pilgrim steps in amice gray;
Who with her radiant finger still'd the roar
Of thunder, chas'd the clouds, and laid the winds,

. . . .

And now the Sun with more effectual beams
Had cheer'd the face of Earth, and dried the wet
From drooping plant, or dropping tree; the birds
Who all things now behold more fresh and green,
After a night of storm so ruinous,
Clear'd up their choicest notes in bush and spray
To gratulate the sweet return of morn.

(IV.409–15, 424–29, 432–38)

Frénicle's *Jésus Crucifié* describes Christ as enduring a dreadful, Satan-inspired storm in the desert during the forty days previous to the verbal temptations, comparing him to a rock withstanding a tempest: "All the Ocean roars, and the wind full of horror/ Accompanies with rumbles his blind fury,/ But the rock holds firm, and repells back again/ The frightening mountains of sea surge."[35] And Giles Fletcher's description of the glorious morn of Easter is verbally so close to Milton's radiant dawn (which also carries overtones of the Easter following the Passion) as to be almost certainly a source:

> But now the second Morning, from her bowre,
> Began to glister in her beames, and nowe
> The roses of the day began to flowre
> In th'easterne garden; for heav'ns smiling browe
> Halfe insolent for joy begunne to showe:
> The early Sunne came lively dauncing out,
>
> .   .   .   .
>
> Th'engladded Spring, forgetfull now to weepe,
> Began t'eblazon from her leavie bed,
> The waking swallowe broke her halfe-yeares sleepe,
> And everie bush lay deepely purpured
> With violets: the woods late-wintry head
> Wide flaming primroses set all on fire,
> And his bald trees put on their green attire,
> Among whose infant leaves the joyous birds conspire
>
> .   .   .   .
>
> Such joyfull triumph, and triumphant cheare,
> As though the aged world anew created wear.[36]

There is even precedent for Milton's epic simile comparing Christ defeating Satan in the temptation to Hercules defeating Antaeus. Sedulius in the *Carmen Paschale* also referred to Satan the Tempter in terms of the Hercules-Antaeus myth: "Thrice rising up with proud spirit to endure,/ After being thrice fallen to earth, thrown down in futile battle."[37] Calling upon other Hercules myths, Bonus compares Satan defeated in the tower temptation to Cerberus, "The unhappy Demon, like Cerberus of the three mouths/ Groaned because of the great beating from Hercules' assault,/ And now lacked the crafty cunning of his three heads," [38] and D'Escorbiac compared Christ victorious over Satan to Hercules defeating the Lernean monster, as well as to a host of other heroes—Samson, Alexander, Caesar, Pompey.[39]

The biblical epic tradition, and especially the Jobean epic material, has obviously provided Milton with general patterns and precepts for his endeavor in the brief epic form, and also with precedents for particular passages. I have not argued that these passages were direct sources, though in the cases of Joseph Beaumont, Giles Fletcher, Quarles, and Fracastoro at least, an influence seems very probable. More important, though, is the recognition of the very considerable degree to which Milton is working within a well-defined generic tradition. This recognition should help to clarify his conception of and his artistic strategy in *Paradise Regained,* and should also further reveal his genius in transforming common biblical epic materials and devices to the requirements of his own transcendent art.

PART TWO · THEME AND DRAMATIC ACTION

*T*HE INDUCTION to *Paradise Regained* (I.1–293) has
the function, among others, of establishing certain
perspectives which control our reading of the entire
poem. Principally, it indicates that Christ's action of overcoming the satanic temptations in the wilderness is inextricably
linked with his emerging understanding of his nature and his
mission. The "identity motif" is not a minor theme, as is sometimes suggested, but is of the very substance of the dramatic
action, for only if Christ comes to understand himself and his
work perfectly can he withstand the temptations of Satan, all
of which present extremely clever parodies, falsifications, or
inadequate statements of that self and that work. The temptation process itself serves as a stimulus to Christ's growth toward
complete understanding.

One important context for regarding the poem's theme and
dramatic action is established in the induction by a series of
ambiguous references to the hero's nature. These, taken together, pose questions about his power and his state of knowledge, as well as, in dramatic terms, about his capacity for
action and growth. The great controlling ambiguity centers
upon the term "Son of God," the title bestowed in a special
way upon Christ at his baptism (the event with which the
action begins) and insistently applied to him with a variety
of meanings throughout the poem. Obviously, as Satan later
remarks, this is a title which "bears no single sense" (IV.517):
Satan himself can claim with some justice, "The Son of God
I also am, or was,/ And if I was, I am; relation stands;/ All
men are Sons of God" (IV.518–20). A most important aspect

of the poem's theme and the central issue in the dramatic encounter between Christ and Satan is the problem of determining, as Satan puts it, "In what degree or meaning thou art call'd/ The Son of God" (IV.516–17).

The induction describes Christ from the perspectives of several different characters, and by this means draws attention to the problem of his nature—the fact that he is, evidently, a man, yet has some kind of claim to divinity by reason of his divine paternity and miraculous birth. The narrator's perspective takes in both terms: he refers to Jesus now as human, now as divine, and indicates by his confident tone that he has at least some comprehension of the mystery involved. In the thematic statement he calls Jesus the "one man" whose firm obedience will recover the Paradise lost by the first man. In the invocation he describes the hero as the "glorious Eremite" led into the desert by the Spirit and brought forth "By proof th'undoubted Son of God" (I.8–11). In the report of the hero's Baptism he recounts God's proclamation of Jesus as "his beloved Son" (I.32), and Satan's view of him as "th'exalted man" (I.36). In his description of Satan's search for Jesus along the coast of Jordan he terms him "This man of men, attested Son of God" (I.122). And in his description of the hero's walk out onto the desert he terms him simply "Son of God" (I.183). The Father's testimony also employs both terms, obviously with full understanding. He affirms the Son's "birth divine," but his emphasis is upon Christ's humanity: Christ is a man "far abler" than Job to resist Satan, he is exposed to temptation to learn the rudiments of his mission, he is "This perfect Man, by merit call'd my Son" (I.150–66). Shifting the emphasis to the divine aspect of Christ, the angelic choir celebrates in prospect the forthcoming glorious victory of the Son of God and, by the statement that the Father "knows the Son," intimates something of the divine relationship (I.173–81). Satan also uses both terms, but his puzzled tone and frequent qualifications reveal his radical uncertainty about the meaning of the title "Son of God." He reports to his followers the Father's testimony that Christ is his "Son belov'd," and he recognizes "The glimpses of his Father's glory" (I.93) in this hero, but he knows also that Christ had a mortal mother and that "man he seems/ In all his lineaments" (I.91–92). It is evident that he cannot imagine what the divine sonship may mean or understand that Christ could be the same as the "first-begot" (I.89–91).

The induction also presents Christ's perspective on himself. He is aware of various testimonies proclaiming him more than man—his mother's assertion that "Thy Father is th'Eternal King, who rules/ All Heaven and Earth" (I.236–37), and the Father's proclamation which "pronounc'd me his,/ Mee his beloved Son" (I.284–85)—but he has no consciousness of himself as the "first-begot" or of any pre-existent state in heaven. Indeed he displays his merely human, limited understanding in his statement that he is led into the desert, "to what intent/ I learn not yet; perhaps I need not know" (I.291–92). The ambiguity with which the term "Son of God" is invested in the induction persists throughout the poem and reaches a climax in the tower scene, in which Christ's comment "Tempt not the Lord thy God" (IV.561) may be understood to refer to the Father simply, or to himself as divine, or to both.

Obviously, there are several possible ways of interpreting the ambiguities regarding Christ's nature and sonship which the induction forces on our attention, and they have very different implications for the interpretation of the ensuing action. For the encounter between Christ and Satan to constitute a genuine dramatic action and a real conflict, Christ's character must be conceived in such a way that the test or temptation is real: he must be able to fall, must be capable of growth, and must be genuinely (not just apparently) uncertain of himself. If he is not so conceived his statements have merely didactic, not personal, meaning, and he is shadowboxing with Satan. All possibility of genuine dramatic action is obliterated in the usual interpretation of Christ in the temptation episode as the divine protagonist always conscious of his divinity: such a view is implied in Allan Gilbert's comment that Christ, as the first-begotten taught directly of God, has no need for the human means offered by Satan though an ordinary man might properly need and use them, and in Douglas Bush's observation that "the sinless divine protagonist of *Paradise Regained* cannot falter, much less fall." [1] Another reading destructive of genuine dramatic conflict sees Christ undergoing the temptation with full consciousness of his divinity—indeed deliberately mystifying Satan about it by his ambiguous answers—but with his divine power held in abeyance so that he might better teach mankind by withstanding all temptation as a man. Elizabeth Pope points out that from patristic times to the seventeenth century this understanding of the temptation episode was dominant in biblical exegesis, and she ascribes this view also to Milton. [2] Often such readings further undercut dramatic conflict by suggesting that Christ experienced the temptation as an allegorical representative of human perfection. Some such understanding would seem to be implicit in Tillyard's comment that the hero of the poem is "partly an allegorical figure" typifying "the way in which the human soul can be regenerated"; in Hughes' observation that Christ in the poem is an "exemplar Redeemer, the Word of Saint John's Gospel, as it fused with the craving of critics and poets of the later Renaissance for a purely exemplary hero in epic poetry"; and in Stein's view that Christ acts in the poem as the perfect man presenting a symbolic pattern of heroic knowledge. [3]

On the other hand, those critics who find some genuine dramatic conflict and some real development of Christ's character in the poem do not agree upon the course this development takes or upon the conception of Christ's nature which makes such development possible. Some see Christ as simply human and therefore capable of dramatic conflict: M. M. Mahood describes him as "the perfect man, as yet scarcely aware of His divine progeniture," and Northrop Frye finds that he withstands the temptations as a human being until the tower temptation, at which time the omnipotent divine power "takes over" the human will which has now fully demonstrated its worthiness.[4] A. S. P. Woodhouse's view has even more dramatic potential: Christ gains "from his experience in the wilderness ... a progressively deeper insight into his own nature as well as into God's purpose," and actually progresses from human beginnings to a full realization of his divinity in the tower scene.[5] Don C. Allen's reading is also dramatic: Christ fluctuates throughout the poem between the divine and the human natures, giving evidence of this alternation by the striking tonal differences of his various speeches:

The fluctuation in this man's knowledge of himself and of his mission is what makes *Paradise Regained* more taut in action than Johnson perceived. In his divine nature Christ knows his identity and foresees his course, but in his human nature the "exalted man" is often uncertain of both. As we read the epic we watch him as he crosses and recrosses the boundary between the two persons, for it is out of this wandering to and fro, out of the humanly uncertain and the divinely sure that Milton gives validity to the test and extracts from it a highly dramatic conclusion.[6]

This variety of opinion arises from the ambiguities regarding Christ's nature which are posed in the induction and continue throughout the poem. Since the uncertainty about the meaning of Christ's sonship occasions much of the tension in the dramatic exchanges between Christ and Satan, and is of primary importance in the development of theme and plot, these ambiguities are artistically necessary, and we cannot expect resolu-

tion of them by simple dogmatic statement. The proper view
of Christ's nature is indeed implicit in the poem itself, but
the fact that many readers for nearly two centuries found
strictest orthodoxy in *Paradise Lost* indicates how easily theological concepts and terms not explicitly defined in a work
of art may be accorded the value most familiar and most
agreeable to the reader. However, for the problem of Christ's
nature, as for so many other difficulties, Milton's *De Doctrina
Christiana* provides helpful guidance. Though we cannot assume in advance a perfect agreement between tract and poem
on this theological issue, yet a general coherence may certainly be expected, given the very high correlation Maurice
Kelley has found between the theological ideas of *De Doctrina*
and of *Paradise Lost.*[7] Accordingly, we may inquire how Milton's treatment of God, of the first-begotten Son of God, and
of the incarnate Christ in *De Doctrina* may help to explain
the hero of *Paradise Regained.*

Both Milton's anti-Trinitarianism and his heterodox view of
the hypostatic union of divine and human in Christ stem from
the same logical quarrel with the orthodox formulas distinguishing the concepts "nature" and "person." Indeed, in Milton's
view the terms "nature" or "essence" (*essentia*), "hypostasis" or
"subsistence" (*subsistentia*), and "person" (*persona*) are virtually identical or are at any rate interchangeable when predicated
of any one intelligent being. Accordingly, in speaking of the
Godhead Milton declares, "God is one ens, not two; one essence and one subsistence, which is nothing but a substantial
essence, appertain to one ens; if two subsistences or two persons be assigned to one essence, it involves a contradiction
of terms." Again he comments, "*essence* and *hypostasis* mean
the same thing."[8] He concludes therefore that to speak of
three persons or three subsistences or three hypostases in one
divine nature or essence (the usual formulation of the doctrine
of the Trinity) is a contradiction. Similarly, in defining the

hypostatic union which comprises the one person of **Christ,** he declares, "the union of two natures in Christ must be considered as the mutual hypostatic union of two essences; for where there is a perfect substantial essence, there must also by an hypostasis or subsistence, inasmuch as they are the same thing," and a little later he includes "person" also as an analogous term: "There is then in Christ a mutual hypostatic union of two natures, that is to say, of two essences, of two substances, and consequently of two persons." [9] Thus he finds also contradictory the orthodox formula for the hypostatic union which describes the Logos as uniting himself in the Incarnation with a human nature rather than with a human person.

The basis of Milton's anti-Trinitarianism is his view of God as the unchangeable, indivisible One. Although God has revealed himself in Scripture in such a way as to accommodate himself to human understanding, and is to be spoken of in accordance with that scriptural presentation of himself, he is really incomprehensible to man—invisible, inaudible, manifested only through the Son who is his Image and his Word.[10] His attributes are Truth, the possession of a most simple essence admitting of no compound, Immensity, Infinity, Eternity, Immutability, Incorruptibility, Omnipresence, Omnipotence, and Unity. He acts in two modes: by internal efficiency, that is, by his decrees, and by external efficiency, "or the execution of his decrees, whereby whatever decrees he has established within himself, he carries into effect outside of himself." [11] His internal efficiency consists of a general decree whereby he has decreed from all eternity whatever he has purposed to do, and also of special decrees concerning the generation of the Son, the creation of the angels, and the predestination to salvation of those men who believe; these special decrees are not said to have obtained from eternity though all of them would necessarily have been in some way incorporated in God's general decree or plan. The Son's generation took place "within the limits of time," not from eternity, since "the decree itself must have been anterior to the execution of the decree";[12] his generation was by external rather than by internal efficiency since Father and Son are different persons.[13]

God's external efficiency is also exercised in the creation of the world through the agency of the Son. That creation is not *ex nihilo* as in the orthodox conception, but from a prime matter which derives in some way from God's own substance: thus matter itself must be substantially inherent in God, God must have produced it out of himself by some process of projection or retraction, and the matter thus produced of God's own substance is indestructible and (in its own nature) incorruptible.[14] Accordingly, though Milton retains the terms "body" and "spirit," they refer (as Raphael's explanations to Adam, *PL* V.469–90, also indicates) to different degrees of refinement of the same "first matter" that is the substance of the whole creation. As Denis Saurat, Maurice Kelley, Walter Curry, and others have shown, this ascription of materiality to God himself, and the concomitant refusal to distinguish fundamentally between angels and men, matter and spirit, is a foundation stone of Milton's thought and is perhaps his most significant and daring departure from orthodoxy.[15]

That Milton showed himself to be a forthright anti-Trinitarian in the *De Doctrina* is denied by few, though there is considerable question as to what variety of anti-Trinitarianism he professes. The orthodox Trinitarian position, established at Nicaea and developed further in the formulations of Athanasius and Augustine, identified three persons in the Godhead distinct in existence or subsistence but one in nature (essence, substance). The Son was therefore understood to be equal to and consubstantial with the Father, and his eternal and natural generation from the Father was illustrated by Athanasius and many others through the metaphors of the sun begetting light and the spring putting forth the brook.[16] The creedal statement at Nicaea described the Son as "only-begotten, *that is, of the substance of the Father, God of God, Light of Light, true God of true God, begotten not made, of one substance [homoousian] with the* Father." [17] The Nicene anathemas denounced a number of Arian opinions which departed from this position: the conception that the Son was produced out of nothingness, that he was created, that he had a beginning, that he is of a different substance from the Father, and that he is subject to moral change or alteration. [18]

Until recently there has been nearly universal agreement that Milton's conception of the Son approximates the Arian position. [19] Arius, insisting upon the oneness of God and the incommunicability of the divine essence, declared that the Son is God only by participation in grace, that he is "neither eternal nor co-eternal nor co-unbegotten with the Father, nor does he have his being together with the Father." Arius also maintained that the Son of God is not generated of the substance of the Father but created out of nothing like the rest of the creation, that he is God's agent for that creation, that he is created by the action of God's will, and that he holds all that he has by God's gift, "life and being and glories." [20] Since he is a creature—albeit unique and distinct from the rest of the creation—he cannot know God's nature or even know fully his own nature; he is mutable and "remains good by His own free will, while He chooseth" as all other creatures do." Distinguishing Milton's viewpoint somewhat from this straightforward Arian position, Louis A. Wood has argued that Milton has closer affinities with the so-called semi-Arians like Basil of Ancyra and Eusebius of Caesarea who affirmed with Arius that the Son is not eternal and not of the same essence as the Father, but modified the Arian statement of his creation from nothingness by declaring that he was of like substance (*homoiousian*, not *homoousian*) with the Father. [22]

Departing radically from this consensus, W. B. Hunter has

recently denied that Milton can be called an Arian at all since
he accepts the view of the Son's generation out of God's substance. Hunter, and J. H. Adamson supporting him, maintain
that Milton's position is closer to that of the early Fathers of
the church who, drawing upon Philo and Plotinus, interpreted
the Trinity in relation to the Neo-Platonic Logos doctrine,
and so viewed the Son as subordinate and in some respects
inferior to the Father, deriving his being and his divine gifts
in some manner from the Father, though still coeternal and
consubstantial with him.[23] Some of the early Fathers such as
Justin Martyr and Tertullian set forth a two-stage Logos theory
deriving from Philo, whereby the Logos (Son) is identified
with the Wisdom of God which always existed within him
(the Wisdom who speaks in Proverbs viii), but was then at
some stage put forth from him as Word and Son. To describe
this natural begetting Tertullian used the familiar "orthodox"
metaphors: God put forth the Word as "the root puts forth the
tree, and the fountain the river, and the Sun the ray"; nevertheless he declares that the "Father is the entire substance, but
the Son is a derivation and portion of the whole."[24] On the
other hand, Origen's theory of the engendering of the Logos
(also identified with the Wisdom of Proverbs viii) resembles
Plotinus' concept of the perpetual emanation of the Logos as
a single, eternal, continuous process:

Who that is capable of entertaining reverential thoughts or feelings
regarding God, can suppose or believe that God the Father ever
existed, even for a moment of time, without having generated this
Wisdom?...Wherefore we have always held that God is the
Father of His only-begotten Son, who was born indeed of Him,
and derives from Him what He is, but without any beginning...
His generation is as eternal and everlasting as the brilliancy which
is produced from the sun. For it is not by receiving the breath of
life that He is made a Son, by *any outward act,* but by His own
nature.[25]

Hunter and Adamson affirm that this Neo-Platonic "subordinationism" was the dominant position regarding the Trinity in the early church, that it was revived by the Cambridge Platonists Henry More and Ralph Cudworth, and that it was never specifically condemned. Hunter concludes that in aligning himself with this position Milton did not consider himself as, and in fact was not, a heretic.

It is true that Milton departs significantly from Arius and resembles the subordinationists in his view of the Son as generated from God's substance: "God imparted to the Son as much as he pleased of the divine nature, nay of the divine substance itself, care being taken not to confound the substance with the whole essence." [26] Thus he could have accepted the Nicene test word, *homoousian,* of the same substance with the Father, in the generic sense, signifying that which is common to several individuals of a class, or as Hunter maintains, in the Stoic sense of a substratum underlying being (senses which the term commonly bore in early Christian thought and which may well have predominated at Nicaea); he could not have accepted it in the sense asserted by Athanasius and accepted in later Catholic theology, numerical identity of substance.[27] However, Milton's understanding of substance is not enough to buttress Hunter's conclusion that "Milton might indeed believe that he was supporting the *homoousian* doctrine, the heart of the Nicene Creed." [28] For as J. N. D. Kelly points out, the Nicene test word was used not so much to define the substantial unity of the Godhead (that came later) as to assert "that the Son was fully God, in the sense of sharing the same divine nature as His Father.... The great issue before the council ... was the Son's co-eternity with the Father, which the Arians denied, his full divinity in contrast to the creaturely status they ascribed to him.... Positively it [the council] was content to affirm the Son's full divinity and equality with the Father, out of Whose being He was derived and Whose nature he consequently shared." [29] But Milton's declaration that the Son may share the Father's substance though not his whole essence prepares for precisely the opposite conclusion: Milton's equation of *essence* with *hypostasis* (individual being or existence) rather than with *substance* is not, as with some of the Fathers, merely a way of strongly affirming the distinction of persons in the Trinity in answer to the Sabellian heresy,[30] but a way of asserting that God's essence, always equated by Milton with the divine nature itself, is radically incommunicable to any other because it can pertain only to one hypostasis or person, the Father, and because its attributes such as Unity and Infinity can in no sense be shared. The following passage indicates Milton's customary manner of using these distinctions to deny the Son's ability to participate fully and automatically in the divine nature which is the essence of the Father:

If...he [the Son] derived his essence from the Father, let it be shown how that essence can have been supremely divine, that is, identically the same with the essence of the Father; since the divine essence, whose property it is to be always one, cannot possibly generate the same essence by which it is generated...Now as the effect of generation is to produce something which shall exist independently of the generator, it follows that God cannot beget a co-equal Deity, because unity and infinity are two of his essential attributes. Since therefore the Son derives his essence from the Father, he is posterior to the Father not merely in rank...but also in essence.[31]

Or again, Milton declares,

the supreme God is self-existent; but he who is not self-existent, who did not beget, but was begotten, is not the first cause, but the effect, and therefore is not the supreme God.... The nature of the Son is indeed divine, but distinct from and clearly inferior to the nature of the Father—for...to be God, and to be in the bosom of God the Father—to be God, and to be from God—to be the one invisible God, and to be the only-begotten and visible, are things so different that they cannot be predicated of one and the same essence.[32]

Or again, with reference to the Son's generation from the Father, Milton observes, "the Father alone is a self-existent God, and...a being which is not self-existent cannot be God."[33] J. N. D. Kelly states that the Arian theology derived some of its elements from the subordinationism of Origen and Dionysius but that "for two of its features...viz. its exaggerated emphasis on *agennesia* [self-existence, the state of being ungenerated] as the indispensable characteristic of Deity, and its rejection of the idea that the Godhead can communicate Its essence, it is difficult to find parallels in these teachers."[34] It is surely significant that Milton emphasized just these two points.

It would seem therefore that Milton denies the basic meaning of the Nicene formulation. Also, it may be queried whether the Miltonic view of the Son's participation in the substance of God really separates the Son much more radically from the rest of creation and really unites him much more firmly to God than the Arian Son created from nothingness. Since for Milton matter also derives in some way from God's substance, the Son must also share that material substance. He may therefore resemble Arius' Son in his relation to the rest of the creation more nearly than he resembles the subordinationists' Logos who by being generated of the substance of God was wholly differentiated from all creatures. Milton's constantly reiterated scriptural terms for the Son are terms which link him with the rest of the creation—"First born of every creature," and "Beginning of the creation of God"; he admits the term "only begotten" as referring solely to the "metaphorical" begetting, that is, to the anointing of the Son as Messiah.[35] Moreover, Milton's willingness to use a variety of terms as synonyms to describe the actual production of the Son indicates that he does not radically separate the Son's production from the rest of creation: "God of his own will created, or generated, or produced the Son before all things, endued with the divine nature." [36]

With regard to the other doctrines anathematized at Nicaea, Milton is even more closely related to the Arian than to the subordinationist position. He explicitly denies the eternity of the Son, whether conceived according to a one- or two-stage Logos theory. For him the Wisdom of Proverbs viii is not the Logos existing from eternity within the Father and later to be manifested, but simply a poetic personification of God's own wisdom.[37] He also explicitly rejects the emanation theory, on the ground that if the Son is eternally begotten he is always in the act of being made and so is never a Son, and also that such words as "to proceed" or to "go forth" from the Father refer to the *mission* of the Son and the Holy Spirit, not to their nature or mode of production.[38] Declaring flatly that "it is impossible to find a single text in all Scripture to prove the eternal generation of the Son" Milton concludes that the texts referring to the Son's literal generation merely "prove the existence of the Son before the world was made." Thus the opening verse of the Gospel of John, "In the beginning was the Word," means simply in the beginning of creation, not "from everlasting." [39] Milton's most emphatic denial of the eternity of the Son turns upon a distinction between God's eternal decree whereby God purposed from all eternity to generate a Son, and his subsequent execution of that decree: "Thus the Son was begotten of the Father in consequence of his decree, and therefore *within the limits of time,* for the decree itself must have been anterior to the execution of the decree." [40]

It is true that Milton is in agreement with several of the subordinationist Fathers as well as with Arius in declaring the Son to have been created by the will of the Father, yet Milton's insistence that it consisted with the perfection of the Father's essence not to beget the Son [41] seems to separate him radically from Tertullian, Origen, and others who constantly used the metaphors of ray from light and stream from fountain to suggest the "natural" and inevitable begetting of the Son. Arius explicitly rejects these metaphors, and it is significant that nowhere in the *De Doctrina* does Milton use them: in the one apparent use of them in his poetry, the "Invocation to Light" in *Paradise Lost,* it is far from obvious that the lines are intended to refer to the Son.[42]

Also, though both Arius and many early Fathers speak of the Son's deriving divine gifts and attributes from the Father, for the subordinationists such a statement normally means that the Father is the source of these attributes in that as Father he is the source of the Son's being and substance, while for Arius (as for Milton) the emphasis is upon the will and the conscious donation of the Father. God's name, attributes, and works are attributed by Milton to the Son, but "in such a manner that they are easily understood to be attributable in their original and proper sense to the Father alone; and that the Son acknowledges himself to possess whatever share of Deity is assigned to him, by virtue of the peculiar gift and kindness of the Father." [43] Both the creative and the redemptive powers are said to belong properly to God, and to be merely exercised through the Son as instrument. Like Arius, Milton insists that the Son is not omniscient since the Father has reserved "some secret purposes" to himself alone, and that he is not omnipotent since he can do nothing of himself but works all miracles by divine assistance.[44] It is further significant that in *Paradise Lost* (V.809–95) Abdiel's warm defense of the right of the Son to rule the angels as their superior makes no claims on the ground of the Son's participation in or derivation from the substance of God, but argues merely on the ground that the Son enjoys that right by the gift of God and because he was God's agent for creating all things.

Moreover, it seems that for Milton as for Arius the Son is mutable since he shares in God's attributes only according to God's good pleasure rather than by nature. Indeed, one of Milton's strongest arguments that the Son cannot be coessential with the Father derives from the fact that he is shown to be mutable in the Incarnation, which the supreme God could never be. Citing Philippians ii:6–8 in reference to the Incarnation, Milton observes,

the phrases "he did not think it," "he made himself of no reputation" (literally, "he emptied himself"), appear inapplicable to the supreme God. For "to think" is nothing else than to entertain an opinion, which cannot be properly said of God. Nor can the infinite God be said to empty himself, any more than to contradict himself; for infinity and emptiness are opposite terms.[45]

If mutable and subject to change like all creatures, then the Son evidently experiences as well the free will and the capacity for moral growth and development which all intelligent creatures enjoy in Milton's (as in Arius') system. Accordingly, the Son's offer in the council in heaven in *Paradise Lost* to suffer and die in order to effect man's redemption is not mere gesture, and God's praise of the Son as showing himself by this offer "By merit more than Birthright Son of God" (III.309) is a testimony to the Son's free and mutable nature.

In Milton's system it is this Son, radically inferior to the Father even in his heavenly condition, who becomes incarnate, and Milton's heterodoxy extends to the conception of that Incarnation. The orthodox statement of the hypostatic union of two natures in the one person of Christ was worked out in several dogmatic statements of the early church, notably at the Council of Ephesus and the Council of Chalcedon, and at the First, Second, and Third Councils at Constantinople.

Chalcedon explained the mode of the union of two natures in Christ by the formula that the Word assumed human nature, body and soul, rather than the person of a particular man: Cyril's Second Letter to Nestorius which was approved at Chalcedon makes this point:

We do not assert that there was any change in the nature of the Word when it became flesh, or that it was transformed into an entire man ... but we say that the Word, in a manner indescribable and inconceivable, united personally [Καθ᾽ ὑπόστασιν] to himself flesh animated with a reasonable soul ... For Scripture does not say "the Word united to himself the person of a man" but "the Word was made flesh." And that means precisely this, that he became partaker of flesh and blood ... but he did not cast aside his being God and his having been begotten of God the Father. He assumed our flesh; but he continued to be what he was.[46]

Chalcedon also insisted that the union of the two natures was a real union, not a mere juxtaposition or indwelling of the Logos, and at the same time that the two natures retained without confusion their distinct characteristics and functions. Christ, the Chalcedon Decree declared, is to be "acknowledged in two natures without confusion, without change, without division, without separation—the difference of the natures being by no means taken away because of the union, but rather the distinctive character of each nature being preserved."[47] The Tome of Leo, approved at Chalcedon, further emphasized the point that each nature retains its own properties and does what is appropriate to it in communication with the other, developing this position through an exposition of the so-called kenosis or "humbling" of the Logos. Leo along with almost all other patristic exegetes understood by kenosis the Logos' voluntary renunciation in the hypostatic union (though not in his ubiquitous divine state) of the glory and the form but not the power and actuality of the Godhead.[48] The key

Scripture text is Philippians ii:6–8: "Who being in ye forme of God, thought it not robbery to be equall with God:/ But made himselfe of no reputation [literally, emptied himself], and tooke upon him the forme of a servant, and was made in the likenesse of men./ And being found in fashion as a man, he humbled himselfe, and became obedient unto death, even the death of the Crosse." Referring to this passage, Leo declared:

> He took on him "the form of a servant" without the defilement of sins, augmenting what was human, not diminishing what was divine; because that "emptying of himself" whereby the Invisible made himself visible, and the Creator and Lord of all things willed to be one among mortals, was a stooping down of compassion, not a failure of power.... Each of the natures retains its proper character without defect; and as the form of God does not take away the form of a servant, so the form of a servant does not impair the form of God.... For each "form" does the acts which belong to it, in communion with the other; the Word, that is, performing what belongs to the Word, and the flesh carrying out what belongs to the flesh. The one of these shines out in miracles; the other succumbs to injuries.... As then—to pass by many points—it does not belong to the same nature to weep with feelings of pity over a dead friend and ... by a voice of command to raise him up to life again.[49]

The Councils of Ephesus and Chalcedon, and the First and Second Councils at Constantinople anathematized a number of heretical views concerning the nature of the union of God and Man in Christ. The most important of the excluded positions were the following: (1) "Docetism," the belief that the Logos assumed no real human body and human nature, but that all his apparently human actions such as eating, drinking, suffering, and dying were illusory. (2) "Arianism," the view that the Logos simply assumed flesh, not human nature, and himself took the place of the human soul in Jesus, thereby experiencing himself the full range of feelings and sufferings attributed to Christ and being capable also of moral growth and development in knowledge. (3) "Apollinarianism," the belief that the Logos took the place of the rational soul (νους), though not of the entire soul in Christ, and thereby directed the Incarnate life and was subject to all its experiences, even suffering; this last provision approaches Theopaschitism since, in contrast to Arius, Apollinaris conceived of the Logos as full participant in the Godhead, equal to the Father. (4) "Nestorianism," the doctrine that not only two natures but two persons coexisted in Christ in a union of juxtaposition, common feeling, and good pleasure, and that in this union the functions and properties of each nature were wholly distinct, the divine incapable of suffering, the human capable of moral growth and movement toward ever closer union with the divine person; [50] Theodore of Mopsuestia often expressed this union through the metaphors of the Logos indwelling in the man Jesus as in a temple, and Nestorius in terms of the divine and human in Jesus making use of the persons of each other. (5) "Monophysitism," the view that while there were two natures before the Incarnation there was but one afterwards, formed by the complete elevation and absorption of the human nature into the divine. [51]

At the Third Council of Constantinople (Sixth Ecumenical Council) one further heresy was anathematized: "Monenergism," or "Monotheletism," which admitted the formula of the two natures in a loose sense, but argued that there was in the incarnate Christ only one redemptive energy and only one will, that of the Logos, which directed the human activities as well as the divine. [52] The Council proclaimed the doctrine of two wills as orthodox:

We also proclaim two natural willings or wills in him and two natural operations, without separation, without change, without partition, without confusion ... two natural wills not contrary ... but his human will following, and not resisting or opposing, but rather subject to his divine and all powerful will. ... We also glorify

two natural operations in the same our Lord Jesus Christ, our true
God, without separation, without change, without partition, without confusion...as the divine preacher Leo most clearly says...
"the Word, that is, performing what belongs to the Word, and
the flesh carrying out what belongs to the flesh." [53]

In his discussion of the incarnate Christ Milton immediately sets aside as untenable two views of the mode of Incarnation. First he repudiates "those who contend for the
merely human nature of Christ," urging again the Son's preexistence as the first born of all creatures, as the agent by
whom God created all things, and as the being generated
from the divine substance.[54] He thereby rejects the Socinian
position which had gained some currency in seventeenth-century England: Socinianism held that the Son came into existence only at the birth of Christ, that he is by nature simply
human, that he was made Lord and given his divine excellence by the gift of the Father and by his own merit, that
he was ignorant of the mind and will of the Father until his
baptism and temptation at which time he was rapt up into
heaven and instructed by God concerning his mission.[55] Milton also repudiates the orthodox view, summarizing its provisions out of Zanchius as follows: the two natures are so
combined in one Christ as to permit him "a real and perfect
subsistence in the one nature, independently of that which
properly belongs to the other"; Christ did not unite with a single man but with human nature; Christ's human nature never
had any separate subsistence independent of the Logos.[56] Milton,
reiterating the argument which he developed earlier with regard to the Trinity, to the effect that the terms "nature," "subsistence," and "person" are interchangeable when used of any
one intelligent being, concludes that the Logos must assume
a *man* since "human nature" cannot exist in abstraction or
separation from some particular human being. He concludes
further that the human nature of Jesus must therefore have

had an independent subsistence before the Logos took it on, and that therefore the one person of Christ is formed of the "mutual hypostatic union of two natures, that is to say of two essences, of two substances, and consequently of two persons." [57] Hunter has argued that these statements seem to make Milton a Nestorian. [58]

Milton specifically refuses to speculate as to the *mode* of this union between the two persons, declaring that we should be content to know simply that the "Son of God, our Mediator, was made flesh, that he is called both God and Man, and is such in reality; which is expressed in Greek by the single and appropriate term, θεάνθρωπος." [59] However, though his observation concerning the union of the two persons would seem to imply a sharp distinction between the properties of the human and divine natures in the new union such as Nestorius insisted upon, Milton's discussion of the actions of Christ after the hypostatic union assumes a unification much more complete and total than even the orthodox theory provides for. He declares that the properties of each nature remain individually distinct after the Incarnation, but he readily admits (as Nestorianism did not) the *communicatio idiomatum* or *proprietatum* whereby what is peculiar to one nature is attributed to both jointly, or what belongs to the compound person may be spoken of as belonging to one nature only. [60] Moreover, he insists that after the hypostatic union has taken place, we may not assign the speeches of Christ variously to his human or to his divine nature:

After the hypostatical union of two natures in one person, it follows that whatever Christ says of himself, he says not as the possessor of either nature separately, but with reference to the whole of his character, and in his entire person, except where he himself makes a distinction. Those who divide this hypostatical union at their own discretion, strip the discourses and answers of Christ of all their sincerity. [61]

This statement would seem to be especially relevant to the dramatic situation of *Paradise Regained,* suggesting that the hero speaks sincerely what he knows.

Furthermore, Milton denies the orthodox view of the mediatorial office, which held that many of Christ's activities—for example, his birth, his temptation, his passion, his death—are the functions of his human nature alone in communion with his divine nature, since the divine nature is incapable of such activity.[62] Rather, Milton insists that the entire work of the mediatorial office is undertaken by Christ in both natures and in his entire person and that no separation or distinction of functions can be made: Christ, he declares, undergoes the birth, circumcision, baptism, temptation, passion, and even the death in his whole person.[63] The Heidelberg Catechism may be taken as representative of the orthodox view that Christ's divine nature was not subject to suffering and that it did indeed sustain and uphold him during his sufferings and at length raised his body to life again,[64] but Milton points to Christ's calling upon his Father during his passion as proof that his divine nature itself was subject to trial and inadequate to sustain him without the Father's assistance:

For if the Son was able to accomplish by his own independent power the work of his passion, why did he forsake himself; why did he implore the assistance of his Father . . . he exclaimed upon the cross, "My God, my God, why hast thou forsaken me?" He whom the Son, himself God, addresses as God, must be the Father; why then did the Son call upon the Father? Because he felt even his divine nature insufficient to support him under the pains of death. Thus also he said, when at the point of death, Luke xxiii.46. "Father, into thy hands I commend my spirit." To whom rather than to himself as God would he have commended himself in his human nature, if by his own divine nature alone he had possessed sufficient power to deliver himself from death? It was therefore the Father only who raised him again to life.[65]

This insistence that Christ was subject to suffering and death in his divine nature also, since the whole of the sacrifice must be slain,[66] would be Theopaschitism were it not for Milton's insistence on the divine nature of the Son as radically inferior to that of the Father and derived from him; Arius' conception of the suffering Logos is saved from Theopaschitism on the same grounds. From all this it is evident that Milton's comments on the hypostatic union provide for the endurance of the properties appropriate to the two natures, but that he persistently refrains from distinguishing among the functions, the words, and the actions of the incarnate Christ so as to ascribe some to one, some to the other, nature.

This begins to sound as if, rather than developing the Nestorian position which he seemed at first to adopt, Milton has instead moved to some variety of Monophysitism, whereby the two persons united in the Incarnation are seen to be fused or joined into one nature. Milton's remarks on the question of Christ's understanding and will align him yet more closely to this position, or rather to the Monothelete development of it. He declares that Christ,

since his assumption of human flesh, remains one Christ ... whether he retains his two-fold will and understanding, is a point respecting which, as Scripture is silent, we are not concerned to inquire. For after having "emptied himself," he might "increase in wisdom," Luke ii.52. by means of the understanding which he previously possessed, and might "know all things," John xxi.17. namely through the teaching of the Father, as he himself acknowledged. Nor is this two-fold will implied in the single passage Matt. xxvi.39. "not as I will, but as thou wilt," unless he be the same with the Father, which, as has been already shown, cannot be admitted.[67]

This formulation appears to deny any basis for the orthodox pronouncement at the Third Council of Constantinople for the twofold will of Christ: Milton offers an explanation as to how, on the assumption of a single, unitary understanding, Christ might come to "know all things," and he explains away one Scripture text which seems to point to a twofold will. This near obliteration of the distinction between the two natures accords with that virtual identification of nature, subsistence, and person which we noted earlier. If Christ is said to have become one person after the Incarnation, Milton cannot find it congenial to think of him as still twofold in his understanding and will, which are of the essence of the person.

How then does Milton understand the Incarnation to have taken place, and what is the nature of the Christ so formed? If his disposition is toward Monophysitism or Monotheletism in regard to the activities and understanding and will of Christ, yet his emphasis upon the divine nature as actually sharing in all the activities usually ascribed to the human nature—even to the suffering and the death—carries him far away from the disposition of the Monophysites to obliterate the human side of Christ through the complete transmutation of the human by the divine. For Milton as for Arius it would seem that the divine is in some important way subsumed in the human, and this raises again the concept of the kenosis or humiliation of Christ, the "emptying" (*sese exinanivit*) which Milton often mentions and explains by citing Philippians ii:6–8. This "emptying," as Hastings points out, was almost universally interpreted by the Fathers as Christ's voluntary renunciation of the glory of God, but it did not imply his actual denuding himself of his power and his divine attributes; indeed Church Fathers and reformers alike held that the Son "emptied himself" only with respect to the hypostatic union, but that he continued to exercise his divine power and attributes outside that union, in his eternal subsistence in the Trinity. But Hastings notes also that Arius' view of a mutable Logos becoming the soul of a suffering, passible man implies an interpretation of kenosis which is very much more literal,[68] and though Milton does not share that aspect of the Arian conception of the incarnate Christ, yet I think for him also the kenosis is literally an emptying of divine attributes and powers. We find one indication of this in the fact that the poems do not show the Son's continuing exercise of divine power and attributes outside the hypostatic union: he does not anticipate any such retention of divine power when he offers to become man in the council in heaven in *Paradise Lost,* and in *Paradise Regained* after the Incarnation he is no longer in heaven communicating with the Father. Again, in the *De Doctrina* Milton cites Philippians ii:6–8 to argue that because the Son was able to "empty himself" this proves that he cannot be one with the Father in essence: "since he emptied himself of that form of God in which he had previously existed, if the form of God is to be taken for the essence of the Deity itself, it would prove him to have emptied himself of that essence, which is impossible." [69] In another place, *De Doctrina* glosses the meaning of "form" in this passage: " 'To be in the form of God' ... seems to be synonymous with being in the image of God." [70] In Milton's reading, then, Philippians ii:6–8 means that the Son emptied himself of whatever of divinity he did enjoy as God's image; the form of which he emptied himself could not have been the essence of the Supreme God because that could not have been emptied out, so it could only have been his own essence or nature as the Image of the Father holding all things at the pleasure of the Father.

From the statements of *De Doctrina,* then, it seems that Milton cannot be exactly classified in terms of any of the common christological positions, that he has indeed constructed his own system as he claimed. Nevertheless, his view of the incarnate Christ, like his view of the Son, has several important resemblances to the Arian position. Specifically, Milton appears to assume a fusion of the divine and human natures and persons into the one person of Christ at the Incarnation,

so that while the individual natures retain their distinct properties, a single person with what seems to be a single understanding and will is formed, all of whose speeches and functions refer to this new self. However, this fusion is not achieved
by commingling and confusing the two natures, but rather,
it would seem, by an emptying out by the divine nature of
that which properly belongs to itself as divine, so that what
is left to operate in the new person is the human element,
the human understanding and will. In Milton's Christology
this is readily possible, since the Son even in his position of
glory in heaven only holds such of the attributes of divinity
as God wishes to bestow upon him by gift, so that he can
experience even there an accession, and presumably also a
diminution, of power and glory. Milton portrays this poetically
in *Paradise Lost* when God bestows an accession of power
on the Son as he goes forth to rout Satan, and again when
God transfers to the Son his own creative power, sending him
forth to create the universe (*PL* VI.710–22; VII.163–96). When
such a Son then empties himself of the "Form of God in which
he had previously existed" he renounces the divine attributes
which he had only by gift not by nature; after such an emptying his personality and understanding and will must be characterized by the human component. But, declares Milton,
"after having 'emptied himself,' he might 'increase in wisdom,'
Luke ii.52. by means of the understanding which he previously possessed, and might 'know all things,' John xxi.17.
namely, through the teaching of the Father." [71] This appears
to mean that the Father might activate the divine element of
Christ's understanding, causing him to gain back what he has
relinquished, or might illuminate him directly regarding his
nature. One might expect that, as this process continues, the
divine personality in Christ would ultimately become the controlling factor, but it might not be necessary to assume a
steady evolution in the regaining of the divine understanding

and will: perhaps, just as the Son enjoyed occasional accessions of power in *Paradise Lost,* the incarnate Christ is the occasional recipient of special divine illumination activating the divine in himself, and may revert to the merely or nearly human on other occasions. Such a view of Christ, drawn from the statements of *De Doctrina,* would seem to describe precisely the hero presented to us in *Paradise Regained*.

Milton's unusual conception of an incarnate Christ who has really emptied himself of divine understanding and will, together with the conventional conception of a puzzled and deluded Satan seeking throughout the temptation to learn whether Christ is indeed divine, provides the basis for a genuine dramatic encounter in the poem, an epic duel transmuted into intellectual and spiritual terms. The induction makes clear that hero and antagonist begin this duel at approximately the same level of knowledge: both are cognizant of the prophecies, both saw the signs at the recent Baptism, both are ignorant of the identity between this Son and the "first-begot." Satan knows that although Christ had a mortal mother he has been pronounced in some sense the Son of God, but he cannot imagine the identity between this humble human being and the divinely powerful first-begotten Son: "His first-begot we know, and sore have felt,/ When his fierce thunder drove us to the deep;/ Who this is we must learn" (I.89–91). Satan saw only the material signs at Christ's baptism—a great prophet who "Pretends to wash off sin," and a "perfect Dove... whate'er it meant" (I.73, 83). He concludes that the prophecy about the seed of the woman bruising his head probably signifies the breaking of all the demoniac empire "of Earth and Air" (I.63), but he expects Christ to achieve this by some form of worldly dominion, appearing "in the head of Nations.../ Their King, their Leader, and Supreme on Earth" (I.98–99). His tone during the first council indicates that he is impressed with the danger, but that he is withal rather confi-

dent that he can oppose "something sudden" (I.96) to prevent
the fulfillment of the prophecy. His optimism gains strength
from his reflections upon his former victory over Adam, and
from the fact that the present voyage promises to be "calmer"
since he need not now traverse Chaos but only the region of
the air which the demons have usurped.

Christ's meditation as he goes forth into the wilderness indicates that prior to his baptism he has learned what he knows
of himself from two sources of knowledge: his Mother's testimony, which has informed him that he is the Son of God,
that his birth is miraculous, and that he is "King of *Israel*
born" who will "sit on *David's* Throne"; and the scriptural
writings, which have taught him that he is the Messiah
"partly" known to the prophets, and that his mission is to
work redemption for mankind through "many a hard assay
even to the death" (I.264). The tentative tone of Christ's first
meditation shows that he does not yet understand what the
prophetic metaphors really mean, and also that he has no
recollection of his previous celestial history as the first-begotten Son. His understanding of his mission is similarly vague:
as a child he thought himself "born to promote all truth,/ All
righteous things" (I.205-6); later he contemplated performing
such valiant deeds as rescuing Israel from Rome and crushing
tyranny through all the earth; at length he concluded that
rule by persuasion was more noble. Evidently divine inspiration figured to some extent in Christ's earlier insights, as in
all true readings of Scripture, but they were gained essentially by human means. However, Christ's first meditation
shows that from the time of his baptism to the moment of
entering the desert he has been in a special way under the
tutelage of divine illumination. At the baptism the Father's
voice itself pronounced him beloved Son, and he knew (as
Satan did not) that the descending Dove was the Holy Spirit.
As he enters the desert he is conscious not only of his limited

human knowledge, being led here "to what intent/ I learn not yet," but also of the guidance of the Spirit and of the availability of the divine illumination to him: "For what concerns my knowledge God reveals" (I.291–93).

This presentation in the induction of hero and antagonist entering upon their great intellectual duel at approximately the same stage of fallible, imperfect knowledge indicates that the dramatic conflict between Christ and Satan over the issues of Christ's nature and mission can be a genuine one. It also suggests something of the way in which that dramatic conflict will develop. Since Milton's Christ has limited human understanding he may be susceptible (as Eve was) to delusion: he may be led to misunderstand and to misinterpret the issues involved in Satan's temptations. The debate-duel between Christ and Satan is envisioned as a "battle of wits" in which both hero and tempter strive for the advantage which accompanies superior understanding. To succeed in perverting Christ Satan will have to understand him perfectly, but Satan is himself the victim of imperfect knowledge and naïveté regarding Christ's nature and mission. To withstand Satan's temptations Christ must refuse all inadequate, partial, or erroneous versions or parodies of himself and his mission and must finally attain to full and perfect understanding.

In this conflict Satan's special advantage will be his firsthand acquaintance with the accumulated knowledge and experience of history, his direct observation of human motives and human weaknesses throughout all time, whereas Christ knows such things only at second hand, through his wide reading in the scriptural and historical records. But more than compensating for this is Christ's special advantage, the gift of divine illumination which he may merit, whereas Satan can rely only upon his own brilliant but now warped intellect, subject to the process Milton described in *Paradise Lost* as attending upon the deliberate and continuing repudiation of God—"hard be hard'n'd, blind be blinded more" (III.200). These different modes of apprehension are to yield vastly different results as both characters endeavor to cope with the ambiguities of Christ's title, Son of God, and with the metaphorical prophecies about Christ and his role. Christ will be led by the Spirit's illumination to imaginative realization of the full, spiritual meaning of the metaphors and the ambiguities, whereas Satan will remain cunning, brilliant even, but ultimately literal-minded, unable to fathom God's metaphors. Yet Satan's very literalism constitutes an aspect of the dramatic situation and of Christ's temptation, for as long as Christ does not wholly understand himself and his role he can conceivably be deluded by the satanic interpretation of his situation.

The dramatic action of the poem, prepared for by the characterization of the principals in the induction, is built upon one great central paradox which virtually transmutes activity and passivity into one another. Satan appears to do all the acting: it is he who dances about Christ in a fever of motion, trying one scheme after another, one argument after another, while Christ seems to be impassive, immobile, unmoved by all of Satan's proposals. Yet it is in Christ's consciousness, not Satan's, that real development and change take place: the challenges of the temptations provide the occasion for Christ's progress through somewhat uneven stages to a full comprehension and definition of himself and the various aspects of his role, whereas Satan for all his feverish activity cannot resolve the puzzle about Christ's sonship and mission until his own defeat and fall force realization upon him. As Allen perceived, the various fluctuations and progressions in Christ's understanding of himself are signaled by changes in tone: his progressive understanding of the meaning of his sonship is attended by a growing certitude of tone as he refers to scriptural metaphor and prophecy, and by an increased calmness and quietness of manner, whereas Satan's progressive frustration is shown by an ever mounting and at length total loss of control over himself and over the course of the action.

The induction prepares us, then, for the development of action and theme in the following terms. During the temptation episode Christ will be in the process of regaining, as Milton expressed it in *De Doctrina,* the divine understanding which he previously possessed by means of the teaching of the Father. However, the conditions of the temptation encounter seem to be that Christ must withstand each of the temptations in terms of his limited human understanding, and that only when he has done so will he merit and attain a special illumination which will bring him to a full, perfect, divine apprehension of that aspect of himself and his mission which has been under attack in each particular temptation. Accordingly, the process of growth is not steady but fluctuating, making for considerable dramatic tension: the action advances through a series of partial climaxes of revelation and understanding until at length the grand climax of full understanding and total victory is achieved on the tower.

*T*HE OTHER issue central to the dramatic action and to the thematic development of *Paradise Regained* concerns Christ's ordained role, or mission. The induction shows both Christ and Satan undertaking their duel with a limited and imperfect knowledge of Christ's mission as well as of his nature. It also establishes the terms for their subsequent debates about that mission. The several allusions in the induction to Old Testament personages prepare for the ensuing exploration of Christ's mission in relation to traditional biblical types. And the references to Christ's office import into the poem the rich meanings contained in the theological concept of Christ's threefold mediatorial office of prophet, priest, and king.[1]

THE USES OF TYPOLOGY: THE REPRISE OF THE PAST

By means of several allusions to Adam and to Job, who were well-nigh universally recognized as major types of Christ, the induction establishes a typological perspective which, at one level, shows Christ searching for his role and Satan challenging it in the light of the mandate of the past—the expectations set in motion by the notable Old Testament and classical figures of Christ and his redemptive action.[2] The allusions to Adam suggest that Christ will appear in *Paradise Regained* as the Second Adam. The thematic statement locates Christ in the wilderness to which Adam was exiled, where, by reliving the first Adam's temptations and reversing his actions, he is to reconstitute the Eden which Adam lost:

> I who erewhile the happy Garden sung,
> By one man's disobedience lost, now sing

> Recover'd Paradise to all mankind,
> By one man's firm obedience fully tried
> Through all temptation, and the Tempter foil'd
> In all his wiles, defeated and repuls't,
> And *Eden* rais'd in the waste Wilderness. (I.1–7)

Satan also draws a parallel between the two temptations. Referring with pride to his deception of *"Adam* and his facile consort *Eve,"* he hopes for a like success from his present similar mission:

> I, when no other durst, sole undertook
> The dismal expedition to find out
> And ruin *Adam,* and the exploit perform'd
> Successfully; a calmer voyage now
> Will waft me; and the way found prosperous once
> Induces best to hope of like success. (I.100–105)

The demonic hosts also see the parallel and expect Satan to repeat his earlier success:

> Unanimous they all commit the care
> And management of this main enterprise
> To him their great Dictator, whose attempt
> At first against mankind so well had thriv'd
> In *Adam's* overthrow. (I.111 15)

The Father also sees the two temptations as analogues, but anticipates a far different outcome from Christ's trial—his "Winning by Conquest what the first man lost/ By fallacy surpris'd" (I.154–55). Allusions to Adam and Eve throughout the poem (e.g., II.131–35, 140–43, 348–49, 369–71; IV.5–7, 613–15) keep the Adam parallel vivid, and maintain it as a continuing frame of reference for Christ's actions.

The allusions to Job in the induction suggest that Christ's temptation is also to be seen as a reprise and heightening of Job's victory over Satan's temptations. This frame of reference is established early in the poem by an echo of Job 1:6–

8,[3] which indicates that Satan has come forth again in his
role as Adversary (the term by which he is known in Job),
that he has been to another assembly (Christ's baptism) at
which he has heard another "exalted man" acclaimed by
God, and that he has again been moved by such testimony
to undertake a temptation:

> That heard the Adversary, who roving still
> About the world, at that assembly fam'd
> Would not be last, and with the voice divine
> Nigh Thunderstruck, th'exalted man, to whom
> Such high attest was giv'n, a while survey'd. (I.33–37)

The Father's comment to Gabriel also refers to Job's temptation as a type of the present action. Christ will prove to be
an abler Job, and Satan will therefore rue his failure to learn
his lesson before: "he might have learnt/ Less overweening,
since he fail'd in *Job,*/ ... He now shall know I can produce a
man/ ... far abler" (I.146–51). The Jobean allusions also recur
throughout the poem, notably at I.364–70, 407–26; III.60–68,
88–95; in the latter two cases Christ himself praises Job as
the noblest of all heroes and models.

    To read such references to biblical—and later to classical—
personages merely as casual allusions or as *exempla* cited by
God or Christ or Satan in support of their arguments or actions, as is usually done, is to miss important dimensions of
Milton's achievement in the poem. These allusions constitute
Milton's adaptation of the typological symbolism which was
constantly used in biblical epic to obtain "epic dimension"
by projecting a particular episode against a broad historical
panorama. Milton's special accomplishment is to make such
typological allusions part of the debate-duel between Christ
and Satan and thus to make them wholly organic not only
to the theme but also to the dramatic movement of the poem
—Christ's discovery of himself and his role through the temp-

tation encounter. The references in the induction to Adam and Job prepare for Christ's effort throughout the poem to consider his situation in terms of the experience of Adam and Job, and in terms also of the other types discussed by Christ and Satan in their dialogues—Moses, Elijah, Daniel, David, Judas Maccabaeus, Hercules, Socrates, and many others. This typological perspective requires that Christ define himself in relation to all those earlier heroes and their histories, becoming at length the summation, the compendium, the completion of them all.

These patterns of typological reference in Milton's poem have gone largely unrecognized, chiefly because of a too facile restriction of typological symbolism to medieval literature and biblical exegesis, on the assumption that Renaissance textual scholarship and the biblical literalism of the Reformation undercut all varieties of allegory. In fact, however, most seventeenth-century biblical exegetes retained typological interpretation of Scripture, only urging some moderation in its use. Typological readings survived the literal and textual emphasis of the Reformers because of the firm basis for them in the New Testament, especially in the Pauline Epistles. Paul refers to the ceremonies of the Law as "a shadow of things to come" (Col. ii:16–17); to the high priest, the tabernacle of the Law, and the rock struck by Moses in the wilderness as types of Christ (Heb. ix:8–11; I Cor. x:4); and most often to Adam as a type of Christ: "Adam ... is the figure of him that was to come/ ... For as by one mans disobedience many were made sinners: so by the obedience of one, shall many be made righteous" (Rom. v:14, 19). Moreover, as Erich Auerbach points out, typological reading of Scripture is not necessarily opposed to a literal and historical emphasis, since the central tradition of typological exegesis both in the patristic period and the Middle Ages was characterized by a "figural realism" which refrained from dissolving type in antitype:

A figural schema permits both its poles—the figure and its fulfillment—to retain the characteristics of concrete historical reality, in contradistinction to what obtains with symbolic or allegorical personifications, so that figure and fulfillment—although the one "signifies" the other—have a significance which is not incompatible with their being real. An event taken as a figure preserves its literal and historical meaning. It remains an event, does not become a mere sign. The Church Fathers, especially Tertullian, Jerome, and Augustine, had successfully defended figural realism, that is, the maintenance of the basic historical reality of figures, against all attempts at spiritually allegorical interpretations.[4]

The tradition of typological exegesis which remained available to Milton might be summarized as follows. From his saturation in patristic literature, he would be aware of Irenaeus' principle of the "recapitulation in Christ"—"When he [the Son of God] was incarnate and made man, he recapitulated [or summed up] in himself the long line of the human race"[5]—a principle which seems to prepare directly for Milton's way of relating Christ to his types in *Paradise Regained*. Milton would also know the several strains of typological symbolism developed by the Fathers. Tertullian, Jerome, Augustine, and other Latin Fathers explained the Old Testament personages and events chiefly in terms of the life of Christ related in the Gospel, though Augustine emphasized also the Old Testament prefigurations of the Christian church and its history. Justin Martyr related the types to the sacraments of the church, Irenaeus working from Jewish tradition stressed the element of eschatological prophecy, and Clement of Alexandria pointed chiefly to Christ figured forth in his members (the church).[6] Origen synthesized the various approaches by taking the Old Testament figures as types of the total reality that is Christ, and therefore as shadowing forth, variously, the historical events of his life as related in the Gospel, his mystical life in the church as a whole or in each individual member who has "put on Christ," or his glorious appearance at the end of time.[7] Such a synthesis obviously prepares for the familiar four levels of scriptural exegesis in the Middle Ages, outlined in characteristic form by Aquinas who based his accompanying affirmation of "figural realism" on the ground that the allegory in Scripture is God's own—that God himself has caused certain real events and persons to signify other real events and persons:

The author of Holy Scripture is God, in Whose power it is to signify His meaning, not by words only (as man also can do), but also by things themselves. So, whereas in every other science things are signified by words, this science has the property that the things signified by the words have themselves also a signification. Therefore that first signification whereby words signify things belongs to the first sense, the historical or literal. That signification whereby things signified by words have themselves also a signification is called the spiritual sense, which is based on the literal, and presupposes it. Now this spiritual sense has a threefold division. For as the Apostle says (*Heb*.x.1) the Old Law is a figure of the New Law, and Dionysius says *the New Law itself is a figure of future glory*. Again, in the New Law, whatever our Head has done is a type of what we ought to do. Therefore, so far as the things of the Old Law signify the things of the New Law, there is the allegorical sense; so far as the things done in Christ, or so far as the things which signify Christ, are signs of what we ought to do, there is the moral sense. But so far as they signify what relates to eternal glory, there is the anagogical sense.[8]

Cassian's explication of "Jerusalem" provides one famous example of this mode of reading: Jerusalem according to history is a city of the Jews; according to allegory it is the church of Christ, according to anagoge it is the heavenly city of God "which is the mother of us all" (Gal. iv:26); according to tropology it is the soul of man. Dante's reading of Psalm cxiv on the subject of the Exodus offers another: "If we consider the *letter* alone, the departure of the children of Israel from

Egypt in the time of Moses is signified; if the *allegory,* our redemption accomplished by Christ is signified; if the *moral meaning,* the conversion of the soul from the sorrow and misery of sin to a state of grace is signified; if the *anagogical,* the departure of the sanctified soul from the slavery of this corruption to the liberty of everlasting glory." [9]

As late as 1634 the medieval *Glossa Ordinaria* in which every passage of Scripture received a fourfold allegorical gloss was reprinted at Anvers, but in general, post-Tridentine Catholic exegetes practiced their typology with greater circumspection. The Douay Bible reaffirmed the typological principle— "Yea al the old Testament is a general prophecie, and foreshewing of the New, which ... is conteyned, and lieth hid in the old" [10]—and its commentary, like the massive and influential commentaries of the Jesuit Cornelius à Lapide and like several of the *Pensées* of Pascal, recognizes many of the established types. But these works decline to relate every detail of literal narrative to an allegorical meaning or to interpret every passage according to four levels.[11] The Reformers and the seventeenth-century Protestant exegetes quarreled even more vigorously with Origen and with those medieval theologians who allegorized everything in Scripture, but nevertheless they allowed and practiced typological interpretation. Luther alluded disparagingly to his experience as an Augustinian friar when he "Allegorized and spiritually signified every particular thing," but he admitted that "Allegories and Spiritual significations ... when they are directed upon Faith, and seldom used, then they are good and laudable." In the prefaces to early editions of Luther's Bible, composed partly by himself and partly by his followers, many of the familiar types are designated—the brazen serpent, Jonah in the whale, the Psalms as presenting the death and resurrection of Christ.[12] Calvin was still more readily disposed to see Christ as "the original paterne of all ye figures," and to interpret the manna, the land of Canaan, David, Moses, and many other Old Testament personages and symbols typologically.[13] Indeed, some of the English Calvinists seem almost to hark back to medieval attitudes. John Weemse in *The Christian Synagogue* asserted the primacy of the literal sense and disparaged the tendency of the Fathers to allegorize everything, but yet he reiterated and employed the old fourfold pattern:

> There is an Allegory in words, and an Allegorie in matter; in words, Metaphors; in matter, Types; in Figures, the Antecedent signifies the thing consequent: & the literall sense is fulfilled before the mystical sense.
>
> . . . .
>
> The Allegoricall application is, when the things in the Old Testament, shadowe out some things in the estate of the new Testament . . .
>
> The Tropologicall, is, when the thing delivered, signifies some other thing to expresse manners . . .
>
> The Anagogicall application, is, when things literally expressed, doe signifie something in heavens blisse.[14]

And the Puritan George Wither in his edition of the Psalms tossed the new circumspection to the winds, arguing that everything in the Old Testament has a figurative as well as a literal meaning: "there is nothing in the *Psalmes,* nor in any place of the Old Testament, written for it owne sake: but all things there, are Types, Figures, Examples, Prophecies, or Parables, to informe or figure out, what should be fulfilled in the New Testament, at the comming of the *Messias:* as appeares by the many testimonies of the *Apostles, Evangelists,* and Christ himselfe." [15]

Milton's relation to this typological tradition is a matter of some dispute. H. R. MacCallam, though he documents the Reformers' continued use of typological interpretation, argues that Milton is more circumspect than most of them, that he distrusts typological reading and makes little use of it in *De*

Doctrina or in his poems.[16] Yet Milton's willingness to admit at least some typological exegesis of the Old Testament, controlled by the attitudes of figural realism and Reformation circumspection, is quite explicit in *De Doctrina:*

No passage of Scripture is to be interpreted in more than one sense; in the Old Testament, however, this sense is sometimes a compound of the historical and typical, as in Hosea xi.1 compared with Matt. ii.15. "out of Egypt have I called my son," which may be explained in a double sense, as referring partly to the people of Israel, and partly to Christ in his infancy.[17]

Indeed, Milton establishes a typological perspective for much of the treatise by comprehending "under the name of CHRIST . . . Moses and the Prophets, who were his forerunners, and the Apostles whom he sent," and he also gives the customary typological reading of David's kingship and Moses' deliverance of the Israelites.[18] In Milton's poetry the problem is to determine when and to what degree the traditional typological associations are being invoked. I remain unconvinced by Michael Krouse's typological interpretation of *Samson Agonistes,*[19] grounded simply upon the traditional understanding of the Samson story and largely unsupported by explicit allusions or statements in the poem inviting such reading. But on the other hand, as I have argued elsewhere,[20] Michael's prophecy in Books XI and XII of *Paradise Lost* is according to Michael's own testimony organized and presented typologically, showing Adam's progeny advancing "from shadowy types to Truth." Similarly, the many biblical and classical allusions to recognized types of Christ in *Paradise Regained* indicate the presence of typological symbolism in that poem.

The typological perspective established in the induction is extended in the poem to include not only other biblical figures but also classical heroes such as Hercules, Oedipus, and Socrates. The tradition of classical typological interpretation was based upon the resemblances between classical and biblical myth—the fallen angels and the Titans, Hercules and Christ, Deucalion's flood and Noah's flood, Orpheus descending to Avernus and Christ harrowing hell. It drew support also from the resemblances between classical and biblical moral teaching, to which Eusebius gave strong testimony in his question, "What else is Plato than Moses speaking Attic Greek?" [21] Of course there could be no tradition of figural realism here: the classical myths were seen as mere stories. The resemblances occurred because the classical myths and moral teachings were simply imitations of the much more ancient biblical materials.[22] This argument could function both to degrade and to exalt the pagan literature, and throughout Christian history these two opposed perspectives and valuations were often maintained at one and the same time. On the one hand, the pagan myths were seen as deformations, corruptions, and even diabolical perversions of truth: as Justin Martyr declared, the demons, learning of Christ, "put forward many to be called sons of Jupiter, under the impression that they would be able to produce in men the idea that the things which were said with regard to Christ were mere marvellous tales, like the things which were said by the poets." [23] But by changing the emphasis slightly, the pagan myths, the Sibylline prophecies, and the writings of Virgil and Plato might be seen as reflections and foreshadowings, however far removed, of Christian truth. Clement of Alexandria exemplifies the more permissive approach of the Greek church in his argument that Greek literature and philosophy constituted a covenant with the Gentiles analogous to the Old Testament covenant with the Jews, both of which were now fulfilled in the Gospel covenant: "from the Hellenic training, and also from that of the law, are gathered into the one race of the saved people those who accept faith ... trained in different Covenants of the one Lord, by the word of the one Lord." [24]

In the late Middle Ages and the Renaissance this positive

emphasis predominated. Albertino Mussato and Boccaccio asserted that the pagan myths tell in a mysterious manner the same things as Holy Scripture, and that the classical poets wrote of Christ.[25] Illuminated manuscripts of Ovid's *Metamorphoses* identified myths of Medea, Aesculapius, Achilles, Theseus, and others as types of the Annunciation, the Crucifixion, the Incarnation, and the Descent to Hades.[26] In the Sistine Chapel the Sibyls occupy niches alternating with Old Testament prophets in testimony to their equation as prophets of Christ. Ronsard's hymn *L'Hercule Chrestien* presented the story of Hercules as "une fiction anticipée de ce que les Prophetes & Sibylles avoient figuré de l'homme-Dieu nostre Seigneur JESUS-CHRIST," and Arthur Golding's translation of Ovid derived classical myths originally "from Holy Writ as from the well from whence all wisedome springs." [27] But for all this, Golding's further comment that the classical myths "went about to turne the truth to toies and lies" shows that, however marked their inclination to regard the classical myths as types, Christian commentators of any age could seldom refrain from noting the inadequacies of these myths when compared with the true Old Testament types. Seventeenth-century commentators were much more disposed than their Renaissance counterparts to point up the false, feigned aspects of the classics: even devotees of the classics such as the Cambridge Platonist Henry More emphasized the groping and mistakes of the pagans which must be rectified in Christ, and Edward Stillingfleet attributed the agreement between classical and biblical stories to the fact that the Greeks had corrupted the biblical originals.[28]

Milton's treatment of classical myth and writing throughout his works manifests just the double perspective and valuation found throughout the Christian tradition. Those critics like Davis P. Harding [29] who draw a sharp contrast between Milton's exuberant Renaissance acceptance of classical myth in early writings such as the *Prolusions, Comus, L'Allegro, Il Penseroso,* and *Lycidas,* and his later denunciation of the classics in *Paradise Regained,* do not I think attend sufficiently to the control of the context. In Milton's early poems and writings on nonbiblical subjects, myth can be explored in its own terms, and can be presented without qualification as a genuine reflection of Christian truth. But in the poems on biblical subjects, which treat the reality of which the myths are mere imitation, a sense of the inadequacy and falseness and even of the diabolical origin of classical myth is always present, though even in such poems the typological significance of classical myth is affirmed by the acceptance of some few classical figures as genuine types of Christ. Milton's first great poem, *On the Morning of Christ's Nativity*—written at the age of twenty-one, when Milton was presumably still enraptured with the classical world—adopts just this attitude. Nearly a third of the poem is given over to a description of the flight of all the denizens of the pagan world at Christ's birth; from the vantage point of the birth of Christ, the rise of the new Sun, all the classical figures are partakers of the satanic realm of darkness and must vanish with the night. At the same time though, Christ is described in terms of two often cited classical types: he is the "mighty *Pan*" now come down to live with the shepherds below (ll. 88–89), and he is an Infant Hercules who in his cradle can control the serpent Satan and his damned crew (ll. 221–28). This treatment of the classical types and the classical world is analogous to that in *Paradise Regained* where, despite Christ's repudiation of classical learning, his final great victory over Satan is described in relation to the victories of Hercules and Oedipus.

Turning again to the induction to *Paradise Regained,* we see now that the references to Adam would automatically arouse certain reader expectations as to how the Adam-Christ relationship might be exploited in the poem, by stimulating the recollection of the various ways in which Adam was a type of Christ. Adam was a rather special type in that his figural relation to Christ was defined chiefly through contrasts rather than, as is the usual emphasis, through resemblances, though of course in all typological symbolism both elements are present. The particular contrast to which Milton points in his thematic statement—Adam's journey from Paradise to the wilderness and Christ's reversal of that journey—was often noted: Ambrose, commenting on Luke iv, observed, "It is fitting to be recorded that as the first Adam was ejected from Paradise into the desert, so the Second Adam returned from the desert to Paradise." [30] The point was reiterated by the seventeenth-century theologian William Cowper:

Sathan tempted the first *Adam* in Paradise, which was the place in all the world, wherein he should have been strongest to resist the Divell ... yet in it Sathan overcame him: But the second *Adam* to recover this losse, encounters with Sathan in the wildernes, a place of all other in the world, meetest for Sathan to tempt a man in; specially to desperation.... The first *Adam* tempted by Sathan, was driven from Paradise to the wildernes, but the second *Adam* by suffering himselfe to be tempted of Sathan, brings home the first againe from the wildernes into Paradise. [31]

A detailed summary of the traditional bases for the typological relationship between Christ and Adam is provided by the seventeenth-century theologian Henry Vertue, quoting Hugh Broughton:

The first *Adam* was made a Soul having life, of Earth earthy: and therefore by the Earthly one came Disobedience, Sin, Judgment, Condemnation, Death. The second *Adam* was made a Spirit, giving life, from Heaven heavenly; and therefore by the Heavenly One came Obedience, Grace, Forgiveness, Justification, Life. *Adam* was made the sixth day, and did eat of the forbidden Tree the sixth hour. *Christ* reforming Man, and healing the Fall, is fastened to the Tree the sixth day, and the sixth hour. *Adam* was made a man without a Father, made not inferiour to the Angels, and lost all. *Christ* was made without a Father, made lower then the Angels, is crowned with Glory, and all the Angels worship him. *Adam* was tempted; *Christ* was tempted. *Adam* lost Salvation at the time of eating: *Christ* brought Salvation to all at the time of eating. *Adam* was made Ruler of the World, and lost it; *Christ* was made Ruler of the World and did hold it....*Adam,* by breaking one commandement, lost all: *Christ,* by fulfilling all the commandements brought life to all....*Adam* was the head of his wife: *Christ* is the head of His Church. *Adam* was a King, a Prophet, and a Sacrificer; *Christ* was a King, a Prophet, and a Sacrificer.[32]

Specifically, as Elizabeth Pope notes,[33] the concept of the "triple equation" identified the three temptations Christ endured with those to which Adam and Eve succumbed, and also with the sins mentioned in I John ii:16, concupiscence of the flesh, concupiscence of the eye, and pride of life, or in other words, the Flesh, the World, and the Devil. Using the Matthew ordering of Christ's temptations (stones, tower, kingdoms), most patristic and medieval exegetes but also many later commentators both Protestant and Catholic—understood these three episodes as, respectively, temptations to gluttony, vainglory or presumption, and avarice or ambition.[34] Joseph Hall's statement is typical:

In every temptation there is an appearance of good, whether of the bodie, of mind, or estate; The first is the *lust of the flesh,* in any carnall desire; the second the *pride* of heart, and life; the third the *lust* of *the eyes:* To all these, the first *Adam* is tempted, and in all miscarryed; the second *Adam* is tempted to them all, and overcommeth. The first man was tempted, to carnall appetite, by the forbidden fruit; to pride, by the suggestion of being as God; to covetousnesse, in the ambitious desire of knowing good and evill: Satan having found all the motions so successefull with the first *Adam* in his innocent estate, will now treade the same steps in his temptations of the second; The stones must bee made bread, there

is the motion to a carnall appetite; The guard and attendance
of Angels must bee presumed on, there is a motion to pride; The
Kingdomes of the Earth, and the glory of them must bee offered,
there to covetousnesse and ambition.[35]

However, several Protestant writers quarreled with the reading of Christ's temptation to change stones into bread as an
invitation to gluttony, agreeing with Calvin that "it is ridiculous, if any man that is hungry desireth meate, that he might
satisfie nature, to referre that to the intemperancie of the
throat." [36] Accordingly, they referred it to the sin of distrust,
in that Christ was invited to distrust the Word and Promise
of God vouchsafed to him at his baptism.[37] This interpretation made for some difficulty in relating the stones temptation
to the first temptation of Adam and Eve, but Christopher
Blackwood's formulation indicates the typical Protestant contrivance: "As he [Satan] overcame the first *Adam* with unbelief of the threatning, Gen. 3.3 [i.e., the threat that death would
result from eating the fruit] so doth he endeavour to overcome the second *Adam* with unbelief of the promise." [38] Evidently, the Christ-as-Second-Adam allusions in the induction
would lead the contemporary reader to expect some treatment of the triple equation in the poem, but it is a measure
of Milton's ingenuity that he meets that expectation in a much
more subtle and complex manner than either the traditional
biblical exegesis or Miss Pope's important study of it would
suggest.

The allusions to Job in the induction also arouse reader expectations, for they reverberate against an exegetical tradition
relating Adam, Job, and Christ in terms of their temptations.
Job himself was understood to be a kind of second Adam, a
perfect or all-but-perfect hero who relived and reversed the
first man's temptation experience by his victory over Satan's
machinations.[39] Developing this contrast, Origen taunted Satan, "Not as long ago do you now come from Adam with

victory, but from Job with confusion. Adam at first you seduced, but Job you did not supplant. Adam you threw forth
from Paradise, but you did not dislodge Job from sanctity."
And on the same point Gregory observed, "So the old enemy
was beaten by Adam [Job] on a dunghill, he that conquered
Adam in Paradise." [40] Job's trial typified Christ's encounter
with Satan in the wilderness, in that both withstood Adam's
temptations, both endured the entire range of temptations,
and Christ in his temptation fulfilled Job's prophecy about
putting a hook into the nostrils of Leviathan (Job xli:2).[41]

More generally, Gregory the Great identified Job as the most
complete Old Testament type of Christ in that he typified
Christ's passion by his own suffering and also prophesied of
him in the famous phrase, "I know that my redeemer liveth"
(Job xix:25).[42] The point was reiterated in the Douay Bible,
"Job *in al his actions, sufferinges, and whole life, was* a special
figure of Christ shewing (*sayth S. Gregorie*) by those thinges
which he did and susteyned, what our Redeemer should do
and suffer: *yea more particularly then most part of the Patriarches.*" [43] Moreover, Job was understood to foreshadow
Christ's mediatorial office: almost everyone identified Job's
sacrifices for his children and friends and his sufferings at
the hands of Satan as types of Christ's priestly sacrifice for
all mankind, and several also termed Job a prophet and a
king, thereby finding in him as in Adam a foreshadowing of
all three aspects of Christ's office.[44] Zeno provides a useful
compendium of the customary typological parallels between Job
and Christ:

Job was called just by God; Christ is Justice itself, from whose
fountain all who are blessed taste... Job was called truthful; the
Lord is the truest of the true... Job was rich; And what is richer
than the Lord who owns all the world and nature, and whose
servants are all the rich... The devil tempted Job three times; so
also according to Scripture he attempted thrice to tempt the Lord.

Job lost the wealth he had accumulated; Christ set aside his heavenly estate out of love for us and made himself a pauper, that we might become rich. The devil killed Job's children in blind fury; the demented Pharisees killed the prophets, the children of the Lord. Job's body was defaced with sores; the Lord took on flesh and was sullied by the crimes of all sinning mankind. Job was urged by his wife to sin; Christ was urged by the Synagogue to follow the corrupt religious practices of the Elders. Job's friends are reputed to have derided him; Both priest and people mocked the Lord. Job sat on a dunghill crawling with worms; Christ dwelt in the true dunghill, that is, the filth of this world, amidst all manner of proud wretches and sensualists, who are veritable worms. Job recovered his health and his wealth; the Lord rising again showed himself not only healed but immortal to those believing in him, and he recovered his mastery over all nature ... Job fathered other children; the Lord also after the loss of his children the prophets "produced" the Holy Apostles. Blessed Job died in peace; the Lord remains blessed eternally, before all age and throughout all ages, and for all ages to come.[45]

Moreover, Job was often identified as a type of the church as well as of Christ on Gregory's principle that whoever foreshadows the head foreshadows also the mystical body:

Because our Redeemer has shewn Himself to be one with the Holy Church, which He has taken to Himself; for of Him it is said, *Who is the Head of us all;* and of the Church it is written, *the Body of Christ, Which is the Church;* whosoever in his own person betokens Him, at one time designates Him in respect of the Head, at another of the Body, so as to have not only the voice of the Head, but also of the Body ... Now that blessed Job maintains the semblance of the Redeemer to come, his very name is a proof. For Job is, if interpreted, "grieving;" by which same grief we have set forth, either our Mediator's Passion, or the travails of Holy Church, which is harassed by the manifold toils of this present life.[46]

Accordingly, Job's experience may typify the church embattled against heresy throughout all history, Job's three friends representing heretics seeking to seduce the church from the truth, and Elihu embodying the proud and arrogant doctor of the church who speaks the truth in a wrong spirit or else the Balaam figure, the gentile mocking the church of God.[47]

The typological allusions to Adam and to Job in the induction thus arouse expectation that Christ will relive and reverse the temptation experience of the first Adam, that he will repeat and surpass Job's notable victory, and that he may also draw upon other typological traditions attaching to these two figures as he presses toward his own definition of himself. Christ's meditative soliloquy as he enters the desert, alluding to several other Old Testament types and figures of himself, prepares for the extension of the typological perspective in the poem and for its dramatic function. Christ indicates that he has pored over "The Law of God.../ Made it my whole delight" (I.207–8); that he has heard and contemplated the prophecy that he is to "sit on *David's* Throne" (I.240); and that he has studied "The Law and Prophets, searching what was writ/ Concerning the Messiah, to our Scribes/ Known partly" (I.260 62). We know by this that his knowledge of his mission has been derived chiefly from the imperfect and "partial" Old Testament prophecies and types, and that these types must therefore be his starting point in the present reflections. His concern now must be to clarify and extend his knowledge, achieving a more complete understanding of his nature and office. Satan's temptation strategy will also begin from the types: he will endeavor to cause Christ to regress from his present state of understanding—to accept inferior types in place of those he has already seized upon—or else to identify himself with the major types in their literal signification and thereby fail to achieve the spiritual understanding and fulfillment of the types which is his peculiar mission. This use of typology poses as part of Christ's puzzling intellectual task in the temptation the problem of how he ought to relate himself to history, how far the past provides a fit model for his actions and wherein he is to redefine its terms in order to become himself the model for the future.

CHRIST'S OFFICE AND THE PROJECTION OF THE FUTURE

The induction to *Paradise Regained* also establishes another frame of reference for the temptation encounter through two references to Christ's office: John is said to be ready to resign to Christ "his Heavenly Office" (I.28) at his baptism, and Christ as he wanders out into the desert muses about how to "Publish his Godlike office now mature" (I.188). The term "office," in reference to Christ's mediatorial office or role, still had in the seventeenth century precise and widely accepted theological meanings and implications, and the reader is hereby alerted to expect these meanings to figure importantly in the conflict and debate between Christ and Satan. By so involving in the temptation episode the functions of Christ's office, which continue in his church throughout all time, Milton can subsume within this episode the entire course of Christ's life, and the history of his church.

With two important differences, Christian theologians were in general agreement about the scope of Christ's mediatorial office, the duties entailed by each of its functions, and the prefiguration of these functions by certain Old Testament types. Some commentators, such as Augustine, Rupert, Hildebertus, and Henry Bullinger, defined Christ's mediatorial office as incorporating the twofold functions of priest and king.[48] Augustine's comment is typical:

For the Lord Jesus Christ, who is the one true King and the one true Priest, the former to rule us, and the latter to make expiation for us, has shown us how His own figure bore these two parts together ... To Him, too, God gave the throne of His Father David, in order that of His kingdom there should be none end. And this was done with the purpose that there might be a mediator between God and men, the man Christ Jesus, to make intercession for us.[49]

But the more usual formula, favored especially by the Protestants because it gave due exaltation to Christ's preaching and teaching role, may be illustrated by Calvin's comment, "the office whiche is committed to hym [Christ] by hys Father, consysteth of three partes. For he is geven bothe a Prophete, a King, and a Preest." [50] Protestant commentators also insisted, in contradiction to the Catholics, that while Christ's prophetic role was continued in his church through the agency of apostles and ministers acting in due subordination to him, his priestly and kingly functions were proper to himself alone and could in no way be shared by others—such as Catholic priests and popes.

The prophetic role comprised Christ's function as teacher and doctor of his church and as illuminator of the souls of his redeemed; its principal Old Testament types were Moses and Elijah. In explicating the prophetic role Luther referred to John viii: "JESUS said unto them [the Jews], first, I am hee that speaketh with you; as if hee would saie, I am your Prophet and Preacher, according as *Moses* told your forefathers [Deut. xviii:18], *I will rais them up a Prophet from among their brethren."* [51] Calvin declared that though the people of God always had prophets, yet the "full lyghte of understandinge was to be hoped for onely at the comminge of Messias," and that, moreover, the office of prophet continues in the church only in due subordination to Christ, who is the end and the fulfillment of all prophecy:

He toke not the anoyntinge [as a prophet] for him selfe alone, that he myghte execute the office of teachinge, but for his whole bodie, that in hys continuall preachinge of the Gospell, the vertue of the Spirit shoulde joyne wythal. But in the meane tyme thys remayneth certayne, that by thys perfection of doctrine whiche he hathe broughte, an ende is made of all prophecys: so that they doe diminish his authoritie, that beinge not content wyth the Gospell, doe patche any forain thynge unto it.[52]

William Ames defined the prophetic role of Christ as "that whereby he hath perfectly revealed the whole Will of God that bringeth salvation," and Joannes Wollebius explained the duties of this role as being "to instruct his Elect in heavenly Truths: the parts whereof are, the external Preaching of Gods will, and the internal illumination of the minde." [53]

The priestly office was identified especially with Christ's sacrificial death on the cross, but also with his continuous intercession for man with the Father; its chief Old Testament types were Melchisedec, Job, and the Jewish high priests. Luther declared that Christ "in his Death...is a Sacrifice offered up for Sins" and that "in making Mediation and Intercession, hee is an High-Priest." [54] Calvin explained that Christ's function as priest is to reconcile us to God: he "by the sacrifice of his death hathe wyped a waie oure gyltynesse, and satisfied for oure synnes," and he also "ys an eternall intercessor." [55] Ames defined the priesthood of Christ as "that whereby he hath purged by sacrifice the sins of men, and obtained the favour of God for them," serving at once as sacrifice, priest, and altar, and Wollebius offered his formula in these terms, "His Sacerdotal office is, to appear for us before God, with full satisfaction, and to intercede for us: the parts whereof are, Satisfaction and Intercession." [56]

Christ's kingly role, exercised both in the church and in the heavenly kingdom, is begun on earth but more perfectly realized at Christ's ascension and restoration to his Father's right hand; its chief Old Testament types were David and Solomon. Both Luther and Calvin designated Christ as an "Everlasting King" ruling a spiritual kingdom, and Calvin specified his kingly duties as follows: to be "an eternal governor and defender of his Churche," and to protect his church so that "it is impossible that the Devell with all the preparation of the woorlde, maye bee able at any time to destroy the Churche." [57] Ames defined the kingship of Christ as that "whereby he doth dispense and administer all things with power and authority, which pertaine to the salvation of man," and Wollebius observed that "His Regal office is, to rule and preserve the Church: the parts whereof are, the Government of the Church, and the destruction of his enemies." [58] In addition, most writers, Protestants and Catholics alike, were agreed that Christ's mediatorial office was exercised in two modes: the Humiliation, which involved his whole life of obedience and fulfilling the law as well as his passion and death, and the Exaltation, which involved his triumphal resurrection, his ascension at which he "spoiled principalities and powers," and his restoration to the right hand of his Father. [59]

Milton's own discussion of Christ's office in *De Doctrina* closely follows the standard formulas of the Protestant theologians, both as to the two modes of its exercise, the Humiliation and the Exaltation, and its three functions—of prophet, priest, and king. Milton defines the three functions as follows:

HIS FUNCTION AS A PROPHET IS TO INSTRUCT HIS CHURCH IN HEAVENLY TRUTH, AND TO DECLARE THE WHOLE WILL OF HIS FATHER....

His prophetical function consists of two parts; one external, namely, the promulgation of divine truth; the other internal, to wit, the illumination of the understanding...

Christ's prophetical function began with the creation of the world, and will continue till the end of all things....

CHRIST'S SACERDOTAL FUNCTION is that whereby HE ONCE OFFERED HIMSELF TO GOD THE FATHER AS A SACRIFICE FOR SINNERS, AND HAS ALWAYS MADE, AND STILL CONTINUES TO MAKE INTERCESSION FOR US....

THE KINGLY FUNCTION of Christ is that whereby BEING MADE KING BY GOD THE FATHER, HE GOVERNS AND PRESERVES, CHIEFLY BY AN INWARD LAW AND SPIRITUAL POWER, THE CHURCH WHICH HE HAS PURCHASED FOR HIMSELF, AND CONQUERS AND SUBDUES ITS ENEMIES....

[Christ] governs not the bodies of men alone, as the civil magistrate, but their minds and consciences, and that not by force and fleshly weapons, but by what the world esteems the weakest of all instruments. Hence external force ought never to be employed in the administration of the kingdom of Christ, which is the Church.[60]

Milton goes on to specify that Christ's kingly role is exercised both in the Kingdom of Grace (the invisible church), which "is at hand," and in the Kingdom of Glory (the millennial kingdom), "which is destined to be made more manifest at his second advent." All three functions are eternal, that is, they "will endure as long as the world shall last." [61]

The references to Christ's office in the induction, besides reminding the reader of the customary definitions of that office and its three functions, also reminds him that Christ's baptism and temptation were almost universally mentioned by Protestant theologians as the two-stage formal inauguration and entry of Christ into his mediatorial office. William Ames emphasized Christ's baptism as a formal initiation:

The Baptisme of Christ was his publick inauguration to the publick performance of his office: therefore in it, the three offices of Christ are affirmed, and confirmed.

They are affirmed by the testimony of the father publickely pronouncing that Jesus Christ is his Sonne, and so that he is appointed a king by him, even that King in whom he is well pleased, that is, a chiefe Priest, who by his intercession should take away the sins of the World, and a chiefe Prophet.[62]

John Udall pointed to the temptation as Christ's "entraunce... into the execution of his office," and Lancelot Andrewes also explained the fast and temptation as the actual beginning of Christ's office: "It may seeme strange, that beeing about to present himselfe to the world, as Prince, Priest, and Prophet, that he would make his progresse into the Wildernesse, and begin with a fast.... Christ from his Baptisme began his calling, and fasted fortie dayes and fortie nights. This His fast (by the new Writers) is called the entraunce into his calling: by the olde Writers, it is called the entraunce into his conflict." [63] Calvin's comment gave special emphasis to the initiatory function of the temptation, suggesting that Christ was somehow transformed by that episode and that he there laid the foundation of his entire role: "Christ went a side into the desert for two causes: First that after the fast of forty dayes as a new man, or rather a heavenly, hee might come forth to execute his office: Then that he shoulde not enter into so hard and notable an office, except he were tryed with temptations, as if hee should so lay the foundation of his first exercise." [64]

Altering the focus somewhat, several Protestant theologians explained the temptation episode as more especially an initiation of Christ into his prophetic office. Christ began to exercise that office by preaching immediately upon leaving the desert, whereas he did not undertake the major aspect of his priestly role until his sacrificial death, or enter into the fullness of his kingly role until his ascension. [65] Accordingly, the temptation was understood to have special import for the ministers who would continue the exercise of Christ's prophetic role in his church. That this view was not limited to Protestants is evident from Aquinas' statement, "no one should take up the office of preacher unless he be already cleansed and perfect in virtue ... Consequently immediately after His baptism Christ adopted an austere form of life, in order to teach us the need of taming the flesh before passing on to the office of preaching." [66] But the Protestants gave the point special emphasis. William Perkins declared that "Christ begins his prophetical office of teaching his church, with temptations." Richard Baxter observed that "Fasting and tryal by temptation were great preparatives to Christ's exercise of his prophetick office: And his ministers should not be strangers to it." John Diodati explained that Christ was consecrated to his prophetic office by baptism, the testimony of God, fasting, and temptations. And Christopher Blackwood affirmed that the temptation was a means of fitting Christ "for his Ministry ... for knowledg of Tentations is one great requisite to make an able Teacher." [67]

Moreover, a number of commentaries on Matthew iv or Luke iv indirectly associate Christ's three temptations with the three aspects of his mediatorial office, though usually the relation is made explicit only with respect to the first temptation which is seen as a special challenge to Christ's prophetic role. William Perkins interpreted the first temptation as an effort to cast doubt upon the prophetic function revealed to Christ at his baptism; he alluded to the kingly role in the next temptation, noting that Satan here "labours with Christ to entertain an earthly kingdome, that so his spirituall kingdome might not be looked after"; and he linked the tower temptation with the priestly role by remarking upon its location on the temple whose rites Christ's priesthood will supplant, and upon the similarity of Satan's challenge, "mitte te deorsum," to that of the crowds at the time Christ was completing his priestly sacrifice on the cross.[68] Thomas Taylor's commentary developed virtually the same relations between the three temptations and the three offices, emphasizing especially the challenge to the prophetic role in the first temptation, where Satan "aimed to overthrow the word of God, so also the faith of Christ in that word." [69]

Considered in terms of these commonplaces, the references to Christ's office in the induction establish the expectation that the poem will be in some way concerned with Christ's discovery of the three functions of his office, and will build upon the traditional understanding that Christ's baptism and temptation served as inauguration and initiation into that office. The Baptism is presented as Christ's formal call to enter upon the public exercise of his office: John was at that time ready to resign "To him his Heavenly Office" (I.28); and Christ indicated that he found in the Baptism and in the testimony of the Father's voice and of the Spirit a grant of new authority:

> I knew the time
> Now full, that I no more should live obscure,
> But openly begin, as best becomes
> The Authority which I deriv'd from Heaven. (I.286–89)

Satan's speech to his cohorts indicates that he has some awareness of the various aspects of Christ's office and that he is trying to fathom their implications for himself. The names of its functions are constantly on his tongue: he refers to the Baptist as the "great Prophet" sent as "Harbinger" to announce Jesus' coming (I.70–71) and remarks that he saw "The Prophet do him [Jesus] reverence" (I.80). Also, he observes that John's baptism was to prepare the people to "do him [Jesus] honor as their King" (I.75), and he raises with his followers the question of how to subvert Jesus, "Ere in the head of Nations he appear/ Their King, their Leader, and Supreme on Earth" (I.98–99). Appropriately, it is the kingly function of Christ's office with which Satan is most concerned, since that is the most immediate threat to the "fair Empire" of earth and air possessed by the demons after the fall of man, and also since the final destruction and punishment of God's enemies is a function of Christ's kingly role.

The Father's explanatory statement about the coming temptation, with its constant shifts in perspective from past to present to future, prepares for the use of subsequent references to and debates about Christ's everlasting office as a means of projecting the entire course of Christ's life and the history of his church. After referring to Job's victory over temptation as a type of Christ's experience, God remarks that Satan,

> now shall know I can produce a man
> Of female Seed, far abler to resist
> All his solicitations, and at length
> All his vast force, and drive him back to Hell,
> Winning by Conquest what the first man lost
> By fallacy surpris'd. But first I mean
> To exercise him in the Wilderness;
> There he shall first lay down the rudiments
> Of his great warfare, ere I send him forth
> To conquer Sin and Death the two grand foes,
> By Humiliation and strong Sufferance:
> His weakness shall o'ercome Satanic strength
> And all the world, and mass of sinful flesh;
> That all the Angels and Ethereal Powers,
> They now, and men hereafter, may discern
> From what consummate virtue I have chose
> This perfect Man, by merit call'd my Son,
> To earn Salvation for the Sons of men. (I.150–67)

Though the first five and one-half lines suggest the action of the temptation episode itself, they evidently refer to the whole course of Christ's life, as is indicated by the transition to the temptation proper in the words, "But first." The subsequent lines suggest still more directly that the temptation is an epitome of Christ's entire role throughout his life and throughout Christian history, for in it he will lay down the "rudiments," or first principles, of his everlasting warfare against Satan, Sin, and Death.

As Christ walks out into the desert he is poised between past and future, eager to learn just what his office involves and how to begin its exercise:

> Musing and much revolving in his breast,
> How best the mighty work he might begin
> Of Savior to mankind, and which way first
> Publish his Godlike office now mature. (I.185–88)

His knowledge of his mission is still indistinct: as a child he had vague aspirations to high endeavor, later he considered undertaking armed conquest over Israel's enemies and indeed against tyranny throughout the earth, but he has already concluded that to rule by persuasion is more glorious. All these tentative possibilities for action are given concrete form and substance in Satan's temptations—not that Satan is clairvoyant, but he is able to judge, on the basis of his vast experience, which modes of life have proved attractive to his opponent. The fact that many of Satan's temptations will recall to Christ courses of action he himself has speculated about must enhance their attractiveness even though Christ has already appeared to dismiss some of these possibilities, for up to this point Christ has been unable to fix certainly upon his proper course of action. However, his past study has led to the beginnings of understanding: Christ perceives something of his prophetic role when he determines that it is "more humane, more heavenly, first/ By winning words to conquer willing hearts,/ And make persuasion do the work of fear" (I.221–23). He has some awareness of his kingly function through the prophecy that he should sit on David's throne and rule an unending kingdom, and through the Magi's testimony that he is "King of *Israel* born" (I.254). And he knows something of his priestly role, for he understands that he must pass "Through many a hard assay even to the death" in order to "work Redemption for mankind, whose sins'/ Full weight must be transferr'd upon my head" (I.264–67). However, the Messiah is only "Known partly" (I.262) to the scribes; now Christ is led forth into the desert in order to achieve through temptation a full self-awareness, and in order to merit a complete revelation from God concerning his mission.

The induction accordingly prepares the reader to regard the temptation about to ensue as a dramatic battle of wits between Christ and Satan in which both participants begin with restricted, imperfect knowledge of Christ's nature as the Son of God, and Christ's office as prophet, king, and priest. It prepares us to expect the dramatic action of the temptation to present Christ's growth in self-knowledge, culminating in his defeat of Satan, and it leads us to expect that the ambiguities arising from the term "Son of God," and from the various possible interpretations of his roles as prophet, priest, and king, will constitute the fundamental issues in the conflict of Christ and Satan. Furthermore, it prepares us to regard the temptation episode in the double perspective of the past and the future, as indeed the turning point between past and future. In the course of the temptation Christ will relate himself to and at length fulfill and subsume the Old Testament and classical types of himself and his role; he will also achieve a full understanding of the three aspects of his mediatorial office which he exercises throughout his entire life and throughout the entire history of his church. In this way Milton establishes the temptation episode, the subject of the brief epic, as the symbolic event at the center of the vast historical panorama, as the true epitome of history.

CHAPTER VIII · THE BREAD-BANQUET
SEQUENCE: PERSONAL FAITH
AND PROPHETIC OFFICE

*A*LTHOUGH the induction to the poem identifies Adam and Job as the major types of Christ's temptation experience, the first temptation contains no allusions to the Christ-Adam parallel, perhaps in part because Milton follows standard Protestant exegesis in defining Christ's first temptation as an invitation to distrust rather than to gluttony (I.355), and the exegetes could relate Adam and Christ only very tenuously in terms of distrust. The Job parallel is kept active through two allusions (I.369–71, 424–26). This is appropriate since, as John Udall points out, Job was constantly incited by his wife and friends to distrust God and to believe himself abandoned by God.[1] But Milton develops the principal themes of the first temptation, faith and prophecy, chiefly by means of other types—the Israelites wandering in the desert, Moses, Elijah, Balaam, the Greek oracles. These two themes, and the particular dramatic situation in which they are embodied, carry over into and receive partial resolution in the highly complex banquet temptation of Book II.

The argument in the first debate-duel between Christ and Satan is multilayered and dense, and the action produces considerable dramatic tension arising chiefly from Satan's disguise and the vexing question of the sonship. Satan's manner throughout the first sequence indicates that he still retains the somewhat precarious confidence he managed to gain during the first consult by recalling his success with Eve. Now again, as with Eve, he adopts a fraudulent disguise, this time as an aged shepherd. But the physical disguise is only part of his posturing and pretense throughout the first temptation. After Christ recognizes him he assumes the deceptive manner of a smooth-tongued, fawning, obsequious inferior, evidently hoping thereby to catch Christ off guard, to lull him into a false security, or perhaps even to win his trust. Accordingly, he returns "smooth" answers to Christ despite his inner "anger and disdain" (I.466–67); he answers Christ's sharp rebukes with feigned humility—"thou art plac't above me, thou art Lord;/ From thee I can and must submiss endure/ Check or reproof" (I.475–77); and he departs at the conclusion of the first encounter, "bowing low/ His gray dissimulation" (I.497–98). This obsequious manner enables him to play upon the title newly emphasized at Christ's baptism—Son of God— without appearing offensive. He can remark with surprise that one called the Son of God is lost in a barren wilderness, and he can propose as if by a sudden flash of insight that if Christ is really the Son of God he can save himself by the miracle of changing stones to bread. He can also insinuate, very subtly, his own counterclaim to be a Son of God: despite his fall he still has liberty to range through earth and air; he still is admitted sometimes into the highest heaven among the "Sons of God"; he still is serviceable to God in tempting and punishing men; he still admires and loves to hear truth though he finds its paths too difficult to follow; and he is really the friend and helper of man through his oracles. The implication is that Christ should admit Satan's claim and should align himself with this "other" Son of God. Very seldom in the first encounter is the obsequious manner even momentarily set aside—perhaps the most obvious case is Satan's apparently innocent but really ironic observation that "no man comes" (I.484) to hear the words of Christ.

In direct contrast to Satan's posturing is Christ's straightforward and "stern" attitude (I.406) as he works out by stages his perception of the disguised shepherd's true identity, as he sharply rebukes Satan's false claims to sonship and prophecy, and as he proclaims himself with confident assurance the new "living Oracle." Christ's development in knowledge, manifested primarily by changes in his tone, will be discussed in detail in relation to the theme of the prophetic role; apparently, after Christ withstands the temptation of the stones at the human level he receives a special illumination from God enabling him to identify Satan as the Father of Lies and himself as the Oracle of God.

The first argument between Christ and Satan operates on two levels simultaneously and is carried forth at each level by references to certain appropriate Old Testament types. The first level supplies a test of Christ's personal faith in a context established by several allusions to that notable Old Testament example of providential guidance, the Israelites' journeying through the wilderness to the Promised Land. The second level offers a test and definition of Christ's public office as prophet, carried forth in part through allusions to the recognized Old Testament types of that prophetic function, Moses and Elijah. Both Christ and Satan refer to and debate about the types. Christ does so as a starting point for his own thinking about his proper mission and office. Satan endeavors to cause Christ to regress from the understanding he has already attained by identifying himself with prophetic types inferior to Moses and Elijah. Or, alternatively, he attempts to bring Christ to a literal understanding, an exact imitation of these noble types in order to divert him from his peculiar mission of going beyond, subsuming, and fulfilling them.

THE TEST OF FAITH: CHRIST AS NEW ISRAEL

Milton associates Christ directly with Israel wandering in the wilderness through Christ's reference to the Fathers fed "here with Manna" (I.350–51); the adverb intimates that Christ is, as it were, retracing Israel's course over the same terrain. This is a wholly appropriate locale for his temptation, for the wilderness in which the Israelites wandered was frequently identified with the symbolic wilderness to which Adam's progeny had been banished after the Fall, and thus it was the proper starting point for Christ's redemptive mission. As the Lutheran Daniel Brenius put it, "John was a preacher in the desert [Matt.] cap.3.1., but Christ was driven from that place into a more desolate solitude, where wild beasts dwelt, to fulfill old types. For the people of Israel, a type of Christ and his Church, were led into the desert, to that place to which Adam, who had been tempted in Paradise, had banished all his progeny out of the promised land. But Christ, the victor over the devil, has recovered paradise." [2] Moreover, patristic, medieval, and Protestant commentators agreed that the Exodus story as a whole foreshadowed Christ's redemption,[3] stating the point in formulations similar to that of the Calvinist Henry Ainsworth: "In *Genesis,* (which historie endeth with the going down of Israel into Egypt,) we have the image of a natural man, fallen from God, into the bondage of syn. In *Exodus,* is the type of our regeneration, and state renewed by Jesus Christ." [4] A further extension of this identification made the Israelites in the desert a figure of the church wandering in the wilderness of this world toward the true Promised Land, the kingdom of heaven.[5] The Red Sea crossing was almost universally identified as a type of our baptism in Christ's saving blood, and the *Biblia Pauperum* presented it also as a type of Christ's baptism in Jordan.[6]

Milton's explicit suggestion that Christ is wandering in that same mythic and actual wilderness earlier traversed by the Israelites activates these typological associations and makes the customary exegesis of the Exodus story an important frame of reference for the temptation of the stones. After coming forth from bondage in Egypt, Israel had wandered for forty years in the wilderness of Sin (Exod. xvi:1) as Christ wandered forty days in the desert. The name "Sin" was explained by many commentators as appropriate for this place of temptation where Israel was brought "to humble thee, and to proove thee" (Deut. viii:2). The place itself is described in Scripture as a "waste howling wildernesse" (Deut. xxxii:10), and "a land of deserts and of pits...a land of drought, and of the shadow of death...a land that no man passed thorow, and where no man dwelt" (Jer. ii:6). Calvin was among those who emphasized the rigors of the place: "What was that waste and barren desert, in which not a crumb of bread, nor a drop of water was to be found, but a grave to swallow up a thousand lives? and therefore it was further called, 'the devastation of horror.'"[7] In that desert the Israelites gave way frequently to doubts, complaints, and murmurings against God. They complained first of hunger, "Would to God wee had died by the hand of the LORD in the land of Egypt, when we sate by the flesh pots, and when we did eate bread to the full: for ye have brought us forth into this wildernes, to kill this whole assembly with hunger" (Exod. xvi:3). God responded to their complaint by sending manna. They cried out again at Massah for lack of water, tempting God by asking, "Is the LORD among us, or not" (Exod. xvii:7), and God sent water gushing forth from the rock struck by Moses' rod (Numb. xx:10 11). The manna and the water from the rock were almost universally interpreted as types of Christ, and often specifically of the Eucharist.[8] Israel also murmured against the manna, demanding flesh: "Who shall give us flesh to eate?/ We remember the fish which we did eate in Egypt freely: the cucumbers and the melons, and the leekes, and the onions, and the garlicke" (Numb. xi:4-5), a complaint which the Psalmist paraphrased (lxxviii:19), "Yea they spake against God: they said, Can God furnish a table in the wildernesse?"

Moreover, the Israelites in the desert fell frequently into

idolatry, provoking Moses to deliver constant warnings to them not to follow false prophets (Deut. xiii), and not to imitate the groves and idols of the pagans (Deut. xvi:21–22). They worshipped the golden calf at the very time Moses was receiving the Decalogue which expressly forbade the making of graven images. Also, they were led into idolatry by the corrupt gentile prophet Balaam, who, prevented by God from cursing the Israelites at King Balac's demand, was said to be the ultimate source of Israel's temptation by the Moabite women to feasting, fornication, and idolatry (Numb. xxv:1–2),[9] and hence was often allegorized as a figure of Satan.[10] The basis for this view of Balaam is provided in Revelation ii:14: "Balaam . . . taught Balac to cast a stumbling blocke before the children of Israel, to eat things sacrificed unto idols, and to commit fornication." Calvin's comment on Balaam's seduction of the Israelites is especially interesting with reference to the banquet scene in *Paradise Regained*:

The Moabitish damsels did not straightway solicit the Israelites to worship their idols, but first invite them to their banquets, and thus tempt them to idolatry; for if mention had been made at first of idol-worship, perhaps they might have shuddered at the atrocity of the crime, to which they allowed themselves to be beguiled by degrees. Now, to be present at a feast which was celebrated in honour of false gods, was a kind of indirect renunciation of the true God.[11]

In *Of Reformation* Milton evoked a similar image, identifying Balaam as the one who devised the devilish policy by which Balac lured the Israelites "from the Sanctuary of God to the luxurious, and ribald feasts of *Baal-peor*."[12]

Numerous commentaries on Christ's temptations provide precedent for Milton's association of those temptations, and especially the first temptation, with the Israelite experience in the desert. Daniel Dyke, for example, declared that one reason why Christ was tempted forty days was "that there might be some answering to the Israelites being forty yccrs in the desert in many trials and temptations." [13] The medieval commentator Rupert worked out perhaps the most elaborate series of parallels and contrasts:

Then was called out of Egypt the youth Israel, the Son of God, the Lord Jesus, after he dwelled in Nazareth where he was reared, after he crossed over the waters in baptism, he was led into the desert by the Spirit and fasted forty days and forty nights, and was tempted, and found faithful in three temptations; for he made void and abolished all the same temptations of the Fathers and children of Israel, who were led from the land of Egypt after crossing over the Red Sea, and being led about and tested forty years in the desert, were tempted and found unfaithful.[14]

Also, observing that all of Christ's replies to Satan's temptations were drawn from the Exodus story, Rupert proceeded to relate each of Christ's temptations to an event in the Exodus account. Rupert identified Israel's sin of gluttony and disobedience in gathering manna on the Sabbath and in craving flesh as the counterpart of Christ's temptation of the stones, citing as evidence Christ's quotation from Deuteronomy viii:3 during that temptation, "He humbled thee, and suffered thee to hunger, and fed thee with Manna, which thou knewest not, neither did thy fathers know: that he might make thee know that man doth not live by bread only but by every word that proceedeth out of the mouth of the LORD doth man live." He identified Israel's tempting God at Massah when they lacked water as the counterpart of the tower temptation on the basis of Christ's allusion to Deuteronomy vi:16 in response to that temptation: "Ye shall not tempt the LORD your God, as ye tempted him in Massah." And he took Israel's worship of the golden calf and other idolatrous acts as counterparts of Christ's temptation to idolatry on the ground that Christ's answer to Satan—"Thou shalt worship the Lord thy God, and him onely shalt thou serve" (Matt. iv:10)—is a slightly altered version of a paraphrase in Deuteronomy of the commandment forbidding idolatry, "Thou shalt feare the LORD thy God; him shalt thou serve" (Deut. x:20).[15] However, most exegetes limited their Israel-Christ comparisons to the first temptation. Paschasius interpreted the stones temptation as an invitation to distrust, paralleling the distrust of the Israelites when they lacked the water subsequently supplied by God from a rock.[16] Samuel Durant explicated Christ's first temptation as intending a reference to God's feeding the Israelites in the wilderness: "il lui a dressé une table, il l'y a nourri l'espace de quarante ans."[17] In similar terms, Thomas Manton paraphrased Christ's reply to the first temptation as meaning, "he that provided forty years for an huge multitude in the desert, he will not be wanting to his own Son, who had now fasted but forty dayes."[18]

Milton builds upon this traditional exegesis, presenting Christ's first temptation and the banquet temptation against the background of Exodus. Christ's desert recalls the horrors of the wilderness of Sin: it is a wild place "with dark shades and rocks environ'd round" (I.194); a "pathless Desert, dusk with horrid shades" (I.296); a place "by human steps untrod" (I.298), where wild beasts glare aloof (I.313). Satan's first disguise as "an aged man in Rural weeds,/ Following, as seem'd, the quest of some stray Ewe" (I.314–15) identifies him as a false shepherd, false pastor, false Moses to lead astray the new Israel. His first words to Christ contain a subtle offer of "guidance" as well as an invitation to distrust: he contrasts Christ's recent exaltation as Son of God at the Baptism with his present abandoned state in the lonely and arid desert where "single none/ Durst ever, who return'd, and dropt not here/ His Carcass, pin'd with hunger and with drought" (I.323–25). These words invite Christ to fear death from lack of food and water, as did the Israelites of old, to believe as the Israelites did that God has abandoned him in the wilderness, and to complain as they did of God's providence. Christ's simple answer, "Who brought me hither/ Will bring me hence, no other Guide I seek" (I.335–36), signals his rejection of the false guidance implied in the comment that he durst not wander here "single."

Satan's response to this is to suggest that only by a miracle can Christ survive in the wilderness. With implicit allusion to the Old Testament type he invites Christ as Son of God to work a miracle similar to that which God worked before for the Israelites in the desert, thus at once providing for himself and for the needy desert dwellers of the present: "So shalt thou save thyself and us relieve/ With Food, whereof we wretched seldom taste" (I.344–45). But Christ draws his answer from Deuteronomy viii:3 in which Moses interprets the manna miracle as a spiritual lesson to the Israelites, and he also cites as evidence of God's providence the Israelites fed in this same wilderness and Moses and Elijah miraculously sustained in a forty-day fast. Milton's development of this first exchange between Christ and Satan through references to the Israelites, Moses, and Elijah may be illuminated by comparison with Joseph Hall's very similar conception:

Satan had taken it for granted, that man cannot be sustayned without bread; and therefore inferres the necessitie of making bread of stones; Our Saviour shewes him from an infallible Word, that hee had mislayed his suggestion; That man lives not by usuall food only, but by every word that proceedeth from the mouth of God; Hee can either sustaine without bread, as he did *Moses* and *Elias,* or with a miraculous bread, as the Israelites with Manna, or send ordinary meanes miraculously, as food to his Prophet [Elijah] by the Ravens, or miraculously multiply ordinary meanes, as the Meale and Oyle to the Sareptan Widdow [who fed Elijah].[19]

At the end of Book I Satan identifies himself as a Balaam figure (I.486–92)—as one who despite his own wickedness is yet a prophet of God. The Balaam identification continues in

Book II with interesting variations. In the second consult Belial plays Balaam to Satan's Balac when he suggests beautiful women as a means to entice Christ to idolatry: "Set women in his eye and in his walk,/ Among daughters of men the fairest found" (II.153–54). Satan scorns the proposal as unworthy of Christ, but he nevertheless incorporates the technique in his own very subtle banquet temptation for the lavish feast offered by Satan to Christ has in attendance women fairer than all the romance heroines, a circumstance recalling the Moabite women who enticed the Israelites to feasting and whoredom as a prelude to idolatry. The feast is offered, moreover, in one of those "groves" the Israelites had so constantly been warned against, a place that was "to a Superstitious eye the haunt/ Of Wood Gods and Wood Nymphs" (II.295–97).

It is important to notice that Christ does not actually experience hunger until Book II. Eliminating the hunger motif from the first temptation permits Milton to set aside the usual associations of that trial with the sin of gluttony and to permit it to function as a temptation to Christ's faith, in which he, like Israel of old, must trust God's providence in the absence of ordinary means. The hunger motif is eliminated by a change in the biblical chronology of events. Matthew iv:2–3 declares that when Christ "had fasted forty days and forty nights, he was afterward an hungred," and that Satan then appeared and urged the temptation of the bread. Milton seems at first to adopt this chronology when he suggests in a transition passage (I.303–13) that Christ wandered forty days in meditations similar to those described, "Nor tasted human food, nor hunger felt/ Till those days ended, hunger'd then at last/ Among wild Beasts." But the first temptation is evidently located toward evening of that fortieth day, before Christ begins to hunger. Neither Christ nor Satan mention that Christ is experiencing present hunger during the first encounter—Satan merely indicates that he *will* find it impossible to survive in this desert place (I.321–25). It is only after the first temptation, as night falls, that the wild beasts mentioned as the companions of Christ's hunger appear upon the dramatic scene (I.502).

In Book II Christ's hunger is explicitly designated as a new sensation: Christ is described as "After forty days fasting.../ Now hung'ring first" (II.243–44), and he declares of himself, "four times ten days I have pass'd,/ ... and human food/ Nor tasted, nor had appetite.../ But now I feel I hunger" (II.245–52). He is somewhat shaken by the new experience and questions, "Where will this end" (II.245); more disturbing, he infers from his hunger pangs that "Nature hath need of what she asks" (II.253), though he reminds himself that God can satisfy that need another way than by supplying food. Satan endeavors to turn this new hunger to his own purposes by again urging upon Christ a literal understanding of the experience of the Israelites and Elijah in the wilderness. If those types of Christ had not been supplied by God they would have perished in this very place, so Christ should expect a similar provision. Christ, however, has been abandoned: "Of thee these forty days none hath regard,/ Forty and more deserted here indeed" (II.315–16). To Christ's answer that these had need whereas he has none, Satan responds ironically, "How hast thou hunger then?" (II.319), echoing Christ's own earlier conclusion that the hunger is itself evidence of need.

In this context the lush banquet which Satan presents comes as a visible embodiment of the presumptuous demand of the Israelites, "Can the Lord furnish a Table in the Wilderness." God has not furnished a table for the new Israel, so the Devil will, and he supplies it with delicacies and luxuries analogous to those which the Israelites craved when they were forced to exist on manna alone. Christ's refusal of the banquet derives from his recognition of the giver: this is the Devil's table, Paul's symbol for the apex of idolatry in I Corinthians x:21, "Yee cannot drinke the cup of the Lord, and the cup of devils: yee cannot be partakers of the Lords Table, and of the table of devils." As the new Israel, Christ will not fall away into idolatry as did the carnal Israel, and the Devil's table, scorned, promptly testifies to its true origin by vanishing away "With sound of Harpies' wings and Talons heard" (II.403).

At this point Christ has demonstrated that he will not simply recapitulate the old type, the carnal Israel, which responded to God's providential guidance by distrust and idolatry, but that he will perfect and fulfill the type. By confirming his own constant faith he confirms his status as the new, spiritual Israel, the fit model for his church which is also a new Israel wandering in the wilderness of this world to the Promised Land.

MOSES, ELIJAH, AND THE PROPHETIC ROLE

The other basic issue in the first temptation is the definition and testing of Christ's mediatorial role as prophet, a thematic concern prepared for by the several commentators who saw the entire temptation episode and especially the first temptation as a specific challenge to that role. Christ begins this theme by relating himself to his great forerunners in the prophetic function, Moses and Elijah. His response to Satan's invitation to distrust shows his consciousness of himself as reliving the experience of both these types with regard to the forty-day fast, and even as wandering in the same wilderness as did Elijah:

> In the Mount
> *Moses* was forty days, nor eat nor drank,
> And forty days *Eliah* without food
> Wander'd this barren waste; the same I now. (I.351–54)

Accordingly, the traditional Christian commentary about Moses and Elijah, especially as regards their relation to Christ's temptation, provides another important context for this first segment of the poem.

Almost all commentators regarded Moses as a type of Christ in respect of his deliverance of the Israelites from bondage.[20] Henry Vertue states the relation as follows: "As *Moses* brought *Israel* from bondage under *Pharoah,* so *Christ* hath set us free from bondage under Satan the Prince of darknesse . . . the Parallels are, *Christ* and *Moses, Satan* and *Pharoah,* bodily and spiritual bondage, *Israel* according to the flesh, and *Israel* according to the spirit."[21] The temptation episode is itself conceived as antitype in Botticelli's companion pictures in the Sistine Chapel which pair together Moses overcoming Pharaoh and Christ overcoming Satan in the temptation. However, most commentators also indicate that Moses presents an imperfect type of Christ's deliverance. As Lapide put it, "Moses bears the figure of the Law and Joshua the figure of Christ, in that just as Moses led the people out of Egypt and Joshua brought them into Canaan, even so the Law liberates believers from impiety, but the Gospel, by grace, introduces them into the heavenly kingdom."[22] In his *De Doctrina* Milton stated the same point: "the imperfection of the law was manifested in the person of Moses himself; for Moses, who was a type of the law, could not bring the children of Israel into the land of Canaan, that is, into eternal rest; but an entrance was given to them under Joshua, or Jesus."[23]

Moses typified Christ also as mediator. The customary presentation of this relationship may be illustrated from the Dutch Annotators: "*Moseh* stood between God and the people in the Covenant of the Law, Gal. 3.19. so is Christ the onely Mediatour between God and his people in the Covenant of Grace."[24] In similar terms, Milton stated that "the name and office of mediator is in a certain sense ascribed to Moses, as a type of Christ."[25] The Old Law given on Mount Sinai, and the New Law proclaimed in the Sermon on the Mount were

paralleled and contrasted by Eusebius and Prosper, and by
Botticelli's companion pictures in the Sistine Chapel, in terms
which suggest at once the relevance and the imperfection of
the Mosaic type.[26] Henry Vertue, quoting Prosper, put the
matter succinctly:

God calling *Moses* into Mount *Sinai,* gave him a Law written in
Tables of Stone, which he was to deliver to the People, which they
carefully keeping, they should receive the Land of Promise. Our
Mediator, the Lord Jesus (of whom *Moses* was a Type) ascending
into the Mount with his Disciples, shews by what means men may
become happy, wrote a Law, not in Tables of Stone, but in the
fleshly Tables of the Heart by the Spirit of God, by which they
may come to enjoy, not Earth, but Heaven.[27]

Still more to the point, most commentators identify Moses
specifically as a major type of Christ's prophetic role. Diodati
describes Moses during the battle with Amalek as saying "I
will look to my office of Prophet, to mediate with God for his
assistance." [28] John Trapp finds in the same passage a manifestation of Christ's entire mediatorial role, with the prophetic
office typified by Moses: "There are that here observe, that
upon the fortieth day after their coming out of *Egypt, Moses,
Aaron,* and *Hur* went up into the Mount, where *Moses's* hands
are thus supported, while *Amalek* is discomfited; and that
Moses the Prophet, *Hur* the Prince, and *Aaron* the Priest, all
put together, were a type of Christ ... our Prophet, Priest,
and Prince." [29] Moreover, most commentators emphasize that
Christ is the fulfillment, the end of the Law and the prophets,
and they gloss the promise in Deuteronomy xviii:18, "I will
raise them up a prophet from among their brethren, like unto
thee, and will put my words in his mouth; and he shall speake
unto them all that I shall command him" as a reference to
Christ at whose coming the Law and the prophets cease.[30]
Peter Martyr's statement is typical:

[To the prophets] it was committed so long to instruct and teach the people in profitable things, untill such time, as Christ which is the head, and wellspring of all prophets should come, upon whose comming the former sort ceased. *For the lawe and the prophets endured untill John* [Matt. xi:13]. That place [Deut. xviii:18] therefore is meant of the other prophets, as of figures and shadowes; but of Christ, as principallie: after whose comming there was no more need of their presence.[31]

Moreover, the relation of Moses and Elijah to Christ as types of the prophetic role was nearly always noted in commentary on Christ's temptation, the feature uniting the three figures being the common forty-day fast. Discussing the common prophetic function, some declared that Moses fasted as proclaimer of the Law, Elijah as restorer of it, and Christ as proclaimer of the New Law; others, that Moses fasted as founder of the Law, Elijah as chief of the prophets, and Christ as giver of the Gospel, which fulfills and supersedes the Law and the prophets.[32] The commentators usually found confirmation for these explanations of the fast as related to Christ's prophetic mission in the appearance of Moses and Elijah at Christ's transfiguration on Mount Tabor. Hall's comment is typical: "Both of them types of Christ: both of them fasted fortie dayes... *Moses* the publisher of the Law, *Elias* the chiefe of the Prophets, shew themselves [on Tabor] to the God of the Law, and Prophets... *Moses* and *Elias* are gone, only Christ is left; the glory of the Law, and the Prophets was but temporary... that only Christ may remain to us intire, and conspicuous." [33]

In some respects Elijah was a closer type even than Moses of Christ's fast in the wilderness and prophetic office. After denouncing the wicked King Ahab who "made a grove" for idols, Elijah fled to Cherith Brook where he was fed first by ravens and then by the widow of Sarepta, whose meal and oil were miraculously multiplied and whose son he raised from the dead (I Kings xvii). According to patristic and medieval commentators Elijah typified Christ "who hungers for our Salvation"; Ahab represented the Devil; the ravens (unclean birds by Jewish law) shadowed forth the priests of the Old Law; the widow, the church of the Gentiles to whom Christ went after rejecting the Jews; and the widow's son, mankind restored by Christ.[34] After chiding Ahab a second time Elijah fled to the wilderness (I Kings xix) where he was twice fed barley cakes and water by an angel, on the strength of which food he went forty days without eating. This event was interpreted by Clement of Alexandria and Joseph Hall as a notable example of temperance, and the Geneva Bible described it as an exercise of Elijah's faith, "to the intent that hee should looke upon nothing worldly, but only trust on Gods providence."[35] In terms of typology Elijah's experience was closely related to Christ's temptation. Joseph Hall described the angelic repast of Elijah as a reprise of the experience of Moses and the Israelites in the desert, and as a type of Christ's experience.[36] Thomas Manton identified the desert where Elijah fasted with that in which Israel wandered and Christ was tempted, and several Fathers interpreted Elijah's angelic repast as a type of Christ's banquet after his temptation.[37] Augustine indicated Elijah's further relation to Christ's prophetic role as the special precursor of John the Baptist (the last prophet before Christ) and as the prophet destined to return to earth before the Last Judgment (Mal. iv:5–6) to convert the Jews by interpreting the Law to them spiritually: "When, therefore he is come, he shall give a spiritual explanation of the law which the Jews at present understand carnally."[38] As a prophet, then, Elijah is associated especially with Christ's temptation and with the restoration and spiritual interpretation of the Law.

We may now examine the development of this prophetic theme through the dramatic interplay between Christ and

Satan. In the course of the first temptation Satan invites Christ
to relate himself to two inferior types of his prophetic role.
He first mentions the Greek oracles, evoking thereby the recollection that the oracles and especially the Sibyls were sometimes viewed as prophets of Christ to the Gentiles.[39] Almost
everyone observed, however, that they were inferior prophets:
Augustine and Lactantius emphasized that they spoke truth
against their will, and taught or at least permitted the people
to worship idols.[40] And Peter Martyr observed that although
God permitted them to tell some truths the better to deceive
those given over to idolatry, they were in fact diabolic parodies
of the prophets: "As God dooth edifie the church by his
prophets: so the divell apishlie counterfeiting God, subverteth
it by his prophets." Peter Martyr also voiced the general
agreement that all oracles ceased at Christ's coming: "The
true God is woont to chase awaie false gods. Wherefore im-
mediatlie upon the birth of Christ, all the oracles of the gods
were put to silence, which before were of great fame and
renowne. For when the light it selfe (which is Christ) was
come into the world, darknes should needs vanish awaie." [41]

Satan also alludes to Balaam as a type of his own prophetic
role and invites Christ to legitimatize and accept that inferior
type by voluntary association with Satan as a Balaam figure.
Many exegetes interpreted Balaam's prophecy in Numbers
xxiv:17—"I shall see him, but not now: I shall behold him, but
not nigh: there shall come a Starre out of Jacob, and a
Scepter shall rise out of Israel, and shall smite the corners of
Moab, and destroy all the children of Sheth"—as referring to
Christ's birth or sometimes to the birth of David as a type of
Christ.[42] The truth of the prophecy was taken as indication
that God sometimes gives his voice to the unworthy prophet,
for Balaam was understood to be a venal, corrupt simoniac
whose readiness to curse Israel at Balac's request (though he
was prevented by God from doing so) marked him as one

who would prostitute his prophetic office for money.[43] Calvin's comment is especially suggestive for Satan's reference to the Balaam type in *Paradise Regained:* interpreting Numbers xxii:40, he declared that Balac bribed Balaam both by money and by a great banquet with "abundance of animals," so that Balaam "might be ashamed to refuse anything to so munificent a king." He remarked also upon the prophetic function which God rather surprisingly granted to Balaam despite his corruption, but he contrasted him sharply with true prophets who

were the organs of the Holy Spirit for all necessary predictions; and the credit due to their prophecies was of an equable and constant character ... Far different was the case with Balaam, and such like, who were only endued with a particular gift, so that they truly foretold some things, and were mistaken in others ... God willed, indeed, that such should exist even among heathen nations, so that some sparks of light should shine amidst their darkness, and thus the excuse of ignorance should be taken away ... It is wonderful that God should have determined to have anything in common with the pollutions of Balaam; since there is no communion between light and darkness, and He detests all association with demons; but however hateful to God the impiety of Balaam was, this did not prevent Him from making use of him in this particular act.[44]

Similarly in his *Apology for Smectymnuus* Milton directly contrasts Moses and Balaam as examples of the true and the false prophet, noting that Moses did not seek reward for exercising his office whereas Balaam did.[45]

Responding to these challenges, Christ displays throughout the first temptation his growing comprehension of his prophetic role: he explores the implications of the major prophetic types, repudiates the inferior types which Satan presents, and at length finds and affirms his own uniqueness as prophet. Milton begins to establish the terms for a test of Christ's prophetic role at the very beginning of the first temp-

tation, by means of Satan's disguise: appearing as a shepherd
in quest "of some stray Ewe" (I.315) Satan is evidently a
parody of the true "Good Shepherd" who seeks after the lost
sheep, and he thereby challenges Christ directly in his role
of prophet and teacher. In this context, Satan's first speech
conveys, besides the offer of guidance and the invitation to distrust, the suggestion that Christ should, as prophet, imitate
Moses in distributing bread to the starved desert dwellers,
thus anticipating the time when he will, in reprise of the
manna in the wilderness, feed the five thousand with bread
and fishes. If Christ will change stones to bread he will both
save himself "and us relieve/ With Food, whereof we
wretched seldom taste" (I.344–45). The elimination of actual
hunger from the first temptation makes this invitation especially apt as a challenge to Christ's prophetic role, for in it
Christ is specifically urged to distrust God's provision for that
office and to believe that its success depends upon his providing in advance for his necessities and those of the other
"shepherds." As Howard Schultz has noted, this contains an
allusion to the whole question of ministerial tithes and church-
supported clergy which will plague the church throughout
its history.[46] Christ's answer, "Man lives not by Bread only,
but each Word/ Proceeding from the mouth of God" (I.349–
50), and his appeal to the examples of Moses and Elijah who
did not make such provision, decisively separate his prophetic role (as exercised by himself and his followers to
come) from any necessary dependence upon material support. Christ here implies that his proper sustenance is the
Word of God, and, conversely, he declares of Satan, "lying is
thy sustenance, thy food" (I.429). In his role as prophet,
then, Christ, the True Bread that has come down from heaven,
the Incarnate Word, is brought to confront and to defeat Satan "compos'd of lies" (I.407).

Christ's developing awareness of his role as prophet is indicated also by his growing certitude in penetrating the disguise of Satan. Immediately after Satan has urged the miracle Christ declares merely that Satan is "other than thou seem'st" (I.347), but as Christ continues his reply he works out exactly who this false shepherd is who has suggested "distrust" to one he has heard proclaimed the Son of God: "Why dost thou then suggest to me distrust,/ Knowing who I am, as I know who thou art?" (I.355–56). The penetration of his disguise forces Satan to shift his ground. He admits his identity but in so doing lays claim himself to the prophetic office. He has served as God's agent in the matter of tempting Job and in deceiving Ahab's prophets (the implication is that he may be serving God again in the present temptation), and he also aids mankind with his oracles and portents. This last claim, developed at length, contains a subtle offer to aid Christ by such means, and conveys an invitation to Christ to identify his own prophetic role with this inferior type. Christ denounces Satan's pretensions with ringing certitude, and is then able by an imaginative re-creation of the scene based upon traditional (Christian) exegesis of the Job story, to describe in complete detail Satan's inner feelings when he came to heaven on the matter of Job,

> As a poor miserable captive thrall
>
> .   .   .   .
>
> Ejected, emptied, gaz'd, unpitied, shunn'd,
> A spectacle of ruin or of scorn
> To all the Host of Heaven. (I.412–16)

He also denounces Satan's claim of service to God as merely an effort to dignify his own malice, he describes precisely how Satan obtains the smattering of truth contained in his oracles, and he flatly rejects Satan's oracles as diabolic parodies of true prophecy serving merely to delude further those given over to idolatry.

At this point Christ appears to win a notable insight into his prophetic office, describing it authoritatively in terms which paraphrase Milton's definition of it in *De Doctrina,*[47] and which also announce the cessation of all the inferior types:

> But this thy glory shall be soon retrench'd;
> No more shalt thou by oracling abuse
> The Gentiles; henceforth Oracles are ceast,
> And thou no more with Pomp and Sacrifice
> Shalt be inquir'd at *Delphos* or elsewhere,
> At least in vain, for they shall find thee mute.
> God hath now sent his living Oracle
> Into the World to teach his final will,
> And sends his Spirit of Truth henceforth to dwell
> In pious Hearts, an inward Oracle
> To all truth requisite for men to know. (I.454–64)

Christ here speaks of the cessation of the pagan oracles, the miraculous sign usually seen as attending upon the birth (but here upon the manifestation) of the Messiah. By referring this sign to the present moment ("henceforth") Christ asserts unequivocally his claim to be the divine Word, the living oracle who will teach the final Word of God, causing thereby the cessation of oracles as well as of all other forms of prophecy. The certitude with which Christ speaks here of his mission contrasts sharply with the doubts and hesitations which marked his meditations as he entered the desert—so sharply that D. C. Allen posits Christ's recollection of his divine preexistence and his encounters with Satan in heaven.[48] That full recollection waits, I believe, upon the tower temptation, but it does seem that Christ has arrived here at some penetrating insight regarding his role. I suggest that by withstanding this first temptation directed at his prophetic office he has merited from God a special revelation regarding this office and that the lines just quoted show him receiving it. Christ cannot call at will upon the divine illumination but it is granted after he has withstood, in all human vulnerability, the test posed. He is in the process of winning back the understanding which he previously possessed by means of the teaching of the Father—"For what concerns my knowledge God reveals."

Though Christ's claim is unambiguous, Satan, the embodiment of the literal mind of evil, cannot fully understand it. Satan shifts ground again and presents himself as a Balaam figure—a miserable liar who yet desires to hear truth in Christ's company—arguing that God himself

> Suffers the Hypocrite or Atheous Priest
> To tread his Sacred Courts,
>
> .   .   .   .
>
>   and vouchsaf'd his voice
> To *Balaam* Reprobate, a Prophet yet
> Inspired. (I.487–92)

Christ here is invited to associate his unique prophetic role with the inferior type that the venal Balaam represents, and thus to associate it voluntarily with falsehood and hypocrisy. This issue also reverberates in the subsequent history of the church, for to invite Satan back as a Balaam figure—an admitted liar and hypocrite who only assumes the posture of a truth-seeker—is to sanction church society based upon outward conformity rather than regeneration, a national church of sinners rather than a congregation of saints. Christ avoids the difficulty which would attend such a voluntary invitation to Balaam-Satan by stating merely that Satan will return or not as God wills.

At this point, after Christ has attained the first significant victory over Satan, and has authoritatively proclaimed his prophetic role as the True Oracle, the imagery indicates his reversion again to the state of simple human vulnerability and uncertainty. His prophetic role is to be further tested, and his understanding of its implications is to be further advanced. His vulnerability is signaled first by the bleak and ominous mood of the final lines of Book I: "now began/ Night with her sullen wing to double-shade/ The Desert; Fowls in thir clay nests were couch'd;/ And now wild Beasts came forth the woods to roam" (I.499–502). It is emphasized also in the long induction to Book II which plays many variations on the theme of doubt, anxiety, and distrust. Mary and the apostles brood anxiously about Christ's disappearance, thinking he may be "only shown" to them for a time and then "caught up to God, as once/ *Moses* was in the Mount, and missing long;/ And the great *Thisbite* who on fiery wheels/ Rode up to Heaven" (II.13–17). Christ himself muses anxiously about the outcome of his experience and his new sensation of hunger, and Satan almost despairs of his undertaking, asking advice in a new council "without sign of boast, or sign of joy,/ Solicitous and blank" (II.119–20). Christ's hunger now leads him to dream, "as appetite is wont to dream" (II.264), of sharing with Elijah the repast brought by the ravens, or of being fed by an angel such a temperate meal as Elijah was given. Christ's allusions here focus on Elijah rather than Moses because Elijah wandered the same desert, because Elijah hungered and was given food whereas Moses was sustained in his fast without hunger, and because Elijah was identified as the prophet who would return to give a spiritual interpretation of the Law. Satan's words, alluding to the provision made for Elijah in the wilderness in contrast to the desertion Christ has experienced in his hunger, invite Christ again to a literal identification with the type; in his dream Christ has already toyed with the notion that he might be supplied like Elijah, but he has already concluded that God is able to sustain him without food despite his hunger.

In this context the banquet temptation takes on other dimensions: God has not sent manna such as sustained the Israelites, or ravens or angels to feed Christ, so Satan will provide for him in the wilderness. The elaborate, sensuous, idolatrous banquet, falsely offered in the guise of a tribute freely presented by Nature, is at once a diabolic parody of the heavenly manna and the temperate repasts offered to Elijah, and an effort to insist upon the literal fulfillment of the types. The banquet temptation also has another facet. Satan presents the banquet as wholly in keeping with the dietary provisions of the Law—"nor mention I/ Meats by the Law unclean, or offer'd first/ To Idols" (II.327–29), but as Michael Fixler has pointed out, he lies.[49] The banquet contains all kinds of "Beasts of chase, or Fowl of game," "Grisamber steam'd" and all kinds of "Fish from Sea or Shore,/ ... of shell or fin" (II.342–46); it therefore admittedly contains forbidden shellfish and grisamber, and probably also some forbidden flesh. Christ is hereby presented with a dilemma: if he refuses the banquet because it contains forbidden foods, he seems to subject himself (and his church) to the dietary prohibitions of the Law which he has come to supersede, or else to be still subservient to the scruple about eating foods offered first to idols, whereas Paul declares that the Christian is free to eat such things, for "the earth is the Lords, and the fulnesse thereof" (I Cor. x:26). Satan has even echoed this Pauline phrase in his statement to Christ, "Hast thou not right to all Created things,/ Owe not all Creatures by just right to thee/ Duty and Service... ?" (II.324–26). On the other hand, if Christ accepts the banquet he will eat at the Devil's table, the very apex of idolatry as Paul makes clear. The banquet is also, it may be noted, a parody of the "fat banquet" of Isaiah xxv:6, "And in this mountaine shall the Lord of hostes make unto all people a feast of fat things, a feast of wines on the lees, of fat things full of marrow, of wines on the lees well refined," which was usually glossed, for example by Luther, as referring to "the call of the Gentiles under the New Covenant."[50]

Christ, however, finds a way of escaping from the dilemma

posed: either to become involved in idolatry or to accept the bondage of the Law and fail to proclaim the new covenant which supersedes the Law. Throughout the second book Christ has been moving toward greater understanding. He has associated himself more often with Elijah, who is to interpret the Law spiritually, than with Moses; he has considered but set aside the expectation that God will deal with him just as with Elijah; he has quite freely entered into the "grove" where the banquet is presented despite the fact that it looks like a place of idolatry, resembling a grove where the "Superstitious eye" might find "Wood Gods and Wood Nymphs" (II.296–97), and also resembling an idolatrous Catholic cathedral, "High rooft, and walks beneath, and alleys brown" (II.293). Christ is however attracted by its beauty and is not put off by appearances: the earth *is* the Lords and the freedom thereof. Now, with regard to the deceptive banquet, Christ refuses it simply on the basis of the giver. It is the Devil's table, the symbol for the height of idolatry, forbidden in the New Law as in the Old as Paul's comment on I Corinthians x:20–21 makes clear: "The things which the Gentiles sacrifice, they sacrifice to devils, and not to God: and I would not that yee should have fellowship with devils./ Yee cannot drinke the cup of the Lord, and the cup of devils: yee cannot be partakers of the Lords Table, and of the table of devils." The idolatrous banquet also alludes to superstitious and idolatrous worship, especially the Roman Catholic mass, which throughout history will seek to mislead the church of which Christ is head. Therefore in repudiating the false banquet here Christ also rejects false priesthood, in preparation for the definition (fully developed in the tower temptation) of his own true priesthood.

More than this, Christ now lays direct claim to lordship over nature, to the freedom from ceremonial restriction which is the mark of the new covenant:

> Shall I receive by gift what of my own,
> When and where likes me best, I can command?
> I can at will, doubt not, as soon as thou,
> Command a Table in this Wilderness. (II.381–84)

Christ's own "Table in the Wilderness" alludes typologically to such future manifestations of his proper "banquet" as the angelic repast which is to celebrate his victory over Satan at the conclusion of the temptation episode, the feeding of the multitude in the wilderness in reprise and fulfillment of the manna type, and the Eucharistic banquet with which his church will be nourished in the wilderness of this world. In addition, by this claim Christ also asserts unequivocally his function as prophet of the New Testament, fulfilling and superseding the Law and the prophets: his spiritual banquet will surpass and supersede the manna and the food supplied to Elijah and he is himself the provider (when and where likes him best) of the fat banquet which will call the Gentiles to the church.

CHAPTER IX · THE BANQUET-WEALTH-GLORY
SEQUENCE: KINGSHIP OVER THE SELF

THE STRUCTURE OF *Paradise Regained* interweaves several thematic motifs in complex counterpoint to the book divisions. Book I presents Christ as Second Israel wandering in the wilderness, and as Second Moses and Second Elijah discovering and at length affirming his prophetic office. This theme extends into Book II, providing one level of meaning in the extraordinarily intricate banquet temptation. At another level, Book II introduces the motif of Christ's kingship. Before Christ can come to terms directly with his mediatorial kingly office, he must display that kingship over the self which in Milton's view constitutes the basis for any kind of public rule or dominion, and which involves perfecting the private moral virtues, controlling desires, and developing the proper attitudes toward power. This motif, the definition and display of Christ's kingship over the self, forms the chief focus in the segment of the poem beginning with Book II and extending through the temptation to glory. It is explored in relation to the triple equation and Christ's situation as Second Adam; in relation to various classical types of Christ who exemplify heroism and ethical knowledge, most notably Hercules and Socrates; and in relation to various Old Testament types, chiefly Daniel and Job.

The dramatic movement in this segment of the poem is marked by steadily mounting tension. One minor climax is Christ's moment of heightened insight after the banquet temptation, and another is Satan's first uncontrollable display of discomfiture precisely at the mid-point of the poem (III.1–4), but the major climactic revelation concerning the kingly office is postponed to the following sequence.

The induction to the second book (II.1–278) displays all of the characters moving from anxiety and doubt to at least partially restored confidence, though all are hampered by imperfect knowledge and misapprehension. The disciples are anxious and dismayed at the disappearance of Christ, but reaffirm their trust as they recall that God has thus far performed his covenant by displaying his Messiah to them. They, however, expect Christ to become a kingly Messiah, ruling a literal kingdom. Mary is filled with "Motherly cares and fears" (II.64), but she regains her patience by reflecting upon the prophecies and especially upon her earlier loss and recovery of Jesus in the Temple; however, she only partially understands how the prophecies can at once proclaim her blessed and also state that a sword will pierce her heart. Satan's doubt and dismay are more profound and continue to center upon the problem of the sonship. In his second consult with the fallen angels he speaks "without sign of boast, or sign of joy" (II.119), wondering whether Christ can be even partly human, so obviously adorned is he "With more than human gifts from Heav'n" (II.137). But, ironically, Satan's confidence is partially restored through that comic variation on the temptation theme in which Belial, playing Satan's role, proposes the allurement of beautiful women as a means of attracting Christ, and Satan, playing Christ's role, rejects the proposal as offering no real enticement to a strong and noble man. This exchange enables Satan to take pride in his own superior understanding of Christ's nature, indicating through his sharp rebuke to Belial and his followers as "False titl'd Sons of God" (II.179) his own awareness that Christ is a very different kind of son. But compounding the irony, Satan's rebuke of Belial's folly in weighing "All others by thyself" in regard to sensuality (II.174) is to redound upon Satan himself in this very sequence, for Satan will foolishly expect Christ to respond as he himself does to things "Of worth, of honor, glory, and popular praise" (II.227). Christ traverses much the same emotional range in this induction: he displays human anxiety about being lost in the desert and experiences a hunger which betokens Nature's need of food, but he quickly reaffirms his confidence in God's ability to sustain him without food.

On the second day Satan returns in a new posture. He is no longer rustic but appears "As one in City, or Court, or Palace bred" (II.300)—that is, he comes now in the character of Prince of This World. Also, he is no longer obsequious and fawning, but presents himself as a knowledgeable man of the world, condescending, officious, expansive to Christ whom he affects to see as naïve and inexperienced in the ways of the world and slack in realizing and asserting his own merits. He now refers to Christ's sonship with deliberate and rather subtle irony. Before the banquet temptation he expresses his great "wonder that the Son of God" should be abandoned in the wilderness when others have been fed there (II.303–14). In presenting the banquet as Nature's tribute to her Lord he remarks twice, ironically, "What doubts the Son of God to sit and eat?" (II.368, 377). In the wealth temptation he insinuates that Christ's divine paternity is of little use to him since his "known" father is a carpenter (II.414). In the glory temptation he suggests that Christ is most unlike his Father (and therefore not a true Son) when he rejects glory.

Christ's matter-of-fact response to the banquet offer, affirming that he has no need of such food and that he will judge the offer by the giver, modulates at length to ringing certitude and challenge as he seems to receive another of those divine illuminations, enabling him now to assert the lordship over Nature due him as the Creator and Son of God (II.381–84). Satan is "malcontent" at Christ's refusal (II.392) but seems not to be seriously discomfited: obviously he did not expect the banquet to succeed with Christ as a sensual attraction though he may well have expected to confuse him with some of the theological complexities discussed in the previous chapter. After making a casual counterclaim to divine sonship and lordship over Nature—"That I have also power to give thou seest" (II.393)—Satan moves immediately to the offer of wealth as a means to kingship. However, when Christ by patient, analytic, almost pedagogic explanation of the uses of wealth and the values and kinds of kingship gives the first extended display of the power of his mind in meeting a strictly ethical challenge in strictly human terms, Satan is for the first time unable to conceal or control his dismay: he stands "A while as mute confounded what to say,/ What to reply, confuted and convinc't/ Of his weak arguing and fallacious drift" (III.2–4). But his mental agility enables him to recover quickly after this defeat. Not in the tones of the obsequious flatterer as in the first temptation, but in those of a knowledgeable and discriminating judge of men, he pays fulsome tribute to the "Godlike Virtues" (III.21) just displayed by Christ, and on this basis tempts him to seek glory. Again Christ is calm and almost pedagogic in explaining the differences between true and false glory, though his tone modulates to scorn as he denounces the brutish conquerers who affect to be Sons of God, and to fervent zeal as he explains the utterly different sources and bases of glory for God and for man. At the end of this sequence Satan is yet more distressed, recognizing that he has most unwisely estimated Christ according to the satanic measure: he "had not to answer, but stood struck/ With guilt of his own sin, for he himself/ Insatiable of glory had lost all" (III.146–48).

CHRIST AS SECOND ADAM: THE TRIPLE EQUATION

The several references to Christ as Second Adam in the poem's induction suggest that the work will utilize in some significant way the traditional triple equation motif, which presents Christ's temptation as a reprise and reversal of Adam's temptation experience. Milton, however, departs from the usual treatment of this theme in that he does not parallel Adam's three temptations with the three biblically reported temptations of Christ, but rather with the wholly original banquet-wealth-glory sequence. Satan speculates about his chances with the old inducements just prior to this sequence: in the second consult he predicts "Far other labor to be undergone/ Than when I dealt with *Adam* first of *Men*" (II.132–33) and warns his followers "lest confidence/ Of my success with *Eve* in Paradise/ Deceive ye to persuasion over-sure/ Of like succeeding here" (II.140–43). But the irony of Satan's situation is evident in the fact that, despite these misgivings, Satan can only urge again these same generic lures which are at the root of all human evil, though he does plan to refurbish and refine them so that the goods offered seem merely "to satisfy/ Lawful desires of Nature," or else to have a show "Of worth, of honor, glory, and popular praise" (II.229–30, 227). It will be recalled that according to the usual exegesis of Eve's temptation, the appearance of the fruit as "good for foode, and ... pleasant to the eyes" constituted a temptation to gluttony or sensual appetite, the promise that it would bring knowledge of good and evil constituted an appeal to avarice and ambition, and the suggestion that eating the fruit would make Adam and Eve "as Gods" was a temptation to pride and vainglory. The Protestant formula for the first temptation interpreted it rather differently, as an invitation to doubt and distrust God's commandment forbidding the fruit. And both Catholic and Protestant accounts emphasized Adam's share in these temptations through his uxorious passion for Eve.[1] Throughout the banquet-wealth-glory sequence Satan invites Christ to identify himself with and imitate the first Adam by giving way before these same temptations.

The undue susceptibility to women, which was Adam's particular sin, is considered in the Satan-Belial exchange and in its crude form is dismissed as a possible enticement for Christ. Yet Satan does include beautiful women and also beautiful boys among the sensual attractions of the banquet scene, presenting them subtly as one of the elements in the panorama of refined sensual pleasure offered to Christ. The narrator's comment that the ladies who participated in the banquet scene were fairer than the ladies of Arthurian romance met "in Forest wide/ By Knights of *Logres,* or of *Lyones,/ Lancelot* or *Pelleas,* or *Pellenore"* (II.359–61) points to later reverberations in history of this aspect of Adam's temptation. Like Christ, these later knights-errant will undertake quests in the wilderness, but unlike him they will prove susceptible to the sensual allurements which overcame the first Adam. As Merritt Hughes notes,[2] the description of Satan's banquet and its setting closely resembles the banquet scene in Tasso's *Gerusalemme Liberata,* by means of which Armida (allegorized as Desire) turns errant knights into fish:

> Under the curtaine of the greene-wood shade,
> Beside the brooke, upon the velvet grasse,
> In massie vessell of pure silver made,
> A banket rich and costly furnisht was,
> All beastes, all birds beguil'd by fowlers trade,
> All fish were there in floods or seas that passe,
>   All dainties made by art, and at the table
>   An hundreth virgins serv'd, for husbands able.[3]

Launcelot, Pelleas, and Pellenore are knights from Malory, all of whom succumbed to the temptations of beautiful women. Launcelot, besotted by wine, was twice led to sleep with the fair Elaine, thinking her to be Guinevere, and was driven mad by the discovery of his infidelity. Pelleas was so violently in love with the scornful Ettard that he submitted to all manner of despiteful and degrading treatment from her. Pellenore's son Percivale, evidently alluded to here under his father's name, was offered after a three-day fast a banquet with "all maner of meetes that he cowde thynke on" and "the strengyst wyne that ever he dranke" by a fair gentlewoman with whom he subsequently went to bed; he was saved from serious sin with the lady, who was "the mayster fyende of helle" in disguise, only by making the sign of the cross which caused the scene to vanish.[4] These romance allusions emphasize Christ's victory over the lure of women, offered not as the crude enticement Belial would have engineered, but in the subtle and deceptive form which was to prove so successful with those later Adam-Christ figures, the knights-errant.

The Protestant reading of Eve's and Christ's first temptation as an invitation to doubt and distrust rather than to sensuality is incorporated in Book II just before the banquet is offered. Of course the doubt-distrust theme echoes throughout the poem, but here the temptation is made very specific as Satan openly invites the now hungry Christ to doubt his sonship and God's providence, "Of thee these forty days none hath regard,/ Forty and more deserted here indeed" (II.315–16). The trust in God which Christ displays in declaring that he has no need of food enables him to withstand Adam and Eve's first temptation as the Protestant formula stated it.

The banquet temptation itself is an analogue to Adam and Eve's first temptation conceived in the traditional manner as a temptation to carnal appetite. The narrator's comment, "Alas how simple, to these Cates compar'd,/ Was the crude Apple that diverted *Eve!*" (II.348–49), suggests that the banquet is to be seen at one level as a magnification of the sensuous appeal of the apple.[5] More than this, the banquet with its lavish abundance of natural goods is presented by Satan in the arid desert as a kind of mock Eden, a diabolic parody of Christ's own mission to raise Eden "in the waste Wilderness." Satan presents

> A Table richly spread, in regal mode,
> With dishes pil'd, and meats of noblest sort
> And savor, Beasts of chase, or Fowl of game,
> In pastry built, or from the spit, or boil'd,
> Grisamber steam'd; all Fish from Sea or Shore,
> Freshet, or purling Brook, of shell or fin. (II.340–45)

Describing these delicacies as Nature's free offering to her Lord, Satan uses terms reminiscent of his address to Eve in *Paradise Lost* as Mistress of Nature,[6] "Owe not all Creatures by just right to thee/ Duty and Service, nor to stay till bid,/ But tender all thir power?" (*PR* II.325–27). Moreover, Satan's assertion, "These are not Fruits forbidden; no interdict/ Defends the touching of these viands pure;/ Thir taste no knowledge works, at least of evil" (*PR* II.369–71), further establishes the parallel with the apple, despite the denial. We know that this banquet is also forbidden, on two counts—it contains foods forbidden by Mosaic law, and it is itself the Devil's table, the very essence of idolatry. In refusing the banquet, then, Christ overcame the substance of Adam and Eve's first temptation according to the conventional formulation. As Jerome put it, "he [Satan] conquered the first man by gluttony [sensuality], but he was conquered by the second man through abstinence." [7]

The temptation to wealth and ambition carries in Milton's poem the meaning customarily associated with the biblical kingdoms temptation through the traditional parallel with Eve's temptation to avarice. Several of the Fathers, for example Gregory the Great, explained the avarice in this formula so that it could accommodate both Eve's desire of forbidden knowledge and the dominion and power involved in the kingdoms temptation: "There is an avarice not only for money, but also for greatness. Rightly therefore that is called avarice which is ambitious for greatness out of measure." [8] Milton associated this broader meaning with his wealth temptation, for Christ is invited to seek wealth as a means of serving an ambition for dominion.

As Miss Pope points out, the offer of glory in Milton's poem incorporates the vainglory and pride usually associated with the tower temptation, the temptation which was equated with the satanic suggestion to Adam and Eve that they would "be as Gods." Miss Pope sees the offer of glory in the poem simply as part of the entire offer of kingdoms and glories to Christ,[9] but it seems rather that the placement of the glory temptation here is intended to complete and to relegate to this segment of the poem the specific treatment of the triple equation and of the Second Adam theme. The language of the temptation to glory invites constant reference to Adam's parallel temptation, for Christ disparages the military leaders and the world conquerors precisely because of their disposition to make themselves like gods. And in direct contrast to Eve, he responds to Satan's invitation to imitate his Father in seeking glory by vehemently refusing to aspire to "That which to God alone of right belongs" (III.141).

In thus reversing Adam's experience in the temptations, Christ proves himself the true Second Adam. The Second Adam motif is to recur again (with much else) in the climactic learning temptation, which will incorporate and greatly refine the lures of pleasure, ambition, and glory, relating them to that paramount cause of Adam and Eve's fall, false wisdom.

THE CLASSICAL HEROES AS TYPES: THE HERCULES MOTIF

Throughout this sequence Christ counters Satan's invitation to imitate the inferior type, Adam, by identifying himself with more worthy types of himself, both classical and biblical. The

two areas of allusion are conjoined because this segment of
the poem concerns moral virtue and right attitudes, the kingdom within which "every wise and virtuous man attains"
(II.468)—classical heroes and philosophers as well as the Old
Testament righteous. Moreover, in this segment of the poem,
as Irene Samuel points out, the sequence of temptations seems
to follow, in reverse order, Socrates' scale of the five kinds of
men and governments outlined in Plato's *Republic*.[10] Belial's
proposal of temptation by women was evidently calculated
to reduce Christ to the effeminate slavery characteristic of
Socrates' tyrannical man who is "drunken, lustful, passionate,"
who finds that "Love is his tyrant," and who consequently is
"miserably degraded and enslaved." The banquet temptation
invites Christ to become Socrates' democratic man who "lives
from day to day indulging the appetite of the hour" and who
enjoys the "freedom and libertinism of useless and unnecessary pleasures." The wealth temptation offers Christ the model
of the oligarchic man who endeavors to "seat the concupiscent and covetous element on the vacant throne [of reason]
and to suffer it to play the great king within him." The glory
temptation invites Christ to identify himself with the timo-
cratic man who is moved especially by "the spirit of contention and ambition" and who is "a lover of power and a lover
of honour; claiming to be a ruler ... because he is a soldier
and has performed feats of arms." At length in the learning
temptation Christ is invited to become the Socratic philosopher, the lover of wisdom.[11] Some Stoic formulations present
a similar scale. In Dio Chrysostom's "Fourth Discourse, on
Kingship" the Cynic Diogenes describes the "three prevailing
types of lives which the majority usually adopt" as follows: "the
first is luxurious and self-indulgent as regards bodily pleasures,
the second, in its turn, is acquisitive and avaricious, while
the third is more conspicuous and more disordered than the
other two—I mean the one that loves honour and glory—and

it manifests a more evident and violent disorder or frenzy, deluding itself into believing that it is enamoured of some noble ideal." [12] This Platonic-Stoic scale became a Renaissance commonplace. [13]

From the classical perspective, both the banquet and the wealth-ambition temptations serve as tests of Christ's temperance in the all-encompassing Stoic understanding of that virtue. Admittedly drawing upon Stoic ethics, Cicero defined temperance as involving the subjection of all the passions; moderation in all things such as raillery, pleasures, amusements; propriety and decorum in the movements of body and spirit; and the proper choice of career in accordance with one's own nature and talents. [14] In his *De Doctrina* Milton defined temperance more narrowly as "the virtue which prescribes bounds to the desire of bodily gratification," [15] and in the poem the term "temperance" is used by the narrator and by Satan in specific reference to Christ's denunciation of the overlush banquet and its "pompous Delicacies" (II.378, 408). But the broader meaning is invoked just after the banquet and wealth temptations, when Christ defines the "kingdom within" in terms of the Stoic definition of temperance, as the rule over all "Passions, Desires, and Fears" (II.467).

In the course of his discussion of temperance, Cicero alludes to the story of Hercules' choice [16] which he derived from Xenophon, who in his turn presents it as Socrates' account of a story he heard from Prodicus:

When Heracles was passing from boyhood to youth's estate, wherein the young, now becoming their own masters, show whether they will approach life by the path of virtue or the path of vice, he went out into a quiet place, and sat pondering which road to take. And there appeared two women of great stature making toward him. The one was fair to see and of high bearing; and her limbs were adorned with purity, her eyes with modesty; sober was her figure, and her robe was white. The other was plump and soft, with high feeding.

Identifying herself as Happiness, but admitting that she is nicknamed Vice by her enemies, the second lady promises Hercules that she will lead him

along the pleasantest and easiest road. You shall taste all the sweets of life; and hardship you shall never know. First, of wars and worries you shall not think, but shall ever be considering what choice food or drink you can find, what sight or sound will delight you, what touch or perfume; what tender love can give you most joy, what bed the softest slumbers; and how to come by all these pleasures with the least trouble.... You shall have the fruits of others' toil, and refrain from nothing that can bring you gain.[17]

However, Hercules follows the first lady, Virtue, who urges him to arduous noble deeds as a means to gain honor.[18]

Though Hercules is not explicitly mentioned during the banquet-wealth temptations, the familiar elements, the moral meanings, and the common iconographical symbols of the story of Hercules' choice are incorporated in these temptations, so that the young Christ repeats here the experience of initiation undergone by the young Hercules. The Hercules motif becomes fully explicit in one of the two climactic epic similes of the poem (IV.562–71) in which Milton presents Hercules' victory over Antaeus (a son of Earth commonly allegorized as representing earthly or sensual desires)[19] as a type of Christ's victory over Satan. It is implicit in Christ's opening meditation when he reviews his youthful aspiration to "subdue and quell o'er all the earth/ Brute violence and proud Tyrannic pow'r" (I.218–19), since Hercules' labors were allegorized in just such terms. But this motif is specifically located in the segment of the poem under discussion by the banquet scene itself, for Renaissance iconographical representations of Hercules' choice regularly presented a banquet scene as the primary symbol of the path of vice or pleasure.[20] Moreover, Satan's references in the discussion with Belial to Alexander and Scipio as notable exemplars of temperance with

respect to women, and his later allusions in the glory temptation to Alexander, Scipio, and Julius Caesar, reinforce the
emphasis upon the Hercules theme in this sequence, for as
A. R. Anderson has shown, all these heroes were identified
in classical times and thereafter as descendants of or successors to Hercules.[21] Satan's allusions to these personages invite
Christ to become another such latter-day Hercules figure.

It has already been noted that Hercules was one of the
two or three classical figures constantly interpreted as types
of Christ even by authors who undertook to eliminate pagan
mythology from their works. Medieval and Renaissance writers often amalgamated him with such recognized Old Testament types as David, Samson, and Jonah, and cited numerous
parallels between the stories of Hercules and Christ.[22] The
analogues noted by Ronsard are typical: both heroes were
Sons of God and a mortal mother; Hercules strangled serpents
in his cradle and Christ escaped in his infancy from Herod;
Hercules achieved his difficult labors and Christ conquered
Sin; Hercules freed Prometheus and Christ freed human nature from the Law and Sin; Hercules repudiated Deianira for
Iole and Christ repudiated the synagogue for the church;
Hercules conquered the many-headed Hydra and Christ conquered Satan; Hercules suffered on Oeta and Christ on
Calvary; Hercules chained Cerberus and liberated Persephone
and Christ overcame hell and liberated mankind.[23] However,
as with all the pagan mythological figures, Christian writers
also viewed Hercules from another perspective: in comparison with the historically real Old Testament figures he is
merely fictional, his feats of conquest over beasts, taken literally, are much inferior to the Christian's feats of conquest
over the self, and his legends are demonic and idolatrous deformations of Christ's deeds.[24] This double perspective operates significantly in the poem, for Satan invites Christ to
follow Hercules in his crude literal reality, whereas Christ

undertakes to relate himself to that figure in his moral and ethical signification.

By the Stoics and Cynics especially, Hercules was transformed from a strong man into a moral hero, a notable example of temperance as regards both sensual pleasures and worldly goods, who, because of this kingship over himself, became Jove's agent for restoring and ruling the earth. Seneca cited Hercules along with Odysseus and Cato as an example of the Stoic wise men, "unconquered by struggles...despisers of pleasure, and victors over all terrors." [25] Epictetus used the relative worldly position of Hercules and of King Eurystheus, whom he served, to derive a moral concerning the relation of temperance to kingship over the self and over others:

God does not give me much, no abundance, He does not want me to live luxuriously; He did not give much to Heracles, either, though he was His own son, but someone else [Eurystheus] was king over Argos and Mycenae, while he was subject, and suffered labours and discipline. And Eurystheus, such as he was, was not king over either Argos or Mycenae, for *he* was not king even over himself; but Heracles was ruler and leader of all the land and sea, purging them of injustice and lawlessness, and introducing justice and righteousness; and all this he did naked and by himself.[26]

The Cynic-Stoic Dio Chrysostom also emphasized Hercules' temperance in ignoring "gold or silver or fine raiment," and he affirmed the relation between Hercules' moral virtue and his public role by retelling the story of Hercules' choice as a test of kingly ideals. Hermes was sent by Zeus to show Hercules two mountain peaks: one, Peak Royal, was approached by a broad safe way and was ruled over by a lady who valued the fruits of the earth and living creatures more than gold and silver; her companions were Justice, Civil Order, Peace, and Law. The other mountain, Peak Tyranny, was approached by a narrow, crooked path and was ruled by a lady who dressed gorgeously, hugged her own gold to herself, and snatched at the wealth of others; her attendants were Cruelty, Insolence, Lawlessness, Faction, and Flattery. As a reward for choosing rightly between these two kingly prospects, Zeus entrusted Hercules with the kingship over all mankind, and his subsequent labors involved going about the world casting down tyrannies.[27]

This Stoic view of Hercules as a model of temperance and right kingly ideals was dominant in the Renaissance. George Sandys allegorized Hercules' conquests over beasts and monsters as representing "the excellency of Virtue in subduing inordinate affections." The Renaissance iconographical handbooks identified the three golden apples from the Garden of Hesperides, with which Hercules was commonly depicted, as symbolizing temperance in regard to anger, to sensual pleasure, and to worldly goods. And the Presbyterian Alexander Ross saw Hercules as "the type of a good king, who ought to subdue all monsters, cruelty, disorder, and oppression in his kingdom."[28]

At the conclusion of the banquet temptation Satan addresses Christ as one whose "invincible" temperance has enabled him to resist the banquet, the path of pleasure, and follow that other path of "high designs,/ High actions" (II.410–11). Satan then recommends and offers wealth as a necessity for achieving such goals, and especially for attaining kingly power, which would seem to be open to a man in Christ's position only by courting the favor of the multitude. As exemplar of such a path to kingship Satan proposes Antipater, one who, according to Josephus, "being well monied, and by nature both factious and industrious, and thorow ambition but badly affected toward *Aristobulus* [then king of the Jews] ... began to stir much trouble":[29] he fomented rebellion against the king, won Roman support, and at length enthroned his son in Israel. A pair of complementary pictures in the *Speculum Humanae Salvationis* shows Antipater on one side displaying his wounds received in battle to Julius Caesar and on this basis defending himself from charges of disloyalty, and, opposite to this, Christ manifesting his wounds to his Father as he intercedes in mankind's defense; the poetic commentary on the pictures interprets Antipater as a type of Christ.[30] In Antipater, then, as in Adam, Satan presents Christ with a recognized but distinctly inferior type of himself, whose actions he ought to imitate only in certain formal details but not in substance.

Christ sets four noble republican Romans over against the corrupt Antipater as nearer analogues of his own case—Curius, Fabricius, Quintius, and Regulus. In Stoic theory these are also latter-day Hercules figures, for though less exalted than Hercules they were favorite Stoic exemplars of temperance and willing poverty conjoined with noble political and military deeds.[31] A tradition also exists for viewing such heroes as quasi-types of Christ: in a passage probably suggestive for Milton's allusions here, Augustine linked together Regulus, Quintius, Fabricius, and Curtius (rather than Curius) as exemplars of virtue surpassing that of most Christians, and Tasso cited the Curzii, Decii, and Marcelli as models of a heroic virtue which is a "shadow and figure" of the divine love of Christ.[32]

Manius Dentatus Curius, the Roman consul who refused to take bribes from the Samnites or from Pyrrhus as an inducement to betray his city, reportedly responded as follows to the Samnites' astonishment at his very simple mode of life: "Curius had lever have domynyon over theym that be ryche, than he hym selfe to have richesse. And as for this golde, whiche ye accounte precious, take it agayne with you, & remembre, that ye can neyther vaynquishe me in batayle, nor corrupte me with money." [33] According to Seneca, the Roman general Caius Fabricius who withstood similar bribery attempts from the same sources thought it "greater than a king's crown to be able to scorn a king's money." [34] Seneca also explained Fabricius' poverty in terms suggestive for the banquet temptation:

Is Fabricius unfortunate because ... he wages war not less on riches than on Pyrrhus? because the roots and herbs on which he dines beside his hearth are those that he himself, an old man and honoured by a triumph, grubbed up in cleaning off his land? Tell me, then, would he be happier if he loaded his belly with fish from a distant shore and with birds from foreign parts? if he aroused the sluggishness of his loathing stomach with shell-fish from the eastern and the western sea? if he has game of the first order, which had been captured at the cost of many a hunter's life, served with fruit piled high around? [35]

Livy praised the Roman dictator Cincinnatus L. Quintius, who was twice called from the plough to become dictator and each time returned again to his poor condition, as a special example to those "who despise all human qualities in comparison with riches, and think there is no room for great honors or for worth but amidst a profusion of wealth," and Augustine cited him as a notable example for Christians. [36] M. Attibius Regulus was honored as a yet more perfect Stoic hero and a yet closer type of Christ in that, as Augustine said, he "was neither corrupted by prosperity, for he remained a very poor man after winning such victories; nor broken by adversity, for he returned intrepidly to the most miserable end." [37] Captured by Carthage and sent to Rome to arrange the release of the Carthaginian prisoners, he persuaded the Roman Senate that such action would not be in their interest, and then voluntarily returned to hideous torture and death in Carthage to honor his pledged word. [38]

At the end of Book II, then, Christ has answered Satan's promulgation of certain inferior types of himself—Adam, the romance knights, Antipater—by presenting himself as Second Hercules and by identifying himself also with those noble

Roman republican Hercules figures who, like Hercules, display temperance with regard to sensual pleasure and worldly gain and also understand rightly the responsibilities of power and rule. Satan derives his next temptation directly from Christ's manifestation of such lofty virtue. Arguing that this virtue will make Christ an infallible counselor and an invincible conqueror of the entire world, Satan urges him to such dominion as a means to win glory, the good "That sole excites to high attempts the flame/ Of most erected Spirits" (III.26–27), and that which led such "erected Spirits" as Alexander, Caesar, Pompey, and Scipio to renounce pleasure and worldly gain just as Christ has done. This is the familiar satanic attempt to foist upon Christ a literal view of the type with which he has identified himself, for these personages have long been recognized as progeny and/or successors of Hercules, and imitators of his temperance. They are, however, heirs to a literal, militaristic definition of Hercules' mission rather than to the moral and typological conception to which Christ has appealed. By these new allusions Satan invites Christ to identify himself with them rather than with Hercules himself and the noble Romans who are his true successors in the moral realm.

Classical tradition viewed Alexander as a descendant of and successor to Hercules, and sometimes as, like him, a son of Jove; the medieval Alexandrian romances provide a basis for seeing him also as a type of Christ.[39] His Hercules-like temperance—the immediate point of Satan's reference to him in speaking to Belial—was emphasized in Plutarch's account of his preserving the chastity of the mother, wife, and daughters of Darius because he thought it "more princely for a king... to conquer himselfe, then to overcome his enemies," and also in the story of his refusing the delicate foods and skilled cooks sent to him by the queen of Casia.[40] In addition, Plutarch imagined a discourse between Alexander and Diogenes the

Cynic in which Alexander defends his military conquests as a Herculean mission of civilizing the world:

Were I not *Alexander,* I would be *Diogenes*...I could willingly employ my whole life and spend my time at my booke and in contemplation, but that I am determined to be a Philosopher in deed and action...[I have] proposed to my selfe to joine together in mutuall societie, Barbarous nations with the Greeks, and by travelling in voiage thorow the earth, to polish and make civill what savage people soever I find....I follow *Hercules,* I take the way of *Perseus.*[41]

But the Stoics denounced Alexander as a false Hercules figure despite his temperance, on the grounds that he enslaved himself by coveting glory, that he pursued false glory by military conquest, and that he wickedly pretended to divine honors. Therefore Seneca vehemently objected to Alexander's relating himself to Hercules,

slave as he was to glory, of which he knew neither the true nature nor the limitations, following the footsteps of Hercules and of Bacchus...Yet what resemblance to him [Hercules] had that mad youth who instead of virtue showed fortunate rashness? Hercules conquered nothing for himself; he traversed the world, not in coveting, but in deciding what to conquer, a foe of the wicked, a defender of the good, a peacemaker on land and sea. But this other was from his boyhood a robber and a plunderer of nations, a scourge alike to his friends and to his foes, one who found his highest happiness in terrorizing all mortals.[42]

And the Stoic Dio Chrysostom offered a very different version from Plutarch's of the encounter between Diogenes and Alexander, in which Diogenes chides the king for failure to attain kingship over the self:

"You are yourself your own bitterest foe and adversary as long as you are bad and foolish."...For he knew that Alexander was a slave of glory..."O perverse man, do not attempt to be king before you have attained to wisdom. And in the meantime...it is better not to give orders to others but to live in solitude, clothed in a sheepskin.... If you will drop your conceit and your present occu-pations, you will be a king, not in word maybe, but in reality." [43]

Cicero, Livy, Seneca, and various Christian writers such as Clement of Alexandria and George Sandys also emphasized Alexander's overweening pride in seeking deification. As Sam-uel Clarke put the case, "He grew so proud and insolent, that he suffered his Souldiers to fall down and worship him like a God. Yea, he commanded his servants, and slaves to do so." [44]

Caesar and Pompey were Hercules figures cast in the Alex-andrian mold. As Plutarch records, Caesar wept bitterly be-cause "king *Alexander* being no older then my selfe is now, had in old time wonne so many nations and countries: and ... I hitherto have done nothing worthy of my selfe." Also, ac-cording to Plutarch, Caesar had gained power by the methods recommended to Christ in the wealth temptation: "he was very liberall in expences, buying (as some thought) but a vaine and short glorie of the favour of the people ... Some say, that before he bare any office in the commonwealth, he was growne in debt, to the summe of thirteene hundred talents." [45] Cicero denounced both Caesar and Pompey as base and wretched, in that "both of them have always re-garded the safety and honor of their country as less important than their own ascendancy and personal interest," and Chris-tians such as Samuel Clarke pointed to Caesar's wicked as-sumption of divine glory in the Alexandrian manner. [46]

Scipio was a special case. He was identified as a Hercules figure by rumors of Jovian parentage; by stories of his Hercu-lean temperance regarding women, manifested in sparing a beautiful Spanish captive betrothed to an enemy soldier; and by the account of his youthful "Hercules' choice" between Pleasure, who urged him to avoid war, and Virtue, who held before him the example of Hercules' destruction of all the monsters throughout the earth. [47] There is some basis in

Cicero's *De Re Publica* for Christ's conditional reference to Scipio as perhaps an exemplar of true glory, for Cicero presents Scipio as spokesman for that glory which is wholly opposed to the "gossip of the vulgar herd," which is attendant upon "excellence," and which is given only by the gods to "men who have served their country well." [48] Yet there is also a basis for Satan's assimilation of Scipio to the Alexandrian company in Lactantius' denunciation of him as one of those militarists who believe

that there is no other way to immortality than to lead armies, to lay waste the territory of others, to destroy cities, to overthrow towns, to put to death or enslave free peoples.... In Ennius Africanus thus speaks: "If it is permitted any one to ascend to the regions of the gods above, the greatest gate of heaven is open to me alone." Because, in truth, he extinguished and destroyed a great part of the human race. Oh how great the darkness in which you were involved, O Africanus, or rather O poet, in that you imagined the ascent to heaven to be open to men through slaughters and bloodshed! [49]

Christ's evaluation of glory in *Paradise Regained* is evidently closely patterned upon those Stoic-Christian texts in which Alexander, Caesar, Scipio, and Pompey served as illustrations of the false renown conferred by the multitude, the false glory attending upon military conquest for world dominion, and the impiety of seeking divine honors:

> They err who count it glorious to subdue
> By Conquest far and wide, to overrun
> Large Countries, and in field great Battles win,
> Great Cities by assault: what do these Worthies,
> But rob and spoil, burn, slaughter, and enslave
> Peaceable Nations, neighboring or remote,
> Made Captive, yet deserving freedom more
> Than those thir Conquerors, who leave behind
> Nothing but ruin whereso'er they rove,

> And all the flourishing works of peace destroy,
> Then swell with pride, and must be titl'd Gods,
> Great Benefactors of mankind, Deliverers,
> Worship't with Temple, Priest and Sacrifice?
> One is the Son of *Jove,* of *Mars* the other,
> Till Conqueror Death discover them scarce men,
> Rolling in brutish vices, and deform'd. (III.71–86)

At length Christ appeals to Socrates as the noblest classical type of himself and as the direct contrast to the glory-seeking world conquerors:

> Poor *Socrates* (who next more memorable?)
> By what he taught and suffer'd for so doing,
> For truth's sake suffering death unjust, lives now
> Equal in fame to proudest Conquerors. (III.96–99)

Behind this statement is a tradition of commentary pointing to Socrates' death for truth's sake at the hands of the Athenian masses as foreshadowing Christ's death, and to his teaching as prefiguring Christ's doctrine. Justin Martyr's statement is especially suggestive:

And when Socrates endeavoured, by true reason and examination, to bring these things to light, and deliver men from the demons, then the demons themselves, by means of men who rejoiced in iniquity, compassed his death ... and in our case they display a similar activity. For not only among the Greeks did reason (Logos) prevail to condemn these things through Socrates, but also among the Barbarians were they condemned by Reason (or the Word, the Logos) Himself, who took shape, and became man, and was called Jesus Christ. ...

Christ ... was partially known even by Socrates (for He was and is the Word who is in every man, and who foretold the things that were to come to pass both through the prophets and in His own person).[50]

Socrates was also seen as a Hercules figure. Plato records that Socrates termed his fruitless searches to find a man wiser than himself as "Herculean labours," Xenophon ascribed the story of Hercules' choice to Socrates, and various legends attributed to him a remarkable, Hercules-like poverty and temperance.[51] A further basis for relating Hercules and Socrates is the curious iconographical portrayal of Hercules among the Celts as an old, bald-headed man carrying the traditional lionskin and club and dragging after him a crowd of men tethered by the ears with chains of gold; this Hercules Ogmius emblem is illuminated by Lucian's comment "that the real Heracles was a wise man who achieved everything by eloquence and applied persuasion as his principal force." [52] The emblem continued to be so drawn and so interpreted in the Renaissance.[53]

Accordingly, when Christ at the conclusion of the glory temptation appeals to Socrates as the noblest classical type of himself, he presents himself at one level as the new Hercules after the Socratic pattern (the teacher of, and willing sufferer for, mankind) rather than after the inferior Alexandrian pattern of the world conqueror.

THE CLASSICAL PHILOSOPHERS AS TYPES: THE SOCRATES MOTIF

By the allusion to Socrates, Christ also identifies himself with the ultimate source of the various ethical principles he has been enunciating throughout this sequence. As Satan observes later in presenting the learning temptation, Socrates was the river

> from whose mouth issu'd forth
> Mellifluous streams that water'd all the schools
> Of Academics old and new, with those
> Surnam'd *Peripatetics,* and the Sect
> *Epicurean,* and the *Stoic* severe. (IV.276–80)

In the banquet-wealth-glory sequence Christ often enunciates classical ethical principles, so frequently indeed that several critics have been led to explain Christ's character primarily in terms of one or another of the classical ethical ideals. Thus

H. J. C. Grierson, E. M. W. Tillyard, and others have ascribed
Stoicism to Christ, Merritt Hughes has traced his resemblance
to Aristotle's magnanimous man, and Irene Samuel has described him as a good Platonist engaged in dialogue with a
sophistical Satan.[54] For excellent reasons no one has suggested
an Epicurean Christ: in the banquet temptation Christ flatly rejects, among other things, the Epicurean ideal of the good life
as the pursuit of refined pleasure. In his *De Finibus* Cicero has
his Stoic spokesman summarize, in terms quite suggestive for
the banquet temptation, the life of the Epicurean wise men,

> with first-rate chefs and confectioners, fish, birds, game, and all of
> the very best; careful of their digestion; with "Wine in flask/ De-
> canted from a new-broach'd cask," . . . with the accompaniment of
> dramatic performances and their usual sequel, the pleasures apart
> from which Epicurus, as he loudly proclaims, does not know what
> Good is; give them also beautiful boys to wait upon them, with
> drapery, silver, Corinthian bronzes, and the scene of the feast,
> the banqueting room, all in keeping.[55]

It seems, though, that instead of identifying himself with one
particular classical ideal from the outset, Christ assimilates
principles common to the Stoics, the Academics, and the
Peripatetics, especially in his definition of the ideal kingship
over self: [56]

> What if with like aversion I reject
> Riches and Realms; yet not for that a Crown,
> Golden in show, is but a wreath of thorns,
> Brings dangers, troubles, cares, and sleepless nights
> To him who wears the Regal Diadem,
> When on his shoulders each man's burden lies:
> For therein stands the office of a King,
> His Honor, Virtue, Merit and chief Praise,
> That for the Public all this weight he bears.
> Yet he who reigns within himself, and rules
> Passions, Desires, and Fears, is more a King;

Which every wise and virtuous man attains:
And who attains not, ill aspires to rule
Cities of men, or headstrong Multitudes,
Subject himself to Anarchy within,
Or lawless passions in him, which he serves.
But to guide Nations in the way of truth
By saving Doctrine, and from error lead
To know, and knowing worship God aright,
Is yet more Kingly; this attracts the Soul,
Governs the inner man, the nobler part;
That other o'er the body only reigns,
And oft by force, which to a generous mind
So reigning can be no sincere delight.
Besides, to give a Kingdom hath been thought
Greater and nobler done, and to lay down
Far more magnanimous than to assume. (II.457–83)

In this passage Christ appears to recognize as types of himself and of his moral teaching the noblest ethical ideals of antiquity—the Aristotelian magnanimous man, the Stoic wise man, the Platonic-Socratic just man or philosopher—but in the course of the sequence he distinguishes among these ideals, and affirms the highest.

Christ's use of the term "magnanimous" in reference to his refusal of a kingdom suggests his relationship to Aristotle's magnanimous man. Aristotle defined the good and happy life as "activity of soul in accordance with virtue," [57] he defined the virtues as means between excessive and defective action and passion, and he prescribed moderation of the passions and desires. Aristotle's magnanimous man is one who leads the life of virtue on the heroic scale:

Now the man is thought to be proud [magnanimous] who thinks himself worthy of great things, being worthy of them ... It is honour that they chiefly claim, but in accordance with their deserts...
Greatness in every virtue would seem to be characteristic of a proud man.... Pride, then, seems to be a sort of crown of the virtues;

for it makes them greater, and it is not found without them.... At honours that are great and conferred by good men he will be moderately pleased ... [But] not even towards honour does he bear himself as if it were a very great thing. Power and wealth are desirable for the sake of honour (at least those who have them wish to get honour by means of them); and for him to whom even honour is a little thing the others must be so to.... He is the sort of man to confer benefits, but he is ashamed of receiving them; for the one is the mark of a superior, the other of an inferior.[58]

Milton's definition in *De Doctrina,* "Magnanimity is shown, when in the seeking or avoiding, the acceptance or refusal of riches, advantages, or honors, we are actuated by a regard to our own dignity, rightly understood," [59] is obviously derived (with some modification) from Aristotle, and the Christ of the poem displays some of the qualities Aristotle enumerates. But Christ's attitude toward wealth and even toward food as wholly unnecessary for his happiness or for his mission is quite at odds with the Peripatetic ideal, which recognized as contributory to happiness such external goods as long life, friends, and moderate "prosperity" on the ground that "it is impossible, or not easy, to do noble deeds without the proper equipment." [60] Christ's denigration of honor stemming from military conquest has no parallel in Aristotle who had Alexander for his pupil, and Christ's definition of magnanimity as involving more often a repudiation of honors than an acceptance of them has little if any warrant in the Aristotelian conception. It has some affinity, though, with the Christianized conception of magnanimity, or heroic virtue, explained by Tasso, Bruno, and Castiglione as the renunciation of the world in order to pursue perfection or the contemplative life.[61] The most important difference is that Aristotle's magnanimous man seeks "honour in accordance with his deserts," whereas Milton's Christ does not seek his own glory, "but his/ Who sent me" (III.106–7).

Again, Christ's behavior in totally rejecting all Satan's offers, and the terms used to describe that rejection—his stated "aversion" to riches and realms (II.457–58), his frequent references to the noted Stoic exemplars of temperance and self-conquest, Satan's observation that he is "unmov'd" by hunger—seem to relate Christ to the Stoic wise man in the rigorous formulation of that ideal which owes much to Cynic asceticism. The Stoics defined man's proper activity as a life according to reason and termed the practice of virtue the sole good and the sole requirement for man's happiness. In his complete self-sufficiency the Cynic-Stoic wise man repudiated sensual pleasure as unworthy of him, found worldly goods and ambitions worthless, took special pride in his ability to withstand pains, and attained not merely the control but the complete elimination of "Passions, Desires, and Fears."

The following statements are typical of the sterner variety of Stoic attitudes. Cicero declares:

How dignified, how lofty, how consistent is the character of the Wise Man as they [the Stoics] depict it! Since reason has proved that moral worth is the sole good, it follows that he must always be happy ... For he will have a better claim to the title of King than Tarquin, who could not rule either himself or his subjects; a better right to the name of "Master of the People" (for that is what a dictator is) than Sulla, who was a master of three pestilential vices, licentiousness, avarice and cruelty.[62]

According to Dio Chrysostom,

The noble man holds his hardships to be his greatest antagonists, and with them he is ever wont to battle day and night ... grappling with hunger and cold, withstanding thirst, and disclosing no weakness even though he must endure the lash or give his body to be cut or burned.... To pleasure he must give the widest berth possible and have none but unavoidable dealings with her. And herein the strongest man is indeed strongest, one might almost say, who can keep the farthest away from pleasures; for it is impossible to dwell with pleasure or even to dally with her for any length of time without being completely enslaved.[63]

Seneca states:

The question has often been raised whether it is better to have moderate emotions, or none at all. Philosophers of our school reject the emotions; the Peripatetics keep them in check. I, however, do not understand how any half-way disease can be either wholesome or helpful.

Pleasure is low, petty, to be deemed worthless, shared even by dumb animals—the tiniest and meanest of whom fly towards pleasure. Glory is an empty and fleeting thing, lighter than air. Poverty is an evil to no man unless he kick against the goads. Death is not an evil.

Learn to be content with little, and cry out with courage and with greatness of soul: "We have water, we have porridge; let us compete in happiness with Jupiter himself." And why not, I pray thee, make this challenge even without porridge and water? For it is base to make the happy life depend upon silver and gold, and just as base to make it depend upon water and porridge.

In what respect is Jupiter superior to our good man? His goodness lasts longer; but the wise man does not set a lower value upon himself, just because his virtues are limited by a briefer span... The wise man surveys and scorns all the possessions of others as calmly as does Jupiter, and regards himself with the greater esteem because, while Jupiter cannot make use of them, he, the wise man, does not wish to do so.[64]

Christ displays here the endurance and self-conquest of the Stoic moral hero, but his perspective differs significantly from that of the Stoics. His self-conquest is not grounded upon his own self-sufficiency but upon his trust in God. He shows genuine concern, not impassivity, when he first experiences hunger, and he is consoled not by the thought that nothing external is necessary to him but by the belief that God can sustain his body without food if need be. He does not disdain or flee from pleasure as unworthy or dangerous but freely enters into the "pleasant Grove,/ With chant of tuneful Birds" (II.289–90) to rest at noonday, and though he shuns the satanic banquet he dreams of sharing a temperate meal with Elijah or Daniel. He does not repudiate absolutely any of the goods offered, or deny them to be goods, but rather he distinguishes: wealth is unnecessary because God can raise men up from poverty; kingship over the self and rule by persuasion are higher forms of rule than civil kingship; true glory is not in military conquest but is given by God to such men as Socrates and Job, for "deeds of peace, by wisdom eminent" (III.91). Most important, in repudiating Satan's invitation to seek Godlike glory in imitation of his Father (III.109–10) Christ formally repudiates Seneca's conception of the Stoic wise man as equal to Jupiter and deserving of even more honor for his perfect virtue.

Ultimately, as Irene Samuel has argued, Christ relates himself most closely to the Socratic-Platonic philosopher or lover of wisdom, whose reason wholly rules over and controls the less noble portions of the soul—the appetitive principle which seeks sensual pleasure and money as well as the passionate part which is concerned with ambition and honor—and who is, accordingly, "most royal... and king over himself." [65] But in the Socratic-Platonic system the goods sought by the less noble portions of the soul are still recognized as goods and may legitimately be sought, though the philosopher will seek first to acquire "justice, temperance, and wisdom" and will estimate all other goods as they conduce to this end:

In the first place, he will honour the studies which impress these qualities on his soul, and will disregard others.... He will be so far from entrusting his bodily habit and sustenance to brutal and irrational pleasures... that he will regard even health as quite a

secondary matter ... He will always desire to attemper the body as
to preserve the harmony of the soul.... He will not allow himself
to be dazzled by the foolish applause of the world, and heap up
riches to his own infinite harm.... He will look at the city which
is within him, and take heed that no disorder occur in it, such as
might arise either from superfluity or from want; and upon this
principle he will regulate his property and gain or spend according
to his means.... He will gladly accept and enjoy such honours as
he deems likely to make him a better man; but those, whether private or public, which are likely to disorder his life, he will avoid.[66]

Finally, the just man can expect that all good things will come
to him in the end: "Then this must be our notion of the just
man, that even when he is in poverty or sickness, or any other
seeming misfortune, these things will bring him finally to some
good end, either in life, or perhaps in death; for the gods
surely will not neglect anyone whose earnest desire is to become just and by the pursuit of virtue to be like God, as far
as man can attain the divine likeness." [67] Similarly, Christ
does not define kingship over the self as the elimination of,
but rather as the rule over, "Passions, Desires, and Fears."
His endurance and apparent repudiation of goods are not
based upon self-sufficiency but upon confidence in God's care:
God can sustain his body without food; he can raise men
from poverty to kingship; and he will give glory to those who
seek "his glory, not thir own" (III.143–44). And Christ, like
the Socratic just man, finds that his trials come to a good end,
for all the goods he has refused on the Devil's terms are attained by or promised to him in greatly exalted form at the
conclusion of the temptation.

In the banquet-wealth-glory sequence, then, Christ states
the high ethical principles common to several of the pagan
schools, displays in his own behavior the heroic ideal of self-
conquest defined by the most rigorous of them, the Stoics,
but finally identifies himself with the ethical perspective of
the Platonic Socrates. This identification will form the starting

point for the learning temptation, in which Satan will invite Christ to a literal and complete identification with the pagan ethical teachers.

THE BIBLICAL TYPES OF KINGSHIP OVER THE SELF

Though it has been useful to consider the classical motifs first in this sequence, since much of the dialogue is carried on in terms of classical ethics, it is time to recall that biblical types are conjoined with and given priority over their pagan counterparts. Daniel is paired with Hercules as a figure with whom Christ identifies himself during his nocturnal sensations of hunger and during the banquet temptation. The linking is wholly appropriate, for traditional exegesis named Daniel as the prime Old Testament example of temperance, continence, conquest over sensuality, and the contemplative life.[68] Though the allusion to Hercules is only implicit in the banquet temptation, both Christ and Satan refer explicitly to Daniel as one subjected to a fast and tempted by exotic food. The narrator recounts Christ's hunger dreams in which Christ imagines himself a "guest with *Daniel* at his pulse" (II.278), that is, sharing the coarse food which the young Daniel, a captive in Babylon, ate and grew fat upon while he abstained for ten days from the delicacies provided him from King Nebuchadnezzar's table (Dan. i:1-6). Satan also refers to that incident in his lying assurances to Christ that the banquet he is offering does not resemble Nebuchadnezzar's: "nor mention I/ Meats by the Law unclean, or offer'd first/ To Idols, those young *Daniel* could refuse;/ Nor proffer'd by an Enemy" (II.327-30). Satan's comment sums up the several motives usually alleged for Daniel's abstention from the king's meat. As Diodati explained, Daniel fasted "either because there might be amongst that food some flesh, which was by the law uncleane: or that had beene consecrated to Idols; or because he feared he should endamage and corrupt his piety and purity through the allurements and pleasures of the Court." [69] However,

Calvinist exegetes tended to view Daniel's refusal chiefly as an exercise of temperance, arguing that he showed his freedom from the ceremonial law and from the scruple regarding meat offered to idols by the fact that he later ate that food. Calvin stated that Daniel "dyd ... chuse rather pulse and most base dyet, not that he thought it unlawfull for him and hys felowes to eate of the kynges meate & to drinke wyne: but he dyd see what a hard thyng it is to kepe a measure in full tables and dayntie fare, and how soone we are deceyved when we are enterteyned and fed delicately." And the Geneva Bible explained that he abstained so that "the king shoulde not entise him by this sweete poyson to forget his religion and accustomed sobrietie." [70]

Christ is a Second Daniel, then, in his refusal to eat forbidden food, and in his refusal to eat delicacies offered by an enemy to undermine his temperance. Moreover, as one of the four major prophets Daniel was a recognized type of Christ's prophetical office, and his abstention from food was interpreted as a type of Christ's fast in the wilderness. [71] Also, the apocryphal story of Daniel's conquest of Bel and the Dragon, both of them figures of gluttony and sensuality, was often presented as a type of Christ's victory in the first temptation: in the various versions of the *Speculum Humanae Salvationis,* pictures of the first temptation are paired with pictures of Daniel unmasking and destroying the idol Bel who supposedly devoured gifts of food really consumed by his corrupt priests, and of Daniel thrusting a bolus of pitch and grease into the Dragon's mouth. [72] We are conscious of Daniel throughout the remainder of this sequence, for his rise from slave to ruler in Babylon makes him an analogue of those biblical figures Christ cites in the wealth temptation. And in the following sequence Christ defines his kingdom in terms of Daniel's prophecy.

In his response to the wealth-ambition temptation, Christ cites David, Gideon, and Jephthah as biblical types analogous to the four noble Romans. In their willing poverty, their modest aspirations, their proper attitudes toward kingship or dominion, these biblical figures are also exemplars of the broader temperance, the kingship over self, which is Christ's dominant concern in Book II.

David became king in fact over the nation of Israel, and Christ meditated, when walking out into the desert, upon the prophecy that he himself would "sit on *David's* Throne" (I.240). Naturally enough, he now thinks again of David's story as a type of his own ultimate elevation, despite poverty, to a public throne, referring to

> the Shepherd lad,
> Whose offspring on the Throne of *Judah* sat
> So many Ages, and shall yet regain
> That seat, and reign in *Israel* without end. (II.439–42)

Christ's identification of himself with David recalls the parallels usually cited as bases for the typological relationship. Henry Vertue summarizes several such parallels, drawn from Athanasius:

David was a Shepherd, and Christ a Shepherd; but *David* of Sheep, Christ of Souls. *Samuel*, a Priest, annointed *David* to be a King; and *John*, as a Priest, baptized our Saviour. *David*, being annointed to be a King, came not presently to the Kingdom, but was content for a long time to serve *Saul*: and so our Saviour, though he was begotten a King from all Eternity, was yet content to serve...*Saul* persecuted David, and Herod persecuted Christ ...*Absalon, Davids* Son, rose up against his Father: and *Judas* rose up against Christ....*David* was annointed by man, but Christ by his Almighty Father.[73]

The comment in the Geneva Bible that "God would exercise him [David] in sundry sortes before he had the use of his kingdome,"[74] offers a basis for close identification of the young David's troubles and adventures with Christ's temptations. In the *Speculum Humanae Salvationis* David's victory over the bear and the lion is paired with and presented as a type of Christ's resistance to the kingdoms temptation (avarice and ambition), and David's defeat of Goliath is similarly related to Christ's overcoming the temptation of the tower (vainglory).[75] The David-Goliath story was also commonly interpreted as a type of Christ's defeat of Satan at the Crucifixion and at the Harrowing of Hell.[76] At this point in the poem, then, Christ sees himself as Second David because he also expects to obtain the throne of Israel after overcoming great difficulties, but the full implications of the Christ-David typology await exploration in the next sequence.

Gideon exemplifies another attitude toward civil kingship— rejection of it—paralleling Christ's rejection of the kingship offered by Satan. As one of the judges called upon to save Israel from her enemies, he typifies Christ as Savior of the world.[77] His humble response to the call of the angelic messenger—"Oh my lord, wherewith shall I save Israel? behold, my family is poore in Manasseh, and I am the least in my fathers house" (Judges vi:15)—was understood to foreshadow Mary's answer to the angel at the Annunciation. Also, his conquest of the Midianites was seen as a type of Christ's conquest over Satan at the Harrowing, and more especially his victory by means of his cross.[78] In the poem Christ cites Gideon as an example of one raised from poverty to greatness, but he serves also as a type of Christ's repudiation of kingship, for he had declared to those offering him ruling power, "I will not rule over you, neither shall my son rule over you: the Lord shall rule over you" (Judges viii:23). In his *De Doctrina* Milton had linked Gideon with Christ as examples of magnanimity in refusing kingdoms, and Peter Martyr also referred to this action of Gideon's as a type of Christ's refusal of civil kingship offered him by the multitude.[79] Moreover, Gideon's story also foreshadows that form of public kingship which Christ asserts as his own particular ideal—"to guide Nations in the way of truth" (II.473)—for the sword Gideon carried into battle was interpreted as a type of the scriptural sword of the Spirit, and the trumpets whose blast brought victory to Gideon's three hundred soldiers were understood to signify "the preaching of the Gospel, now spread abroade throughout the whole worlde." [80]

Jephthah exemplifies another conception of kingship relevant to Christ's situation, for Jephthah attains to the judgeship only after rejection by his own people and the sacrifice of his own flesh. Christ's reference to him in the poem alludes to his disinheritance by his legitimate brethren as the son of a harlot, "Thou shalt not inherit in our fathers house, for thou art the sonne of a strange woman" (Judges xi:2), a rejection commonly interpreted as a type of Christ's rejection and passion brought about by the Jews. Henry Vertue states the common analogues, quoting Augustine:

The name *Jephte* signifies *opening:* so Christ opened to his Disciples the sense of the Scriptures concerning himself: *Luke* 24-27. *Jephte's* Brethren rejected him, and cast him out of his Father's house, objecting to him, that he was a Bastard ... So delt the chief Priests with Christ ... *Jephte* fled; and so did Christ ... *Jephte's* Brethren, that cast him out, turn to him, and seek him, that they might be saved by him from the *Ammonites:* which clearly fore-signifies, that they, who rejected him, turning to him, finde Salvation in him. [81]

More especially, Jephthah's sacrifice of his daughter in accordance with his vow was interpreted by the Fathers and many later exegetes as typifying, in Prosper's words, "the Lord Jesus, our only Judge and Captain [who] ... offered up his flesh, as his only Virgin Daughter." [82] Jephthah is then a type of Christ as a suffering and sacrificing ruler; his specific classical analogue in this sequence is Regulus, who also sacrificed his own flesh.

As all the virtues of the noble classical types were at length subsumed in Socrates, to whom Christ related himself at the conclusion of the glory temptation, so are the noble qualities of the biblical types—temperance, willing poverty, kingship over the self, lofty ideals of public kingship, patient suffering— subsumed in Job, whose name Christ links with that of Socrates, but whom he praises as a yet greater hero. We are made conscious of Job earlier in this sequence when Satan echoes one of Job's comforters in describing Christ as "Lost in a Desert here and hunger-bit" (II.416).[83] At the conclusion of the glory temptation Christ refers not once but twice to Job as the apex of human heroism. The sources and bases of this common view of Job have been discussed above,[84] but we may cite here as of special relevance to the themes of this sequence, Drexelius' assertion of Job's superiority to all the notable classical heroes, even Regulus:

History, both sacred and profane, proposed exceptional men in all ages as examples of virtue to be emulated. Homer produced King Agamemnon as a very prudent prince in whom virtue can be contemplated by others even as in a mirror. In the same way Achilles is displayed to our eyes. So also Maro set forth Aeneas as a wise and pious king. So also the poets sang of Hercules, unconquerable by the will of his stepmother, destroying all the monsters of the earth and subduing all by labor and patience. So Xenophon extoled Cyrus and showed that king as a specimen of all royal and heroic virtues. But it would be sensible for these good writers to cease speaking of those who stood as merely imitators [of Job] in worth...None [was] greater than Regulus who kept faith in rendering himself up to the enemy and exhibited patience and constancy in suffering torture. Up to the present day the praise of this man is held in memory on three counts: one of his justice, another of his fortitude, a third of his admirable patience. But farewell, my Regulus, our Job triumphs more gloriously in all three.[85]

Christ's first reference to Job, alluding to that heavenly scene wherein God exalted Job as a just man and thereby provoked Satan's envy and desire to tempt him, points directly to Job as type of Christ by recalling the very similar scene which in the poem preceded Christ's temptation:

> This is true glory and renown, when God
> Looking on th'Earth, with approbation marks
> The just man, and divulges him through Heaven
> . . . .
> thus he did to *Job*. (III.60–64)

A later reference praising Job above all others for his "deeds of peace," his "wisdom eminent," his patience and temperance (III.91–92), further emphasizes Christ's conception of Job as the most notable type of his own heroic role. We may recall at this point the tradition specifically linking Job's temptations to Christ's (and Adam's) in terms of the triple equation, and that Job as sinless hero, as great sufferer, as prophet of Christ's coming, and as prefiguration of Christ's three offices of prophet, priest, and king, was distinguished by many exegetes as the most complete type of Christ.[86]

Thus, at the conclusion of the banquet-wealth-glory sequence, during which Satan sought to overcome Christ by means of Adam's temptations, Christ identifies himself most closely with Job who had already conquered Satan on this same ground. He also links Job and Socrates together as exemplifying the highest ideals of moral virtue and as presenting the most perfect types of himself in antiquity. But Socrates and Job also represent, traditionally, the highest ideals of wisdom in their respective cultures. The Socratic and Jobean wisdom will be directly contrasted in the learning temptation, when Christ will be forced to distinguish between them and ultimately to pass beyond both these types to the assertion of his own unique wisdom.

*W*ITH the words, "But to a Kingdom thou art born,
ordain'd/ To sit upon thy Father *David's* Throne"
(III.152–53), Satan shifts the frame of reference
from the kingdom within to the public realm. The sequence concerning the inner kingdom has involved kingly
power and glory considered as objects of desire, but Satan
now suggests to Christ that whether or not he values such
goods in themselves, he is nevertheless called to be some
kind of king. He may not rest in the achievement of perfect
kingship over the self but must assume a public kingly office.
This theme was touched upon in the glory temptation, when
Satan observed that Christ's perfect virtue itself constitutes a
natural call to public service, but it becomes dominant with
Satan's reference here to Christ's divinely ordained kingly role.
This third major segment of the poem is principally concerned
with the challenge to and the full revelation of Christ's kingly
office, and, most appropriately, the temptations addressed to
Christ in this character are set forth as public displays of
specific kingdoms, Parthia and Rome.

In introducing this theme Satan refers to King David, whom
Christ has already mentioned as the chief Old Testament type
of his kingly office in his opening meditation and in the wealth-
ambition temptation (II.439–42). Repeating his earlier strategy Satan now alludes to David (and Judas Maccabaeus),
inviting Christ to identify his kingly role completely with those
Old Testament exemplars and types of it, whereas Christ must
discover in the course of the temptation precisely how he
ought to fulfill the type in spiritual terms, and how he is to
move beyond the Davidic kingdom to discover and affirm his

own unique kingly office. In *De Doctrina* Milton defines Christ's kingdom as existing in two stages: the Kingdom of Grace (the invisible church), which is at hand, and the Kingdom of Glory (the millennial kingdom), which is to come.[1] Accordingly, the dialogue throughout this sequence alludes frequently to the exposed position of the church in its encounters with the world throughout history, but also to its confident expectation of glorious triumph in the millennium. Indeed, as Fixler has pointed out, one important aspect of Satan's craft is to invite Christ to confuse the two stages of the kingdom, to inaugurate the millennial rule over all the earth when his business is rather to establish the wholly spiritual Kingdom of Grace, the church.[2] Throughout this present sequence, then, we are made especially aware that the temptation episode subsumes not only the Hebrew and classical past but all subsequent Christian history.

The dramatic action in this portion of the poem rises to a climax in which Christ gains another divine insight into his mission, this time into the full implications of his kingly office. Again, much of the dramatic tension develops over the matter of Christ's nature—the problem of the sonship. In the highly charged transition passage between the temptations to glory and to Parthia, Satan emphasizes yet another paternity for Christ identifying him as David's son and heir, "ordain'd/ To sit upon thy Father *David's* Throne;/ By Mother's side thy Father" (III.152–54). The transition passage also marks a significant turning point in the battle of wits, as Christ for the first time attacks Satan directly, challenging him to account for his implausible pose of solicitude about the kingdom:

> But what concerns it thee when I begin
> My everlasting Kingdom? Why art thou
> Solicitous? What moves thy inquisition?
> Know'st thou not that my rising is thy fall,
> And my promotion will be thy destruction? (III.198–202)

Satan's reply is masterly. He is "inly rackt" (III.203) and shows
it, giving vent to the anxiety and dismay that have been welling
up in him from the beginning of the poem:

> I would be at the worst; worst is my Port,
> My harbor and my ultimate repose,
> The end I would attain, my final good.
> My error was my error, and my crime
> My crime; whatever, for itself condemn'd,
> And will alike be punish'd; whether thou
> Reign or reign not; though to that gentle brow
> Willingly I could fly, and hope thy reign,
> From that placid aspect and meek regard,
> Rather than aggravate my evil state,
> Would stand between me and thy Father's ire
> (Whose ire I dread more than the fire of Hell)
> A shelter and a kind of shading cool
> Interposition, as a summer's cloud.
> If I then to the worst that can be haste,
> Why move thy feet so slow to what is best. (III.209–24)

As Stein has argued, the despair and agony and recklessness
sounded in this speech are genuinely moving,[3] but our sym-
pathy, I would suggest, is almost immediately deflected by a
new and appalling apprehension of Satan's corruption, as we
realize that what looks like a genuine emotion, a "moment
of truth" on Satan's part, can like everything else be manipu-
lated by him for his own ends. We know that he does not
really seek the Port of Worst but is even here trying to corrupt Christ so as to avoid it; we see the audacity of his
suggestion that Christ become priest and mediator for him instead of his designated conqueror; and we gasp at the rhetorical craft which can turn all this to account in framing an
argument to urge Christ to hasten to his own kingdom.

Moving quickly from this contested ground, Satan then presents the remarkable vision of Parthia, both as a means to
give the inexperienced, rustic Christ some acquaintance with

courts, and also as a display of the means which Christ needs
to make him truly David's son and heir—armed might and
control over the ten lost tribes which alone can install him
"In *David's* royal seat, his true Successor" (III.373). Christ's
answer shows his developing understanding of the metaphor
of the Davidic sonship: he recognizes that he does not need
the lost tribes to hold that title, and he has full confidence
that at the proper time he will not be "slack" in endeavoring
what is needful for his kingdom (III.398). His tranquil observation of the pageant of Parthia gives way to scornful commentary on the weakness and ostentation of "fleshly arms"
and at length to a bitter denunciation of the idolatrous lost
tribes, yet his ire is soon transmuted into an almost ecstatic
vision of the reclamation of these tribes by God's providence
in his due time. Another undercurrent in the dramatic situation here is Christ's continuing counteroffensive against Satan
—"But whence to thee this zeal?" (III.407).

The Parthian encounter leaves Satan visibly worsted: he is
"Perplex'd and troubl'd at his bad success," and he is conscious of Belial-like error in that he had "no better weigh'd/
The strength he was to cope with, or his own" (IV.1, 8–9).
Now desperate, Satan goads himself to produce a yet more
magnificent spectacle, the stunning pageant of Rome, and a
yet more brilliant rhetorical presentation of it. He offers Rome
to Christ with a further play on Christ's ambiguous sonship,
suggesting that Christ become the heir of the childless
Emperor Tiberius. He also continues his own parody of
Christ's divine sonship, claiming that he himself has received
all power on earth, and "by that right" gives it to Christ.
Christ is "unmov'd" by the Roman pageant as by the Parthian
and demonstrates his steadily mounting confidence by his
continued counterattack against Satan, this time sparked with
witty irony as he demands whether, instead of expelling the
wicked Tiberius, he ought not "Expel a Devil who first made

him such" (IV.129). At length, after withstanding at the human level all these temptations regarding his kingship, Christ apparently receives another of those flashes of divine understanding, after which he can cite Daniel's metaphors of the tree and the stone evidently with full comprehension of their meaning for his kingdom. He can also lay claim to full knowledge of the means to his kingdom which we know that he did not have as he entered the desert: "Means there shall be to this, but what the means,/ Is not for thee to know, nor me to tell" (IV.152–53).

Satan's next move seems to many readers flagrantly undramatic, since, after Christ has categorically refused the kingdoms offered apparently as a free gift. Satan can hardly expect him to accept a new offer of them with the price tag of idolatry boldly attached. Actually, however, the passage functions brilliantly in the dramatic interplay of the poem, for it marks a new stage in Satan's mounting discomfiture and humiliation. His statement is a desperate face-saving maneuver: recognizing that Christ has regarded all his offers as "slight" and valueless, he here attempts to prove their value by citing their high price—a not uncommon manner of proving worth in this world. Satan also reiterates here his own claim to the divine sonship, asserting that he has received the kingdoms (presumably from God), and that he may therefore give them "to whom I please" (IV.164). Responding in zealous anger Christ continues his counteroffensive against Satan, flatly denying Satan's claim to the kingdoms of this world since they are God's and therefore his own by right of his sonship: "Wert thou so void of fear or shame,/ As offer them to me the Son of God,/ To me my own, on such abhorred pact" (IV.189–91). His "Get thee behind me" (IV.193) asserts unequivocal power over Satan, and his comment, "plain thou now appear'st/ That Evil one, Satan for ever damn'd" (IV.193–94), intimates full comprehension of Satan's nature as blasphemer of God.

ISRAEL: CHRIST'S KINGDOM AND FALSE ZEAL

The lines from the conclusion of the glory temptation to the beginning of the temptation of Parthia (III.150–226) serve as a kind of induction to this third segment of the poem, and also as a link between the two major temptations of Book III. Two themes—power and time—organize Book III. Both of them are introduced in the glory temptation through the discussion of the great world conquerors all desirous of winning fame while young. The induction passage, our present concern, invites Christ to seize "Occasion's forelock" (III.173) and to take up arms to win back his kingdom, Israel, at once. The kingdom of Parthia is then presented as especially notable for its armed might, which Christ comes "just in time" to view and utilize as a means to win back his kingdom. Christ's final speech in Book III, after which the narrator proclaims him *"Israel's* true King," wholly repudiates urgency and force as in any way involved in Christ's kingdom and assigns the establishment and maintenance of that kingdom to God's "due time and providence."

The induction is also a temptation, in its own right, to false conceptions of "Zeal and Duty" (III.172). At the level of private morality, Satan builds upon Christ's zeal for God's glory displayed in his refusal to seek glory for himself, and tempts him now to act from motives of false zeal rather than glory. At the public level, Satan invites Christ to a very simplistic understanding of his duty as king—to take up arms himself and seize David's throne, the literal Israel, at once. Moreover, this temptation especially invites Christ to a false apprehension of the uses of time: he is invited to seize his kingdom at the wrong time, in the throes of false zeal, rather than under providential guidance.

As an exemplar of zeal and duty Satan cites the great Jewish military leader Judas Maccabaeus, frequently identified in biblical commentary as a type of Christ. In the second century B.C. the priestly family known as the Maccabees took up arms against the profanations of the Temple and the Law perpetrated by Antiochus IV (Epiphanes), king of Syria; after many battles Judas won back and purified the Temple, and his brother Simon effected the political independence of Judaea in 142 B.C.[4] The Maccabees and the Hasmonaean dynasty descending from them united the functions of the high priesthood and the kingship. Satan asserts that the Roman emperor Tiberius is desecrating the Temple and the Law at the present time just as Antiochus did of old and concludes that Jesus should take up arms at once, imitating Judas who "indeed/ Retir'd unto the Desert, but with arms" (III.165–66).

In traditional biblical exegesis Judas Maccabaeus was identified as a type of Christ on several counts. In iconography Judas' purifying the Temple was often presented as a type of Christ's driving the money changers out of the Temple. Some commentators took Judas' great victory over Seron as a type of Christ's victory over Satan at the Crucifixion. And almost everyone interpreted Judas' defeat of Antiochus as a type of Christ's conquest over Antichrist, since the "little horne" who was to "destroy the mighty, and the holy people" mentioned in Daniel's prophecy (Dan. viii:9–25) was almost always identified both as Antiochus IV and Antichrist.[5] Diodati, for example, states that the little horn was Antiochus, "the most cruell, subtill, and pestilent persecutor that ever the Church had...and also...Antichrist, the last deadly enemy of the Christian Church: as Antiochus had been of the Jewish."[6] The reference in the poem to Antiochus also reinforces the Daniel motif introduced at the beginning of the kingdoms sequence, in preparation for Christ's definition of his own kingdom in terms supplied by Daniel's prophecy.

However, many commentators on Maccabees and Daniel warned against a literal interpretation of the Maccabean type such as Satan sets forth here, for they saw in the fusion of priestly and royal power effected under the Hasmonaeans a grave danger to the Christian church. Calvin observed that this united kingship and priesthood was not only "sold and made a marchandise, but it was bought with mutuall slaughters and parricides," and Milton declared that the Hasmonaeans "plundered David's sepulchre, and began to keep foreign soldiers, and to invest the priesthood with a kind of regal power." [7] The Maccabean type could be interpreted rightly only in spiritual terms, as a figure of Christ's unique fusion of the royal and priestly offices; its spiritual meaning for the Christian church was suggested in Luther's interpretation of the Maccabees' sword as the type of the "good Holy Gospel ... wherewith God's servants faithfully come to grips with the contemporary Anti-Christ." [8]

Christ's answer displays his understanding that zeal and duty consist first of all in waiting upon God's time, avoiding both passivity and false zeal. He insists that neither he nor Satan will determine the time for establishing the kingdom, but God alone will do so, "He in whose hand all times and seasons roll" (III.187). Echoing Ecclesiastes iii:1, "To every thing there is a season, and a time to every purpose under the heavens," Christ confidently asserts that "All things are best fulfill'd in their due time,/ And time there is for all things" (III.182–83). Both his answer and manner display that right moderation of zeal urged by Calvin:

Nothing is better, than to leave unto his [God's] pleasure the moments of times, and opportunitie of matters, and not to prevent his providence by our hastinesse, in which except we rest altogether, we stoppe up the way against his vertue and power. ... He alloweth no heate, that men are stirred unto of their owne accord, but alway requireth moderation of zele, the only rule whereof is this, that we move neither tongue, nor feete, nor handes, before he him selfe commaundeth us. [9]

Also, Christ opposes Satan's invitation to a false conception of kingly duty derived from a literal interpretation of the Maccabean type through an implied reference to that most complete Old Testament type of his kingly role, David. The Geneva Bible's comment that David was exercised by God "in sundry sortes before he had the use of his kingdome," and Milton's observation in *Eikonoklastes* that David, "by suffering without just cause, learnt that meekness and that wisdom by adversity, which made him much the fitter man to raigne," [10] offer close parallels to Christ's comment here about the procedure God may have designed for his Son's assumption of his kingdom:

> What if he hath decreed that I shall first
> Be tried in humble state, and things adverse,
> By tribulations, injuries, insults,
> Contempts, and scorns, and snares, and violence,
> Suffering, abstaining, quietly expecting
> Without distrust or doubt, that he may know
> What I can suffer, how obey? who best
> Can suffer, best can do; best reign, who first
> Well hath obey'd. (III.188–96)

This induction concludes with Christ's challenge to Satan to account for his own sense of urgency, since Christ's assumption of his kingdom will mean Satan's downfall. Satan's answer, whatever the psychological state which prompts it, functions as a devious invitation to Christ to corrupt his kingly office just as he had before invited Christ to degrade his prophetic role through voluntary association with Satan-as-Balaam, that is, with hypocrites and false prophets (I.483–92). Here Satan seems to suggest that Christ become *his* king, protecting and shielding him—

> to that gentle brow
> Willingly I could fly, and hope thy reign,

> From that placid aspect and meek regard,
> Rather than aggravate my evil state,
> Would stand between me and thy Father's ire. (III.215–19)

But of course Christ's proper kingly function with respect to Satan, which Christ affirms in resounding tones at the conclusion of this sequence, is to conquer and destroy Satan and all his kingdom.

PARTHIA: CHRIST'S KINGDOM AND CIVIL POWER

Satan's offer of Parthia builds upon Christ's repeated identification of himself with David; in it Satan suggests that Christ become literally a Second David, seeking after David's physical kingdom, Israel, by David's means—the use of armed force. Following upon the temptation to take over Israel at the wrong time, this temptation emphasizes the wrong means. Preparatory to the offer of Parthian force Satan suggests that Christ's hesitancy to act may stem from inexperience:

> The wisest, unexperienc't, will be ever
> Timorous and loth, with novice modesty
> (As he who seeking Asses found a Kingdom)
> Irresolute, unhardy, unadvent'rous. (III.240–43)

The allusion is to Saul (I Sam. ix–x), and the implication is that Christ is behaving like Saul, who was at length rejected by God for disobedience, rather than like David, who obtained the kingdom for himself and his progeny.

The mount from which Christ views the kingdoms again underlines his association with several of the types previously mentioned. The reader of *Paradise Lost* will recall that the mountain from which Michael showed the history of the world to Adam is explicitly associated with the mountain of Christ's temptation:

Not higher that Hill nor wider looking round,
Whereon for different cause the Tempter set
Our second *Adam* in the Wilderness,
To show him all Earth's Kingdoms and thir Glory. (*PL* XI.381-84)

The relation of these two mountains emphasizes again the
Adam motif: Christ is another Adam seeing a world under
the dominion of Sin and Death, though with its ugliness now
fraudulently masked. The prospect from the mount also recalls
the Moses-Christ relation—the parallel which John Lightfoot
along with several others drew between "the Lords shewing
to *Moses* from a high Mount all the kingdomes of *Canaan,* and
saying, *All these will I give to the children of Israel,* and the
Devils shewing to *Christ* all the kingdomes of the earth, and
saying, *All these will I give thee.*" [11] In these terms, Christ appears as a Second Moses being shown a false promised land,
though of course in another sense all the earth is his promised
inheritance. But the prospect of the kingdoms from the mountain suggests especially the situation of David, who built his
citadel and castle upon Mount Sion, and who was promised
by God a settled kingdom: "I will appoint a place for my
people Israel, and will plant them, that they may dwell in a
place of their owne, and move no more: neither shall the children of wickednesse afflict them any more" (II Sam. vii:10).
On the mount Christ is a Second David being offered again
the literal Israelite kingdom, but now by Satan rather than
by God.

Satan offers Parthia to Christ specifically as the means to
his kingdom, and he asserts its value as such a means on two
grounds. First, he declares that only by possessing Parthia
can Christ become the new David, since the Parthian Empire
controls the territory in which now dwell the ten lost tribes
of Israel carried away by the Assyrians in 726 B.C. David,
after becoming king of Judah, was by league anointed king

at Hebron over both Israel and Judah: "all the Elders of Israel came to the king to Hebron; and king David made a league with them in Hebron before the LORD: and they anointed David king over Israel/... And in Jerusalem he reigned thirtie and three yeeres over all Israel and Judah" (II Sam. v:3, 5). With characteristic literalism Satan declares that if Christ is to be the new David and sit "on the Throne of *David* in full glory" (III.383) he must also control the united tribes, and to do this he must control Parthia:

> Choose which thou wilt, by conquest or by league.
> By him thou shalt regain, without him not,
> That which alone can truly reinstall thee
> In *David's* royal seat, his true Successor,
> Deliverance of thy brethren, those ten Tribes
> Whose offspring in his Territory yet serve. (III.370–75)

In the second place Parthia is offered to Christ as providing the only power—military force—by which Christ can hope to obtain and to maintain his kingdom. The emphasis in the spectacle of Parthia upon military formations, impressive cavalry displays, and skilled weaponry leads to the symbolic identification of Parthia with the might of the state and its armies. David's kingdom of old had to be conquered: both before and after his enthronement David engaged in well-nigh constant wars with the supporters of Saul, with the Philistines, with the Amalekites, and with other heathen, and he had to win his capital city, Jerusalem, from the Jebusites by battle. Christ, Satan suggests, must expect to do the same. The narrator's comparison of Parthian might to the chivalry of Charlemagne gathered for the siege of Albracca further identifies Parthia with great and misused military force, for the *Orlando Innamorato* records that many of Charlemagne's knights were enticed to this siege through Angelica's deceit and thereby defaulted in their proper service to their king.[12]

Besides presenting Parthia as a means to Christ's kingdom

in the double sense just described, Satan also presents it as heir to the territory and power of the first three of the four great empires described in the prophecy of Daniel, thereby reinforcing the Daniel motif present throughout the temptation of the kingdoms. Daniel interpreted Nebuchadnezzar's dream of the image made of four metals—gold, silver, brass, and iron—and his other dream of the four fierce beasts, as referring to the four great empires of the ancient world. Most commentators identified these empires as Babylonia, Persia, Macedonia (Greece), and Rome and explained that the proliferation of the Roman Empire into several smaller kingdoms was signified by the ten toes of the statue and the ten horns of the fourth beast.[13] Jerome and Augustine departed from the usual exegesis somewhat in that they conflated Assyria and Babylonia in the first empire.[14] The passage in *Paradise Regained* seems to assume Jerome's reading: it refers to the Assyrian Empire explicitly as the "golden" empire, and links Babylonia to Assyria as a kingdom equally "ancient"; it then refers to the Persian Empire through mention of the great Persian emperor Cyrus and the Persian cities Persepolis, Bactria, and Ecbatana; finally it alludes to the Macedonian Empire by reference to the cities of Selucia and Antioch which were centers of its power, and also by reference to the conquest of the king of Antioch by the Parthians. Satan therefore offers the ancient kingdoms associated with the first three empires of Daniel's prophecy as now comprehended in Parthia. In doing so he also prepares for his culminating offer of Rome as the fourth and greatest of the empires, as well as for Christ's definition of his own kingdom in terms of Daniel's metaphor of the stone which was to crush Nebuchadnezzar's image, symbolically destroying all the worldly kingdoms.

The offer of Parthia as the means whereby Christ could win and maintain his kingdom has many ramifications for the continuing history of the church. Parthia is symbolically the power of the civil state, and Satan's offer of it represents, essentially, a temptation to the use of civil power for the establishment and maintenance of the church. Assuming an ecclesiastical context for this temptation as for all of the others, Howard Schultz identifies Parthia as the Genevan type of militant Protestantism; however, this identification causes him to allegorize the ten lost tribes as "Christians in thrall to Rome," [15] a reading not justified by the text which, as has been seen, explicitly declares the tribes to be enslaved in Parthian territory. The identification of Parthia as the power of the civil state is further strengthened by the close parallel between Milton's comment on the relations between church and state in his tract *Of Civil Power* and Christ's comment in the poem on the worthlessness of Parthian arms for his purposes. The tract declares that "Christ rejects outward force in the government of his church...to shew us the divine excellence of his spiritual kingdom, able without worldly force to subdue all the powers and kingdoms of this world, which are upheld by outward force only," [16] and in the poem Christ describes the Parthian military display as

> Much ostentation vain of fleshly arm
> And fragile arms, much instrument of war
> Long in preparing, soon to nothing brought,
>
> . . . .
>
> Plausible to the world, to mee worth naught. (III.387–93)

However, Parthia is not to be read simply as an allegory of civil power, but rather in the typological perspective which controls the references to Old Testament and classical figures. Its relations with Israel are historically real, but they are also made to reflect something of the continuing problem of church and state throughout time, and perhaps especially in Milton's own time. Satan's statement that Parthia has been "of late/ Found able by invasion to annoy/ Thy country, and captive lead away her Kings" (III.364–66) suggests the continuing persecution of the church by the civil power. And the situation of the ten tribes, enslaved by Parthia but more enslaved by their own vices and idolatries, has a contemporary analogue in the situation of the English Protestants who, by inviting the restoration of Charles II, submitted themselves to something very like Papist idolatry in the English church and so deserved enslavement by the civil state.

Christ's rejection of the Parthian kingdom and its force as a means to the throne of Israel has behind it a very considerable exegetical tradition which drew from the David story a moral lesson regarding the rejection of armed might. Many, especially among the Fathers, identified the battle of David and Goliath as the type of Christ's spiritual victory over Satan in the temptation, and saw David's shedding of his armor as typifying the repudiation of armed might by Christ and his church. They also explained the five stones which David carried, from among which he chose one to kill Goliath, as symbolizing the five books of the Pentateuch from among which Christ used only one, Deuteronomy, as the source for the Scripture quotations with which he defeated Satan.[17] Commentators also pointed to the biblical verses forbidding David to build a temple to God because he was a man of warfare and blood to emphasize the difference between the Davidic kingdom and that peaceful kingdom to be ruled by his son— Solomon/Christ. God said to David, "Thou hast shed blood abundantly, and hast made great warres: thou shalt not build an house unto my Name, because thou hast shed much blood upon the earth in my sight./ Behold, a sonne shall bee borne to thee, who shall be a man of rest . . . / He shall build a house for my Name" (I Chron. xxii:8–10). As Augustine explained, "Solomon built this temple to the Lord, in type and in figure indeed the future Church and body of Christ . . . therefore as he had built that temple himself, so the true Solomon our Lord Jesus Christ, the true peaceful king, has built the temple for himself." [18]

As the true peaceful king, Christ responds to the Parthian offer by decisively separating his kingly office and its exercise in his church from any use of or league with civil power—from anything resembling the Roman church's direct exercise of such power, or the practice in Anglican or Calvinist national churches of calling upon the magistrate's sword to carry out ecclesiastical policy. Tillyard's assertion that Milton has here repudiated warfare generally and turned his back upon his own role in the English Civil War [19] ignores this context. In the glory temptation Christ asserted that Scipio's defensive war to save his country might be glorious if undertaken for motives of genuine patriotism, and there is no reason to suppose that Milton ever saw the Civil War as anything other than a patriotic defensive war. In the Parthian episode Christ simply asserts that force can play no role in his own kingdom, the church. Christ concludes this exchange by throwing back to Satan, who has been urging upon him the literal Davidic example, the fact that Satan had also tempted David "to the pride/ Of numb'ring *Israel*" (III.409-10); the reference suggests that Satan by his insistence that Christ restore the ten tribes and number them in his kingdom is tempting Christ to the same kind of pride—that is, to trust in numerical strength or force.

Christ's decisive refusal to attempt to regain the ten tribes, together with his bitter comment that they deserve their slavery by their idolatry and that if restored they would only fall away again, seems at first an unwarrantably harsh repudiation of the imperfect. But the subsequent lines greatly modify this harshness by their vision of the final, peaceful restoration of the lost ones by God's providence, in his own time:

Yet he at length, time to himself best known,
Rememb'ring *Abraham,* by some wond'rous call
May bring them back repentant and sincere,
And at their passing cleave the *Assyrian* flood,
While to their native land with joy they haste,
As the Red Sea and *Jordan* once he cleft,
When to the promis'd land thir Fathers pass'd;
To his due time and providence I leave them. (III.433-40)

These lines echo Isaiah's eloquent description of the millennial kingdom, which Milton termed the Kingdom of Glory and saw as the final exaltation awaiting the Kingdom of Grace, the church. This context not only reinforces Christ's insistence that his methods be those of peace, in direct contrast to the worldly force employed by all other kingdoms, but also shows in compelling metaphor the basis for Christ's confidence that the peaceful kingdom will ultimately prevail, that it will at length achieve the inner change required for a true restoration of the ten lost tribes, and that it will transform the earth:

The wolfe also shall dwell with the lambe, and the leopard shall lie downe with the kid: and the calfe and the yong lion, and the fatling together, and a little childe shall leade them....

They shall not hurt nor destroy in all my holy mountaine: for the earth shall be full of the knowledge of the Lord, as the waters cover the sea ...

And it shall come to passe in that day, that the Lord shall set his hand againe the second time, to recover the remnant of his people which shalbe left, from Assyria, and from Egypt ...

And there shalbe an high way for the remnant of his people, which shalbe left from Assyria; like as it was to Israel in the day that hee came up out of the land of Egypt.

(Isa. xi:6, 9, 11, 16)

Christ's paraphrase of Isaiah's prophecy to define his kingdom's peace serves to suggest by metaphor and symbol the transformation of the mountain from which Christ views worldly armed might into the holy mountain of his own glorious kingdom, and also prepares for Christ's later reference to Daniel's prophecy to define his kingdom's power. These echoes and quotations show Christ using prophecy as a means of seeing beyond the literal Davidic type in order to reach a more complete understanding of his kingly office, which is precisely the role defined for prophecy by Augustine:

In the service of prefiguring this King in that earthly kingdom of the people of Israel, King David stood forth pre-eminent ... [But] from that period ... at which they received the land of promise and began to have kings, in order to preclude the supposition that the promise of the Christ who was to be their Liberator had met its complete fulfillment in the person of any one of their kings, Christ was prophesied of with greater clearness in a number of prophecies; not only by David himself in the book of Psalms, but also by the rest of the great and holy prophets.[20]

After Christ has used prophecy to attain such a spiritual understanding of his role, he is referred to by the narrator as *"Israel's true king"* (III.441), that is, as the new, peaceful king of the new Israel, the invisible church, which utterly repudiates force but which will ultimately prevail as the holy millennial kingdom.

ROME: CHRIST'S KINGDOM AND THE KINGDOM OF ANTICHRIST

The Roman Empire is the fourth empire of Daniel's prophecy. It is represented by the legs of iron and feet and toes of iron and clay in Nebuchadnezzar's image, and also by the fourth beast "dreadful and terrible, and strong exceedingly," with great iron teeth and ten horns. Both symbols insist upon the tremendous strength of this fourth empire, exceeding all the rest, and also upon its proliferation into several parts. Satan offers Rome to Christ as a universal empire extending in all directions, North, East, South, West, and he equates it explicitly with "all the world" (IV.105), thereby tempting Christ to seek a substitute empire, the world, in place of his own spiritual realm. In the Parthian temptation Christ was offered the wrong means for the attainment of his own kingdom, Israel; but here he is offered the wrong kingdom. He and his church throughout history are invited to confuse the spiritual kingdom, the invisible church, with the world itself and specifically with the worldly Roman Catholic church, both of which are traditionally identified as Antichrist in Protestant exegesis. Behind this opposition of the mundane and the spiritual kingdoms is of course Augustine's contrast of the City of God and the City of Man, and also Augustine's identification of Rome as the "head of this earthly city of which we speak." [21]

The magnificent Roman pageant is a true climax to the entire kingdoms theme which began with the banquet temptation, for it gathers together into a kind of compendium all the enticements and temptations of the world formerly offered to Christ singly, and greatly enhances their magnificence and grandeur. This city has "ample Territory, wealth and power,/ Civility of Manners, Arts, and Arms,/ And long Renown" (IV.82–84). Its glory is evident in the magnificent buildings and especially the elegant royal palace, which are like "Houses of Gods" (IV.56). Its power is manifested by the Roman legions and cohorts, and by the fact that "All Nations now to *Rome* obedience pay" (IV.80). Rome also can engage Christ's zeal and duty and charity, providing an opportunity for him to rescue the Roman people enslaved by the brutish Tiberius. And it also provides a means for obtaining and maintaining Christ's own kingdom: "without the highest attain'd/ Will be for thee no sitting, or not long/ On David's Throne" (IV.106–8). With nice irony, Christ indicates his perception that Rome is indeed a compendium of all the previous worldly temptations when he picks Satan up on his one omission, the Roman counterpart of the banquet temptation:

> though thou should'st add to tell
> Thir sumptuous gluttonies, and gorgeous feasts
> On *Citron* tables or *Atlantic* stone,
>
> .   .   .   .
>
> Their wines of *Setia, Cales,* and *Falerne,*
> *Chios* and *Crete,* and how they quaff in Gold,
> Crystal and Murrhine cups emboss'd with Gems
> And studs of Pearl, to me should'st tell who thirst
> And hunger still. (IV.113–21)

Christ's reference to his continuing hunger further relates the banquet episode, the beginning of the kingdoms sequence, to this climactic completion of the sequence.

Rome, besides being identified as the great compendium of that worldliness which is the antichristian opposite of Christ's spiritual kingdom, is specifically identified through several features of the description as the Roman church—in Protestant eyes the embodiment of all worldliness and the great Antichrist depicted in the Book of Revelation. Rome's Imperial Palace, with its "compass huge, and high/ The Structure, skill of noblest Architects,/ With gilded battlements, conspicuous far" (IV.51–53), may suggest St. Peter's; the banquet described above with rare wines quaffed in rich vessels suggests the Mass and the vessels used in its celebration; the constant "issuing forth or ent'ring in" of the "Praetors, Proconsuls to thir Provinces/ ... in robes of State" (IV.62–64) may suggest the prelates and bishops moving back and forth between Rome and their own districts. Just such an identification of Antichrist as at once the epitome of worldliness and also as the Roman church may be seen in Milton's *Of Reformation:* "right truly it may be said, that *Antichrist* is *Mammons* Son. The soure levin of humane Traditions mixt in one putrifi'd Masse with the poisonous dregs of hypocrisie in the hearts of *Prelates* that lye basking in the Sunny warmth of Wealth, and Promotion, is the Serpents Egge that will hatch an *Antichrist* wheresoever ... though his cheife Kennell be at *Rome.*" [32]

The traditional Protestant commentary upon the temptation of the kingdoms provides bases for Milton's identification of Rome as the chief kingdom offered to Christ, for his allusion to the Roman church through this identification, and for his interpretation of the temptation of the kingdoms as prefiguring the continuing conflict of the true church in relation to the antichristian Church of Rome throughout history. Perkins observes:

Note a further reach of Sathan in this promise of these earthly kingdomes, even to overthrow Christs spirituall kingdome. Satan knew wel that if Christ were the true Messias, he should be a King, and have a kingdom, though not earthly, yet spirituall in the hearts and consciences of men, which should bee the ruine of his kingdome; and therfore he labours with Christ to entertain an earthly kingdome, that so his spirituall kingdome might not be looked after. And looke as he seeks to deale with Christ the head, so he perseveres against the Church which is his body; for Gods church hath it ministery, which in it nature is a soveraignty, to be exercised in the dispensation of the word: now the Devill hath laboured by all meanes to bring this ministery wherein the Churches spirituall soveraigntie doth consist, to become an earthly lordship and dominion, that by this meanes he might overturne it, and make it fruitlesse in the building and upholding of Christs spirituall kingdome: and how he hath prevailed this way, the church of Rome doth shew to all the world.[23]

Lightfoot explained the temptation of the kingdoms in similar terms:

If wee come to ponder, by weighing and considering the state of the world at this time, it will appeare, that the object that the Devill presented *Christ* withall in this spectacle, was *Rome,* her Empire and glory. For I. That Empire is called by the very name of *all the world, Luke* 2.1. . . . Where was there any pompe or worldly glory to bee seene any where upon all the earth at this time, but what belonged to the *Roman* state? nay, where was there almost any Country or kingdom, but was within the compasse and do-

minion of that Empire?...The *Roman* stories that describe the
State of *Rome* at these times, doe give an abundant account of
her wealth, pompe, power, revenues, extent, and largenesse even
to the amazement of the Reader, they were all so vast ... [Satan]
doth offer to seat *Christ* in the very throne of *Antichrist,* and would
perswade the singular seed of the woman, to become the singular
seed of the Serpent, and his owne heire placed by himselfe in his
owne seat.... When *Satan* cannot at the entrance of the Gospel,
perswade Christ by all the pompe of Rome, to do like *Antichrist,* hee
setteth up *Antichrist* at *Rome,* to bee an enemy to the Gospel, in
all the continuance of it.[24]

Furthermore, referring to the evil Tiberius, Lightfoot, like
Milton, intimates that his viciousness is a foreshadowing of
papal degeneracy and persecution: *"Tiberius* was...a man
of such subtlety, cruelty, avarice, and bestiality...as if in
this very beginning of the Gospel, hee were produced of such
a constitution, to teach us what to look for from that cruell
and abominable City, in all ages and successions." [25]

Christ responds to the offer of Rome by affirming that his
own kingdom is wholly spiritual in nature and manner of
rule. He "was not sent" to expel the brutish Tiberius (or a corrupt and licentious pope), but he will expel "a Devil who
first made him such" (IV.129). Neither will he undertake to
save from slavery the Roman people (or the Roman Catholics) who have so degenerated from their initial virtue, for
no one can "of inward slaves make outward free" (IV.146).
His kingly mission and that of his church is thereby defined
as the expulsion of devils and the restoration of man's inner
freedom, a wholly spiritual function which has no relation to
Rome, whether considered as worldliness simply, or as the
worldly ecclesiastical dominion of the Roman church.

At length, by the use of two metaphors from Daniel, both
of which suggest the growth of Christ's church from small
beginnings to final domination of all the earth, Christ affirms

the power, the universality, and the ultimate victory of his kingdom, though spiritual, over all worldly kingdoms and over Rome itself as the compendium of them all. The tone of the pronouncement manifests Christ's confidence, and his full understanding of all the implications of his kingly office:

> Know therefore when my season comes to sit
> On *David's* Throne, it shall be like a tree
> Spreading and overshadowing all the Earth,
> Or as a stone that shall to pieces dash
> All Monarchies besides throughout the world,
> And of my Kingdom there shall be no end:
> Means there shall be to this, but what the means,
> Is not for thee to know, nor me to tell. (IV.147–53)

The tree is that tree which was "in the midst of the earth, and the height thereof was great./ The tree grew, and was strong, & the height thereof reached unto heaven, and the sight thereof to the end of all the earth" (Dan. iv:10–11). The stone is that stone cut out of the mountain without hands which Nebuchadnezzar saw in his vision as falling upon and crushing the great image which represented the four empires of the world:

> Thou sawest till that a stone was cut out without hands, which smote the image upon his feet that were of yron and clay, and brake them to pieces.
>
> Then was the yron, the clay, the brasse, the silver, and the gold broken to pieces together, and became like the chaffe of the summer threshing floores, and the wind carried them away, that no place was found for them: and the stone that smote the image became a great mountaine, and filled the whole earth.
>
> And in the dayes of these kings shall the God of heaven set up a kingdome, which shall never be destroyed: and the kingdome shall not bee left to other people, but it shall breake in pieces, and consume all these kingdomes, and it shall stand for ever.
>
> (Dan. ii:34–35, 44)

The stone's miraculous origin is explained by some commentators as suggesting Christ's incarnation, and its miraculous expansion as signifying the wholly spiritual increase and multiplying of Christ's church. The Dutch Annotators interpret the stone itself as meaning

that the person and kingdome of Christ should at first be mean and of no respect among men upon earth, as a stone is a mean and base thing in comparison of gold and silver that were in that image ... Our King, Christ ... shall according to his humane nature proceed from the kingdome of Juda ... and break in pieces the aforesaid kingdomes, and change the kingdom of David into a spirituall and everlasting kingdome.[26]

Similarly, the Geneva Bible explained the stone's action as signifying "that all the kingdomes of the worlde are transitorie, and that the kingdome of Christ shall onely remayne for ever"; the Geneva commentary identified the stone itself as

Christ, who was sent of God, and not set up by man, whose kingdome at the beginning should bee small and without beautie to mans judgement, but should at length growe and fill the whole earth, which hee calleth a great mountaine ... And this kingdome, which is not onely referred to the person of Christ, but also to the whole body of his Church, and to every member thereof, shalbe eternall.[27]

Moreover, traditional commentary links this stone with that which David used to smite Goliath, both of them presenting, as Cyprian put it, "a strong and lively emblem of the victory gained over Satan and all his servants."[28] David's victory typifies Christ's victory at the temptation specifically, and Daniel's prophecy looks forward to that ultimate and total defeat which will come at the end of time. Christ's kingship involves the peaceful rule over his church as he affirms after the Parthia temptation, and also the conquest of its enemies as he asserts after the temptation of Rome. The stone subsumes both motifs: the weakness with which David confronted and conquered the armed Goliath as a type of Christ and his church combating Satan and the world by Scripture only; and also the omnipotence and universality of the spiritual power which will ultimately confound all worldly kingdoms.

Satan's bold invitation to Christ to worship him reveals that the condition implicit in all the offers of the kingdoms sequence is idolatry, for to desire these worldly goods immoderately, or to suppose them to be in any sense needful for the establishment of Christ's kingdom, is idolatry of the things of this world, and therefore of its Prince. This concluding episode also provides an occasion for Christ's further declaration of the scope of his office, for just as at the conclusion of the stones episode Christ exploded Satan's claim to oracles by revealing himself as the divine oracle and prophet, so now Christ asserts his own rightful kingship over all the realms the Prince of This World has usurped:

> The Kingdoms of the world to thee were giv'n,
> Permitted rather, and by thee usurp't,
> Other donation none thou canst produce:
>
> .   .   .   .
>   Wert thou so void of fear or shame,
> As offer them to me the Son of God,
> To me my own, on such abhorred pact,
> That I fall down and worship thee as God?
> Get thee behind me; plain thou now appear'st
> That Evil one, Satan for ever damn'd. (IV.182–84, 189–94)

CHAPTER XI · ATHENS: LEARNING, KINGSHIP, AND PROPHECY

*A*FTER his resounding defeat at the conclusion of the kingdoms sequence, Satan speaks "with fear abasht" in an effort to placate Christ's formidable ire, and also to win continuing opportunity for his temptation. Assuming a humble posture he admits Christ's victory over him, but the humility disguises his continued ironic questioning of Christ's sonship, and his implicit assertion of his own claim to divine sonship, Godship even, by reason of his power over earth and air:

> Be not so sore offended, Son of God,
> Though Sons of God both Angels are and Men;
> If I to try whether in higher sort
> Than these thou bear'st that title, have propos'd
> What both from Men and Angels I receive,
> Tetrarchs of fire, air, flood, and on the earth
> Nations besides from all the quarter'd winds,
> God of this world invok'd and world beneath. (IV.196–203)

Then, having made his counterclaim, Satan affects a casual dismissal of these kingdoms and directs his astonishing ingenuity to the construction of a new and even more wonderful pageant, just when the reader is sure that he has exhausted all his skill in displaying Roman grandeur. Moreover, Satan presents this climactic offer of Athens in the most persuasive and eloquent terms—in language itself evoking and imitating the elegance, nobility, and loveliness of the ideal described. Satan's brilliant strategy in this temptation is to offer a kingdom which is the embodiment of precisely that nonmaterial good—classical learning—which seems to be requisite to

Christ's accomplishment of the functions of his office as he himself has just defined them. Satan offers the kingdom of learning as necessary for Christ's kingly rule by persuasion, and also for his prophetic function of teaching God's final Word. This context reminds us that those Old Testament figures with whom Christ has identified himself most closely as types and prophets of these two offices—Moses, Daniel, and Job—were said by many commentators to have assimilated much of the pagan learning of their own times.[1] The proposition before Christ in the learning temptation is that he follow this precedent.

Satan's rhetoric in presenting his argument is masterful, and like Comus' rhetoric it has provoked some critics to rage against Christ's harsh repudiations of such noble offers, and has moved others to a condescending pity for what they take to be Milton's subconscious tensions about learning and his masochistic flagellation of himself here for his earlier love of it. R. M. Adams sees in Christ's speech only a "provincial contempt of the classics," and "a feeling for the Christian dispensation as not only supplementing but cancelling pagan reason." W. B. C. Watkins declares that Milton here "negates learning like an Alexandrian bonfire" and "rips to shreds the passion of fifty years." Douglas Bush finds it painful "to watch Milton turn and rend some main roots of his being." George Sensabaugh explains the "strange pronouncements upon intellectual curiosity and humane studies" as stemming from a "deep disillusion." And E. M. W. Tillyard senses in the passage a mood of "mortification or masochism" in which Milton "goes out of his way to hurt the dearest and oldest inhabitants of his mind: the Greek philosophers, his early love Plato included, the disinterested thirst for knowledge, the poets and orators of Greece and Rome."[2]

Any analysis of the theme and dramatic movement of the poem must explain why Christ renounces so categorically all the realms of knowledge, sometimes in a tone of matter-of-fact objective analysis, sometimes in a tone of harsh denunciation. Classical philosophy is "false, or little else but dreams,/ Conjectures, fancies, built on nothing firm" (IV.291–92), since the philosophers are "Ignorant of themselves, of God much more,/ And how the world began, and how man fell/ Degraded by himself, on grace depending" (IV.310–12). The classical poets are greatly inferior to the Hebrew poets since they sing "The vices of thir Deities, and thir own" (IV.340), and if one removes their "swelling Epithets thick laid/ As varnish on a Harlot's cheek" they will be found to be "Thin sown with aught of profit or delight" (IV.343–45). The classical orators are far below the Hebrew prophets in teaching "The solid rules of Civil Government" (IV.358).

It is tempting to follow Howard Schultz in reading this wholesale renunciation of classical learning in the strictly ecclesiastical terms consonant with his interpretation of the entire poem as a quasi-allegory in which Christ as head of the church confronts its enemy Antichrist and enunciates counsels of perfection meant "not primarily for the Christian layman, but for the church and its ministers."[3] On this reading, Christ's repudiation of learning means simply that he and the ministers of his church have no need of human learning to perform the offices of teaching and ruling the church, and the passage offers a precise analogue to the argument concerning the education of the ministry outlined in Milton's antitithe tract, *The Likeliest Means to Remove Hirelings out of the Church* (1659). However, the previous discussion has demonstrated that at least the sizable segment of the poem comprising the banquet-wealth-glory temptations cannot be given a strictly ecclesiastical interpretation since it concerns the kingdom within "Which every wise and virtuous man attains" (II.468).[4] I hope the discussion has also shown that the poem presents Christ as a dramatic character seeking out and finding his total mission rather than simply as allegorical representative of and spokesman for his church.

Yet, since the offer of Athens follows immediately upon the offers of Parthia and Rome, which are direct challenges to Christ's exercise of his proper kingly rule over the church, it might be expected that the learning temptation would also be primarily or entirely ecclesiastical in its import. The text gives partial support to such a reading, for learning is offered as a necessity for Christ's prophetic (teaching) role and also for his kingly function of ruling by persuasion:

> And with the *Gentiles* much must thou converse,
> Ruling them by persuasion as thou mean'st,
> Without thir learning how wilt thou with them,
> Or they with thee hold conversation meet?
> How wilt thou reason with them, how refute
> Thir Idolisms, Traditions, Paradoxes?
> Error by his own arms is best evinc't. (IV.229–35)

Classical oratory is suggested to Christ as the source of the principles of statecraft needed for his kingdom, and classical philosophy as offering the ethical knowledge needed for his teaching. An ecclesiastical frame of reference is further developed by Christ's answer:

> Think not but that I know these things; or think
> I know them not; not therefore am I short
> Of knowing what I ought: he who receives
> Light from above, from the fountain of light,
> No other doctrine needs. (IV.286–90)

This statement closely parallels the position Milton assumed in *The Likeliest Means* (1659) on the vexed question of ministerial learning.

In that tract, a contribution to the tithe and learned-ministry controversies, Milton had answered the tithe supporters' argument that tithes are necessary to reimburse ministers for the expense of their university education by the assertion that the minister's learning is entirely from above: "it is a fond error, though too much beleevd among us, to think that the universitie makes a minister of the gospel; what it may conduce to other arts and sciences, I dispute not now: but that which makes fit a minister, the scripture can best informe us to be only from above; whence also we are bid to seek them." [5] But the argument of the tract moves beyond the strictly ecclesiastical issue of ministerial learning and speaks also to the question of the private man's pathway to spiritual truth. For both minister and laity, Milton asserts, the path is precisely the same—Scripture and the illumination of the Spirit of God: "Therefor are the scriptures translated into every vulgar tongue, as being held in main matters of belief and salvation, plane and easie to the poorest: and such no less then thir teachers have the spirit to guide them in all truth." [6] In the same tract, however, Milton assumes that ministers generally will be learned: he refers to the biblical commentaries, manuals, and other aids available in English to the minister, proposes that the state erect libraries in which the minister might study, and outlines a plan for training prospective ministers in languages and arts in local preparatory schools. Moreover, in his *De Doctrina* Milton states a number of "requisites for the public interpretation of Scripture" which presuppose learning: "knowledge of languages; inspection of the originals; examination of the context; care in distinguishing between literal and figurative expressions; consideration of cause and circumstance, of antecedents and consequents; mutual comparison of texts; and regard to the analogy of faith." [7] I have argued elsewhere that the apparent discrepancy in the argument of the tract is resolved by the implicit distinction Milton makes between the doctrines of the arts, sciences, and philosophies, and the skills derived from human learning such as methods of textual analysis, knowledge of languages, and the like. The

first is wholly useless to the minister or to the seeker after
spiritual truth since his doctrine must come only from above,
but the second, though not essential, will normally be useful
to the minister in explicating God's Word.[8] This is precisely
the position Christ assumes at the beginning of his answer
to Satan in the learning passage: whether or not he knows
the classical texts, they are irrelevant to his mission, as "other
doctrine" is useless and misleading in relation to the "Light
from above."

The concepts enunciated in the tract and implicit in the
poem—that spiritual truth comes only from above, that human learning is wholly irrelevant in the spiritual order, that
the minister must not commingle the doctrines of human
learning with the divine revelation—are central to reformed
Protestantism. The biblical *locus classicus* for them is I Corinthians ii:4–5, "And my speech, and my preaching was not with
entising words of mans wisdome, but in demonstration of
the Spirit, and of power:/ That your faith should not stand
in the wisedome of men, but in the power of God."

The centrality of these attitudes may be illustrated in the
following extracts. Zwingli declared that a man properly approaches Scripture only when he,

despairyinge of hys owne witte and reason, wholly, doth altogether
submit and humble hym selfe, & confesseth that he knoweth
nothinge but hanging wholly upon God, doth geve a diligent eare,
to his inspiratyon ... But he is sayde to have nothyng, whiche doth
ingerate and bryng to the scriptures his owne carnall and fleshly
sense ... The wordes of the spirite, are manifeste and cleare, the
doctryne of god, is lightsome, illuminatyng teaching, and certifiyng
mans heart and mynde, of his salvation, without any patchyng
of humayne reason. ... Wherfore we do see that the symple wyttes
of ye disciples, were taughte of God, to thys ende, that wee myghte
learne too seeke all the knowledge of heavenly things in God
onely.[9]

The English Congregationalist Joshua Sprigge citing I Corinthians ii:2 linked Paul's abrogation of human learning in preaching to an argument that Christ's kingdom must be in no way dependent upon the power of the world:

For I, determined not to know any thing among you, save Jesus Christ, and him crucified, 1 Cor. 2 . . . Christs death is thus *avenged* upon the glory of the world, whilest the power and greatnesse of this world is *reprobated* and rejected from most *noble* uses and honourable services, namely, from ministring *in* his kingdome: Goe, says Christ to *mans wisdome* and humane Eloquence, I will have none of thee in preaching my Gospel; and returne to the scabbard, says he to the *Magistrates sword* . . . Thus Christ reprobates parts and learning . . . and he brings down the mighty things of the world, by the weake; and things that *are,* by things that *are not, that no flesh may glory in his presence, but he that glorieth, let him glory in the Lord,* that neither our *faith,* nor the Ordinances *successe, should stand in the wisdome of men.*[10]

Similarly, the Baptist Samuel How sharply differentiated the role of learning in the order of nature and in interpreting Scripture:

I doe acknowledge it [learning] in it selfe to be a good thing, and good in its proper place, which is for the repayring of that *decay which came upon man for sin* . . . but bring it once to be a *help to understand the mind of God in the holy Scriptures,* and there it is *detestable filth, drosse, and dung* in that respect, and so good for nothing, but [to] *destroy, and cause men to erre.*[11]

These precepts were constantly invoked in Protestant polemic to refute the view of philosophy as *ancillae theologiae* held by Roman Catholics and many Anglicans, and during the Civil War they were turned against the conservative Presbyterians who also upheld church establishment, tithes, and a university-trained ministry. For all their interest in universities, though, the Presbyterians did not deny in theory these central

Protestant principles relating to the autonomy of the spiritual order, and, on the other hand, comparatively few Protestants took up the position of the radical sectaries and the Fifth Monarchists that learning is useless even in the natural order and that ignorance is a positive advantage to the minister or the seeker after religious truth.[12]

This context illuminates one aspect of the learning temptation in *Paradise Regained,* but in the final analysis that temptation cannot be seen wholly in ecclesiastical terms or even in the broader terms (also explored in Milton's tract) of the Christian's proper approach to scriptural revelation. Satan offers Athens to Christ in all of its fifth- and fourth-century glory as a compendium of Gentile knowledge, and therefore as the embodiment of wisdom as Parthia was the embodiment of power and Rome of grandeur and magnificence. Moreover, this wisdom is offered by Satan not simply as it is necessary to Christ's peculiar mission and that of his church, but as the highest good in the scale of ethical goods offered to Everyman's choice, as the virtue needed to complete both the contemplative and the active lives. Augustine's statement of the relation of wisdom to the active and the contemplative lives is especially relevant to the terms in which Satan presents the temptation:

As the study of wisdom consists in action and contemplation, so that one part of it may be called active, and the other contemplative—the active part having reference to the conduct of life, that is, to the regulation of morals, and the contemplative part to the investigation into the causes of nature and into pure truth—Socrates is said to have excelled in the active part of that study, while Pythagoras gave more attention to its contemplative part ... To Plato is given the praise of having perfected philosophy by combining both parts into one.[13]

Satan evidently addresses Christ as one who wishes to combine (like Plato) the contemplative and active lives, that is, as Satan interprets these terms, the life of learning and the life devoted to the exercise of moral virtue in the world. Remarking upon Christ's early attraction to "contemplation," Satan defines the wisdom appropriate to the life of contemplation to be the wide-ranging, universal knowledge of all things in the world: "as thy Empire must extend,/ So let extend thy mind o'er all the world,/ In knowledge, all things in it comprehend" (IV.222–24). He also offers wisdom, defined as classical ethical knowledge, as that which is necessary to perfect Christ's kingdom within and so to prepare for Christ's own active life in the world—"These rules will render thee a King complete/ Within thyself, much more with Empire join'd" (IV.283–84). Accordingly, he praises the tragedians as "teachers best/ Of moral prudence" (IV.262–63) and extols Socrates (whom Christ had commended so highly for his moral excellence in the banquet-wealth-glory sequence) as the one who turned philosophy away from idle speculation and toward ethics, and who was himself the source of the ethical teaching of the various schools. Satan's comment that "sage Philosophy . . / From Heaven descended to the low-rooft house/ Of *Socrates*" (IV.272–74) alludes to Cicero's quotation of Varro on the subject of Socrates' special achievement in philosophy, a comment constantly reiterated in the Renaissance:

It is my view, and it is universally agreed that Socrates was the first person who summoned philosophy away from mysteries veiled in concealment by nature herself, upon which all philosophers before him had been engaged, and led it to the subject of ordinary life, in order to investigate the virtues and vices, and good and evil generally, and to realize that heavenly matters are either remote from our knowledge or else, however fully known, have nothing to do with the good life.[14]

Classical learning is, then, offered to Christ as the source of the wisdom which he will need not only as a public figure to achieve his destined role as king and prophet of his church, but also as a private man to lead the contemplative life and to perfect the kingdom within.

However, if the learning temptation cannot be given a strictly ecclesiastical interpretation, it must nevertheless be read in theological terms. The issue here is the contrast between the role of learning in the order of nature and its role in the order of grace. The subject of the debate is the concept of wisdom—whether its substance is natural learning or revelation, whether its source is God or man. It has not been generally recognized that Satan makes of wisdom a wholly mundane thing. Although the lures in the panorama of Athens are greatly exalted and refined, Athens may be seen to be, like Rome, a compendium of the earlier worldly enticements. The ambition here proposed to Christ is not for simple dominion over Athens, but rather for association with the intellectual richness of its life which will lead to a dominion of the mind "o'er all the world" (IV.223). The glory offered is the opportunity to "Be famous . . . / By wisdom" (IV.221–22) after the example of Socrates. And replacing that other grove containing the Epicurean banquet is the "Olive Grove of *Academe*" whose sensory delights are directed to a much more refined sensibility. There

> the *Attic* Bird
> Trills her thick-warbl'd notes the summer long;
> There flow'ry hill *Hymettus* with the sound
> Of Bees' industrious murmur oft invites
> To studious musing; there *Ilissus* rolls
> His whispering stream. (IV.245–50)

Moreover, Satan's stated definition of wisdom as knowledge of all things "in the world" and as knowledge relating to moral virtue would be wholly unacceptable to Christians in the Augustinian tradition, who labeled the first kind of knowledge *scientia* rather than *sapientia,* and the second sort as *prudentia* or else as an aspect of *scientia.*[15] Even the classical philosophers Satan cites did not define wisdom in these earth-bound terms. Plato considered wisdom to be the contemplation of the eternal, immutable, and intelligible ideas, and his Idea of the Good is a quasi-mystical concept. The Stoics defined wisdom as the knowledge of both human and divine things: "Sapientia est rerum humanarum divinarumque scientia." In the Augustinian Christian tradition the wisdom appropriate to the contemplative life is knowledge of God, and the apex of the kingdom within is occupied not by the moral virtues ordered by prudence but by the theological virtues—faith, hope, charity—made known through God's revelation and given through his grace.[16]

In assuming a radical distinction between knowledge (*scientia*), which derives from the study of the things of the world, and wisdom (*sapientia*), which comes only from above, Milton's Christ is defending a Christian commonplace prevalent from Augustine's time through the seventeenth century. The distinction was, interestingly enough, often developed through allusions to and commentary upon Job xxviii, especially the following verses:

But where shall wisedome be found? and where is the place of understanding?

Man knoweth not the price thereof; neither is it found in the land of the living.

It cannot bee goten for golde, neither shall silver be weighed for the price thereof.

God understandeth the way thereof, and he knoweth the place thereof.

Then did hee see it, and declare it; he prepared it, yea and searched it out.

And unto man he said, Behold, the feare of the Lord, that is wisedome: and to depart from evill, is understanding.

(xxviii:12–13, 15, 23, 27–28)

Augustine's seminal exegesis of these verses and especially of the twenty-eighth verse, which he renders on the authority of the Septuagint version, "Ecce pietas est sapientia; abstinere autem a malis est scientia," [17] sets the precedent for the direct opposition of *sapientia* and *scientia*. In the passage cited above in which he identified exemplars of wisdom from both the active and the contemplative spheres, Augustine defined wisdom in human, philosophical terms, but when the Jobean context establishes a theological perspective, he completely separates wisdom from human knowledge:

Having examined a great number of passages from the Holy Scriptures, I find it written in the Book of Job, that holy man being the speaker, "Behold, piety, that is wisdom; but to depart from evil is knowledge." In thus distinguishing, it must be understood that wisdom belongs to contemplation, knowledge to action. For in this place he meant by piety the worship of God, which in Greek is called Θεοσέβεια. For the sentence in the Greek MSS has that word. And what is there in eternal things more excellent than God, of whom alone the nature is unchangeable? And what is the worship of Him except the love of Him, by which we now desire to see Him, and we believe and hope that we shall see Him; and in proportion as we make progress, see now through a glass in an enigma, but then in clearness?... Discourse about these and the like subjects seems to me to be the discourse itself of wisdom. But to depart from evil, which Job says is knowledge, is without doubt of temporal things.... And therefore, whatsoever we do prudently, boldly, temperately, and justly, belongs to that knowledge or discipline wherewith our action is conversant in avoiding evil and desiring good ... When a discourse then relates to these things, I hold it to be a discourse belonging to knowledge, and to be distinguished from a discourse belonging to wisdom, to which those things belong, which neither have been, nor shall be, but are; and on account of that eternity in which they are, are said to have been, and to be, and to be about to be, without any changeableness of times. [18]

Augustine's use of the Job passage to support a conception of wisdom as wholly derived from and wholly concerned with the divine, and his sharp distinction between this wisdom and that ethical knowledge which is of human derivation and focus, presents a close parallel to Christ's attitude in *Paradise Regained*. At the conclusion of the banquet-wealth-glory sequence Christ had appealed both to Socrates and Job as teachers and exemplars of the highest moral and ethical knowledge, though he left no doubt that he considered Job to be the more perfect of the two. Now, using his accustomed strategy, Satan begins the learning temptation by inviting Christ to identify himself completely with the lesser of these two types— Socrates—and he changes the terms of the discourse so as to equate moral knowledge, for which Christ had earlier honored Socrates, with wisdom. Given this new context, Christ now disparages as lacking in wisdom the same classical philosophers whose ethical teachings he had before echoed and praised, and, vehemently denying that wisdom can be of mundane origin, Christ identifies himself in effect with the more adequate conception of wisdom associated with Job in the Augustinian Christian tradition.

Though the Scholastics modified the Augustinian position by attributing the name of wisdom to metaphysics and natural theology as well as to revelation, many medieval and Renaissance Christian writers such as Filelfo, Lyra, Nicolas of Cusa, John Colet, and Ficino identified themselves with and expanded the Augustinian position. They agreed for the most part that wisdom (*sapientia*) is the knowledge of the divine things of God; that absolute wisdom is God himself; that human wisdom is piety, faith in and worship of God according to his revelation; that the ancients were not wise themselves but only seekers after wisdom as Socrates admitted when he declared that he knew nothing; that knowledge of temporal human things or of mere moral virtue is not *sapientia* but *scientia,* or *scientia* and *prudentia.*[19] Juan Luis Vives stated these conclusions succinctly: "Perfect wisdom is to know this Religion: to live according to it, is perfecte Vertue ... This is eternall life, sayth Christ our lord, to knowe the father, & whom he sent among us, Jesus Christ his sonne. This is the course of most absolute wisedom, wherof the first steppe is, to Knowe thy self, and the last of all to know God." [20]

Throughout the Renaissance Job xxviii was a favorite text for defining the Christian conception of wisdom. Filelfo, citing Job's "pietas est sapientia," declared:

Therefore that which is of wisdom is that by which eternal and unchangeable things are contemplated. The inferior realm of knowledge is versed in temporal and mutable things, and in action. Knowledge, therefore, is not otherwise different from wisdom than action from contemplation. He who therefore is most learned, is most holy; the Apostle Paul shows this most clearly with this comment: Therefore to one man by the Spirit is given the word of wisdom, but to another the word of knowledge is according to his own spirit. This principle also did most innocent Job teach, saying, Therefore *pietas* is wisdom, but to abstain from evil is knowledge. In this distinction is declared clearly that wisdom is contemplation and knowledge, action. *Pietas,* therefore in this place is the virtue by which we worship God.... Knowledge therefore is that which is developed according to the precepts of the works of human life.[21]

Calvin also drew from Job xxviii the conclusion "that our reason and understanding extende no further, then too the things heere bylowe, and which concerne the present life. But if we woulde mounte up too the kingdome of heaven, and seeke the things that perteyne too the everlasting life: there wee fayle and are utterly blinde ... If wee intende too knowe what is meete for us, let us desire God too shewe it by hys holy spirite." [22] Similarly, John Trapp observed that the wisdom described in Job xxviii is "supernal and supernatural ... such as cannot be fathomed or found out by humane abilities, or by natural reason. But God *revealeth* it unto *his by his Spirit.*" Joseph Caryl also declared that this wisdom is reserved to "those who are holy and believing," and that Christ himself is "the publisher of this truth" in Scripture and to the conscience by the Spirit.[23]

The distinction between *sapientia* and *scientia* in the Christian discourses on wisdom was often attended by just the kind of disparagement of classical learning and of the philosophical schools that is found in Christ's response in *Paradise Regained.* Like the poem, these texts cite the patristic argument that the Bible is a compendium of all other learning, and indeed the original source of Gentile knowledge.[24] Also like the poem, these passages refer to Socrates' famous comment that he knew only that he knew nothing as evidence that the ancients themselves eschewed any claim to true wisdom. Again like the poem, such disparagements often followed upon a commendation of the classical writers for moral virtue or knowledge of natural things; it is only from the perspective of Christian wisdom that they were denounced as absurd and foolish. And, when allowance is made for the dramatic situation in the poem, the tone of Christ's denunciation of the schools does not seem noticeably harsher than that of many similar Christian comments on classical learning.[25] Lactantius, for example, observed that "Socrates, though he was the most learned of all the philosophers ... so despised, derided, and cast aside the learning in which the philosophers then boasted, that he professed that very thing as the greatest learning, that he had learnt that he knew nothing." [26] Luther's comment on classical learning in comparison with revelation certainly matches or surpasses in acerbity the learning passage in Milton's poem:

The wisdom of the *Grecians,* in comparison of the wisdom of the Jews, is altogether Beastial, for without God, no wisdom nor true understanding can bee, the wisdom of the *Grecians* consisteth in an external virtuous and civil conversation, but the end of the wisdom of the Jews (such as are upright and Godly) is to fear God and to trust in him. The wisdom of the world is the wisdom of the *Grecians,* from whence *Daniel* nameth all the Kingdoms of the world (according to their kindes) Beasts and ignorant Cattle.[27]

Peter Martyr identified the philosophers as the sources of the "vain conceit" which Paul warned against in Colossians: *"Paule* reprooveth that philosophie, which is corrupted through the inventions of men, and ambitious contentions of philosophers....Wherfore the apostle saith; *Through philosophie and vaine deceit*...And who doubteth, but that the fate and impassibilitie of the Stoiks, the perpetuall doubting of the Academiks, and the idle and unoccupied deitie of the Epicures, was this vaine deceit." [28] Even the Cambridge Platonist Nathanael Culverwel, for all his devotion to the classics, can invoke telling metaphors to display the darkness and tawdryness of classical philosophy in comparison with revelation:

You may see *Socrates* in the twilight, and lamenting his obscure and benighted condition, and telling you that his Lamp will shew him nothing but his own darknesse. You may see *Plato* sitting down by the waters of *Lethe,* and weeping because he could not remember his foormer notions. You may hear *Aristotle* bewailing himself... that his *abrasa tabula* has so few, and such imperfect impressions upon it.

. . . .

The Candle of *Socrates,* and the candle of *Plato,* the Lamp of *Epictetus,* they did all shine before men, and shine more then some that would fain be call'd Christians. Nature makes a very fine show, and a goodly glittering in the eye of the world, but this Candle cannot appear in the presence of a Sun; all the paintings and varnishing of Nature, they please and enamour the eyes of men, but they melt away at the presence of God. The Lamp of a Moralist may waste itself in doing good to others, and yet at length may go out in a snuffe, and be cast into utter darknesse.[29]

The Jobean commentators are especially disposed to enumerate the errors of the schools in contrast to Job's wisdom. One anonymous commentator observes that Job teaches us to bear adversity better than any of the philosophers,

of the which none hath taught anything purely in this matier. The Epicures call us from the crosse to delectacion, & pleasure. The peripatetiques counte sickenesse, povertie, reproche, and disworshippe among the greatest eivilles that can be. Certaine Stoicques doe counsaile men that be in daunger either to breake their own neckes, either to hang, or kil themselves, or by some other violente death to shift from their peine. And other teache other things more foolishe.[30]

And, as Edna Newmeyer has pointed out,[31] Theodore Beza's disparagement of the schools in his commentary on Job closely resembles in substance and tone the comparable passage in *Paradise Regained*:

Some of the chiefest of them [the Greek philosophers] have not beene ashamed to say, that there is no certen knowledge to be had of anything [the Skeptics].

. . . .

Who knoweth not the wicked opinion of the *Epicures* attributing all things to the concourse or meeting of their small motes which they call *Atomi?* who knoweth not that the *Stoicks* sliding from one extreame to another, have tied god by the chaines as it were, of midle and secondary causes? who knoweth not that the *Peripatet-icks,* the wittiest of all the rest, have shut out the event of al things from Gods providence?

. . . .

We have here . . . in *Job's* person a most rare example. . . . by so much more excellent then all the precepts of the *Platonists* and *Peripatet-icks,* by how much deeds are better then words, and action is to be preferred before vaine and idle speculation. But among the rest of *Jobs* vertues, the invincible constancie of his godly minde, most wonderfullie sheweth it selfe; condemning both that iron disposition and unsensiblenes of the *Stoicks,* and also whatsoever

the Philosophers babble of their vaineglorious fortitude and Mag-
nanimitie...For surelie wee do not reade of any (except the onely
Sonne of God, in whome all things were perfit in the highest
degree) who...did with greater courage and constancie wrestle
with and passe through those miseries, as did this our Champion.[32]

What has been happening in the learning temptation is now
evident. Satan has offered Christ human knowledge (*scientia*),
terming it wisdom (*sapientia*); he has offered it in place of
the true wisdom from above, and as a means of obtaining
certain goods which only wisdom itself can gain—the life of
contemplation, the perfection of the kingdom within, and the
accomplishment of Christ's prophetic and kingly offices.
Christ's vehement rejection of knowledge offered in place of
wisdom is firmly grounded in the tradition which identifies
God as the substance and source of wisdom; the question of
the role of knowledge in its own sphere, the natural order,
is never at issue in this passage. The context thus wholly
accounts for Christ's changed attitude toward classical learning, which he used and highly praised during the ethical
debate on the kingdom within, but which he degrades and
pronounces to be almost worthless when it is presented as
wisdom and viewed from the standpoint of the eternal wisdom made available to man through revelation.

It may be, as Schultz argues, that the harshness of tone in
this passage owes something to Milton's recent involvement
in the learned-ministry controversy. But since (as has been
seen) tone as well as substance can be matched in much other
commentary on Christian wisdom, there seems to be no warrant for regarding this passage either as testifying to some
basic change in Milton's earlier humanistic attitude toward
learning, or as inviting a purely ecclesiastical interpretation.
One finds close parallels in contemporary commentary on wisdom and knowledge even for the passage which most dis-
tresses modern readers, that in which Christ denounces the

reading of many books and seems to suggest that only those
who have no need of books can properly use them:

> However, many books
> Wise men have said are wearisome; who reads
> Incessantly, and to his reading brings not
> A spirit and judgment equal or superior
> (And what he brings, what needs he elsewhere seek)
> Uncertain and unsettl'd still remains,
> Deep verst in books and shallow in himself,
> Crude or intoxicate, collecting toys,
> And trifles for choice matters, worth a sponge;
> As Children gathering pebbles on the shore. (IV.321-30)

The biblical source in Ecclesiastes xii:12, "of making many
bookes there is no end; and much studie is a wearinesse of
the flesh," provides part of the context in which this passage
demands to be read, and the rest is supplied by such contemporary parallels as Quarles' verse meditation on Job xxviii:

> The Morall sayes, All Wisedome that is given
> To hood-wink't mortals, first, proceeds from heaven:
> Truth's errour, Wisedom's, but wise insolence,
> And light's but darknesse, not deriv'd from thence;
>
> . . . .
>
> Wisdom's the Card of knowledge, which, without
> That Guide, at random's wreck't on every doubt:
> Knowledge, when Wisedome is too weak to guide her
> Is like a head-strong Horse, that throwes the Rider:
> Which made that great Philosopher avow,
> He knew so much, that he did nothing know.[33]

Christ's disparagement of classical poetry may seem especially harsh, and perhaps cannot be wholly accounted for in
terms of context and tradition. Nevertheless, this attitude is
far from unique, and it can be paralleled in the writings of
the Fathers as well as in thematic statements by Christian

poets of various periods who desired to extend the hegemony of the true faith over the domain of the Muses.[34] In the learning temptation the pagan poets are presented to Christ as sources of true wisdom, and Christ responds by damning them for their "Gods ridiculous" and for the "vices of thir Deities, and their own" (IV.340, 342), though he admits that some were teachers of moral prudence. Christ's unfavorable comparison of them to the biblical poets, and his conclusion that biblical poetry is not only manifestly superior in truth but also in art, is really a reiteration of Milton's statement in *The Reason of Church Government* that the lyric poetry of the Bible excels all other "in the very critical art of composition."[35] Both statements evidently stem from Milton's refusal to separate form and content in poetry, or, to put it another way, from his Platonic refusal to separate truth and beauty.

Finally, Christ's observation that the classical orators, though "Statists indeed,/ And lovers of thir Country" (IV.354-55), were far inferior to the prophets echoes Milton's comment in the *Defensio* that Scripture contains the highest formulation of the mere natural law regarding civil government.[36] Yet the references here to the prophets who "with our Law, best form a King" (IV.364) have special relevance to this King and his church (as do the comments about government throughout the poem). Christ's reference to the prophets reinforces the movement throughout this entire temptation away from the Law and the literal types to the prophetic interpretation of the types in terms of metaphor and symbol, the prophets being those who, according to John Smith, were able "in these types and Shadows, which were Symbols of some spiritual things, to behold the Antitypes."[37]

In the learning passage, then, three definitions of wisdom are under discussion. The first is the classical, with Socrates as its source and prime exemplar; it is offered to Christ by Satan and functions here as an inferior type of Christ's own wisdom. The second is the Jobean formula which recognizes *sapientia* as wholly divine; it is brought to bear upon this passage by the earlier pairing together of Socrates and Job, and by the whole tradition contrasting the two in terms of wisdom. The third is Christ's own unique role as the "Image" of the Father's wisdom.

In this passage Christ appears in some respects as a Second Socrates living over again the experience of Socrates recorded in the *Apologia*. In that dialogue Socrates explains that he sought to prove false the oracle which pronounced him wisest of men by examining all the claimants to wisdom—philosophers, public men, poets, artisans—and that he found their claims worthless. Similarly, Christ in this passage analyzes all the classical pretenders to wisdom and finds them useless for his purposes. Socrates concludes with the suggestion that wisdom is divine, proposing that what the oracle really meant in declaring him wisest of men is that "the wisdom of men is worth little or nothing.... He, O men, is the wisest, who, like Socrates, knows that his wisdom is in truth worth nothing." [38] But Christ is a Second Socrates who goes far beyond the type, for he does not rest his claim to wisdom on the discovery that he knows nothing. He recognizes that even as ethical teachers the philosophers cannot carry out Socrates' noblest precept— know thyself—without the understanding of the Fall, and of Grace, and of man's creation by God, but must remain "Ignorant of themselves, of God much more" (IV.310). Over against this inferior type Christ identifies himself with the Jobean insight, "pietas est sapientia," with its concomitant recognition that wisdom per se is only from above: thus he recognizes God as the object of contemplation, the giver of the revelation that leads to self-knowledge, the source of the theological virtues which perfect the inner kingdom, and the revealer of the spiritual truth which alone guides the church.

But more than this, there is an obvious basis in traditional

Christian commentary for the identification of Christ himself
as the incarnate wisdom of God. The customary exegesis of
John i identifies the Logos with the Son of God, the incarnate
Word, and the exegesis of Proverbs viii:22–23 identifies the
Son with Wisdom, who declares, "The LORD possessed me in
the beginning of his way, before his works of old./ I was set
up from everlasting, from the beginning, or ever the earth
was." Milton's anti-Trinitarianism modifies the identification
of the Son incarnate in Christ as the eternal Wisdom, for this
attribute is proper only to the Father. Yet Milton's presentation of the Son in *Paradise Lost* as the visible Image of the
Father, rendered able, by special grant from the Father, to exercise the Father's omnipotence in expelling the angels from
heaven, and to utilize the Father's creative energy in forming
the world, prepares the reader to see Christ here as one who
may be the Image of the Father's wisdom. That is, he may ex-
press as much of the divine wisdom as God sees fit at any time
to devolve upon him. In this context the words with which
Christ begins his answer to Satan's learning temptation carry
a *double-entendre* of which Christ himself is not yet fully
aware, for they point beyond Job's understanding of wisdom
to Christ's own unique status as the True Oracle, the one who,
as Image of the Father's wisdom, may communicate in a special way with the Fountain of Light: "he who receives/ Light
from above, from the fountain of light,/ No other doctrine
needs" (IV.288–90).

*I*N THE storm-tower sequence, the dramatic conflict between Christ and Satan intensifies steadily, building to
a grand climactic moment of self-discovery and self-
manifestation for both of these characters. Christ and Satan
have been moving throughout the poem toward opposite poles
with respect to self-control and control over the external action, and in this sequence they assume ultimate positions.
When Satan returns Christ to the wilderness after the temptation of the kingdoms he can no longer maintain even the pretense of civility. His irony is now blatant and crude: "What
dost thou in this World? The Wilderness/ For thee is fittest
place" (IV.372–73). As Christ's comment makes clear, the cha-
otic upheaval of the storm is the expression of Satan's inner
disintegration and frenzy: "Ambitious spirit, and wouldst be
thought my God,/ And storm'st refus'd, thinking to terrify/
Mee to thy will" (IV.495–97). Against this physical and psy-
chic storm Christ presents the diametrically opposed image
of perfect order and tranquillity. He endures the storm "with
untroubl'd mind," he is "patient," "unshaken," "unappall'd in
calm and sinless peace" (IV.401, 420, 421, 425), and he answers Satan's expressed concern about his dismal night with
a witty counterthrust which exasperates Satan to fury: "Mee
worse than wet thou find'st not; other harm/ Those terrors
which thou speak'st of, did me none" (IV.486–87). The beautiful morning after the storm offers objective testimony to the
fact that the control of events has now passed completely
out of Satan's hands.

Following the storm Satan returns to tempt Christ in his

"wonted shape"—which evidently means in his own demonic shape, appropriate to him now that he has no more guiles and gifts to offer but can only display the violence and brutality which comprise his essential self. His loss of control causes him to assert brazenly the point he had endeavored to insinuate subtly throughout the poem—that he is himself a "Son of God," and that Christ can lodge no special claim to divine sonship. This assertion is a further instance of Satan's unintentional self-revelation for it testifies to the blindness and self-delusion which have prevented him from learning anything fundamental about Christ's nature during the entire temptation episode, but in addition it shows Satan's now desperate attempt to use his own uncertainties to evoke doubts in Christ concerning his sonship:

> Then hear, O Son of *David,* Virgin-born;
> For Son of God to me is yet in doubt:
>
> . . . .
>
> Therefore I thought thee worthy my nearer view
> And narrower Scrutiny, that I might learn
> In what degree or meaning thou art call'd
> The Son of God, which bears no single sense;
> The Son of God I also am, or was,
> And if I was, I am; relation stands;
> All men are Sons of God; yet thee I thought
> In some respect far higher so declar'd. (IV.500–501, 514–21)

Concluding that he has found Christ proof against temptation, "To th'utmost of mere man both wise and good,/ Not more" (IV.535–36), Satan asserts that his next move is devised to discover unequivocally "what more thou art than man,/ Worth naming Son of God" (IV.538–39). Accordingly, the tower episode functions both as a temptation and as an ultimate test of identity. And it is in this episode, as I will argue below, that the various themes and also the dramatic action centering upon the discovery of Christ's mission and his nature are drawn together and resolved in the single gesture of Christ's calm stance on the tower. Here Christ endures the ultimate test of the kingdom within, violence and the threat of death; he achieves a full understanding of and typologically figures forth his sacrificial priestly office; and he is vouchsafed the final revelation of his divine sonship.

The nocturnal storm and the tower episode continue to develop the twin motifs, present throughout the poem, of Christ's private moral virtue and his public office. As contrivances of Satan's rage and violence these incidents seek to reduce Christ, in his private capacity, to fear and terror, as is indicated by the narrator's twice-repeated statement that all Satan's "darts" and "devices" are now spent (IV.366, 443), that he comes now "Desperate of better course, to vent his rage/ And mad despite," and that he is "swoln with rage" (IV.445–46, 499). Under these attacks Christ displays patience and fortitude, the virtues Everyman needs to repel or to endure the onslaught of evil.[1]

Milton's creation of an extra-biblical episode involving fear and terror finds some warrant in commentary on the temptation episode. One basis for it is the customary interpretation of Psalm xci as referring to Christ's temptation, inasmuch as this Psalm is the source of Satan's reference in the tower temptation to God's promise of angelic rescue to his faithful, "he shall give his Angels charge over thee: to keepe thee in all thy wayes./ They shall beare thee up in their hands: lest thou dash thy foote against a stone" (Ps. xci:11, 12). The adjacent verses which describe encounters with the sources of fear and terror could therefore be easily attached to the temptation episode:

Thou shalt not be afraid for the terror by night: nor for the arrow that flieth by day:

Nor for the pestilence that walketh in darknesse; nor for the destruction, that wasteth at noone day.

Thou shalt tread upon the Lion, and adder: the young Lion and the dragon shalt thou trample under feet. (Ps. xci:5, 6, 13)

In Eusebius' interpretation the beasts of this passage referred literally to the wild beasts among whom Christ wandered, and symbolically to "the devil himself, and the ruling evil powers that follow him" whom Christ overcame in the temptation; also the "terror by night" referred to demons attacking Christ in the night, and the "arrow by day" to the words Satan flung at Christ during the temptation.[2]

Moreover, though the Fathers customarily explained the tower temptation simply as a temptation to vainglory and presumption, and though the Reformers interpreted it as primarily a temptation to Christ to use presumptuous means of descending from the tower when he might descend normally by the stairs,[3] several of the Protestants made terror and despair important aspects of the episode. Labeling the tower incident a "violent and hellish temptation," Thomas Taylor explained that Satan's violent transportation of Christ to the tower might be seen as "a meanes...of shaking Christs faith with terror and feare what might become of him, being now delivered into the hands of Satan." [4] And John Trapp spoke for many Calvinists in interpreting the tower temptation as an effort to drive Christ to despair and suicide:

Here our Saviour is tempted to self-murther, by an old Manslayer. And when *Moses, Elias, Jonas* and others of the best sort of Saints were in a fit of discontent, and grew weary of their lives, wishing for death, Divines doubt not but Satan gave a push at them with his ten horns, to dispatch, and ease themselves of the present trouble, by cutting off their own days. A dangerous and hideous temptation.[5]

In Milton's presentation, however, these motifs of terror and violence are not subsidiary but central, and the tower episode is at one level an attempted murder of Christ. Most of the exegetes understood that Christ was placed upon a narrow ledge of the Temple where he would be able to stand (with some difficulty) if he chose,[6] but Milton's Satan places Christ on the topmost spire where by human power alone he cannot stand. That Satan expects Christ to fall is evident from his scornful remark, "to stand upright/ Will ask thee skill" (IV. 551–52), and by the narrator's observation that Satan, amazed, "Fell whence he stood to see his Victor fall" (IV.571). The storm sequence acts as an induction and as a preparative to the tower episode, inviting Christ to see himself alone and unsheltered, denied the heavenly protection promised the people of God in Psalm xci, subjected in the present to the fury of the "Fierce rain" and "stormy blasts" (IV.412, 418), and expecting in the future only "dangers, and adversities and pains" (IV.479). Satan evidently hoped that as a result of this experience Christ's confidence in God's protection would be shaken so that he would waver and fall when placed upon the precarious spire, or else that he would give way to a "death wish" as a means of escaping present and future troubles, or else that he would be driven by the insinuated doubts about his nature and God's protection to cast himself down in order to test himself and God.

Christ's patience and fortitude in the storm scene are presented with implicit, though not explicit, allusion to Job. At the conclusion of the offer of Athens Christ identified himself with Jobean wisdom rather than with Socratic ethical knowledge, so that we expect Satan, in accordance with his usual strategy, to derive his next temptation from that identification. The descriptions of Christ in the storm scene as "patient," "calm," and "unshaken" indicate that he is indeed displaying that virtue for which Job was the universally recognized pattern.[7] The storm itself recalls the several Jobean tempests: a violent wind destroyed Job's house and children, God spoke to Job from a whirlwind, and Job on his dunghill, according to Chrysostom, endured storms both real and metaphorical:

"though assaulted on all sides by a flood like this, when there raged about him a fearful storm, clouds, rain, lightnings, whirling winds, and waterspouts, he remained himself unmoved, seated as it were in the midst of this surge, thus awful and overwhelming, as in a perfect calm, and no murmur escaped him." [8] The description of Christ enduring the storm is very similar indeed:

> the Clouds
> From many a horrid rift abortive pour'd
> Fierce rain with lightning mixt, water with fire
> In ruin reconcil'd: nor slept the winds
> Within thir stony caves, but rush'd abroad
>
> . . . .
>
> while thou
> Satt'st unappall'd in calm and sinless peace. (IV.410-25)

After the stormy night Satan approaches Christ rather in the character of a Jobean comforter, intimating that the storm in some way signifies God's or Nature's displeasure with Christ: "This Tempest at this Desert most was bent;/ Of men at thee" (IV.465-66), whereas Christ rightly discerns that the fearful signs (like Job's boils) are "not sent from God, but thee" (IV.491).

After Christ has imitated Job with respect to patience and fortitude, Satan progresses to the next stage of his customary temptation strategy and invites Christ to identify himself literally and completely with his type. Satan's declaration that Christ has now proved himself "th'utmost of mere man both wise and good,/ Not more" (IV.535-36) asserts that Christ has matched the highest human exemplar of both moral virtue and wisdom—previously identified in the poem as Job. Satan's continuing literalism of mind as well as his temptation tactic keep him from recognizing or admitting that Christ has already overmatched Job in the storm episode, for Christ has not given vent to any of Job's complaints, laments, or declarations of God's desertion,[9] and Satan also ignores the striking declarations which Christ has hitherto made about his mission and office. Satan's suggestion to Christ that he is no more than a perfect man like Job constitutes the last desperate attempt to deter Christ from a full realization of his unique, divine nature and mission, and hence from that final, determinate conquest over satanic violence and death which the divine power alone can achieve.

The storm-tower sequence also challenges Christ as a public figure in his priestly role, the third aspect of his mediatorial office. According to Diodati, Christ's priesthood involves his continual intercession for mankind, but principally his offering "himself as a Sacrifice to his Father, to expiate the sins of the whole world," at the Crucifixion.[10] The storm-tower episodes foreshadow the final defeat of Sin and Death at the Crucifixion, the defeat which the Father earlier prophesied that Christ would accomplish "By Humiliation and strong Sufferance" (I.160). There is warrant for linking the theme of Christ's priesthood with the Jobean motif in the storm-tower sequence, since even exegetes who paid scant attention to typology identified Job's suffering as a type of Christ's passion and death, and his sacrifices offered for his children and friends as a type of Christ's priestly intercession.[11]

Commentary on the tower temptation often linked that temptation directly with Christ's priestly office. Perkins and Diodati recalled that the scene of this episode, Jerusalem, was the center of the Old Law which Christ's priesthood would supplant, and the place where his death would found the new dispensation.[12] Thomas Taylor pointed out that the Temple upon which Christ was placed held the symbols of Christ's priesthood in the Old Law: the sanctum had "the altar of incense for sweete perfume... an holy type of Christ, who offered himselfe on the altar of the crosse, a sacrifice of sweet smell to God his Father," and also "the rod of *Aaron* which had budded, a type of the Priesthood of Christ, who in the world seemed a dead branch and drie, but after his death and resurrection beganne again to flourish." [13] Joseph Hall saw in Satan's violent transportation of Christ to the tower a foreshadowing of the violence accorded him at the Crucifixion: "What was *Pilate,* or the Jewes that persecuted thine innocence, but limbs of this Devill? And why are wee then amazed, to see thee touched and locally transported by the heade, when wee see thee yeelding thy selfe over, to bee crucified by the members?" [14] Several others, with John Knox, conflated Satan's words at the tower temptation with the taunts of the crowds at the Crucifixion: "It is the same tentation whilk the Divill objectit to him be the princes and the preistis in his grevous tormentis upon the cross. For this thai cry, 'Yf he be the Sone of God, lat him come doun fra the cross and we sall beleif in him.' " [15]

Building upon such traditional exegesis Milton contrived his storm and tower sequence to foreshadow and epitomize Christ's passion and death. The comments that Satan's darts are now spent, that he returns at this point only to vent his rage, are in keeping with the usual explanations of Luke iv:13, to the effect that the Devil left Christ "for a season" after the temptation only to return, as Aquinas put it, *"not to tempt Him, but to assail Him openly* ... at the time of His passion." [16] The narrator's comment that Satan "knew his power/ Not yet expir'd" (IV.394–95) when he returned Christ to the wilderness seems an allusion to Christ's words to the soldiers who came to seize him at Gethsemane, "this is your houre, and the power of darknes" (Luke xxii:53). Paraphrasing this verse Diodati related it to the Passion, as "the time in which God suffereth you to practise your rage against me: and the Devill who is the Prince of darknesse, to do all his endeavours through you, to seek to destroy and put me out who am the light of the world, and the sun of righteousness." Thomas

Taylor applied the verse to the Passion and also to the tower temptation: "This was the houre of the power of darknes, wherein Satan was allowed to take all advantages to further his temptation." [17] Milton's emphasis in the storm sequence upon "Darkness" and "louring night" (IV.398, 399) relates that incident to the period of the Passion in which Christ directly confronted the power and violence of the Prince of Darkness in the execution of his priestly office.

In developing this motif of Christ's priestly sacrifice, Milton worked out quite precisely his allusions to the passion, death, and exaltation of Christ. Satan predicts the events of Christ's passion before sending the storm which (he says) confirms that prediction: "Sorrows, and labors, opposition, hate,/ Attends thee, scorns, reproaches, injuries,/ Violence and stripes, and lastly cruel death" (IV.386–88). The imagery used to describe the storm,

> either Tropic now
> 'Gan thunder, and both ends of Heav'n; the Clouds
> From many a horrid rift abortive pour'd
> Fierce rain with lightning mixt, water with fire
> In ruin reconcil'd: nor slept the winds
> Within thir stony caves, but rush'd abroad
> From the four hinges of the world, and fell
> On the vext Wilderness, whose tallest Pines
> Though rooted deep as high, and sturdiest Oaks
> Bow'd thir Stiff necks, loaden with stormy blasts,
> Or torn up sheer: ill wast thou shrouded then,
> O patient Son of God, yet only stood'st
> Unshaken; nor yet stay'd the terror there.
> Infernal Ghosts, and Hellish Furies, round
> Environ'd thee, some howl'd, some yell'd, some shriek'd,
> Some bent at thee thir fiery darts (IV.409–24),

points to the violent upheavals of nature recorded at Christ's death—the three hours' darkness over all the earth, the earthquakes, the splitting of rocks, the opening of graves (Matt. xxvii:51–52). The reference to Christ as "Ill ... shrouded" looks forward to Christ's death and burial, while the description of him as sustaining the attack of "Hellish Furies" suggests the descent into hell.

After all this, Christ's witty remark to the returning Satan, "Mee worse than wet thou find'st not" (IV.486), shows his refusal to be intimidated by mere threats and portents, but also his understanding, grounded upon faith in God, that the violence to come will not permanently harm him, and that his wholly voluntary acceptance of his suffering, priestly role will culminate in his exaltation. This implication is clarified by John Diodati's paraphrase of Christ's remarks about his passion in John xiv:30, "The Devill is going to bend all his forces ... to bring me to nothing ... but as he hath no right in me that am without sin: so hath he no actuall power to do with mee according to his will: and my death shall not bee through any endeavour of his, but because I voluntarily submit my selfe to my Fathers will about the salvation of the world." [18] The description of the restoration of nature to beauty, holiness, and peace after the storm has a close verbal resemblance to the description of Easter morn in Giles Fletcher's *Christs Victorie, and Triumph,*[19] and suggests the final conquest over darkness and death achieved at the first Easter. The glorious dawn "Came forth with Pilgrim steps in amice gray" and "still'd the roar/ Of thunder, chas'd the clouds, and laid the winds" (IV.427–29), thereby reaffirming the power of light over darkness, the victory present and to come of the Son/Sun of God over the Prince of Darkness, and the restoration of Edenic beauty to the earth:

> And now the Sun with more effectual beams
> Had cheer'd the face of Earth, and dried the wet
> From drooping plant, or dropping tree; the birds

> Who all things now behold more fresh and green,
> After a night of storm so ruinous,
> Clear'd up their choicest notes in bush and spray
> To gratulate the sweet return of morn. (IV.432–38)

The tower episode actualizes the violence threatened and portended in the storm scene, suggesting the Crucifixion in which Christ submitted himself to satanic violence and, paradoxically, overthrew it by that very submission. In addition to this the tower scene points to Christ's ascension, since it shows Christ's conquest of Satan in his kingdom of the air. Lancelot Andrewes relates the three notable "assumptions" of Christ in a manner suggestive for Milton's conflation of them here: "the Divell assumpted Christ [to carry him to the Temple]...And as he suffered this Assumption, so afterwards, *Luk* 9:51. his second Assumption, was to goe to *Jerusalem* to suffer; and so at the last he came to his third and last Assumption, to be received up into glorie, 1 *Tim* 3:16." [20] The series of events pointed to in the tower temptation is clarified by Milton's summary in *Paradise Lost* of the events attending upon and following after the Crucifixion, the moment of the fulfillment of the promise to Adam and Eve that the seed of the woman would bruise Satan's head. Then Jesus

> Saw Satan fall like Lightning down from Heav'n,
> Prince of the Air; then rising from his Grave
> Spoil'd Principalities and Powers, triumph't
> In open show, and with ascension bright
> Captivity led captive through the Air,
> The Realm itself of Satan long usurpt,
> Whom he shall tread at last under our feet. (*PL* X.184–90)

In *Paradise Regained* Satan's falling awestruck as Christ stands unmoved suggests that other "fall" at Christ's death; Christ's escape from death foreshadows his resurrection; and the angelic banquet and hymn honoring Christ as "Son of the most

High, heir of both worlds" (IV.633) foreshadows his enthronement at the right hand of the Father.

Moreover, the typological perspective of the poem whereby
the temptation story is made to embody and foreshadow the
whole mission of Christ and his church supports Schultz' suggestion that the storm-tower sequence also figures forth the
continuation of Christ's suffering and triumph in the church
throughout history.[21] The storm imagery suggests the church
subject to persecution by Satan and the world, and also suggests the violence and terror of the Last Day when according
to one poetic description,

> The earth shall tremble, the hills also
> Shall sink and perish, the mountain peaks
> Bow down and topple, the terrible roar
> Of the fierce sea confound the minds of men.[22]

Similarly, the glorious dawn following after the storm represents the millennial reign of Christ and his saints, the tower
scene suggests that last grand battle wherein Christ will overthrow Satan, and the angelic banquet symbolizes the church's
communion which celebrates Christ's priestly sacrifice and
which itself prefigures the "marriage supper of the Lamb."

Though the focus in the storm-tower sequence is on Christ's
Jobean patience and his priestly role, this sequence also subsumes many earlier motifs. As Dick Taylor notes,[23] Satan presents a new challenge to Christ's prophetic role by his suggestion that the starry configurations portend for Christ "many
a hard assay/ Of dangers, and adversities and pains" (IV.478–
79), and by his interpretation of the ominous storm as a confirmation of the portents; portents, we recall, were among the
prophetic devices Satan laid claim to in Book I (l. 395). This
satanic prediction is hardly a new revelation to Christ, for even
during his first meditation he understood enough of his priestly
role to know,

                              my way must lie
          Through many a hard assay even to the death,
          Ere I the promis'd Kingdom can attain,
          Or work Redemption for mankind, whose sins'
          Full weight must be transferr'd upon my head. (I.263–67)

But he refuses to corrupt his prophetic role by recognizing the
stars and the storm as portents of his forthcoming passion,
identifying these correctly as "false portents, not sent from God,
but thee" (IV.491). Satan also challenges the kingly role anew
when he asserts that the dangers to come will render the
attainment of the promised kingdom highly uncertain: since
Christ has missed the perfect season for establishing it, it may
prove to be merely "Allegoric . . . as without end,/ Without
beginning" (IV.390–92). But Christ shows his awareness that
suffering and death constitute the very pathway to his kingdom. Moreover, Christ in this sequence wins back the last
realm which Satan has usurped as a result of man's fall. At
the conclusion of the sequence on the kingdoms, Christ, by
scorning all the worldly goods offered by Satan, had won
back and reclaimed all the earthly kingdoms taken over by
the Prince of This World. Now, by enduring the storms, the
tempests, the awesome portents, and the terrifying exposure
in air on the pinnacle of the tower Christ breaks the magical
and demonic power of the Prince of the Air and reclaims this
last domain.

  But in addition to all this, the tower temptation is structured
by Satan as an identity test, as the ultimate challenge to
Christ's divine sonship, and in a manner which ironically up-
sets Satan's expectations it does indeed bring both Christ and
Satan to complete realization and manifestation of themselves.
Satan supposes in his scornful challenge to Christ that he has
allowed for all the possibilities. If Christ is a mere man he
must fall from the spire upon which he has been placed; if

he is divine he will save himself by a miracle; and if he is
uncertain he may cast himself down to test himself and God:

> There stand, if thou wilt stand; to stand upright
> Will ask thee skill; I to thy Father's house
> Have brought thee, and highest plac'd, highest is best,
> Now show thy Progeny; if not to stand,
> Cast thyself down; safely if Son of God. (IV.551-55)

But what happens is quite beyond the limited satanic imagina-
tion. Christ simply stands; he shows his divinity not by miraculous escape on Satan's terms but by calmly maintaining the
impossible position into which Satan has thrust him, being
sustained in this action-passion by the Father as he will be
later at the Crucifixion here prefigured.

The single line of the poem which renders Christ's answer
to Satan and his response to the tower challenge is notably
ambiguous: "Tempt not the Lord thy God; he said and stood"
(IV.561). Christ may refer here to the Father only, or to
himself only, or to both; he may stand by the power of the
Father, or by his own power. The ambiguity serves, I believe,
to permit Christ's phrase to function on two levels. As an
answer to Satan's temptation to presumptuous action it refers
as in the Mosaic source (Deut. vi:16) to the evil of tempting
or testing the Father. But in relation to the identity challenge
the words refer, I think, to Christ himself, indicating that he
is now given to understand, at this climactic moment, the full
meaning of his divine sonship—his nature as the Image of the
Father—and that he is also permitted to exercise the divine
power in standing where standing is impossible. His affirmation is of course the result of the Father's illumination as the
standing is an expression of the Father's power, for in Milton's
view even in heaven the Son does not exercise divine preroga-
tives by his own right, but only as the Father devolves them
upon him. I suggest then that Christ here is not merely the

recipient of a miracle of divine protection but that in this moment he completes his journey to self-understanding through the teaching of the Father and, as he achieves the ultimate in passive endurance, he is enabled to turn this very passion into a dramatic act of conquest over Satan—"he said and *stood.*" The syntax refers both the standing and the statement to Christ as subject, yet we know that the standing is certainly a miracle of the divine power, for by human power alone Christ could not stand in this place. It seems reasonable to suppose that the miracle of full illumination accompanies that other miracle, and that the attribution of both the statement and the standing so unqualifiedly and forcefully to Christ indicates that he has now become again (as before in heaven) the conscious agent of the divine power in working the defeat of Satan.

This reading is supported by the dramatic movement of the poem to this moment of climax. Throughout the temptation, at lesser climactic moments, a sudden increased certainty and authority in Christ's manner and tone have signified his reception of specific revelations regarding the various functions of his office, granted to him in each case after he has withstood all the satanic challenges directed against those functions. Thus after the temptation of the stones he declared himself God's living oracle in recognition of his prophetic role, after the banquet temptation he affirmed his own table in the wilderness in anticipation of his priesthood, and after the temptation of the kingdoms he cited with full comprehension Daniel's metaphors regarding the power of his kingdom and implied also his full understanding of the means to it. Christ's simple statement on the tower rings with certainty and assurance beyond anything else in the poem. It suggests that Christ, after patiently enduring satanic violence and attempted murder, has come to understand fully the sacrificial priestly office he here prefigures, has had revealed to him his nature as the Image of the Father, and is now permitted to exercise the divine power in standing. These several climactic realizations are conflated in this episode, for the divine understanding and the divine power are necessary to Christ's conquest over satanic violence and death in the Ascension, the aftermath of his priestly sacrifice, and also to that final, determinate victory of the divine power over Satan at the end of time, both of which are also prefigured on the tower.

This understanding of the passage is also reinforced by the reactions of Satan falling "smitten with amazement" and "struck with dread and anguish" (IV.562, 576), which indicate that at last, in total defeat, he knows his victor as before he knew his conqueror in heaven and will know him again in this role at the end of time. It is hardly to be supposed that Satan would comprehend Christ's nature before Christ himself does. Satan in one moment comprehends and falls defeated as Christ in one moment comprehends and stands victorious; and it is the full manifestation of Christ's nature in the miraculous action-passion of standing which reacts upon, and manifests fully, and so defeats the satanic nature, revealing the unsubstantiality and powerlessness of evil. This reading is further supported by the angelic hymn terming Christ "True Image of the Father" and identifying him unequivocally as the first-begot. It might be argued that the angelic hymn itself reveals to Christ his divine nature, but this lyric of praise seems not to have the dramatic force of a climactic revelation of identity. Rather it purports to be, and I think is, a hymn celebrating the complete victory the Son has already achieved and the full illumination he has already merited, honoring him in terms which he already fully understands.

After this climactic moment when Christ stands and Satan falls, and in these actions each fully knows himself and the other, the rest is recapitulation and future projection. The final similes likening Satan's fall to the falls of Antaeus and the

Sphinx emphasize over again the two motifs of Christ's personal virtue and his mediatorial office. The Antaeus allusion recalls Christ's earlier identification as Second Hercules, the perfect exemplification of moral virtue.[24] The Hercules-Antaeus conflict, in which Hercules smothered "in air" the giant who gained new strength by every contact with his mother Earth, was described by Lucan as Hercules' hardest combat, and was usually interpreted as an allegory of reason's conquest over all sensual or earth-bound passions and desires.[25] This simile alludes to Christ's perfect command over the kingdom within; to the absolute freedom he has won for his kingdom, the church, from any necessary reliance upon the things of this world; to the exercise of the mediatorial kingly office of expelling demons and redeeming man from inner slavery; and to the priestly sacrifice in his passion and death of everything mortal about him—his human body and life itself. The Sphinx simile alludes to Christ's attainment of true wisdom. Oedipus defeated the Sphinx by solving the riddle whose answer is "Man," and Christ defeats Satan because he possesses true self-knowledge and knowledge of the human condition. Also, as prophet, Christ is the teacher of that divine wisdom from above which alone can defeat the monster whose riddling temptations threaten all mankind.[26]

The angelic hymn restates the scope of the temptation episode as a discovery of Christ's nature and an epitome of his entire mission and office—its prefiguration in history and its extension in the church. Such a perspective has a near analogue in Lightfoot's concluding comment to his exegesis of the temptation episode: "Thus hath Christ been shewed the Son of God by the voice of the Father, and annointed for the great King, Priest, and Prophet visibly by the Holy Ghost: And thus hath hee shewed his power and command over the evill Angels; and the good Angels have owned his Lordship and dominion over themselves; and thus every way attested,

is hee presently to appeare amongst men as the Minister of
the Gospel." [27] The hymn suggests this large scope chiefly by
ambiguities of tense and conflations of time, by means of
which Christ's nature is celebrated as already fully manifested,
and his office is celebrated as already achieved but also as
just beginning. The angels celebrate Christ as the "True Image
of the Father" (IV.596) and the "debeller" of Satan from
heaven, but note that he *"still"* expresses that same "Godlike
force" in the wilderness (IV.601-2). They declare that he
has *"now* ... aveng'd/ Supplanted *Adam,"* that he has *"regain'd* lost Paradise," and that "A fairer Paradise is founded
now" (the "paradise within thee, happier far" of *PL* XII.587),
since he has now made men secure against the Tempter (*PR*
IV.606-8, 613). But they also assert that Christ is come *"to* rein-
stall" Adam's sons in that Paradise where they *"shall dwell*
secure," and that Satan "like an Autumnal Star/ Or Lightning ... *shalt fall"* from heaven (IV.615-20).[28] Thus, Eden is
already restored, but Christ is yet to install it, we have just seen
Satan's fall occur, but it is yet to come—at the Crucifixion, and
at the end of time. Moreover, the phrases "in all her gates *Abaddon* rues/ Thy bold attempt" and "hee all unarm'd/ *Shall
chase* thee with the terror of his voice/ From thy Demoniac
holds" (IV.624-28) conflate Christ's present victory against the
powers of hell (Abaddon is the term for hell in Job xxviii:22)
with his future casting forth of the demons from men into
swine (Matt. viii:29-32), and with the Harrowing of Hell
where as King of Glory he will throw open all of hell's gates.
The final angelic paean celebrates Christ's full attainment of
his kingly role as "heir of both worlds" and "Queller of Satan"
but then urges him to *"Now* enter" upon "thy glorious work"
and *"begin* to save mankind" (IV.633-35).[29] Christ has won
the complete victory but the battle is just beginning; he has
saved mankind, but he is yet to do so.

Thematically the implication is that because Christ has now

come to understand himself fully and because he has now been exercised in all the "rudiments" or root concerns of his great warfare (I.157) according to the Father's prediction, he has in effect already won the victory, has already expressed his total office which has now merely to be worked out in time. Structurally, as in *Paradise Lost,* after the end is foreseen the perspective shifts back to the beginning again and the Second Man, like the first, goes forth to live out the history that has been shown or epitomized: Christ returns "private" to his mother's house to await the new beginning. The angelic hymn uses ambiguities of tense and conflations of time to show in retrospect what the Father's speech by means of the same devices displayed in prospect—that the temptation episode is the epitome of Christ's total role, the embodiment of the entire Christian theology of redemption, the turning point of history. As such it is the fitting complement to the epic of the Fall and the proper subject for the Miltonic brief epic.

PART THREE · THE ART OF THE POEM

CHAPTER XIII · SOME ASPECTS OF NARRATIVE METHOD, STRUCTURE, AND STYLE

*T*HIS study has approached *Paradise Regained* as companion poem to *Paradise Lost* rather than as sequel or postscript. Deriving as it does from a somewhat different generic tradition than *Paradise Lost,* this brief New Testament epic has its own distinct subject and focus. The subject of *Paradise Lost,* fully explored in that poem and needing no sequel, is the fall and restoration of man. The focus is upon the condition of mankind manifested in and extending from the story of Adam: even the supernatural actions apparently outside this focus such as the fall of Lucifer, the warfare of Christ in heaven, and Michael's prophecy of Christ's forthcoming redemption are presented in terms of their effect upon man's state. *Paradise Regained* treats some of the same material, but here the focus is upon Christ the hero. Mankind is involved in the story since Christ has a human nature and is the redeemer of mankind, yet we do not identify totally and automatically with this hero as with Adam, but only partially and by deliberate choice. The subject of *Paradise Regained,* then, is Christ's heroic achievement and mission in its deepest significance and broadest ramifications. These differences in subject matter, form, and focus in Milton's two epic poems naturally give rise also to important differences in narrative method, structure, and style.

THE NARRATIVE VOICE

The first few lines of *Paradise Regained* point to a conception of the epic narrator quite different from that obtaining in *Paradise Lost.* In the brief epic, as in the longer work, the

epic narrator is not simply to be equated with Milton but is
a conscious creation serving specific aesthetic functions.[1] Perhaps the primary characteristic of the narrative voice of *Paradise Regained* is the easy, confident tone. In his invocation
the narrator proposes to sing of deeds hitherto "unrecorded"
and "Above heroic" (I.15–16), but his claims and aims are
not accompanied, as they are in the opening lines of *Paradise
Lost,* by an insistence in image and statement upon the difficulties of his task and upon his own inner darkness and chaos
as an analogue of that first darkness and chaos upon which
the Spirit brooded. The new confidence stems in part from
the narrator's previous experience of the Spirit's aid and his
previous success in singing of the happy Garden: "I who ere-
while . . ."; "inspire,/ As thou art wont." Another basis for this
confidence may be the greater familiarity of the new material.
Christ's temptation takes place on earth, not in the unfamiliar
reaches of the eternal places, and the time is the narrator's
own time—after the Fall. But the most important reason is
surely the narrator's changed situation and perspective, a
change consonant with and indeed deriving from the story he
now treats. In *Paradise Lost* the narrator identified himself
very closely with his falling and fallen first parents, referring
to Adam and Eve as to none of the other characters by intimate, proprietary epithets: "our Grand Parents," "our general
Mother," "Our first Father," "our general Ancestor," "our cred-
ulous Mother," "our Father penitent." [2] He further emphasized
his condition as fallen man by his frequent and repeated invocations to the Muse and the Spirit, by his treatment of his own
physical blindness as a kind of analogue to spiritual blindness,
and by his confessed difficulty in reascending, as narrator,
from hell's terrain to the light of God.[3] In *Paradise Regained,*
by contrast, the narrator presents himself in quite another
character through the titles he uses to signify his relation to
his hero. Most often he refers to Christ formally as the "Son

of God," emphasizing thereby the important dramatic and thematic motif of Christ's divine sonship, and indicating as well that his own and mankind's identification with this hero cannot be complete. But his second title for his hero, used only slightly less often than the other, is an intimate, proprietary epithet analogous to those attaching to Adam in the longer epic—"our Savior." The narrator's two titles for Christ are significantly linked in the final lines of the poem, "Thus they the Son of God our Savior meek/ Sung Victor" (IV.636–37). The constant use of the epithet "our Savior" reveals that the narrator does not now think of himself primarily as man fallen but as man restored and redeemed through Christ's heroic action. He can therefore sing of Christ's victory with confident expectation that he will share in it by being victorious over all his poetic difficulties, and he can invoke the Spirit once only, describing him as a hawk with "prosperous wing full summ'd" for a successful flight, since this is the same Spirit who led the "glorious Eremite" into the desert and returned him victorious (I.8–17).

This conception of the epic narrator as man redeemed, as self-styled follower and imitator of his hero, helps to explain certain other differences from *Paradise Lost* in narrative manner and method. In the brief epic the narrator appears much more objective: he records what happens, what is said, what seems to be the case, and he refrains from commenting upon and evaluating the speeches and actions of the characters as he does continually in *Paradise Lost* to the dismay of many critics.[4] However, this apparent restraint derives not from objectivity, but from the almost complete fusion of the narrator's point of view (as redeemed man) with that of his Redeemer who is present in person to comment upon and to evaluate Satan's various poses and temptations, thereby rendering additional narrative evaluation superfluous. Given this perspective, in which the hero is presented from the vantage point of a

narrator who sees him as the Savior and has taken him
as model, there is an inevitability and even an appropriateness in the often lamented fact that Christ sounds at times
like "Milton himself imagined perfect." [5] The close identification with his hero leads the narrator on two occasions to depart radically from his seeming objectivity and
thereby to reveal his true stance. At the conclusion of Book III
he cheers Christ's victory and points to its broad implications
in man's moral history, "So fares it when with truth falsehood
contends" (III.443); here the pat moralistic tone and the dis-
concerting rapidity of the shift of perspective make the line
poetically inept. However, the other departure from the objective manner, the narrator's pathetic apostrophe to his hero
during the storm scene, is wholly successful:

> ill wast thou shrouded then,
> O patient Son of God, yet only stood'st
> Unshaken; nor yet stay'd the terror there.
> Infernal Ghosts, and Hellish Furies, round
> Environ'd thee, some howl'd, some yell'd, some shriek'd,
> Some bent at thee thir fiery darts, while thou
> Satt'st unappall'd in calm and sinless peace. (IV.419-25)

In his discussion of *Paradise Regained* as a meditative poem
Louis Martz cites this passage as the "affectionate colloquy,"
the outpouring of the heart which traditionally concludes a
meditation. [6] But nearer precedents for such apostrophes are
provided by the epic tradition. For example, Virgil apostro-
phizes Dido before her suicide (*Aeneid* IV.408-11), and in
Paradise Lost when the narrator contemplates Eve moving
inexorably toward that act which brought with it the fall of
the narrator himself and of all mankind he addresses Eve
directly in tones filled with emotion:

> O much deceiv'd, much failing, hapless *Eve*,
> Of thy presum'd return! event perverse!

> Thou never from that hour in Paradise
> Found'st either sweet repast, or sound repose;
> Such ambush hid among sweet Flow'rs and Shades
> Waited with hellish rancor imminent
> To intercept thy way, or send thee back
> Despoil'd of Innocence, of Faith, of Bliss. (*PL* IX.404–11)

Similarly, in *Paradise Regained* the epic narrator is overcome with emotion and is moved to apostrophize his hero when he treats the episode symbolic of the Passion, the event through which that hero has saved the narrator and all mankind.

STRUCTURE

Although the earlier analyses of theme and action have necessarily considered structure also, the structural complexity of this brief epic can best be appreciated in an overview. The poem's architectonic quality is achieved by two methods: the repetition with variation of certain recurrent motifs, and the setting of various structural patterns against each other in an elaborate counterpoint. At first view the poem divides into three unequal segments, with the first and third temptations balancing each other and flanking the long kingdoms temptation rather like the prologue and epilogue to an extended narrative. Viewing the structure in this way, Roy Daniells has likened the poem to a baroque church such as Santa Maria della Salute, whose three separable architectural components are dominated by the large central element and unified by certain devices of perspective.[7] Lengthy inductions preface each of these three major segments of the poem (the storm scene serves this function in relation to the tower temptation) thereby reinforcing the tripartite structure. This structural organization is further underscored by the use of the three major temptations to present three separate aspects of the theme, with each aspect worked out on two levels of action. As a private man, Christ withstands in each temptation a characteristic human vice and exhibits its contrary virtue. In the first temptation he withstands the invitation to doubt and despair, showing perfect faith and confidence in the Father; in the second temptation he withstands the intemperance, avarice, and vainglory to which Adam succumbed, showing perfect temperance, contentment, and humility; and in the third temptation he withstands the fear and terror evoked by Satan's violence, showing Jobean patience and fortitude. As a public figure, Christ through these three temptations learns about and is exercised in the three functions of his mediatorial office, and by that same token defeats Satan in the three aspects of *his* public role: the True Prophet defeats Satan, the Father of Lies, in the first temptation; the True King of the church and of the world dethrones Satan, Prince of This World, in the kingdoms temptation; and the suffering Priest exposed in darkness and in air overthrows the Prince of Darkness and Prince of the Air in the tower temptation.

However, several other patterns provide a counterpoint to this basic tripartite structure. From one perspective the entire poem functions as a single structural unit, presenting the conflict between Satan and Christ over the proper interpretation of Christ's title, Son of God: in this pattern the various temptations build steadily through several lesser climaxes to the grand climactic moment on the tower in which Christ realizes and affirms his divine nature and Satan falls in amazement. From still another viewpoint one might distinguish four rather than three basic structural divisions. Since the public and private themes develop concomitantly in the first and third temptations but sequentially in the kingdoms temptation, that episode accordingly breaks into two segments at the point at which Satan shifts the discussion from the private to the public realm with his remark, "But to a Kingdom thou art born" (III.152).[8] The segment dealing with the public kingdom has a kind of induction of its own in the deeply personal exchange between Christ and Satan, during which Satan asserts his desire to seek the Port of Worst. Still another structural counterpoint within the temptation of the kingdoms, overlaying this two-part division, is its organization according to the traditional tripartite scale of ethical goods, *Voluptaria* (the banquet), *Activa* (wealth, glory, kingship over Parthia and Rome), and *Contemplativa* (learning).

Furthermore the division of the poem into four books provides an additional counterpoint playing off against all these structural patterns, in that each book emphasizes its own particular thematic motif. Book I is wholly concerned with the challenges to faith which may attack the private man or the public prophet. Book II explores the motif of intemperance either as related to bodily enjoyments or to external possessions and honors. Book III adumbrates the concepts of "time" and "force" either as related to personal glory or to the public mediatorial kingdom. Book IV presents a series of climaxes, each outdoing the last in scope and effect—Rome, Athens, then the final victory and revelation on the tower.

Adding further richness and complexity to the poem, and also greater cohesiveness and unity, is the interlocking of the various structural patterns and of the individual temptations so that each new offer subsumes, with variations, certain basic elements in that which has just preceded it. The banquet temptation carries over from the temptation of the stones the elements of Christ's hunger and abandonment and the invitation to doubt and despair. The wealth-ambition temptation carries over from the banquet the motifs of Christ's neediness and of his temperance, here displayed in regard to worldly goods. The glory temptation explicitly builds upon the previous incident, presenting glory as the end for which wealth and kingdoms are means: "Thou neither dost persuade me to seek wealth/ For Empire's sake, nor Empire to affect/ For glory's sake" (III.44–46). The temptation to false zeal and duty builds upon Christ's expressed desire to seek the glory of God rather than his own. The offer of Parthia incorporates both the motif of glory won through force and conquest and the motif of Christ's duty to win back his own kingdom, Israel. The temptation of Rome is more complex, for as the kingdom of this world it subsumes all of the previous lures, rendering them all more grand and magnificent: it has banquets, riches, glory, dominion, martial power, and, in addition, noble arts. Athens provides a yet more impressive climax: as the most seductive worldly kingdom it includes all the previous lures—sensual pleasure, wealth, glory, and dominion—but ennobles them so as to make them more attractive to a refined sensibility. Moreover, as false wisdom Athens presents the ultimate challenge to Christ's faith and prophetic role as defined in the first temptation. The storm temptation also subsumes earlier elements: the false portents again challenge Christ's prophetic role, and the predicted difficulties besetting the kingdom challenge his kingly role, while the major function of the scene is to present Christ as suffering priest. The tower scene serves as the grand climax, showing Christ victorious in all three roles; as suffering priest he sustains the violence of Satan, Sin, and Death and overcomes all three; as True Prophet, Second Oedipus, he puts down the riddling tempter who would devour all mankind; as king he fulfills that aspect of his kingly role which involves the destruction of Satan and all his works.

THE STYLE: DICTION

The language of *Paradise Regained* is usually said to be flat, colorless, and austere in comparison with that of *Paradise Lost*. Kenneth Muir has compared it to the style of Dryden's *Religio Laici* as "fitter for discourse and nearer prose," and Martz has described *Paradise Regained* as a meditative poem whose "middle style" resembles that of Virgil's *Georgics*.[9] However, the language of *Paradise Regained* incorporates most of the epic stylistic features and most of the kinds of poetic figures found in *Paradise Lost,* albeit in lesser profusion and in a somewhat muted tone. The question is posed therefore as to whether, and on what grounds, the style of the poem can be termed an epic style, and how it accommodates the decorum imposed by the subject.

For one thing, this decorum dictates that Satan avoid the splendid and swelling oratory which he employs to such remarkable effect in the councils and the temptation scenes of *Paradise Lost.* His very different manner and style of address in the brief epic results not so much from his continued decline and degeneration after his sin (though this is a factor) but primarily from the fact that Satan is too intelligent a rhetorician not to adapt his tactics to the very different circumstances which he here meets. He does not now require the elevated, stirring, emotion-laden rhetoric he used in the first scenes in hell in *Paradise Lost* to rouse his followers from despair, to establish his own power and position, and to win support for his own plan. In the first council of the new epic he needs merely to inform his followers—now comfortably established and reasonably content in their usurped kingdoms of earth and middle air—of this new danger, in such a way that they will not be too greatly alarmed, and will give him a new grant of authority to act. The second council, which includes the exchange between Satan and Belial, offers a closer analogue to the great consult in *Paradise Lost,* but here the council is not stage-managed; Satan genuinely wants helpful suggestions to help him meet the unprecedented challenge offered by Christ. Satan's answer to Belial in this council parodies Christ's own manner of speaking to Satan throughout the poem, and this fact offers a clue to Satan's new rhetoric. In his conversations with Christ in this poem Satan is evidently attempting to imitate Christ's own reasonable, precise speech; he is trying to make his proposals sound like an objectification

of Christ's own thoughts, like the discourse of his alter ego.
He must therefore eschew the temptation style of *Paradise
Lost*—swelling phrases, mock-indignation, an onrushing tor-
rent of fine-sounding words covering faulty logic—and must
work instead through subtle nuances of suggestion, intimation,
and irony sounded above a ground base of seemingly calm
and ordered rationality. The narrator also, as redeemed man,
models his speech on Christ's, and so must also show reason
and restraint in his description of the characters and their
conflict. It is then to be expected that *Paradise Regained* will
differ considerably from *Paradise Lost* in tone and style,
though Milton has taken pains to elevate and ennoble these
aspects of his brief epic by incorporating many of the expected
epic stylistic features.

One such feature is the formal epic descriptive passage,
modeled upon those descriptions of banquets, military pageants, noble cities, and awesome tempests which are customary in epic. Milton has found a way to make such descriptions
wholly organic to his poem by treating them as part of Satan's
temptation strategy: he has a banquet and a storm scene described by the narrator, a martial pageant (Parthia) and a noble
city (Rome) described partly by Satan and partly by the
narrator, and the grand panorama of Athens presented wholly
by Satan. Such passages employ elevated and sublime language further exalted by vivid imagery and sonorousness, for
in these instances Satan pretends to be, and the narrator genuinely is, moved to soaring eloquence by the impressiveness
and splendor of the scenes.

The epic catalogue is another epic stylistic device used with
some frequency in *Paradise Regained*. Though these catalogues are briefer than those in *Paradise Lost,* they also elevate the language through the massing together of evocative
and sonorous names. The poem contains several catalogues—
of the places where the disciples sought Christ after his bap-

tism; of the classical nymphs seduced by Belial and the classical gods he impersonated in doing so; of the nymphs and knights whom the attendants in the satanic banquet resemble; of the various ancient kingdoms subsumed in the Parthian Empire; of the places from which the Parthian horsemen came; and of the places near and far which are now tributary to the Roman Empire.[10]

The brief epic has also a few epic similes, though their comparative paucity is sometimes cited as further evidence that Milton abandoned the epic high style in this poem. However, it must be remembered that Milton did not employ epic similes in all parts of *Paradise Lost* but used them almost entirely in relation to the fallen angels or to Adam, concentrating them especially in Books I and II, where they serve an essentially proleptic function. Similes are almost entirely omitted from the dialogue portions of *Paradise Lost*—the council in heaven, Raphael's discourse with Adam in Books VII and VIII, the domestic dispute of Adam and Eve, Michael's prophecy [11]—as if inappropriate to them. So it is not surprising that the brief epic, which is more than two-thirds dialogue, offers occasion for only six such similes. But, however sparingly used, these similes do help to heighten the style of the poem as it builds to a climax (five of the six similes appear in Book IV). Moreover, they help to throw the theme of the higher heroism into relief, for this classical epic stylistic device is restricted wholly to descriptions of Satan or of the satanic values. The first simile addresses itself to the ancient epic ideal of miltary' prowess, comparing the Parthian military forces to the martial strength of Charlemagne's knights gathered to storm Albracca (*PR* III.337–44). The other five similes, all in Book IV, characterize Satan in defeat. Three of them make up a finely graded sequence of comparisons for Satan's now compulsive temptation behavior, offering first a human analogue, then one in the animal kingdom, and finally one in inanimate nature, thereby imaging in the sequence itself Satan's steady disintegration and loss of control:

> But as a man who had been matchless held
> In cunning, overreach't where least he thought,
> To salve his credit, and for very spite
> Still will be tempting him who foils him still,
> And never cease, though to his shame the more;
> Or as a swarm of flies in vintage time,
> About the wine-press where sweet must is pour'd,
> Beat off, returns as oft with humming sound;
> Or surging waves against a solid rock,
> Though all to shivers dash't, th'assault renew,
> Vain batt'ry, and in froth or bubbles end;
> So Satan ... (IV.10–21)

The two longer epic similes, whose rich thematic implications and appropriateness have been suggested above,[12] compare Satan's defeat by Christ to Antaeus' defeat by Hercules and to the Sphinx's destruction by Oedipus.

The fact that these last two similes are built upon recognized typological associations points to the presence of another, and hitherto unexplored, variety of "epic simile" in the poem. In some sense the many typological allusions throughout the poem may be seen as a kind of condensed epic simile, for they all set up implied comparisons and contrasts with Christ on the basis of recognized and familiar associations between type and antitype. By implication and ramification, then, they present extended comparisons which, like the traditional epic simile, often relate the present action to past and future events. This condensed figure is at once appropriate to the shorter scope of the brief epic, and is also a suitable contrast to the standard epic simile, which is used here only in relation to the satanic values.

The poetic language of *Paradise Regained* is further enriched by several pervasive image patterns which function as

submerged metaphors, subtly commenting upon the antagonists and the action. One such pattern presents Christ as rock
in opposition to Satan as spirit of the air. Satan "Flies to his
place" in "mid air" to hold his consistory (I.39), he is "Into
thin Air diffus'd" (I.500) after the failure of his first temptation, and he gathers all the powers of the air—storm, tempest,
lightning, thunder—to terrify Christ in the storm scene. On
the other hand, Christ's allusion to Daniel's metaphor for his
kingdom as a "stone that shall to pieces dash/ All Monarchies
besides" (IV.149–50) relates the rock image to Christ, and
after the storm episode Satan declares that Christ has shown
himself "Proof against all temptation as a rock/ Of Adamant"
(IV.533–34). The two images are directly opposed in the simile
comparing Satan's compulsive temptations to "surging waves
against a solid rock,/ ... [which] in froth or bubbles end" (IV.
18–20); the final phrase aptly comments upon the unsubstantiality of the power of air and storm when confronted with
the rock that is Christ.

More pervasive is the light-darkness imagery identifying
Christ as source of light in conflict with Satan as the power
of darkness. The fallen angels' habitat in mid-air partakes of
darkness—Satan's "gloomy Consistory" takes place "Within
thick Clouds and dark tenfold involv'd" (I.41–42)—but it partakes also of light for Satan by contriving man's fall has led
his followers from "Hell's deep-vaulted Den to dwell in light,/
Regents and Potentates, and Kings, yea gods/ Of many a pleasant Realm" (I.116–18). However, this partial light is promptly
measured against the standard of God's supernal light as he
appears "in full frequence bright/ Of Angels" (I.128–29). The
desert is presented as an image of the world as yet under the
power of darkness, that is, under Satan's domination: it is a
place "with dark shades and rocks environ'd round" (I.194),
a "pathless Desert, dusk with horrid shades" (I.296), a place
double-shaded by "Night with her sullen wing" (I.500). Christ

comes into this place as light-bearer. In Book I he is "our Morning Star then in his rise" (I.294), an influence which is to dispel the darkness and a star to replace that other, fallen morning star and light-bearer, Lucifer. At the conclusion of the first night Christ is associated with a still more immediate forerunner of the dawn, the "Herald Lark":

> Thus wore out night, and now the Herald Lark
> Left his ground-nest, high tow'ring to descry
> The morn's approach, and greet her with his Song.
> As lightly from his grassy Couch up rose
> Our Savior,
>
> .   .   .   .
>
> Up to a hill anon his steps he rear'd,
> From whose high top to ken the prospect round. (II.279–86) [13]

Later, in replying to the learning temptation Christ identifies himself as one who is in direct contact with the source of light itself, as one who "receives/ Light from above, from the fountain of light" (IV.289). During the second night—the storm scene—Christ is wholly given over to the power of darkness, but the redeemed narrator observes that this darkness (like evil itself) is unsubstantial: "Darkness now rose,/ As daylight sunk, and brought in louring night,/ Her shadowy offspring, unsubstantial both,/ Privation mere of light and absent day" (IV.397–400). The description of the glorious morning scene which follows evokes the traditional Son/Sun conceit: the dawn dispels the storm raised by Satan *"To tempt the Son* of God with terrors dire./ *And now the Sun* with more effectual beams/ Had cheer'd the face of Earth" (IV.431–33).[14] This Son/Sun verbal association presents Christ himself as source of light, "cheering" and renewing the darksome and sin-marred earth. When Satan reappears to urge the significance and meaning of the storm, he is explicitly identified as "The Prince of darkness" (IV.441), and the angels' final paean associates Christ directly with the light of God: "True Image of the Father, whether thron'd/ In the bosom of bliss, and light of light/ Conceiving" (IV.596–98). Christ is then the light, as he is the rock.

A pervasive image pattern relating to hunger and food has been traced in detail by Lee Cox.[15] This imagery identifies Satan as the purveyor of false nourishment to body and spirit, and Christ as the recipient and purveyor of the true nourishment for soul and body which is from God. Christ endures throughout the poem a twofold hunger, his physical hunger being a kind of metaphor for the spiritual hunger fed only by God's word. In the first temptation the physical hunger is only imminent: Satan predicts that Christ will die "pin'd with hunger and with drought" (I.325) and urges him to provide bread from stones. Christ's answer refers to God as the source of both physical and spiritual food: "Man lives not by Bread only, but each Word/ Proceeding from the mouth of God, who fed/ Our Fathers here with Manna" (I.349–51). Then he declares of Satan, "lying is thy sustenance, thy food" (I.429), and proclaims himself the "living Oracle" of God (I.460). After this temptation Christ is "with holiest Meditations fed" (II.110), and even when he feels the torment of bodily hunger he testifies to his greater need for and satisfaction from spiritual food: "And from the sting of Famine fear no harm,/ Nor mind it, fed with better thoughts that feed/ Mee hung'ring more to do my Father's will" (II.257–59). To assuage his physical hunger Christ dreams of receiving providential food from God like that given Elijah or Daniel but is offered instead the lavish satanic banquet. In the wealth temptation Satan continues to taunt Christ with his "hunger-bit" condition (II.416), and later Christ in rejecting the "sumptuous gluttonies, and gorgeous feasts" of the Romans mentions that he does yet "thirst/ And hunger still" (IV.114, 120–21). The second night Christ goes to his rest still "Hungry and cold" (IV.403). But after the tower scene Christ's physical hunger is sated by "A table of Celestial Food, Divine,/ Ambrosial . . ./ That soon refresh'd him wearied, and repair'd/ What hunger, if aught hunger had impair'd,/ Or thirst" (IV.588–93). The banquet also symbolizes the satisfaction of his hunger to know and do his Father's will, and the suggestion of the communion points to his own status as the True Bread of life, the Word of God.

The martial imagery establishes yet another submerged metaphor, the temptation as duel or single combat between hero and antagonist. The invocation addresses the Spirit who brought Christ "Into the Desert, his Victorious Field/ Against the Spiritual Foe" (I.9–10). The lines introducing the action— "Now had the great Proclaimer with a voice/ More awful than the sound of Trumpet, cried/ Repentance, and Heaven's Kingdom nigh at hand" (I.18–20)—evoke the suggestion of a herald with a trumpet calling knights to do battle in the lists. The metaphor of the duel is continued through references to the "Adversary" appearing at an "assembly fam'd" where he "Would not be last" and where he "survey'd" a while "th'exalted man, to whom/ Such high attest was giv'n" (I.33–37). God speaks as monarch setting the conditions for a joust or single combat: he expects his Son to overcome Satan, "Winning by Conquest what the first man lost," and also to lay down in the wilderness "the rudiments/ Of his great warfare" against Sin and Death (I.154, 157–58). Also the angelic choir proclaims that Christ is entering "his great duel, not of arms,/ But to vanquish by wisdom hellish wiles" (I.174–75). Moreover, Christ's victories over the three major temptations are described in warlike terms: his teaching will "retrench" Satan's oracles (I.454); his kingdom will "to pieces dash" all other kingdoms (IV.149); his calm stance on the tower "smites" Satan with amazement and casts him to hell (IV.562). At the conclusion of the poem the Hercules-Antaeus simile reinforces this metaphoric pattern by explicitly comparing Christ's temptation to that notable mythical duel. Finally the angelic hymn lauds Christ in his role of "Queller of Satan," the victor in single combat: he is "with Godlike force endu'd"; he long ago did "debel" and cast Satan out of heaven; now he has given Satan a wound which anticipates and symbolizes the "last and deadliest wound" to come (IV.602–34).

Wordplay, evoking multiple meanings and adding resonance in many passages, is also a prominent aspect of style in *Paradise Regained;* as Christopher Ricks has shown, such wordplay is of the very essence of Milton's style in *Paradise Lost.*[16] The most common devices employed in the brief epic are etymological metaphors which call forth an older and more vividly pictorial sense of a word along with a modern sense, puns which also are often based upon etymology, and verbal reflections or echoes, often ironic.

The narrator uses such devices frequently. His reference to Satan as being "with the voice divine/ Nigh *Thunderstruck*" (I.35–36)[17] calls upon the vivid metaphorical meaning, struck by thunder, and suggests also the Titans or the falling Vulcan struck by Jove's thunder: this latter implication is reinforced a little later as Satan recalls how "his fierce thunder drove us to the deep" (I.90). This metaphor also carries the further suggestion that in the present conflict Satan is and will be thunderstruck not by the power of God but simply by the voice divine, the Word. A further example is in the reference to Satan's "gloomy *Consistory*" (I.42). This word carries its general meaning of a council or a council chamber, but it has also a special ecclesiastical signification—the meeting of the pope with his cardinals to deliberate the affairs of the church[18]—which initiates the poem's frequent association of Satan with the antichristian Roman church seen as deriving from him. The narrator also uses supposedly etymological puns, as in the description of the ravens abstaining from the food they brought to Elijah, "Though *ravenous*" (II.267–69).

Christ's speech has little verbal play of this kind: the conscious use of it would require a perspective which he does not yet have on past and future events, and its unconscious appearance in his speech would seem indecorous. Yet in the passage explaining that he "held it more humane, more heavenly, first/ By winning words to conquer willings hearts,/ And make persuasion do the work of fear;/ At least to *try,* and teach the erring Soul/ Not wilfully misdoing" (I.221–25), he does seem to call upon several senses of the word *try. Try* carries the sense of attempt, and also the sense of separating or distinguishing good from bad, as pure metal from dross; the word may also recall to us the fact, as yet unknown to Christ, that he will ultimately try the good and the wicked in a judicial sense, assigning fitting rewards and punishments.

Appropriately, the Father makes the most extensive and most conscious use of etymological puns and metaphors, for he is the one who has complete knowledge of all events, and who is aware of all the conditions of the contest. When he declares to Gabriel about Christ, "To show him worthy of his birth divine/ And high prediction, henceforth I *expose*/ To Satan; let him tempt and now *assay*/ His utmost subtlety" (I.141–44), he puns on the several meanings of *expose:* to abandon or lay open to danger (probably the primary meaning); but also, continuing the single combat metaphor, to exhibit openly and display for admiration; and even, to set forth or explain. He also puns on *assay.* Because of the syntax we are momentarily in doubt whether Satan is to assay Christ's subtlety or his own, and both meanings are relevant: Satan is to put to proof, try, or tempt Christ's subtlety, and also to practice by way of trial his own subtlety. Moreover, the Father's comment that Christ will win "what the first man lost/ By *fallacy* surpris'd" (I.154–55) refers in general to deception and trickery, but also to the more precise meaning of deception by sophistry, by false and unsound arguments, which is especially pertinent to Adam's and Christ's trial. Finally the comment that Christ will defeat Sin and Death "by Humiliation and strong *Sufferance"* suggests both his actual suffering and also the patience and endurance he displays.

In Satan's speech the puns, metaphors, and verbal echoes are nearly always unconscious and ironic. He executes a deliberate pun in his scornful remark to Christ, "Of thee these forty days none hath regard,/ Forty and more *deserted* here indeed" (II.315–16), punning upon Christ's abandoned situation in the desert. In an earlier line the pun is unconscious: "With granted leave *officious* I return" (II.302). Satan means, of course, that he returns in an obliging and dutiful manner, and perhaps desires to suggest also that the leave given him to return is somehow official, but that other meaning of *officious,* unduly forward in pressing services, meddlesome, is exactly descriptive of Satan's manner here, and he thus characterizes himself unknowingly. Also, he uses an etymological pun that works against his own argument when he includes among the famous kingdoms which constitute modern Parthia, *"Babylon* the *wonder* of all tongues" (III.280). He means of course that all men speak admiringly of Babylon as one of the seven wonders of the world, but when we recall that in *Paradise Lost* Babylon is identified with the Babel of Genesis xi:1–9, the origin of the confusion of tongues, we see that Satan's term of praise ironically degrades the city.[19] Satan's speech is also characterized by certain verbal echoes which work ironically as we recall the earlier uses. Satan's reference to the authority granted him by his followers "Consenting in *full frequence"* (II.130) echoes God's conversation with Gabriel undertaken "in *full frequence* bright/ Of Angels" (I.128–29), suggesting thereby the absurdity of the satanic imitation of God. Also, as prelude to his presentation of the various kingdoms Satan declares that these sights will educate that inexperience which makes Christ "Irresolute, unhardy, unadvent'rous" and will cause him

to "quit/ Those *rudiments*" (III.243-45); the allusion to
Christ's supposed rusticity and inexperience ironically recalls
the Father's use of the term *rudiments* to indicate that Christ
would learn in the desert the first principles of his great warfare
against Satan.

THE STYLE: SYNTACTICAL AND SOUND PATTERNS

The assertion that the style of *Paradise Regained* is comparatively plain or prosy also seems to receive support from
consideration of its syntactical constructions, sound patterns,
and rhetorical figures. As Tillyard observes, the unit of rhythm
is generally shorter than in *Paradise Lost* and the long suspended or periodic sentences creating what T. S. Eliot has
termed the "almost...physical sensation of a breathless leap"
are much less typical.[20] Martz points out that the Latinate
constructions, the inversions, and the ellipses of *Paradise Lost*
are much less common here, and that the syntax instead displays the "normal, supple, easy movement of an educated
mind." [21] The range of sound and musical effects is also less
spectacular and according to J. B. Broadbent rhetorical figures
are less abundant than in the long epic.[22] Nevertheless, in these
areas as in that of diction *Paradise Regained* will be found to
use the same devices as *Paradise Lost,* albeit with restraint
and with close attention to the decorum dictated by the
subject.

That *Paradise Regained* has shorter rhythmic and syntactical units can be readily demonstrated. A single sentence in
the brief epic often extends over fifteen lines of verse, but
seldom over twenty-five or thirty lines, as is very common in
Paradise Lost. The thematic statement of *Paradise Lost,* for
example, is a single sentence extending over seventeen lines
of verse, while that of *Paradise Regained* is a seven-line sentence. In both poems the invocation comprises a single sentence of ten lines, but in *Paradise Lost* the introduction to

the narrative describing Satan's fall to hell is a surging period of thirty lines while the comparable introduction to the narrative in *Paradise Regained* incorporates only fifteen lines. Several considerations may help to account for the difference: the shorter poem might well seem unbalanced if constructed of such long units; the new subject does not require these periods to create, as they do in *Paradise Lost,* the sensation of physical motion and tremendous energy; the narrator, now confident of himself as redeemed man, does not need them as he does in *Paradise Lost* to suggest the large inclusiveness and tremendous difficulty of his subject; they are not appropriate to Christ who uses comparatively terse, pointed sentences to image the precision and rigor of his mind; and they are not suitable for Satan who is endeavoring to imitate Christ's mode of speech. Nevertheless, the brief epic exploits such occasions as are offered for the very long suspended sentence. One use is to show the full complexity of a problem out of which at length some decision or determination of action evolves. An example is the twenty-six-line sentence which begins Christ's meditation in Book I, recounting Christ's growing apprehensions of his mission which culminate in his perception that persuasion is more heavenly than conquest (I.201–26). Another case is the thirty-line sentence unit concluding Satan's exchange with Belial in the second consult, in which Satan elaborates the great difficulty of appealing to Christ through sensual beauty, and evolves another strategy of attack through "manlier objects" and hunger (II.205–34). A second use is to convey the sense of multiplicity within unity, and periods having this function appear with increasing frequency in the descriptive passages of Book IV as the poem builds to its climax. Satan's description of Rome begins with a long sentence of seventeen lines followed by another of nineteen lines (IV.44–79), and then in a tremendous burst of rhetorical energy Satan presents the entire panorama of Athens as a single sentence of forty-eight lines (IV.236–84); these syntactical suspensions suggest the manifold and almost innumerable glories comprehended in these single places. Similarly the narrator collects into a single sentence of twenty-five lines all the terrors and horrors of the storm which attacks Christ (IV.401–25), and the angelic choir begin their celebration of Christ's victory with a twenty-two-line sentence expanding upon the many facets and implications of Christ's conquest (IV.596–617). An even more subtle use of the long period is Christ's résumé of Satan's catalogue of the Roman glories, in which Christ ironically undercuts each element by his rephrasing, and then brilliantly deflates the entire collection by his witty concluding question:

> Nor doth this grandeur and majestic show
> Of luxury, though call'd magnificence,
> More than of arms before, allure mine eye,
> Much less my mind; though thou should'st add to tell
> Thir sumptuous gluttonies, and gorgeous feasts
> On *Citron* tables of *Atlantic* stone,
> (For I have also heard, perhaps have read)
> Their wines of *Setia, Cales,* and *Falerne,*
> *Chios* and *Crete,* and how they quaff in Gold,
> Crystal and Murrhine cups emboss'd with Gems
> And studs of Pearl, to me should'st tell who thirst
> And hunger still: then Embassies thou show'st
> From Nations far and nigh; what honor that,
> But tedious waste of time to sit and hear
> So many hollow compliments and lies,
> Outlandish flatteries? then proceed'st to talk
> Of the Emperor, how easily subdu'd,
> How gloriously; I shall, thou say'st, expel
> A brutish monster; what if I withal
> Expel a Devil who first made him such? (IV.110–29)

An examination of the word order in *Paradise Regained* reveals that the Latinate inversions are neither so numerous nor so striking as in *Paradise Lost,* but yet they are used with some frequency, often to throw special emphasis upon key words by means of the artificial arrangement. The pathos of the apostles' plaint, "Alas, from what high hope to what re-lapse/ Unlook't for are we fall'n" (II.30–31), is largely due to the suspension of the thought and the withholding of the verb so that the very contours of the sentence imitate a "falling" from a height. Similarly, Christ's ironic comment to Satan after the storm, "Mee worse than wet thou find'st not; other harm/ Those terrors which thou speak'st of, did me none" (IV.486–87), achieves its power chiefly by the placement of the negatives in final position.

Paradise Regained also makes significant use of the fluid or liquid syntax which Ricks has found to be so characteristic of *Paradise Lost*[23]—constructions which introduce subtle nuances and ambiguities of meaning by admitting of more than one reading, or perhaps by utilizing the slight hesitation of the voice at the end of the poetic line before it moves on to complete the syntactical unit to convey a fleeting sugges-tion of a meaning other than the stated meaning. This last device reinforces the metaphor discussed previously of John the Baptist as herald with trumpet opening the lists between Satan and Christ: "Now had the great Proclaimer with a voice/ More awful than the sound of Trumpet, cried/ Repent-ance" (I.18–20). The brief withholding of the word *repentance* by the line-ending enables the metaphor to create its effect before we are brought to concentrate on the literal story. The device is used again to produce an ironic overtone in Satan's observation that the demons now "Must bide the stroke of that long threat'n'd wound,/ At least if so we can, and by the head/ Broken be not intended all our power/ To be infring'd" (I.59–62). The slight hesitation after *power* invites first the reading, the metaphorical wound means the breaking of all our power, which we recognize as precisely the effect Christ's

victory will achieve, but then Satan adds the verb *infringed*
to control *power,* thereby modifying his interpretation and
rendering it much less accurate. A somewhat more complex
example which employs both the line-ending and liquid syntax
is the description of Satan's action in summoning the first
consult: he "with envy fraught and rage/ Flies to his place,
nor rests, but in mid air/ To Council summons all his mighty
Peers,/ Within thick Clouds" (I.38–41). Two meanings and
two senses of *but* are involved: we read first that Satan can
rest nowhere except in mid-air as that is now his *place;* then,
attending to the entire syntactical unit, we read that Satan
flies without resting until he reaches mid-air where he assem-
bles his council.

Perhaps even more important to the style of *Paradise Regained* than the devices just discussed are its many rhetorical
schemes, especially iterative schemes—figures which derive
their force both from sound repetition and word order, and
which according to Puttenham affect both sound and sense.[24]
Though Broadbent's observation that the iterative schemes
are less numerous in *Paradise Regained* than in *Paradise Lost*
is no doubt quantitatively true, yet especially in the dialogue
portions of the brief epic they occur very frequently and seem
to serve an even more significant function than in the long
epic. Through structural balance and sound repetitions they
elevate and stiffen the language, providing the impression of
a patterned verbal duel analogous to a single combat. Yet at
the same time, paradoxically, they contribute to the impression of spontaneous speech, of a progressive and dramatic
working out of meanings and understandings as Christ and
Satan talk. More paradoxical still, those speeches which most
critics designate as containing the greatest emotional realism
and sincerity are among those contrived with the greatest
rhetorical art.

One need not identify and label each of the rhetorical figures of iteration or parallelism to appreciate the complex patterns Milton weaves, though a brief résumé of the most common of these figures may aid the analysis of the few examples which follow. In the first place, the brief epic employs a good deal of rhyme not only in terminal but also in medial or beginning position in the lines: there is actual *rhyme, identical rhyme* (*antistrophe*), *near rhyme* (perhaps the commonest variety), and what Broadbent calls *anti-rhyme*—using opposites in rhyming position to create the effect of an oxymoron.[25] Also, the poem has many varieties of sound/word/phrase repetitions: *alliteration* (*paroemion*), associating and balancing related or contrasting terms; *epanalepsis,* beginning and ending a line with the same word; *epizeuxis,* repeating words adjacent to each other; *anadiplosis,* starting a line with the last word of the line before; *anaphora,* using the same word or phrase to begin several successive clauses; *antimetabole,* repeating a phrase or clause and inverting it; *antithesis,* coupling together contrary words or phrases; *ploce,* repeating a single word with a few words interspersed;[26] *traductio,* repeating a word in a different grammatical form, often with punning effect; *prosono masia,* using homophonous words close to one another, often as a quasi-pun; *epanados,* expanding a statement by repetition and amplification of key words. Finally, Milton uses a variety of rhetorical schemes built upon the similarity or paralleling of various syntactical units to achieve a repetitive effect: *brachylogia,* a series of disjunctive words separated only by commas; *parison,* a series of phrases in parallel construction; *climax,* the interweaving of clauses by using the word which ends the first clause to begin the subsequent one, and so forth; *asyndeton,* a series of parallel phrases without conjunctions; *polysyndeton,* a series of words or phrases joined by conjunctions.

Such schemes are found in the speech of the narrator, of God the Father, and of Mary but are most common in the exchanges between Christ and Satan, with the significant exception of Satan's lofty descriptive passages. Analysis reveals a very close similarity in Satan's and Christ's use of the schemes, although Christ's speeches have some edge in regard to tightness of organization; the similarity lends further support to the observation that Satan in this poem is endeavoring to sound like Christ's alter ego, to imitate the voice of reason itself.

A first example may be taken from part of the exchange between Christ and Satan in Book I. Upon being discerned in his disguise, Satan moves at once to highly patterned speech as if to demonstrate the rationality of his case by his own controlled, rational discourse:

> Though I have *lost*
> Much luster of my native brightness, *lost*
> To be belov'd of God, I have not *lost*
> To love, at *least* contémplate and admire
> What I see excellent in *good, or fair,*
> *Or virtuous;* I should so have *lost* all sense.
> What can be then *less* in me than desire
> *To see* thee and approach thee, whom I know
> Declar'd the Son of *God, to hear* attent
> Thy wisdom, and *behold* thy *God*like deeds?
> *Men* generally think me much a foe
> To all *mankind:* why should I? they to me
> Never did wrong or violence; *by them*
> I *lost* not what I *lost,* rather *by them*
> I *gain'd* what I have *gain'd,* and *with them* dwell
> Copartner in these Regions of the World,
> If not disposer; lend them *oft my aid,*
> *Oft my advice* by presages and signs,
> And answers, oracles, portents and dreams,
> Whereby they may direct their future life.
> Envy they say excites me, thus to gain
> Companions of my misery and *woe.*

At *first* it may be; but *long since* with *woe*
Nearer acquainted, now I feel by proof
That fellowship in pain divides not smart. (I.377-401)

The italics (which I have supplied here and in subsequent
passages) will call attention to some of the patterns: the elaborate ploce on *lost* reinforced by identical end rhyme and the
near rhymes *least* and *less* as well as by the contrasting word,
gain'd; the parison in the organization of lines 389-91; the interlocking of lines 393-94 by anadiplosis. One of the subtlest
effects is the ironic *double-entendre* of line 383. Satan, carried along by the sound pattern established through the emphatic repetitions of *lost* in several lines, asks, "What can be
less in me than desire/ To see thee," meaning, of course, How
can I have anything less than a desire at least to see and talk
with thee. However, the word arrangement ironically suggests
the opposite and truer meaning, that there can be nothing
Satan desires less than thus to confront and listen to Christ.

Christ responds to this passage with a speech using the same
kinds of rhetorical schemes, with, if anything, even more intricate patterning:

Deservedly thou griev'st, compos'd of *lies*
From the *beginning,* and in *lies* wilt *end;*
Who boast'st re*lease* from Hell, and *leave* to *come*
Into the *Heav'n* of *Heavens;* thou *com'st* indeed,
As a poor miserable captive thrall
Comes to the place where he before had sat
Among the Prime in Splendor, now depos'd,
Ejected, emptied, gaz'd, unpitied, shunn'd,
A spectacle *of ruin* or *of scorn*
To all the *Host* of *Heaven;* the *happy* place
Imparts to thee no *happiness,* no joy,
Rather *inflames* thy torment, representing
Lost bliss, to thee no more communicable,
So never more *in Hell* than when *in Heaven.*

But thou art servicable to *Heaven's* King.
Wilt thou impute to obedience what thy fear
Extorts, or pleasure to do ill *excites?*
What but thy *malice mov'd* thee to *misdeem*
Of righteous Job, then cruelly to *afflict* him
With all *inflictions?* But his patience won.
The other service was thy chosen task,
To be a *liar* in four hundred mouths;
For *lying* is thy sustenance, thy food.
Yet thou pretend'st to *truth;* all Oracles
By thee are giv'n, and what confest more *true*
Among the Nations? That hath been thy craft,
By mixing somewhat *true* to vent more *lies.* (I.407–33)

Here the elaborate traductios on *come, heaven, happy, lies, truth, afflict;* the antithesis of *truth/lies;* the frequent near rhymes such as *extorts/excites* and *imparts/inflames* contribute to the progression of the argument in which Christ, by slightly altering the senses and grammatical forms of the words Satan has used, overthrows his pretenses. And the single-line bracylogia at line 414 provides a fine formal embodiment of Christ's scorn.

This highly schematized language which yet achieves a conversational tone is by no means unique: it can be matched in nearly all the formal argument between Christ and Satan, especially in the passages on wealth, glory, zeal, arms, learning, and the meaning of the storm. Rather than cite additional illustrations of interchange between the two, I will consider two short passages, one by Satan and one by Christ, where the rhetorical patterning achieves rather special effects. The first is Satan's speech in response to Christ's formal challenge in Book III, a speech which critics usually interpret as a genuine emotional outburst, an intensely dramatic moment in the relation of the two antagonists.[27] The interesting point is that this emotion accompanies, indeed is conveyed by, one of the most elaborately patterned passages in the entire poem, clear evidence that for Milton contrived rhetoric is in no way antithetical to psychological realism or dramatic intensity:

> To whom the Tempter inly rackt replied.
> Let that *come* when it *comes;* all hope is lost
> Of my reception into grace; what *worse?*
> For where *no hope is left, is left no fear;*
> If there be *worse,* the expectation more
> Of *worse* torments me than the feeling can.
> I would be at the *worst; worst* is my Port,
> My harbor, and my ultimate repose,
> The end I would attain, my final good.
> *My error* was my *error,* and my *crime*
> My *crime:* whatever, for itself condemn'd,
> And will alike be punish'd; whether thou
> *Reign* or *reign* not; though to that gentle brow
> Willingly I could fly, and hope thy *reign,*
> From that placid aspect and meek regard,
> Rather than aggravate my evil state,
> Would stand between me and thy Father's *ire*
> (Whose *ire* I dread more than the *fire* of Hell)
> A *shelter* and a kind of *shading cool*
> Interposition, as a *summer's cloud.*
> If I then to the *worst* that can be *haste,*
> Why move thy feet so slow to what is *best.* (III.203–24)

The patterning is very intricate: ploce and traductio and epi-zeuxis throughout on *worse, worst;* ploce on *error, crime, reign;* a true rhyme *ire/fire* that has a punning effect; a near rhyme *haste/best* which images the relation of these two concepts in Satan's mind; an alliteration which relates *shading cool* and *summer's cloud.* Yet for all this contrivance, appropriate to the formal intellectual duel, Satan's cry is made to sound spontaneous.

The opening lines of Christ's reply to the learning temptation are remarkable for being perhaps the most tightly ordered and rigidly patterned segment of the entire poem. This is wholly appropriate for Christ here speaks as the voice of true wisdom, manifesting that wisdom in the perfect control and justness of his speech:

> *Think not* but that *I know* these things; or *think*
> *I know* them *not; not* therefore am I *short*
> Of *knowing* what I *ought:* he who receives
> *Light from above, from the fountain* of *light,*
> No other doctrine needs, though granted *true;*
> But these are *false,* or little else but *dreams,*
> *Conjectures, fancies,* built on nothing firm. (IV.286–92)

Most remarkable, and unparalleled elsewhere in the poem, are the two epanalepses repeated within four lines of each other: line 286 begins and ends with *think,* line 289 with *light.* The passage has also a traductio on *know* functioning in antithesis to *think,* and also in the climactic series of terms, *think, know, light, true.* The slant rhyme *short/not/ought,* the ploce *I know/ I know,* the parison *from above, from the fountain* further knit the passage together. Then this tightly woven, precise statement respecting Christ's true wisdom is set off against the inferior learning which he will soon describe by the antithesis *true/false,* and also by the bracylogia *dreams,/Conjectures, fancies.*

One other passage, this time from the narrator's speech, deserves special attention: the climactic epic similes celebrating Christ's victory over Satan. The narrator's speech is not usually so intricately patterned as this, but as he here celebrates the victory of Christ, whose perfect reason has renewed his own and that of all mankind, he most appropriately attains a precision and economy and emphasis which match that of Christ himself. The patterning serves to elevate and ennoble the language and also to re-emphasize the central themes: the ploce on *tempt,* the traductio on *proud,* the ploce and traductio and rhyme and epizcuxis echoing through the entire passage on *fell/fall*—which are then related by slant rhyme to *foil* recalling the metaphor of single combat—set up the pattern *pride-fall-foil.* Other features are the ploce on *solv'd,* and the very effective polysyndeton of line 579:

> Tempt not the Lord thy God; he said and stood.
> But *Satan smitten* with amazement *fell*
> As when Earth's Son Antaeus (to compare
> Small things with greatest) in *Irassa strove*
> With *Jove's Alcides,* and oft *foil'd* still rose,
> Receiving from his mother Earth new *strength,*
> *Fresh* from his *fall,* and *fiercer* grapple join'd,
> Throttl'd at length in th'Air, expir'd and *fell;*
> So after many a *foil* the Tempter *proud,*
> Renewing *fresh* assaults, amidst his *pride*
> *Fell* whence he stood to see his Victor *fall.*
> And as that Theban Monster that propos'd
> Her riddle, and him who *solv'd* it not, devour'd,
> That once found out and *solv'd,* for grief and spite
> Cast herself headlong from th'Ismenian *steep,*
> So *struck* with dread and anguish *fell* the Fiend,
> And to his crew, that sat consulting, brought
> Joyless triumphals of his hop'd success,
> *Ruin, and desperation, and dismay,*
> Who durst so *proudly* tempt the Son of God.
> So Satan *fell* ... (IV.561-81)

The style of *Paradise Regained,* then, no less than its relationship to generic traditions and its vast all-inclusive theme, supports the poem's claim to the status of brief epic. Coleridge's encomium on the work as "in its kind...the most perfect poem extant"[28] is perhaps the appropriate final tribute to Milton's consummate art in conceiving his brief epic according to the demands of the higher moral and spiritual heroism and in executing it without sacrificing either epic dimension or the decorum appropriate to this very special subject. The perfection is not merely formal, for the poem in large measure succeeds in its attempt to incorporate, evaluate, and order the whole complex of Classical-Judaeo-Christian values which constitute the intellectual heritage of Western man. The particular ordering vision, like all human things, is partial. But the poem's dramatic situation—Christ's search in the wilderness to comprehend his nature and discover his mission, his subsumption of the past but rejection of its dead literalisms, his abjuration of the many evil or ignoble or imperfect or less perfect modes of action which would preclude attainment of the highest concept of personal excellence and mission—presents a myth of human process, of human striving toward ideals of comprehension and order, of wisdom and noble action which must remain relevant and powerful as long as such ideals hold any meaning for us.

NOTES

ABBREVIATIONS

ANCL   Ante-Nicene Christian Library, ed. Alexander Roberts and James Donaldson (24 vols.; Edinburgh, 1867–72)

CE   *The Works of John Milton,* ed. Frank A. Patterson *et al.* (18 vols.; New York, 1931–38)

CSEL   Corpus Scriptorum Ecclesiasticorum Latinorum (80 vols.; Vienna, 1866–1964)

Douay Bible   *The Holie Bible ... by the English College of Doway* (2 vols.; Douai, 1609)

EETS   Early English Text Society

ELH   *ELH: A Journal of English Literary History*

Geneva Bible   *The Bible: That is, the Holy Scriptures ... Whereunto Are Adjoyned Briefe Summaries of Doctrine ... by Theodore Beza: And Also Short Expositions ... Englished by L. Tomson* (London, 1590)

HDB   *Dictionary of the Bible,* ed. James Hastings (5 vols.; New York, 1911–12)

HTR   *Harvard Theological Review*

JEGP   *Journal of English and Germanic Philology*

JHI   *Journal of the History of Ideas*

LCC   Library of Christian Classics, ed. John Baillie *et al.* (26 vols.; Philadelphia, 1953–57)

LF   A Library of Fathers, ed. E. B. Pusey *et al.* (40 vols.; Oxford, 1843–61)

Loeb   The Loeb Classical Library

MGH   Monumenta Germaniae Historica, Auctores Antiquissimi (15 vols.; Berlin, 1877–1919)

MLN   *Modern Language Notes*

MLQ   *Modern Language Quarterly*

MP   *Modern Philology*

N&Q   *Notes and Queries*

Pat. Graec.   Patrologiae Cursus Completus, Series Graeca, ed. J.-P. Migne (166 vols.; Paris, 1857–66)

Pat. Lat.   Patrologiae Cursus Completus, Series Latina, ed. J.-P. Migne (221 vols.; Paris, 1844–64)

PL   *Paradise Lost*

PMLA   *Publications of the Modern Language Association*

PQ   *Philological Quarterly*

PR   *Paradise Regained*

SEL   *Studies in English Literature, 1500–1900*

SP   *Studies in Philology*

SSCC   Scripturae Sacrae Cursus Completus, ed. J.-P. and V. S. Migne (28 vols.; Paris, 1837–45)

UTQ   *University of Toronto Quarterly*

NOTES

CHAPTER I

1. *The Holy Bible, Conteyning the Old Testament and the New* [AV] (London, 1612). Unless otherwise specified, subsequent biblical references are to this edition, a copy of which has manuscript notes in Milton's hand.

2. See for example: E. M. W. Tillyard, *Milton* (London, 1930), pp. 302–12; Denis Saurat, *Milton, Man and Thinker* (London, 1944), p. 233; Douglas Bush, *English Literature in the Earlier Seventeenth Century, 1600–1660* (Oxford, 1962), p. 412; W. B. C. Watkins, *An Anatomy of Milton's Verse* (Baton Rouge, La., 1955), p. 124; H. J. C. Grierson, "John Milton," *The Criterion*, VIII (1928), 254; G. F. Sensabaugh, "Milton on Learning," *SP*, XLIII (1946), 258–72.

3. Watkins, *Anatomy*, p. 104.

4. David Masson, *The Life of John Milton* (7 vols.; London, 1859–94), VI, 654–55.

5. In *John Milton: Complete Poems and Major Prose*, ed. Merritt Y. Hughes (New York, 1957). All subsequent quotations from the text of Milton's poems are from this edition. Citations from Milton's prose works are to volume and page of the Columbia *Milton* (*CE*).

6.   Ille ego, qui quondam gracili modulatus avena
       carmen, et egressus silvis vicina coegi
       ut quamvis avido parerent arva colono,
       gratum opus agricolis; at nunc horrentia Martis
       Arma virumque cano...

This echo is recognized by Tillyard, *Milton*, p. 322, by Arnold Stein, *Heroic Knowledge* (Minneapolis, 1957), pp. 6–7, and by Louis L. Martz, "*Paradise Regained*: The Meditative Combat," *ELH*, XXVII (1960), 224–25, but none of them admits its force as an assertion of the epic nature of *Paradise Regained*. Indeed, Martz and Tillyard relate the poem to Virgil's *Georgics* on the basis of this echo and of the four-book structure, though it would seem that the lines in question assert instead the poem's epic character.

7. Tillyard, *Milton*, p. 316. Cf. Tillyard, *The English Epic and Its Backgrounds* (London, 1954), p. 447.

8. The positions, respectively, of Tillyard, *Milton*, p. 318; Howard Schultz, "Christ and Antichrist in *Paradise Regained*," *PMLA*, LXVII (1952), 790–808; Bush, *Earlier Seventeenth Century*, p. 413; Stein, *Heroic Knowledge*, pp. 4–8; Kenneth Muir, *John Milton* (London, 1955), p. 167; Martz, "Meditative Combat," pp. 223–47. However, A. S. P. Woodhouse, "Theme and

Pattern in *Paradise Regained,*" *UTQ,* XXV (1955–56), 167–82, sees the poem
as a "brief epic."

9. *CE* III, Part I, 237–38.

10. Parker, "On Milton's Early Literary Program," *MP,* XXXIII (1935–36),
49–53.

11. Tillyard, *English Epic,* pp. 4–15.

CHAPTER II

1. For patristic and later Christian writers cited by Milton see J. P. Pritchard,
"The Fathers of the Church in the Works of John Milton," *Classical Journal,*
XXXIII (1937–38), 79–87. A partial list includes Philo, Diodorus Siculus,
Clement of Alexandria, Origen, Cyprian, Lactantius, Athanasius, Basil, Proco-
pius, Sulpicius Severus, Ambrose, Chrysostom, Jerome, Augustine, Theodoret,
Prudentius, Gregory the Great, Isidore of Seville, Erasmus, Luther, Calvin,
Grotius, Pareus, Bucer, Diodati, Bullinger.

2. Josephus, *Against Apion* II.14, 281, trans. H. St. J. Thackeray [*Works*]
(Loeb [8 vols.; London, 1926–63]), I, 297, 405; Clement, *Stromata* I.xxi; VI.iii,
trans. William Wilson (ANCL, Vols. IV, XII [Edinburgh, 1867, 1869]), IV,
425; XII, 219; Isidore, *Etymologiarum* I.xxxix.9–18, Pat. Lat. LXXXII, 118–20;
Jerome, "Epistle LIII, Ad Paulinum," Pat. Lat. XXII, 540–49, commonly printed
as preface to the Vulgate.

3. See E. R. Curtius, *European Literature and the Latin Middle Ages,* trans.
W. R. Trask (New York, 1953), pp. 219–20; Origen, *Contra Celsum* IV.21;
VII.30, trans. Henry Chadwick (Cambridge, Eng., 1953), pp. 197–98, 418–19;
Clement, *Stromata* V.iv, xiv; VI.iii, v, viii, ANCL XII, 233–34, 282–89, 319,
327–28, 339–42; Clement, *Protreptikos, or Exhortation to the Heathen,* ANCL
IV, 19–20.

4. Philo, *De Vita Contemplativa,* trans. F. H. Colson [*Works*] (Loeb [10
vols.; London, 1929–62]), IX, 163–67; Josephus, *Jewish Antiquities* II.xvi.4;
IV.viii.44, Loeb, IV, 317, 621–23; Eusebius, *Evangelicae Praeparationis*
XI.v.514*b–c,* trans. E. H. Gifford (Oxford, 1903), p. 551; Jerome, "Preface to
Job," Pat. Lat. XXVIII, 1140–41.

5. Jerome, *ibid.;* Cassiodorus, *De Schematibus et Tropis,* Pat. Lat. LXX,
1269–80; Bede, *De Schematis et Tropis Sacrae Scripturae,* Pat. Lat. XC, 175.
See also Curtius, *Latin Middle Ages,* pp. 46–47.

6. Certain aspects of this tradition have been discussed by Charles M. Jones,
"Milton's Brief Epic," *SP,* XLIV (1947), 209–27; Israel M. Baroway, "The
Hebrew Hexameter: A Study in Renaissance Sources and Interpretation," *ELH,*
II (1935), 66–91; and Leonard Siger, "The Image of Job in the Renaissance"
(Ph.D. dissertation, The Johns Hopkins University, 1960).

7. S. R. Driver and G. B. Gray, *A Critical and Exegetical Commentary on
the Book of Job* (International Critical Commentary [2 vols.; New York,

1921]), I, lxv; W. Taylor Smith, "Job," *HDB*, Vol. II; Jerome, "Ad Paulinum," Pat. Lat. XXII, 545.

8. Baba Bathra 14*b*, 15*a*, 15*b*, The Babylonian Talmud, ed. I. Epstein (London, 1935), I, 69–77.

9. Origen, *Contra Celsum* VI.43, pp. 359–60; Eusebius, *De Demonstratione Evangelica*, Pat. Graec. XXII, 51.

10. For example: Jerome, *Quaestionum in Genesim*, Pat. Lat. XXIII, 971; Philippus Presbyterius, *In Historiam Job Commentariorum* (Basle, 1527), pp. 3, 144–46; Nicholas of Lyra [*Postilla in Universa Biblia*] (Strasbourg, 1480), Job; Robert Bellarmine, *De Scriptoribus Ecclesiasticis, Opera Omnia* VII (Cologne, 1617), col. 2; Joannes Piscator, *Commentariorum in Omnes Libros Veteris Testimenti* (Herborn, 1644), III, 7; Victorinus Strigelius, *Liber Job* (Leipzig [1571]), pp. 2–3; Franciscus Titelmann, *Elucidatio Paraphrastica in Librum Job* (Antwerp, 1547), preface.

11. Origen?, *In Job Commentarius, Opera Omnia*, ed. Charles Delarue (4 vols.; Paris, 1733–59), II, 850–51; Olympiodorus and Chrysostom, in Niceta, *Catena Graecorum Patrum in Beatum Job*, ed. Patrick Junius (London, 1637), preface; Augustine, *City of God* XVIII.47, trans. Marcus Dods (New York, 1950), p. 658; [Prosper], *De Promissionibus et Praedictionibus Dei*, Pat. Lat. LI, 750–51; Isidore, *De Ortu et Obitu Patrum*, Pat. Lat. LXXXIII, 136; Gregory the Great, *Moralia in Job* (LF, Vol. XVIII [Oxford, 1844]), p. 15; *Glossa Ordinaria*, Pat. Lat. CXIII, 747–51; Rabanus Maurus, *De Universo*, Pat. Lat. CXI, 50; Theodore Beza, *Job Expounded*, trans. ? (London [1589?]), preface; Augustinus Steuchius, *Enarrationes in Librum Job* (Venice, 1567), fol. 5ᵛ; Hieremias Drexelius, *Jobus Divinae Providentiae Theatrum* (Antwerp, 1655), p. 31; Douay Bible I, 1059; John Downame *et al.*, *Annotations upon All the Books of the Old and New Testament* (London, 1645), n.p. (argument to Job).

12. John Calvin, *Sermons . . . upon the Booke of Job*, trans. Arthur Golding (London, 1574), p. 2; Thomas Cajatan, *In Librum Job Commentarii* (Rome, 1535), fols. 2ᵛ–3; Sir Walter Raleigh, *The History of the World*, Part I (London, 1614), p. 398; John Trapp, *Annotations upon the Old and New Testament* (5 vols.; London, 1654–64), II, 1–2 (introduction to Job); Edward Leigh, *Annotations on Five Poetical Books of the Old Testament* (London, 1657), Prolegomena; John Selden, *De Jure Naturali & Gentium, Works*, ed. David Wilkins (London, 1726), I, 746–49.

13. Baba Bathra 14*b*, 15*a*, 15*b*, Babylonian Talmud I, 71–75; Moses Maimonides, *The Guide for the Perplexed*, trans. M. Friedländer (London, 1904), p. 296; Martin Luther, *Colloquia Mensalia*, trans. Henrie Bell (London, 1652), pp. 361–62.

14. Polychronius, and Julianus of Halicarnassus, in *Catena*, preface; Steuchius, *Enarrationes*, fol. 3ᵛ; Arthur Jackson, *Annotations upon . . . the Five Doctrinall, or Poeticall Books* (London, 1658), preface; John Diodati, *Pious and Learned Annotations upon the Holy Bible* (London, 1648), pp. 284–85 (argument to Job).

15. Gregory, *Moralia,* LF XVIII, 15; Suidas, *Index Scriptorum,* Pat. Graec. CXVII, 1283; Lancelot Andrewes, *XCVI Sermons* (London, 1629), pp. 425–26.

16. John Lightfoot, *The Harmony, Chronicle and Order of the Old Testament* (London, 1649), pp. 44–46; Hugo Grotius, *Annotata ad Vetus Testamentum* (Paris, 1644), I, 298; Joannes Oecolampadius, *In Librum Job Exegemata* (Geneva, 1553), preface.

17. Origen?, *In Job, Opera* II, 851. See also Bellarmine, *De Scriptoribus, Opera* VII, 3–4; Drexelius, *Jobus,* pp. 21–22; Titelmann, *In Job,* preface; Gasparus Sanctius, *In Librum Job Commentarii* (London, 1625), p. 5; Douay Bible I, 1060 (argument to Job).

18. Calvin, *Sermons ... upon ... Job,* p. 2; Beza, *Job Expounded,* preface, chap. xxxviii; Leigh, *Annotations,* Prolegomena; Trapp, *Annotations* II, 2; Joannes de Pineda, *Commentariorum in Job* (3 vols.; Venice, 1608), I, chaps. i–iii of preface; Joannes Quistorpius, *Annotationes in Omnes Libros Biblicos* (Frankfurt, 1648), p. 384; Balthasar Corderius, *In Librum Job* (SSCC, Vol. XIII [Paris, 1861]), cols. 221–30; *The Dutch Annotations upon the Whole Bible,* trans. Theodore Haak (London, 1657), argument to Job.

19. Caryl, *An Exposition ... upon ... Job* (12 vols.; London, 1643–70), I, 6.

20. Senault, *The Pattern of Patience, in the Example of Holy Job,* trans. ? (London, 1657), preface.

21. Jerome, Pat. Lat. XXVII, 223–24: "Denique quid Psalterio canorius, quod in morem nostri Flacci, et Graeci Pindari, nunc iambo currit, nunc Alcaico personat, nunc Sapphico tumet, nunc semipede ingreditur? Quid Deuteronomii et Isaiae cantico pulchrius? Quid Salomone gravius? Quid perfectius Job? Quae omnia hexametris et pentametris versibus, ut Josephus et Origines scribunt, apud suos composita decurrunt."

22. Jerome, Pat. Lat. XXVIII, 1140: "hexametri versus sunt, dactylo spondaeoque currentes: et propter linguae idioma crebro recipientes et alios pedes, non earumdem syllabarum, sed eorumdem temporum."

23. *Ibid.,* 1145–82. Jerome's other translation of Job, taken from the Septuagint, is in prose (Pat. Lat. XXIX, 61–118).

24. Arator, "Epistola ad Vigilium," Pat. Lat. LXVIII, 80–81; Aldhelm, *Opera,* ed. Rudolfus Ehwald (MGH, Vol. XV [Berlin, 1919]), pp. 63–64; Albertus Magnus, *Commentarii in Job,* ed. Melchior Weiss (Fribourg, 1904), col. 10.

25. Googe, quoted in Thomas Warton, *History of English Poetry* (3 vols.; London, 1840), III, 365.

26. Lodge, *Defence of Poetry, Music, and Stage Plays,* in *Elizabethan Critical Essays,* ed. G. G. Smith (2 vols.; Oxford, 1904), I, 71.

27. Steuchius, *Enarrationes,* fol. 3^V; Titelmann, *In Job,* preface; Quistorpius, *Annotationes,* p. 384; Leigh, *Annotations,* p. 1; Trapp, *Annotations* II, 2.

28. Pineda, *In Job* I, chap. iv of preface: "Genebrard. affirmat Moysem Spondaicis versibus repraesentasse Jobi historiam ... Marianus Victorius in annotat. ad Epist. 122. Hieronym. ait se invenisse experimento versus libri Job esse Hexametros ex Spondeo, Dactylo, & aliis pedibus, ut Trocheo, Iambo, &

Proceleumatico currentes, non tam syllabarum, quam temporum in eis habita ratione... Certè suam poësim esse in sacris Scripturis, & suam Carminis metrique mensuram cultam ab Hebraeis, constitutum est apud omnes doctores sacros... Poësim verò, & carminum Heroïcorum scientiam, non omninò intercidesse Hieronymi tempore, docte colligit Andraeas Masius... Revocare & docere, summo cum labore conantur alii: vide libellum R. David Jahaiae de metris Hebraicis, quem Latinum reddidit Gilb. Genebrardus." Cf. Gilbert Genebrardus, *Chronographiae* (London, 1609), p. 78.

29. Mercerus, *Commentarii in Jobum* (Amsterdam, 1651), p. 19 (preface): "Conatus sum juxta ea quae monet Hieronymus, multos versus ad dimensionem pedum revocare. Sanè plerosque dimensus hexametros esse comperi, verùm ubi pro dactylo & spondaeo passim alii pedes juxta linguae idioma, ut dicebat Hier. occurunt."

30. Drepanius, "Exhortatio ad Legenda Sacra Volumina," Pat. Lat. LXI, 1089.

31. Isidore, *Etymologiarum* I.xxxix.9-11, Pat. Lat. LXXXII, 118-19: "Heroicum enim carmen dictum, quod eo virorum fortium res et facta narrentur. Nam heroes appellantur viri quasi aerei, et coelo digni propter sapientiam et fortitudinem; quod metrum auctoritate caetera metra praecedit, unum ex omnibus tam maximis operibus aptum quam parvis, suavitatis et dulcedinis aeque capex... Omnibus quoque metris prius est. Hoc primum Moyses in cantico Deuteronomii, longe ante Pherecydem et Homerum... Unde et apparet antiquius fuisse apud Hebraeos studium carminum quam apud gentiles. Siquidem et Job, Moysi temporibus adaequatus, hexametro versu, dactylo spondaeoque decurrit."

32. Bede, *De Arte Metrica*, Pat. Lat. XC, 162-63, 174: "Coenon est, vel mictun, in quo poeta ipse loquitur, et personae loquentes introducuntur, ut sunt scripta et *Ilias* et *Odyssea* Homeri, et *AEneis* Virgilii; et apud nos historia beati Job." Cf. Diomede, *Ars Grammatica*, Book III, in *Grammatici Latini*, ed. Henrich Keil (7 vols.; Leipzig, 1855-80), I, 482.

33. Rabanus Maurus, *De Universo* XV.ii, Pat. Lat. CXI, 420.

34. Suidas, *Index Scriptorum*, Pat. Graec. CXVII, 1283: "Jobus. Habes philosophi hujus praemia. Habes et ejus librum, Homerica et Platonica Musa suavius quid canentem, qui nec fabularum nec alienarum calamitatum narrationem praedicat, vel audacissimum Achillem, aut callidissimum Ulyssem, quibus caedes sunt triumphus, et mulierum stupra, praeclara facinora; sed Satanam describit a nudo quidem et inermi et solo superatum..." (Text in Latin only.)

35. Mantuan, *Parthenice Mariana*, ed. J. B. Ascensius [Paris, 1502], Apologeticon; *Uranie*, st. 50, *Du Bartas His Divine Weekes and Workes*, trans. Joshua Sylvester (London, 1621), p. 530.

36. Strigelius, *Job*, pp. 1-2; Sanctius, *In Librum Job Commentarii* (London, 1625), p. 1; Chemnitius, *Dissertatio Theologica... de Persona et Libro Hiobi* (Jena, 1688), sig. C2^V; Steuchius, *Enarrationes*, fols. 4^V-5.

37. Renan, *Le Livre de Job* (Paris, 1882), p. xlvi. See W. B. Stevenson, *The*

Poem of Job (London, 1947), pp. 21–22; "Job," *HDB*, Vol. II; "Job," *Encyclopaedia Britannica*, 14th ed., Vol. XIII.

38. "Job," *HDB*, Vol. II; Archibald MacLeish, *J. B.* (London, 1959); John Owen, *Five Great Skeptical Dramas of History* (London, 1896); H. M. Kallen, *The Book of Job as a Greek Tragedy, Restored* (New York, 1918).

39. Driver, *An Introduction to the Literature of the Old Testament* (9th ed.; Edinburgh, 1913), p. 411.

40. For example: E. C. Baldwin, *Types of Literature in the Old Testament* (New York, 1929); R. G. Moulton, *The Book of Job: A Dramatic Poem Framed in an Epic Story* (New York, 1902); J. F. Genung, *The Epic of the Inner Life, Being the Book of Job* (Boston, 1891), pp. 25–29. E. M. W. Tillyard, *The English Epic and Its Backgrounds* (London, 1954), p. 5, indicates that he considered the work for inclusion in the epic category but finally omitted it on the ground that it "does not contain enough."

41. Luther, "Preface to the Book of Job" (1524), *Works*, ed. H. E. Jacobs *et al.* (Philadelphia, 1932), pp. 383–84; Calvin, *Sermons…upon…Job*, pp. 37–47; Beza, *Job Expounded*, preface. See also George Hutcheson, *An Exposition of the Book of Job* (London, 1669); [Joseph Hall], *A Plaine and Familiar Explication…of the Whole Divine Scripture* (London, 1633), chap. iii; *Biblia Sacra*, ed. Immanuel Tremellius and Franciscus Junius (London, 1585), n.p. (argument to Job); Geneva Bible, fols. 179^V–180^V (argument to Job). See also the annotations on Job cited above, of Trapp (p. 27), Piscator (pp. 1–11), the Dutch Annotators (argument to Job and chaps. iii, xlii), and Downame *et al.* (Job, argument and chap. iii).

42. Quistorpius, *Annotationes*, p. 383, records the Anabaptist opinion.

43. Luther, *Tischreden* 475, ed. Karl Drescher (6 vols.; Weimar, 1912–21), I, 209: "Und ist schier wie ein *Argumentum Fabulae;* wie man ein Spiel agirt und hält, in welchem etliche Personen eingeführt werden, da Einer mit und nach dem Andern redet und disputiret, wie ihm ums herz ist, und wie ers meinet, daher est auch der Meister genommen und beschrieben hat; wie Terentius seine Comödien; damit er hat wollen anzeigen ein Erempel der Geduld…. Der ebräische Poet und Meister dieses Buchs, er sey nu gewesen, wer er wolle, hat solche *Tentationes* und Anfechtung gehabt, gesehen, erfahren, und also beschrieben. Gleichwie Virgilius den theuren Helden Aeneam beschreibet, und führet ihn durch alle Wasser, Meer und Herbergen, macht einem feinen, politischen Welt-und Kriegsmann aus ihm." Cf. *Tischreden* 279, I, 117.

44. Beza, *Job Expounded*, preface.

45. D'Albiac, *Le Livre de Job* ([Geneva], 1552), p. 16; Oecolampadius, *In Job*, preface; Mercerus, *In Jobum*, preface; Brentius, *Hiob cum Piis et Eruditis …Commentariis* (Hagenau, 1527), epis. ded.

46. Origen?, *In Job, Opera* II, 851–90; Origen, "Selecta in Job," Pat. Graec. XII, 1031–50; Chrysostom, "Fragmenta in Beatum Job," Pat. Graec. LXIV, 505–656; Jerome, *Commentarii in Librum Job*, Pat. Lat. XXVI, 655–850; Zeno, "De Job," Pat. Lat. XI, 439–43; Ambrose, *De Interpellatione Job et David,*

Pat. Lat. XIV, 797–850; Peter of Blois, *Compendium in Job,* Pat. Lat. CCVII, 795–826; Jacques de Vorigine, *Legenda Aurea,* trans. William Caxton (1527); and the Jobean annotations or commentary of Philippus Presbyterius, Gregory the Great, Nicholas of Lyra, the *Glossa Ordinaria,* the Douay Bible, Pineda, Steuchius, and Corderius cited above.

47. Gregory, *Moralia,* LF XVIII, 20–21.

48. Origen, "Selecta in Job," Pat. Graec. XII, 1033:
Ὡς τις ἀθλητὴς ἐν σταδίῳ κέκραγα, καὶ οὐδαμοῦ τὸ χρῖμά μου ἐπανίσταται. ἔτι γὰρ παλαίω.

49. Chrysostom, "Fragmenta," Pat. Graec. LXIV, 521, 525:
ἦχέ τις ἡμέρα, ἐν ἦ τὸ θέατρον ἠνοίχθη, καὶ ὁ ἀθλητὴς κατέβη πρὸς τὰ παλαίσματα . . . . Ἐχ τούτου μανθάνομεν, ὅτι ἐβούλετο μὲν ὁ Θεὸς τὸν Ἰὼβ πειρασθῆναι, χαθάπερ τις ἀθλητὴν ἔχων γενναῖον. διὰ γὰρ τοῦτο ἐρωτᾷ τὸν διάβολον, ἵνα αὐτῷ δῷ ἀφορμὴν τῆς πάλης, οὐχ ἤθελε δὲ αὐτὸς παρασχεῖν τὴν ἀφορμήν, . . .

50. Olympiodorus, *Commentarium in Beatum Job,* Pat. Graec. XCIII, 15:
Ἐπειδὴ δὲ μέγας ἦν ἀθλητής, καὶ ὁ τῶν ἀποστατιχῶν δυνάμεων ἄρχων διαβολος δι' ἑαυτοῦ [ἴσ. χατ' αὐτοῦ] κατέβη πρὸς τὸν ἀγῶνα, ὁ τοὺς ἑαυτοῦ στεφανίτας ἀναχηρύττων Θεός, πάντα παθεῖν συνεχεχώρηχε τὸν δίχαιον, καὶ πάσας ἐνέγχαι τοῦ πολεμίου τὰς πληγάς, ὡς ἄν μήτις αὐτῷ πρόφασις ὑπολειφθῆ. Cf. cols. 25, 28–29, 36, 456. See also Gregory Nazianzen, "Oratio XXIV," Pat. Graec. XXXV, 1101; Didymus Alexandrinus, "Fragmenta in Job," Pat. Graec. XXXIX, 1129; Athanasius Alexandrinus, "Fragmenta in Job," Pat. Graec. XXVII, 1345.

51. [Prosper], *De Promissionibus,* Pat. Lat. LI, 750–51; Methodius, *Fragments,* trans. William R. Clark (ANCL, Vol. XIV [Edinburgh, 1869]), pp. 227–28; Tertullian, "Of Patience," trans. S. Thelwall (ANCL, Vol. XI [Edinburgh, 1869]), pp. 227–28; Cassiodorus, *De Schematibus,* Pat. Lat. LXX, 271.

52. Prudentius, *Psychomachia,* trans. H. J. Thomson [*Works*] (Loeb [2 vols.; Cambridge, Mass., 1949–53]), I, 291.

53. Gregory, *Moralia,* LF XVIII, 34, 23.

54. Stunica, *In Job Commentaria* (Toledo, 1584), pp. 44–62; Pineda, *In Job* I, 69; Corderius, *In Librum Job,* SSCC XIII, 282.

55. Geneva Bible, fol. 180ᵛ (argument to Job); Beza, *Job Expounded,* preface; chap. iii (preface). See also Sebastiano Castalione, *Biblia . . . cum Eiusdem Annotationes* (Basle, 1551); Joannes Cocceius, *In Job* (Franeker, 1644); and the commentary and annotations of Diodati and Hutcheson.

56. Holland, *An Exposition of the First and Second Chapter of Job* (London, 1596), epis. ded.

57. Caryl, *Job* I, 341.

58. Origen?, *In Job, Opera* II, 857: "Sicut admirabilis ille Job . . . quia Abraham per Deo dilectam fidem est imitatus, & quia Isaac in verissima castitate est sectatus, & Israel in perspicua cordis puritate appropinquavit, & Melchisedech in filiorum immolatione, & Joseph in castitate, & Moysi in mansuetudine, &

Samueli in justitia, & Lazaro in passione judicii...Ergo quia omnium sanctorum sanctitatis particeps effectus est beatus Job." (Text in Latin only.)

59. Origen, *Enarrationes in Job,* Pat. Graec. XVII, 64:

Καὶ χαθάπερ στρατιώτης γενῖανος, χαὶ εἰδὼς νυχτομαχεῖν, τειχομαχεῖν, πεζομαχεῖν, ναυμαχεῖν, χαὶ τοξεύειν, χαὶ δόρυ σείειν, χαὶ σφενδόναις χαὶ ἀχοντίοις, χαὶ παντὶ τρόπῳ μάχης περιγίνεσθαι τῆς ἐναντίων χαὶ πανταχοῦ χρατεῖν. οὕτω δὴ χαὶ ὁ γενναῖος ἐχεῖνος ἅπαντα πειρασμὸν μετὰ πολλῆς ἥνεγχε τῆς ἀνδρίας, τὸν ἀπὸ πενίας, τὸν ἀπὸ λιμοῦ, τὸν ἀπὸ νόσου, τὸν ἐξ ὀδύνης, τὸν ἀπὸ παίδων ἀπωλείας, τὸν ἀπὸ τῶν φίλων, τὸν ἀπὸ τῶν ἐχθρῶν, τὸν ἀπὸ τῆς γυναιχὸς, τὸν απὸ τῶν οἰχετῶν.

60. Chrysostom, "Fragmenta," Pat. Graec. LXIV, 570; Tertullian, "Of Patience," ANCL XI, 227–28; Ambrose, *De Interpellatione,* Pat. Lat. XIV, 798–99; Diodati, *Annotations,* argument to Job; Cocceius, *In Job,* epis. ded.

61. See Dominico Comparetti, *Vergil in the Middle Ages,* trans. E. F. M. Benecke (London, 1895), pp. 60–118.

62. Jerome, "Ad Paulinum," Pat. Lat. XXII, 545.

63. Pineda, *In Job* I, chap. viii of preface.

64. Senault, *Pattern of Patience,* preface.

65. Chemnitius, *Dissertatio,* sigs. D3ᵛ–D4ᵛ; Caryl, *Job* I, 8.

66. Gregory, *Moralia,* LF XVIII, 137–38. Cf. Origen?, *In Job, Opera* II, 878–79; and Chrysostom, "Fragmenta," Pat. Graec. LXXIV, 557.

67. Gregory, *Moralia,* LF XVIII, 26.

68. See for example: Jerome, *In Librum Job,* Pat. Lat. XXVI, 655–64, 848–49; and Gregory, *Moralia,* LF XVIII, 26–27.

69. See above mentioned Jobean annotations and commentary of Didymus, Gregory Nazianzen, Olympiodorus, Zeno, Philippus Presbyterius, Ambrose, Rabanus Maurus, the *Glossa Ordinaria,* the Douay Bible, Corderius, Pineda, Titelmann, Sanctius, Drexelius.

70. See Jobean commentary and annotations, cited above, of Calvin, Beza, the Geneva Bible, Brentius, Oecolampadius, Strigelius, Lancelot Andrewes, Piscator, Hutcheson, Caryl.

71. See Edward D. Coleman, *The Bible in English Drama* (New York, 1931), pp. 78–79; Alfred Harbage, "Census of Anglo-Latin Plays," *PMLA,* LIII (1938), 624–29; Leicester Bradner, "A Check-List of Original Neo-Latin Dramas by Continental Writers Printed before 1650," *PMLA,* LVIII (1943), 621–33; Siger, "Image of Job," pp. 323–37; Hardin Craig, *English Religious Drama of the Middle Ages* (Oxford, 1955), p. 365.

72. Manley, *The Affliction and Deliverance of the Saints: Or, the Whole Book of Job Composed into English Heroicall Verse Metaphrastically* (London, 1652).

73. Quarles, *Job Militant* (London, 1624).

74. In *Du Bartas His Divine Weekes and Workes,* pp. 886, 994. See also prefatory matter in 1641 edition.

75. *Ibid.,* p. 895.

76. Morillon, *Paraphrase sur le Livre de Job* (Paris, 1668), sigs. A8, E3^v (preface): "Le sacré texte nous apprend, que dés la naissance du monde, il se fist un grand combat dans le Ciel; mais j'ose dire qu'il s'en est fait un plus grand sur la Terre, lors que cette Armée épouventable attaque l'invincible Job; Le premier ne paroissoit point surprenant, il s'y trouvoit beaucoup de rapport & d'égalité; les esprits combatoient les esprits, & le nombre des combatans de part & d'autre estoit à peu prés semblable: Mais que peut-on voir de si prodigieux que le second? un homme seul, un homme mortel est exposé à la rage de tous les esprits infernaux . . . Si le serviteur fidele aprés un travail assidu, a droit d'esperer la recompense de son maistre, & si la couronne est deüe au vainqueur qui a vaillamment combatu, qui pourroit disputer à Job la gloire d'être couronné apres tant de victoires & de triomphes. Il n'a plus d'ennemis en teste, tout l'Enfer est vaincu, & les Demons n'oseroient plus se presenter devant un Heros si redoutable."

77. Le Cordier, *L'Illustre Souffrant ou Job* (Paris, 1667), pp. 1-2:

> QUITTONS ces grands Heros, à qui l'ancienne Histoire
> Fait offrir de l'encens au Temple de Memoire;
> Ces Cesars immortels, dont les exploits vaillans
> Sont figurez au Ciel sous des Astres brillans;
>
> .   .   .   .
> Laissons au Grand Virgile élever un AEnée,
> Jusqu'à braver Junon, malgré la Destinée.
> Comme au fameux Ovide orner de toutes parts
> Les traits de Cupidon sous le Foudres de Mars.
>
> .   .   .   .
> Mais chantons un seul Homme, à qui la patience
> Donna plus de valeur, d'esprit, & de science,
> De courage, de feu, de force à celebrer,
> Que tous ceux que l'Histoire auroit pû me nombrer.

78. Aurelius, *Jobus, sive de Patientia* (London, 1632).

79. J[acobus] D[u Port], ΘΡΗΝΟΘΡΙΆΜΒΟΣ, *sive Liber Job* (Cambridge, Eng., 1653), epis. ad lectori.

80. Mellius de Sousa, *In Librum Job Paraphrasis Poetica* (London, 1615).

81. [Henry Oxenden], *Jobus Triumphans* ([London], 1656).

82. *Ibid.*, p. 25:

> JOB tamen invictus perstans, fortissimus unus
> Qui fuit in terris, animis ingentibus iras
> Istorúmque tulit fastus, inimicáque verba,
> Et postquàm casus animo, superaverit omnes,
> Invicto dominantem antè prostravit & ipsum
> Inferni regem, triste & mirabile monstrum,
> Huic Pater omnipotens victori praemia reddit.

83. *Ibid.*, pp. 27-28:

> Dum spoliatorem spoliat, Satanamque repellit,
> Invictis animis, & tela immissa retorquet,
> Dúmque argumentis hostes confundit acutis,
> Et sese totis opponens viribus Orcum
> Servitio premit, & toti dominatur Averno.
> Macte tuâ laude hâc JOB nam sic itur ad astra,
> Per tua supplicia, & cruciatus tendimus omnes
> In caelum, via difficilis, sed certa, cruenta,
> Sed clara; excordi forsan mentuenda, sed illi,
> Qui JOBI invictam gerit alto in pectore mentem
> Non formidanda est, quandò calcavit eandem
> CHRISTUS, & hoc ipso conscendit tramite caelum.

84. Aylett is author of two other brief epics: *Susanna: Or, the Arraignment of the Two Unjust Elders* (London, 1622), and *D[avid's] Troubl[es] Remembred* (London, 1638), as well as of an adaptation of Du Bartas' *Uranie*, called *Urania, or the Heavenly Muse,* in *Divine and Moral Speculations in Metrical Numbers* (London, 1654). See Frederick M. Padelford, "Robert Aylett," *Huntington Library Bulletin,* No. 10 (October, 1936), pp. 1-48.

85. Aylett, *Joseph* (London, 1623), pp. 1-2.

86. *Ibid.*, p. 91.

87. Beaumont, *Psyche: Or Loves Mysterie in XX Cantos, Displaying the Intercourse betwixt Christ and the Soule* XVIII.33-34 (London, 1648), p. 350.

88. *Ibid.,* XVIII.41, 45, 46, pp. 350, 351.

89. Blackmore, *A Paraphrase on the Book of Job* (London, 1700), preface.

90. *Ibid.*

CHAPTER III

1. Aristotle, *Poetics,* in Gilbert, *Literary Criticism, Plato to Dryden* (New York, 1940), p. 114.

2. For example, the *Little Iliad* (4 books), the *Aithiopis* (5 books), and the *Nostoi* (5 books), all of which were described by Proclus (*ca.* A.D. 140) in the *Manual of Literature.* See Leonard Whibley, *A Companion to Greek Studies* (Cambridge, Eng., 1931), pp. 126-27.

3. See Charles M. Gayley and Benjamin P. Kurtz, *Methods and Materials of Literary Criticism: Lyric, Epic, and Allied Forms of Poetry* (Boston, 1920), pp. 515-16.

4. M. Marjorie Crump, *The Epyllion from Theocritus to Ovid* (Oxford, 1931), pp. 22-24, defines the epyllia as short, highly formalized poems usually treating a single and often a romantic incident in the life of a hero or heroine; other classical examples are Callimachus' *Hecale* and Catullus' *Peleus and Thetis.*

5. Martz, *"Paradise Regained:* The Meditative Combat," *ELH,* XXVII (1960), 224–25.

6. Virgil, *Georgics* III.1–48.

7. *CE* XVIII, 194. Milton's entry quotes from "Hymn Ten" on Romanus of Antioch.

8. See P. O. Kristellar, *The Classics and Renaissance Thought* (Cambridge, Mass., 1955), pp. 90–91, and E. R. Curtius, *European Literature and the Latin Middle Ages,* trans. W. R. Trask (New York, 1953), p. 260. The patristic epic poets were published in famous Renaissance collections of Christian poetry, notably those of Aldus Manutius [*A Collection of Ancient Christian Poets*] (3 vols.; Venice [1501–4]); Georgius Fabricius, *Poetarum Veterum Ecclesiasticorum Opera Christiana* (Basle, 1564); and Margarinus de la Bigne, *Magna Bibliotheca Veterum Patrum, et Antiquorum Scriptorum* (15 vols.; Cologne, 1622). Juvencus and Sedulius had each appeared in over thirty editions by the mid-seventeenth century. They were also constantly cited as literary ancestors and exemplars by Renaissance poets striving to write biblical epic or by Renaissance editors presenting contemporary efforts. For example, by Mantuan, *Parthenice Mariana* [Paris, 1502], Apologeticon; Henricus Petreus Herdesianus' preface to Fracastoro's *Joseph* (Frankfurt, 1578), p. 407; Joannes Klockus, *Christiados Priscae et Novae Libri XII* (Ursel, 1601), sig. B5ᵛ; Estiene de Sanguinet, *La Dodécade de l'Evangile* (Bergerac, 1614), verse dedication; Giles Fletcher, *Christs Victorie, and Triumph in Heaven, and Earth* (Cambridge, Eng., 1610), To the Reader.

9. *Mansus,* ll. 7–15, 51. See discussion of the allusions to Mantuan in Harris F. Fletcher, *The Intellectual Development of John Milton* (2 vols.; Urbana, Ill., 1956), I, 239–42. Allusions to Joshua Sylvester's *Du Bartas* discussed in David Masson, *The Life of John Milton* (7 vols.; London, 1859–94), I, 89–99, in H. C. H. Candy, "Milton's Early Reading of Sylvester," *N&Q,* CLVIII (1930), 93–95, and in George C. Taylor, *Milton's Use of Du Bartas* (Cambridge, Mass., 1934). Allusions to Giles Fletcher discussed in Herbert E. Cory, *Spenser, the School of the Fletchers, and Milton* (Berkeley, Calif., 1912). The Index to the Columbia *Milton* records several probable allusions to these and other biblical epic poets. See also E. M. W. Tillyard, *The Miltonic Setting* (Cambridge, Eng., 1938), pp. 165–204, for a convincing argument regarding Milton's keen awareness of contemporary poetic trends.

10. Burton O. Kurth, *Milton and Christian Heroism; Biblical Epic Themes and Forms in Seventeenth Century England* (Berkeley, Calif., 1959), has related Milton's heroic ideals in *Paradise Lost* and *Paradise Regained* to contemporary English biblical poems, but the tradition upon which Milton draws is much more extensive. Milton's *Ad Patrem,* ll. 77–85, testifies to his early acquaintance with Italian and French as well as Latin, Greek, and Hebrew.

11. Curtius, *Latin Middle Ages,* p. 462.

12. Juvencus, *Evangeliorum,* ll. 1–24, ed. Johannes Huemer (CSEL, Vol. XXIV [Vienna, 1891]), pp. 1–2:

Immortale nihil mundi conpage tenetur,
Non orbis, non regna hominum, non aurea Roma,
Non mare, non tellus, non ignea sidera caeli.
Nam statuit genitor rerum inrevocabile tempus,
Quo cunctum torrens rapiat flamma ultima mundum.
Sed tamen innumeros homines sublimia facta
Et virtutis honos in tempora longa frequentant,
Adcumulant quorum famam laudesque poetae.
Hos celsi cantus, Smyrnae de fonte fluentes,
Illos Minciadae celebrat dulcedo Maronis.
Nec minor ipsorum discurrit gloria vatum,
Quae manet aeternae similis, dum saecla volabunt
Et vertigo poli terras atque aequora circum
Aethera sidereum jusso moderamine volvet.
Quod si tam longam meruerunt carmina famam,
Quae veterum gestis hominum mendacia nectunt,
Nobis certa fides aeternae in saecula laudis
Inmortale deçus tribuet meritumque rependet.
Nam mihi carmen erit Christi vitalia gesta,
Divinum populis falsi sine crimine donum.
Nec metus, ut mundi rapiant incendia secum
Hoc opus; hoc etenim forsan me subtrahet igni
Tunc, cum flammivoma discendet nube coruscans
Judex, altithroni genitoris gloria, Christus.

13. Sedulius, *Carmen Paschale* I.17–26, ed. Johannes Huemer (CSEL, Vol. X [Vienna, 1885]), pp. 16–17, and *Opus Paschale,* CSEL X, 176–77. In the opening passage of the *Opus,* a prose recension of the material treated in the poem, Sedulius declared that the subject matter of classical poetry is "scelerata temporum gesta, nonnulla etiam probrae narrationis arte composita," and he proposed to himself another model, "cur ego, qui decacordo psalterio inter beati dogmatis choros Daviticae modulationis cantus exercens spiritalia reverenter dicta respondeo."

14. See above, pp. 11–17; see Dominico Comparetti, *Vergil in the Middle Ages,* trans. E. F. M. Benecke (London, 1895), pp. 60–118. Maphaeus Vegius (fifteenth century) wrote a "thirteenth book," commonly appended to the *Aeneid* until the mid-seventeenth century, in which Aeneas is shown enjoying a heavenly apotheosis; see Anna C. Brinton, *Maphaeus Vegius and His Thirteenth Book of the Aeneid* (Stanford, 1930), pp. 1–28.

15. Sedulius, "Epistola ad Macedonium," CSEL X, 4–6.

16. Victor, *Alethias,* ll. 119–26, ed. Carolus Schenkl (CSEL, Vol. XVI [Vienna, 1888]), p. 363 (Precatio).

17. Avitus, "Ad Apollinarem Episcopum," Pat. Lat. LIX, 324: "Quippe cum licentia mentiendi, quae pictoribus ac poetis aeque conceditur, satis procul a

causarum serietate pellenda sit. In saeculari namque versuum opere condendo, tanto quis peritior appellatur, quanto elegantius, imo, ut vere dicamus, ineptius falsa texuerit. Taceo jam verba illa vel nomina, quae nobis nec in alienis quidem operibus frequentare, ne dicam in nostris conscribere licet: quae ad compendia poetarum, aliud ex alio significantia plurimum valent. Quocirca saecularium judicio, qui aut imperitiae, aut ignaviae dabunt, non uti nos licentia poetarum, plus arduum quam fructuosum opus aggressi, divinam longe discrevimus ab humana existimatione censuram.... salubrius dicente clerico non impletur pompa quam regula, et tutius artis pede quam veritatis vestigio claudicatur. Non enim est excusata perpetratione peccati libertas eloquii. Nam si pro omni verbo otioso quod locuti fuerint homines, rationem redhibere cogentur (*Matth.* XII, 36) agnosci in promptu est, illud periculosius laedere, quod tractatum atque meditatum et antepositum vivendi legibus, loquendi lege praesumitur."

18. Some later editions, including the CSEL, present Sedulius' poem in five books by dividing the very long third book. But Sedulius' "Epistola ad Macedonium" seems to point to a four-book structure: "quatuor igitur mirabilium divinorum libellos, quos ex pluribus pauca conplexus usque ad passionem et resurrectionem ascensionemque Domini nostri Jesu Christi quatuor evangeliorum dicta congregans ordinavi, contra omnes aemulos tuae defensioni commendo" (CSEL X, 12). The great Renaissance editors Aldus, Fabricius, and La Bigne respect the four-book division.

19. Proba, *Cento,* ed. Carolus Schenkl (CSEL, Vol. XVI [Vienna, 1888]), pp. 569–609.

20. Dracontius, *Carmen de Laudibus Dei,* Pat. Lat. LX, 679–902. Eugenius, a seventh-century bishop of Toledo, produced a drastic cutting and re-ordering of Dracontius' poem (Pat. Lat. LXXXVII, 369–88).

21. In some editions the five books of Avitus' poem are presented as separate poems along with a sixth, *De Virginitate.* But the title *De Spiritalis Historiae Gestis,* supplied in Avitus' "Epistle XLV" (Pat. Lat. LIX, 262), seems to relate to these five books as a unit, but not to *De Virginitate.* Also, the ending of the fifth book suggests that the work is conceived as a five-book epic: "Quae pius explicuit per quinque volumina vates,/ Nosque tubam otipula sequimur, numerumque tenentes/ Penimus hoc tenui cymbae nunc littore portum."

22. Arator, *De Actibus Apostolorum,* ed. A. P. McKinlay (CSEL, Vol. LXXII [Vienna, 1951]). Fortunatus (sixth century) records that an oral recitation of the work according to ancient epic custom was ordered by Pope Vigilius to take place in A.D. 544 at the Church of St. Peter in Chains: see Rémi Ceillier, *Histoire Générale des Auteurs Sacrées et Ecclésiastiques* (16 vols.; Paris, 1858–69), XI, 197–98.

23. Prudentius, ed. H. J. Thomson [*Works*] (Loeb [2 vols.; Cambridge, Mass., 1949–53]).

24. Avitus, *De Spiritalis* I.177–207, ed. Rudolfus Peiper (MGH, Vol. VI [Berlin, 1883]), p. 208; Virgil, *Aeneid* I.257–96.

25. F. P. G. Guizot, *Histoire de la Civilisation en France* (Paris, 1840), II,

67–77, finds Avitus' poem so dramatic as to invite comparison with *Paradise Lost*. See also Eleanor S. Duckett, *Latin Writers of the Fifth Century* (New York, 1930), pp. 91–92.

26. Victor, *Alethias* I.178–83, 213–22; II.405–558; III.646–789, CSEL XVI, 370, 371–72, 400–405, 431–36.

27. For some particular typological allusions in Avitus see *De Spiritalis* I.160–70; IV.493–501, 639–58; V.704–21, MGH VI, 207, 249–54, 273–74.

28. Sedulius, *Carmen Paschale* V.217–19, CSEL X, 130; Virgil, *Aeneid* II.404–16. See also the application of Virgil's apostrophe to Dido viewing the launching of Aeneas' ships to Herod viewing the massacre of the Innocents: *Aeneid* IV.408–11; *Carmen Paschale* II.127–30, CSEL X, 53.

29. See the opening lines of Florus of Lyons, *In Natale Sanctorum Joannis et Pauli* (ninth century), cited in F. J. E. Raby, *A History of Christian Latin Poetry from the Beginnings to the Close of the Middle Ages* (Oxford, 1927), p. 199; also Prologus to Otfried, *Evangelienbuch* (Basle, 1571, *ca.* 840 lines), pp. 1–9. Though Otfried's poem is not in Latin it derives from that tradition, being an avowed attempt to do in the vernacular what the patristic poets did in their own language.

30. Odo, *Occupatio*, ed. Antonius Swoboda (Leipzig, 1900); *The Non-Dramatic Works of Hrosvitha*, ed. Sister Mary Gonsalva Wiegand (St. Louis, Mo., 1936), pp. 14–65.

31. Gerson, *Josephina*, in *Opera Omnia*, ed. Lud. Ellies du Pin (5 vols.; Antwerp, 1706), IV, 743–84.

32. About 1630 a MS now known as Junius XI was discovered by Archbishop Ussher and was presented by him to Francis Dujon (Junius) of Leyden; an edition was printed by Junius in Amsterdam in 1654, and then the MS was returned to England. Masson, *Life of Milton* VI, 557, speculates as to whether Milton might have seen the Junius MS before he became blind and considers it just possible. Scholars no longer accept the attribution of these three poems to Cædmon.

33. For text, discussion of dating, and other problems see *The Cædmon Poems*, trans. Charles W. Kennedy (London, 1916); Bernhard Ten Brink, *Early English Literature*, trans. H. M. Kennedy (London, 1891); George Philip Krapp, *The Junius Manuscript* (Anglo-Saxon Poetic Records, Vol. I [New York, 1931]), pp. v–xxxvi.

34. For *Judith*, see Albert S. Cook, *Judith, an Old English Epic Fragment* (Boston, 1889). For the *Heliand*, see *Der Heliand, oder die Altsächsische Evangelienharmonie*, ed. C. W. Grein (Cassel, 1869).

35. *Genesis*, ll. 409–14, in Krapp, *Junius Manuscript*, p. 16.

36. See especially ll. 1196 ff., 1995 ff., 2731 ff., 2902 ff., 4933 ff.

37. See Kennedy, *Cædmon Poems*, pp. liv–lvii; James W. Bright, "The Relation of the Cædmonian *Exodus* to the Liturgy," MLN, XXVII (1912), 97–103.

38. See Kennedy, *Cædmon Poems*, pp. lxiv–lxx; Krapp, *Junius Manuscript*,

pp. xxxiii–xxxvi; Merrel D. Clubb, *Christ and Satan* (Yale Studies in English, Vol. LXX [New Haven, 1925]).

39. Lines 1–3, in Krapp, *Junius Manuscript,* p. 135:

> þæt wearð underne   eorðbuendum,
> þæt meotod hæfde   miht and strengðo
> ða he gefestnade   foldan sceatas.

40. See Watson Kirkconnell, *The Celestial Cycle* (Toronto, 1952). The three-part celestial cycle which provides the content and context for much Christian epic poetry comprises the battle in heaven at which Lucifer was defeated, the creation and fall of man, and the redemption by Christ.

41. See translation in Kennedy, *Cædmon Poems,* p. 153; ll. 122–24, in Krapp, *Junius Manuscript,* p. 139:

> þes ðe ic ær gecwæð
> þæt ic wære seolfa   swægles brytta,

42. See translation in Kennedy, *Cædmon Poems,* p. 172; ll. 698–707, in Krapp, *Junius Manuscript,* pp. 157–58:

> Wite þu eac, awyrgda,   hu wid and sid
> helheoðo dreorig,   and mid hondum amet.
> Grip wið þæs grundes;   gang þonne swa
> oððæt þu þone ymbhwyrft   alne cunne,
> and ærest amet   ufan to grunde,
> and hu sid seo   se swarta eðm.
> Wast þu þonne þe geornor   þæt þu wið god wunne,
> seoððan þu þonne hafast   handum ametene
> hu heh and deop   hell inneweard seo,
> grim græfhus.

43. Among French poems, the twelfth-century *L'Estoire Joseph* and *Genesis,* the thirteenth-century *Exodus,* and Gautier de Belleperche's *Maccabees.* See *Les Traductions de la Bible en Vers Français au Moyen Age,* ed. Jean Bonnard (Paris, 1884), pp. 11–41, 105–19, 123–24, 125–26, 168–76. English poems preserving from the older epic the typical alliterative line, tags of oral delivery, some exciting action, dramatic dialogue, and characteristic diction are the thirteenth-century *Story of Genesis and Exodus,* ed. Richard Morris (EETS, Vol. VII [London, 1865]); *Jacob & Joseph, or the Story of Joseph,* ed. Arthur S.

Napier (Oxford, 1916); *Susannah, or Seemly Susan,* in *Minor Poems of the Vernon MS, Part II,* ed. F. J. Furnivall (EETS, Vol. CVII [London, 1901]), pp. 626–36; and the poems of the fourteenth-century "Pearl Poet," *Pearl, Cleanness, Patience,* and *Sir Gawaine,* ed. I. Gollancz (EETS, Vol. CLXII [London, 1923]).

44. Such as the tenth-century French *Passion* (516 lines), in *Les Plus Anciens Monuments de la Langue Française,* ed. Edward Koschwitz (Leipzig, 1902); the thirteenth-century English *Southern Passion* (2,250 lines), ed. Beatrice Daw Brown (EETS, Vol. CLXIX [London, 1927]); and the thirteenth-century English *Passion of Our Lord* (706 lines), in *An Old English Miscellany,* ed. Richard Morris (EETS, Vol. XLIX [London, 1872]), pp. 38–57.

45. *The Northern Passion,* ed. Frances A. Foster (EETS, Vols. CXLV, CXLVII, CLXXXIII [London, 1913, 1916, 1930]), CLXXXIII, 1.

46. The dream vision is also used in the very long *Le Pelerinage Jhesucrist* by Guillaume de Deguilleville, ed. J. J. Stürzinger (London, 1897).

47. For example: the English *Northern Passion* and the French twelfth- to thirteenth-century *Passion,* ed. Frances A. Foster (EETS, Vol. CXLVII [London, 1916]), pp. 102–25; the fourteenth-century *Le Livre de la Passion (ca.* 2,500 lines), ed. Grace Frank (Paris, 1930); the Italian fourteenth-century *La Passione del N. S. Gesu Christ (ca.* 1,364 lines) probably by Nicolo Cicerchia [Florence, 1483?].

48. Saint-Marc Girardin, *Tableau de la Littérature Française au XVIe Siècle* (Paris, 1862), p. 194, argues that the Gospel of Nicodemus itself is a true Christian epic by reason of its matter and its narrative force.

49. Gaston Paris, ed., *Trois Versions Rimées de L'Evangile de Nicodème* (Paris, 1885), prints the imaginative version of André de Coutances and two other paraphrases; the English paraphrase is edited by William H. Hulme (EETS, ex. ser., Vol. C [London, 1907]), pp. 23–136, and has examples of romance diction especially at ll. 1441, 1759–64; the *Harrowing, ibid.,* pp. 2–22, is almost entirely in dialogue and may have been conceived or presented as an interlude.

50. See Olin H. Moore, "The Infernal Council," *MP,* XVI (1918–19), 169–93, and Mason Hammond, *"Concilia Deorum* from Homer through Milton," *SP,* XXX (1933), pp. 1–16. Claudian in his *In Rufinum* contrives a council summoned by Allecto to attack the peace of the world, in the course of which Megaera declares that she has nurtured a monster, Rufinus, the embodiment of all evil, and departs to incite him to this purpose. Claudian's *De Raptu Proserpine* also contains such a council.

51. *Develis Perlament,* ed. F. J. Furnivall (EETS, Vol. XXIV [London, 1867]), pp. 41–57.

52. Petrarch, *De Familiari* X.4 (1348 or 1349), in *Petrarch, the First Modern Scholar and Man of Letters,* trans. James Harvey Robinson (New York, 1898), pp. 261–64; Boccaccio, *Genealogia Deorum Gentilium* XIV.viii, xiii, in *Boccaccio on Poetry,* trans. Charles G. Osgood (Princeton, 1930), pp. 46, 64–65; Boccaccio, *Life of Dante,* in Gilbert, *Literary Criticism,* pp. 208–11.

53. *De Familiari* X.4, *Petrarch, the First Modern Scholar*, pp. 266–75.

54. Pico the Younger, *De Rerum Praenotione* (1506–7), and *Examen Vanitatis Doctrinae Gentium, & Veritatis Disciplinae Christianae* III.iii, cited in Bernard Weinberg, *A History of Literary Criticism in the Italian Renaissance* (2 vols.; Chicago, 1961), I, 255–56.

55. Teobaldo Mannucci, better known as Aldus Manutius or Aldo Manuzio (1450–1515), was the founder of the Aldine Press. The preface to his famous *Collection of Ancient Christian Poets* (which included Prosper, Prudentius, Sedulius, Juvencus, Arator, Proba, Gregory Nazianzen, and others) asserts that he had been unable to find a single learned man able to repeat the first lines of these poets and undertakes to introduce the learned to these worthy examples of Christian poetry. This statement is an exaggeration, for Mantuan in the Apologeticon to his *Parthenice Mariana* (1481) had already placed himself in the line of descent of Juvencus and Prudentius as a writer of sacred verse.

56. Petrarch, *De Familiari* X.4, *Petrarch, the First Modern Scholar*, pp. 261–62; Boccaccio, *Life of Dante*, in Gilbert, *Literary Criticism*, p. 211; Mantuan, *Parthenice Mariana*, sig. A2ᵛ; Jacobus Bonus, *Sub Figura Herculis Christi Praeludium* [Rome, 1526]; Aelius Nebrissensus, ed., *Thalichristia* by Alvarus Gomez de Ciudad Real [Alcala, 1522], Preface to Reader.

57. Bonus, *De Vita & Gestis Christi* [Rome, 1526], Dedication:

> Dextera virtutum domini mihi sancta canenti
> Hoc exigit opus, quod nulla incendia, nullas
> Horret aquas, ullum nec ab aethere labile tempus.
> Aut formidati tonitrus, aut fulminis iras.
> Stat quia luce Dei, coeli quia mole tenetur,
> Aeternaeque virent aeterno in vertice laurus.
> Non hic arma virum miramur Apolline ficto,
> Infandique graves iras agitamus Achillis,
> Aut per inane vagum vento iactamus Ulixem,
> Non falso quae multa movent Helicone poetae.

58. Mario A. Di Cesare, *Vida's Christiad and Vergilian Epic* (New York, 1964), pp. 74–75, calls attention to one notable exception which I have not seen, the *Davideis* (fifteenth century, 14 books) by the Croatian humanist Marko Marulic, which was well known in Italy. However, Marulic's preface indicates his christological emphasis: "In almost all details I consider David to foreshadow Christ."

59. See above, note 50. In the *Filocolo*, the devils, enraged by the victory of Christ at the harrowing of hell, call a council to guard against further encroachments.

60. In biblical epic Allecto, and the Furies modeled upon her, are commonly shown hurling snakes or fiery brands into the breasts of their victims, and usually assume a disguise to deceive them as Allecto deceived Turnus in the guise of an aged priestess of Juno.

61. Statius, *Achilleid* II.86–167, trans. J. H. Mozley [*Works*] (Loeb [2 vols.; London, 1928]), II, 589–95.

62. Gomez for his purity and elegance of style was known as the Spanish Virgil. Another long poem on the life of Mary is the *Theotocon* (fifteenth century, 4 books, *ca.* 3,800 hexameters), ascribed to the Florentine theologian Joannes Dominicus, Corellanus, in *Nuova Raccolta d'Opuscoli Scientifici et Filologici* (Venice, 1768), Vols. XVII–XIX; it describes, sequentially, the ancestry and life of Mary and Christ, the glorification of Mary in heaven, and the various churches built in her honor.

63. Valle, *Jhesuida* [Augsburg, 1473?], written about 1445, often republished. Valle was also known as Hieronymus de Vallibus or Girolamo Padovano. See Roberto Cessi, "Un Poemetto Cristiano del Secolo XV," *Raccolta di Studi di Storia e Critici Letteraria* (Pisa, 1918), pp. 683–91.

64. Mutius (Muzio), *De Triumpho Christi* (Venice, 1499 [edition used: Cologne, 1550]).

65. Ilarione, *La Crisias*, ed. J. B. Pitra, in *Spicilegium Solesmense Complectens Sanctorum Patrum Scriptorumque Ecclesiasticorum* (4 vols.; Paris, 1858), Vol. IV. Ilarione (Hilarion) was a fifteenth-century Benedictine.

66. A very brief discussion of these poems appears in Paul Van Tieghem, *La Littérature Latine de la Renaissance* (Paris, 1944), pp. 123–27, and in John Sparrow, "Latin Verse of the Renaissance," *Italian Renaissance Studies: A Tribute to the Late Cecilia M. Ady* (London, 1960), pp. 354–409.

67. Mantuan, *Parthenice Mariana* (Bologna, 1481 [edition used: Paris, 1502]). The *Parthenice* was often re-edited after 1481; the Bologna, 1501, edition and most subsequent editions contain two additional parts, one treating the life of Catherine of Alexandria, the other, the lives of various feminine saints such as Margaret, Agatha, Lucy, and Apollonia. Mantuan, general of the Carmelite order, was also author of pastorals and secular epics.

68. Some other humanist brief epics contrived according to this pattern are the vernacular Italian poems of Antonio Cornazano, *La Vita & Passione de Christo* (1518, 3 books, *ca.* 3,180 lines in terza rima), and *La Vita de la Gloriosa Vergine Maria* (1518, 8 chapters, *ca.* 935 lines in terza rima), both of which resemble in many respects the medieval Passion or saint's life. Both appeared in the edition used (Venice, 1518). In 1472 the first poem appeared under the title *De Fide: Et Vita Christi,* although the text is Italian.

69. Sannazaro, *De Partu Virginis* (Naples, 1526). Sannazaro (1456–1530) is best known for his vernacular pastoral *Arcadia* [Venice, 1502]. He began writing the *De Partu* in 1500 but did not complete it until 1521; the original title was *Christiados.*

70. Cf. *Aeneid* IX.446; *De Partu* II.384, fol. E^v.

71. *De Partu* I.8–14:

> Nec minus o Musae vatum decus: hic ego vestros
> Optarim fonteis: vestras nemora ardua rupes:

Quandoquidem genus e coelo deducitis: & vos
Virginitas: sanctaeque juvat reverentia famae.
Vos igitur: seu cura poli: seu Virginis huius
Tangit honos: monstrate viam: qua nubila vincam:
Et mecum immensi portas recludite coeli.

72. Vida, *Christiad* (Cremona, 1535). Vida (1490?–1566) was made bishop of Cremona in 1532; a member of the order of the Canons Regulars of the Lateran, he was commissioned by Pope Leo X to compose the *Christiad* and given a benefice at Frascati so that he might enjoy a poet's ease for his task.

73. Di Cesare's study, *Vida's Christiad and Vergilian Epic,* demonstrates the poem's subtle and sophisticated transmutation of Virgil at the level of theme and structure, if not always of style, a transmutation reaching far beyond the rather rigid precepts for Virgilian imitation laid down in Vida's own *De Arte Poetica* (Rome, 1527).

74. Fracastoro, *Joseph,* in *Opera Omnia* (Venice, 1555 [edition used: Frankfurt, 1578]). The poem was translated into English and completed by Joshua Sylvester in *Du Bartas His Divine Weekes and Workes* (London, 1621). Fracastoro (Hieronymus Fracastorius), 1483–1553, doctor, poet, and astronomer, was perhaps best known for his didactic poem, *Syphilis.*

75. Pierius, *Jonas Propheta* (Tübingen, 1555); Godran, *Judith Viduae Historia* (Dijon, 1569).

76. Walther, *Monomachia Davidis et Goliae* (Zurich, n.d.).

77. Folengo, *L'Agiomachia,* ed. Antonio Rafanelli (Salerno, 1898); Godran, *Historia Crucis Dominicae* (Dijon, 1565).

78. Strasburgus, *Orationes Duae Carmine Heroico Scriptae, et Publice Recitatae in Celeberrima Academia Lipsensi: In Prima Oratione Describitur Christi Victoris & Satanae Pugna in Deserto. In Altera est Hypotyposis Judicii Divini contra Lapsum Hominem....* (Leipzig, 1565). The *Oratio Prima* is dated March 10, 1565, the *Oratio Secunda* April 21, 1565, and the titles suggest that something in the nature of oral recitation was attempted. A reversal of the two poems would place them in proper sequential order as regards subject matter. Both poems praise the Protestant theologian Victorinus Strigelius as a teacher of heavenly truth and poetic art.

79. Sig. A5: "Dicere victoris Christi Satanaéque duellum,/ Montibus in vastis inter deserta ferarum/ Invia, confectum verbo, & coelestibus armis."

80. Sig. [A8ᵛ]: "levibus primum experiatur in armis/ Tyro rudimentum, & magnis se praeparet ausis."

CHAPTER IV

1. Du Bellay, *La Lyre Chrestienne,* in *Oeuvres de l'Invention de l'Autheur,* published with *Quatriesme Livre de l'Enéide* (Paris, 1552 [edition used, in *Les Oeuvres Françoises,* Paris, 1569]). The French poet and critic Joachim

Du Bellay was a member of the Pléiade, a group devoted to the development of the French language and the imitation in it of all the classical genres, especially the long heroic poem; Pléiade style was characterized by elaborateness and a mixture of classical and Christian references. Du Bellay's *La Deffence, et Illustration de la Langue Françoyse* (Paris, 1549) is a manifesto of the group.

2. Lapini, *Letiöne ... nella quale si Ragiona in Universale del Fine della Poesia* (Florence, 1567), sigs. D1^V–D4^V; Gambara, *Tractatio ... de Perfectae Poëseos Ratione Agitur* (Rome, 1576), pp. 11–12.

3. In his dedicatory epistle to Girolamo Fracastoro's *Joseph* (Frankfurt, 1578), pp. 395–408. Similarly, Georgius Fabricius in the dedicatory epistle to his *Poetarum Veterum Ecclesiasticorum Opera Christiana* (Basle, 1564) vigorously defended the early Christian poets included in his very influential collection against the charge of the learned humanist Lorenzo Valla that they comprised a muddy stream of Latinity, by urging that less limpid waters are often the most healthful.

4. In Du Bartas, *La Muse Chrestiene* (Bordeaux, 1574), republished in revised form in *Les Oeuvres* (Paris, 1579). For an extensive history of the Urania influence, see Lily B. Campbell, *Divine Poetry and Drama in Sixteenth-Century England* (Berkeley, Calif., 1955).

5. Stanzas 48–50 in Joshua Sylvester's translation, *Du Bartas His Divine Weekes and Workes* (London, 1621, pp. 529–30). The French version (Paris, 1579, sig. P^V) reads:

> La liaison des vers fut jadis inventeé
> Seulement pour traitter les mysteres sacrés
> Avec plus de respet: & de long tems aprés
> Par les carmes ne fut autre chose chantée.

> Ainsi mon grand David sur la corde tremblante
> De son lut tout-divin ne sone rien que Dieu.
> Ainsi le conducteur de l'Exercite Hebrieu,
> Sauvé des rouges flôs, le los du grand Dieu chante.

> Ainsi Judit, Debore, au milieu des gend'armes
> Ainsi Job, Jeremie accablés de douleurs,
> D'un carme bigarré de cent mile couleurs
> Décrivoint saintment leur joyes & leurs larmes.

6. Valvasone, *Angeleida* (Venice, 1590), epis. ded.; La Pujade, *La Muse Chrestienne,* in *Les Oeuvres Chrestiennes,* Part II (Paris, 1604), fols. 63–66. See also the Bartas-like argument for a New Testament poetic subject by the French poet and critic Jean Vauquelin de la Fresnaye, *L'Art Poétique Francois,* Book III, in *Les Diverses Poesies* (Paris, 1612), pp. 82–3, 108–10; and Louis Le Laboureur's argument that Christ's story constitutes a worthy epic subject, in the preface to his *La Magdalaine Pénitente* (Paris, 1643), sig. E2: "Il n'y a

point de conquerant qui ait si bien merité de sa patrie que Jesus-Christ a merité de tous les hommes en general, & dont les victoires soient si solemnelles & si importantes que celles que ce Monarque du Ciel a remportées sur les Demons pour nostre salut."

7. James I, *The Essayes of a Prentise, in the Divine Art of Poesie* (Edinburgh, 1585); Sylvester, *Fragments and Other Small Workes of Bartas* (London, 1605). *Uranie* appeared subsequently in various editions of Sylvester's *Du Bartas* (London, 1608, 1611, 1613, 1621, 1641, etc.).

8. Southwell, *Saint Peters Complaynt* (London, 1595); Stradling, *Divine Poemes. In Seven Severall Classes* (London, 1625), pp. 74–86; J[oseph] F[letcher], *Christes Bloodie Sweat* (London, 1613); Aylett, *Urania*, in *Divine and Moral Speculations in Metrical Numbers, upon Various Subjects* (London, 1654).

9. Trissino, *La Poetica*, Parts I–IV (Vicenza, 1529), p. ii; and *La Quinta et la Sesta Divisione della Poetica* (Venice, 1562). Possevino, *Tractatio de Poesi & Pictura Ethnica, Humana, & Fabulosa* (Rome, 1593), fols. [1–3^V].

10. See for example, Giovanni Battista Pigna, *Gli Heroici* (Venice, 1561).

11. Sassetti, *Sopra Dante (ca. 1573)*, MS BNF VII, 1028, fols. 4^V–5, Biblioteca Nazionale, Florence, cited and translated in Bernard Weinberg, *A History of Literary Criticism in the Italian Renaissance* (2 vols.; Chicago, 1961), I, 530–31. I am indebted to Weinberg's penetrating analyses and comprehensive bibliography for some of the material in this section.

12. Denores, *Discorso . . . intorno à que' Principii, Cause, et Accrescimenti, che la Comedia, che la Tragedia, et il Poema Heroico* (Padua, 1586), in Weinberg, *Literary Criticism* I, 317; Spenser, "Letter to Raleigh," 23 Jan. 1589, *Works*, ed. J. C. Smith and E. de Selincourt (Oxford, 1950) pp. 407–8; Frénicle, *Jésus Crucifié* (Paris, 1636), sig. O (Preface).

13. Tortoletti, *Juditha Vindex et Vindicata* (Rome, 1628), pp. 184–85, 191–96.

14. Daniello, *La Poetica* (Venice, 1536), pp. 11, 42; Varchi, *Della Poesia*, in *Lezzioni* (Florence, 1590), p. 616; Capriano, *Della Vera Poetica* (Venice, 1555), sig. C^V. Trissino in the dedicatory epistle to *La Italia Liberata da Gothi* (Rome, 1547) declares that his epic presents not only things useful for war, "ma ancora ornamento ad alcune altri parti del vivere humano."

15. Bonciani [*Difesa di Dante*], MS Ricc., 2435, fol. 117, Biblioteca Riccardiana, Florence, in Weinberg, *Literary Criticism* II, 903. Cf. Varchi, *L'Hercolano* (Florence, 1570), pp. 248–57.

16. Giovanni Battista Marino, *L'Adone* (Venice, 1623). The Paris, 1623, edition appeared with Jean Chapelain's prefatory "Lettre ou Discours de M. Chapelain à M. Favereau . . . sur le Poëme d'Adonis du Chevalier Marino."

17. Scaliger, *Poetices* I.ii (Lyons, 1561), p. 5; [Puttenham?], *The Arte of English Poesie* (London, 1589), pp. 33, 50–51; Meres, *Palladis Tamia. Wits Treasury* (London, 1598), p. 282.

18. Joannes Klockus (Johann Kloch), *Christiados Priscae et Novae Libri XII*

(Ursel, 1601), sig. C (Prefatio); Campanella, *Poetica* (Rome, 1944; wr. *ca.* 1596), pp. 91–167, in Weinberg, *Literary Criticism* II, 907–8; see William Alexander, *Anacrisis* (London, 1634), in *Critical Essays of the Seventeenth Century*, ed. J. E. Spingarn (3 vols.; Oxford, 1908), I, 186.

19. Francesco Robortello, *In Librum Aristotelis de Arte Poetica Explicationes* (Florence, 1548), pp. 93, 219, 290; Jacopo Mazzoni, *Della Difesa della Comedia di Dante* III.vi (Cesena, 1587), pp. 409–17; Frénicle, *Jésus Crucifié*, preface; Le Laboureur, *La Magdalaine Pénitente*, sig. I2; Drayton, *Moyses in a Map of His Miracles* (London, 1604), preface.

20. Campanella, *Poetica*, p. 167, in Weinberg, *Literary Criticism* II, 908; Vauquelin, *L'Art Poetique Francois*, pp. 108–10; Philippe Le Noir, *Emanuel, ou Paraphrase Evangélique* (Paris, 1638), Advertissement; Robert Arnauld D'Andilly, *Poème sur la Vie de Jésus-Christ*, st. 1–3 (Paris, 1634); Jean de Saint-Peres, *La Vie de Joseph* (Paris, 1648), preface.

21. See for example, Giraldi Cinthio, *Discorsi...intorno al Comporre de i Romanzi* (Venice, 1554), p. 69.

22. See for example, A. Sebastiano Minturno, *L'Arte Poetica* (Venice, 1563), p. 31.

23. See R. C. Williams, "Methods of Treatment of the Epic as Discussed by Sixteenth Century Critics," *Romantic Review*, XII (1921), 276–85; Minturno, *L'Arte Poetica*, pp. 25–38.

24. Tortoletti, *Juditha*, p. 290; Klockus, *Christiados...Libri XII*, Prefatio.

25. Pigna, *I Romanzi* (Venice, 1552), pp. 25–26, 45; Cinthio, *Discorsi... intorno*, pp. 19–22; Le Noir, *Emanuel*, Advertissement.

26. *La Sepmaine, ou Création du Monde* (Paris, 1578); thirty editions appeared in less than six years, as well as translations into Latin, English, Italian, Spanish, and Dutch. *La Seconde Sepmaine* (Paris, 1584–1608). See *The Works of Guillaume de Salluste, Sieur Du Bartas*, ed. U. T. Holmes *et al.* (3 vols.; Chapel Hill, N.C., 1935–40).

27. Du Bartas, *Seconde Sepmaine*, Advertissement, cited in [Thomas Lodge], *A Learned Summary upon the Famous Poeme of William of Saluste Lord of Bartas* (London, 1621), n.p.

28. *Judit*, in *La Muse Chrestiene* (Bordeaux, 1574), republished in *Oeuvres* (Paris, 1579). The second edition was translated by Thomas Hudson as *The Historie of Judith* (Edinburgh, 1584) and by Sylvester as *Bethulians Rescue* in [Jean Bertaut], *The Parliament of Vertues Royal* (2 vols.; London, 1614). In his folio edition of Du Bartas' *Divine Weekes* (1621) Sylvester includes both his own translation and that of Hudson.

29. Hudson's translation in Sylvester's *Du Bartas* (1621), p. 683.

30. Tasso, *Il Goffredo* [afterward, *Gerusalemme Liberata*] (Venice, 1581), English trans. Edward Fairfax, *Godfrey of Bulloigne: Or the Recovery of Jerusalem* (London, 1600); *Di Gerusalemme Conquistata* (Rome, 1593). The "Allegoria" appeared with *Il Goffredo* (Venice, 1581). *Discorsi...dell' Arte Poetica, et in Particolare del Poema Heroico* (Venice, 1587); *Discorsi del Poema Heroico* (Naples [1594?]).

31. Ariosto, *Orlando Furioso* (Ferrara, 1516, 40 cantos; Ferrara, 1532, 46 cantos); Ronsard, *Les Quatre Premiers Livres de la Franciade* (Paris, 1572).

32. Tasso, *Il Mondo Creato* (Viterbo, 1607).

33. Tasso, *Della Virtù Heroica* (Venice, 1582), fols. 8–9.

34. R. A. Sayce's excellent study, *The French Biblical Epic in the Seventeenth Century* (Oxford, 1955), which is limited to Old Testament poems, finds Du Bartas and the Counter Reformation baroque sensibility the all-pervasive influences upon French biblical epic. However, this view must be modified when the New Testament poems are considered. In the years in question France produced at least ten Christiads and five Magdaliads.

35. Valvasone, *Angeleida*, epis. ded; Klockus, *Christiados...Libri XII*, Prefatio; Michel Foucqué, *La Vie, Faictz, Passion, Mort, Résurrection, et Ascension de Nostre Seigneur Jésus Christ* (Paris, 1574), pp. 20–22; Frénicle, *Jésus Crucifié*, preface.

36. Drayton, *Moyses*, preface.

37. Fletcher, *Christs Victorie, and Triumph in Heaven, and Earth, over, and after Death* (Cambridge, Eng., 1610), To the Reader.

38. For example: In Latin, Joannes Mellius de Sousa, *In Librum Job* (London, 1615); Patrick Adamson, "Jobus, sive de Constantia," in *Poëmata Sacra* (London, 1619); Jacobus Lectius, *Jonah, seu Poetica Paraphrasis*, in Theodore Beza, *Poëmata Varia* (Geneva, 1614); Joannes Petrus Lotichus, *Holofernes* (2d ed.; Frankfurt, 1625). In English, William Forest, *History of Joseph* (London, 1569); John Marbecke, *The Holie Historie of King David* (London, 1579); William Hunnis, *The Life and Death of Joseph*, in *Hunnies Recreations* (London, 1595). Also, several paraphrases by Francis Quarles: *Job Militant* (London, 1624); *Hadassa: Or the History of Queene Ester* (London, 1621); *A Feast for Wormes...the History of Jonah* (London, 1620); and *The Historie of Samson* (London, 1631). In French, Jean de Saint-Peres, *La Vie du Saint Patriarche Tobie* (Paris, 1648), and *La Vie de Joseph*.

39. Dolce, *La Vita di Giuseppe* (Venice, 1561).

40. Du Bellay, *La Monomachie* (Paris, 1560); Brach, *Monomachie,* in *Les Poemes* (Bordeaux, 1576); Belleau, *Les Amours,* in *La Bergerie* (2d ed.; Paris, 1572). The poet and critic Vauquelin, also associated with the Pléiade though not actually a member, began his unfinished poem on David, the *Israelide,* at about this time; the only remnants of it are in his *L'Art Poetique Francois.*

41. Coignard (Mme de Mansencal), *Judith,* in *Oeuvres Chrestiennes* (Tournon, 1595). See also Thierry Petremand, *Paraphrase de l'Admirable Histoire de la Saincte Heroyne Judith* (Lyons, 1578).

42. *Noahs Floud* and *David and Goliath* were published for the first time in *The Muses Elizium* (London, 1630). In this edition the *Moyses* is titled *Moses, His Birth and Miracles* and appears without the 1604 preface.

43. Fuller, *Davids Hainous Sinne* (London, 1631).

44. Oriet, *La Susanne* (Paris, 1581). Oriet is also author of *Le Livre de l'Esther* (Paris, 1584), which begins *ab ovo* and has very few epic devices. D'Urfé, *Hymne de Saincte Susanne,* in *Le Premier Livre des Hymnes* (Lyons, 1608); Montchrestien, *Susane,* published in *Les Tragedies . . . Plus une Bergerie et un Poeme de Susane* (Paris [1601?]).

45. Aylett, *Susanna: Or, the Arraignment of the Two Unjust Elders* (London, 1622); *Joseph* (London, 1623); *D[avid's] Troubl[es] Remembred* (London, 1638). For attribution of the last, which appeared anonymously, see *B.M. General Catalogue,* and Frederick M. Padelford, "Robert Aylett," *Huntington Library Bulletin,* No. 10 (October, 1936), pp. 1–48.

46. Ceba, *La Reina Esther* (Genoa, 1615); Millieus, *Moyses Viator: Seu Imago Militantis Ecclesiae Mosaicis Peregrinantis Synagogae Typis Adumbrata* (London, 1636, 1639). Another long poem on a single hero is the unpublished French *Judic* of Anne D'Urfé (wr. *ca.* 1599–1620, 3 books, unfinished, described in Sayce, *French Biblical Epic,* pp. 72–73), which probably represents the first French attempt to produce a full-scale epic (12 books) on a biblical subject. Another example is François Perrin's *Histoire Tragique de Sennachérib* (1599, 9 books, *ca.* 2,550 alexandrines). The English *Jonathan: An Heroicke Poeme Intended* by William Alexander, published in *Recreations with the Muses* (London, 1637), was evidently also conceived as a full-scale neoclassical epic on a martial Old Testament subject though only one book was completed.

47. Murtola, *Della Creatione del Mondo* (Venice, 1607); Passero, *L'Essamerone* (Naples, 1608); Gamon, *La Semaine* (Geneva, 1599); D'Aubigné, *La Creation,* first published in *Oeuvres Complètes* (6 vols.; Paris, 1873–92), III, 325–44; Saint-Martin, *La Nature Naissante* (Paris, 1667). Cf. Maury Thibaut de Maisières, *Les Poèmes Inspirés du Début de la Genèse a l'Epoque de la Renaissance* (Louvain, 1931).

48. Valmarana, *Daemonomachie: Sive, de Bello Intelligentiarum super Divini Verbi Incarnatione* (Vienna, 1627), Book I published in [*Collection of Sacred Latin Poetry*], ed. William Lauder (London, 1753); Peyton [*The Glasse of Time, in the First Age*] (London, 1620); Alexander, *Doomsday* (London, 1637).

49. Taubmannus, *Bellum Angelicum* (Leipzig, 1604), selections in Lauder.

50. Scève, *Microcosme* (Lyons, 1562).

51. Masenius, *Sarcotis* (Cologne, 1654 [edition used: ed. J. Dinouart, Paris, 1757]). Other poems treating Adam's fall, but having less epic quality, are, in English, Francis Sabie's *Adams Complaint* (London, 1596, 1 book, *ca.* 516 lines in 6-line stanzas); in Italian, Giovanni Sorenzo's *I Duo Primi Libri dell'Adamo* (Bergamo, 1606, 2 books, *ca.* 1,440 lines in ottava rima; and, in Latin, Caspar Barlaeus' *Paradisus: Sive Nuptiae Primorum Parentum Adami & Evae* (Amsterdam, 1643, 1 book, *ca.* 900 lines), in Lauder.

52. Fletcher, *Historie of the Perfect-Cursed-Blessed Man* (London, 1629); Ramsay, *Poemata Sacra* (Edinburgh, 1633).

53. Folengo, *La Humanità del Figliuolo* (Venice, 1533).
54. Mellius de Sousa, *In Librum Job...assesserunt de Reparatione Humana* (London, 1615). The conjunction of the two works suggests some consciousness of a typological relation between Job and Christ. Ross, *Virgilii Evangelisantis Christiados Libri XIII* (London, 1638); Ross has another cento (1 book, *ca.* 1,620 lines) which is a brief summary of the Gospel story, *Virgilius Evangelisans; sive Historia...Jesu Christi, Virgilianis Verbis...Descripta* (London, 1634). See also Othon Gryphius, *Virgilii Centones* (Ratisbon, 1593, 1 book, *ca.* 2,750 hexameters), and Stephen Pleurreus' *Aeneis Sacra* (Paris, 1618, 1 book, *ca.* 3,430 hexameters).
55. Montreulx, *Jésus Christ en l'Authel* (Paris, 1607); D'Escorbiac, *La Christiade, ou Poëme Sacré* (Paris, 1613); D'Argent, *La Sepmaine...Contenant l'Histoire de la Seconde Creation ou Restauration de Genre Humain* (Sedan, 1629); Sanguinet, *La Dodécade* (Bergerac, 1614).
56. Donadeus, *De Bello Christi* (Messina, 1614).
57. La Pujade, *La Christiade,* in *Oeuvres Chrestiennes.* La Pujade is also the reputed author of *La Mariade* (Bordeaux, 1605, 12 books) which I have not seen. The poem is mentioned in Raymond Toinet's *Quelques Recherches autour des Poèmes Heroïques-Epiques Français du Dix-Septième Siècle* (2 vols.; Tulle, 1899, 1907), I, 78. Some other poems—the Italian *La Christiade, Poema Heroico* of Marcantonio Laporelli (Rome, 1618, 24 books, *ca.* 4,500 lines in terza rima), and the French works *Emanuel, ou Paraphrase Evangélique* by Le Noir (1638, 15 books, *ca.* 10,000 alexandrines), and *Poëme sur les Merveilles de Jésus-Christ* by Charles de Bouques (Paris, 1642, 5 books, unfinished)—are simply straightforward sequential accounts of Christ's life, without flashback, recitals, or other epic apparatus.
58. Fraunce, *The Countesse of Pembrokes Emanuel* (London, 1591).
59. Marino, *La Strage de gli Innocenti* (Venice [1610?]); Richard Crashaw translated Book I, "Sospetto d'Herode," into English and published it in his *Steps to the Temple* (London, 1646).
60. More [Morus], *Laus Christi Nascentis* (Paris, 1655 [edition used: *Poëmata,* Paris, 1669]). This More is evidently the French clergyman whom Milton castigated in the *Defensio Secunda,* erroneously taking him to be the author of the Royalist denunciation of the regicide, *Regii Sanguinis Clamor ad Coelum Adversus Parricidas Anglicanos* (The Hague, 1652).
61. Another brief French Christiad, also on the subject of Christ's passion and death, but with little epic dimension or epic quality, is P. Bigres, *Jesus Mourant* (Paris, 1644, 1 book, *ca.* 1,580 alexandrines).
62. Du Port [Franciscus Portus], *De Messiae Pugna* (Paris, 1621). There is an earlier French version in two books (*ca.* 4,860 lines), *Le Triomphe du Messie* (Paris, 1617).
63. Tansillo, *Le Lagrime di S. Pie[t]ro* [wrongly attributed to Cardinal de Pucci] (Venice, 1560); published in Tansillo's name as *Le Lagrime de San Pietro* (Vico Equense, 1585). Tansillo began the work about 1539.

64. Valvasone, *LaGrime di Santa Maria Maddelena* (Carmagnola, 1588), published with Tansillo's *Lagrime* (Venice, 1592); Campeggi, *Le Lagrime di Maria Vergine* (Bologna, 1617).

65. Nostradame, *Les Perles, ou les Larmes de la Saincte Magdeleine* (Toulouse, 1606); Robinson, *The Life and Death of Mary Magdalen* (wr. *ca.* 1620), unpublished until Oskar Sommer's edition (EETS, ex. ser., Vol. LXVII [London, 1899]).

66. Remi de Beauvais, *La Magdeleine* (Tourney, 1617).

67. M[ichel] de Marolles, *Traité du Poëme Epique* (Paris, 1662), p. 38: "De sorte que nous le trouvons chez les François, chez les Italiens & chez les Latins Modernes, dans les mesmes pensées, les mesmes comparisons, & les mesmes inventions. Je voy presque par tout des Dieux assemblez au Conseil, jusques dans le Poëme des Couches de la Vierge de Sannazare. Je voy par tout des Sibyles agitées, des Propheties d'une longue & illustre posterité, des Cerberes, des Furies, & des Champs Elysiens. Iris ou Mercure, n'y manquent jamais. Neptune est toûjours esgalement inconstant, & Junon dépite, Apollon & les Muses sont incessamment invoquez pour en estre inspirez: & bien que ce ne soit toûjours sous les mesmes noms, ce n'est pourtant que pour dire la mesme chose, avec la seule difference le plus souvant que ce n'est pas si agreablement."

68. Nicolas Courtin's *Charlesmagne Penitent,* in *Poësies Chrétiennes* (1687, 5 books, *ca.* 2,800 alexandrines), is an interesting late exception; it presents Charlemagne in later life as a Job-like figure, conquering himself through suffering.

69. Perachon, *Poëme sur la Naissance de Jésus-Christ* (Paris, 1665; see preface to 1669 edition).

70. Godeau, *Saint Paul. Poëme Chrestien* (Paris, 1654), sig. A3^V: "Quoy que Saint Paul soit le plus grand Heros du Christianisme, je n'ay jamais consideré cét ouvrage come un Poëme heroïque... Je say bien que par les régles il ne peut estre digne de ce nom, autre que la mauvaise forme que je luy ay donnée... Le martyre de Saint Paul n'est pas de soy une matiere fort riche. Car, enfin, il n'y paroist autre chose à dire, sinon, qu'il a eu la teste tranchée, ce qui est fort vray-semblable, mais ce qui n'est point merveilleux, & par conséquent, ce qui ne peut estre le sujet d'un Poëme heroique."

71. Clarke, *Christiados... Libri 17* (Bruges, 1670).

72. LesFargues, *David* (Paris, 1660), sig. E2: "J'ay mieux aymé faillir contre les methodes de l'art que contre les principes de la Religion"; [Jacquelin?], *Hélie* (Paris, 1661); Julien-Gatien Morillon, *Joseph, ou l'Esclave Fidele* (Paris, 1679); see above, pp. 28–31, for Job paraphrases.

73. Saint-Amant, *Moyse Sauvé* (Paris, 1653), sig. E2 (preface): "Je n'ay ni principal Heros agissant, ni grandes Batailles, ni Sieges de Villes à produire. Mon Ouvrage n'est que d'un jour entier, au lieu qu'il faut que l'epique soit d'un an ou environ." Saint-Amant is also author of a fragment, *Joseph et Ses Frères en Egipte* (Rouen and Paris, 1658), which he claimed to have

written some thirty years earlier and to have published in 1658 as a fragment so as to avoid having to complete this early piece. It is almost devoid of epic apparatus.

74. Pech, "Discours aux Dames," in *Judith* (Toulouse, 1660), sig. A4^V: "J'ay voulu plustost luy donner le Tiltre de Saint que d'Heroïque, par ce que je n'ay point-eu de combats à descrire, & que mon Heroïne ne l'a esté que dans la derniere action de mon ouvrage, qui en est la principal sujet, par tout ailleurs elle n'y paroist que comme une Veufe affligée, Pieuse, & Saincte, qui songe à tout autre chose qu'à des exploits guerriers."

75. Coras, *Jonas, ou Ninive Penitente* (Paris, 1663), p. 8: "Je ne donne pas à cet Ouvrage le titre de Poëme Heroïque, parce que je n'ay pas esté persuadé que le sujet que j'y traite, en pust soûtenir la dignité. Ce n'est pas que la voix de Jonas n'ait produit des miracles que surpassent ceux qui peuvent partir de la main des plus grans Héros, & je trouve le seule conversion de Ninive qu'il opéra par sa prédiction, beaucoup plus merveilleuse que la prise de Troye. On doit pourtant considerer, que Jonas n'estoit pas un Guerrier, mais un Prophète; qu'il n'a pas assiégé Ninive avec une armée...il faut considerer...qu'il combat les ennemis avec la parole, & non pas avec l'espée."

76. Coras, *Josué, ou la Conqueste de Canaan* (Paris, 1665), preface; *Samson* (Paris, 1665), preface; *David, ou la Vertu Couronée* (Paris, 1665), preface.

77. *Josué*, preface: "J'ay préféré une briéveté forte & vigoureuse à une longueur énervée & languissante."

78. Desmarets, *Marie-Madeleine, ou la Triomphe de la Grace* (Paris, 1669), preface; *Esther* (Paris, 1670), preface. See also his *La Deffense du Poëme Heroïque* (Paris, 1674).

79. Cotin, *Poësies Chrestiennes* (Paris, 1668).

80. Boileau, *L'Art Poetique*, in *Oeuvres Diverses* (Paris, 1674), pp. 124–28; also, "Lettre du Sieur D. ou B. à l'Autheur du *Jonas* & du *David*" [Paris, 1668]. Le Bossu, *Traité du Poëme Epique* (Paris, 1675), pp. 8, 97, 124, 144–48.

81. Cowley, *Davideis, or, a Sacred Poem of the Troubles of David*, in *Poems* (London, 1656).

82. Davenant, *Gondibert, an Heroik Poeme* (London, 1650), preface; Hobbes, *Answer*, in Spingarn II, 55–64.

83. Cowley, *Poems*, sig. B2^V (preface).

84. *Ibid.*, sig. B2^V.

85. *Ibid.*, sig. B3.

86. *Ibid.*, sig. B^V.

87. *Ibid.*, p. 24*n*.

88. *Ibid.*

CHAPTER V

1. *CE* IX, 111; XVII, 253, 241.

2. See above, pp. 20–25.

3. See above, p. 66.

4. See above, p. 91.
5. See above, pp. 25–28.
6. Quarles, "Meditation 3," *Job Militant* (London, 1624), sigs. D2ᵛ–D3.
7. See above, pp. 32–35.
8. Gregory, *Moralia in Job* (LF, Vol. XVIII [Oxford, 1844]), p. 97.
9. See for example, Joseph Caryl, *An Exposition ... upon ... Job* (12 vols.; London, 1643–70), VIII, preface: [Job gives] "an account or narrative of the whole course of his life in the dayes of his prosperity, both in his publick Capacity as a Magistrate, throughout the 29th Chapter ... as also in his private capacity." Cf. Quarles, "Meditations 11, 13, 15," *Job Militant.*
10. See above, pp. 21–25.
11. Gryphius, *Virgilii Centones* (Ratisbon, 1593), ll. 1–5:

> Ille ego, qui quondam non inferiora secutus,
> Prima rudimenta & levium spectacula rerum,
> Structa meis manibus gracili modulatus avenâ:
> Majus opus moveo. Magno nunc ore sonandum
> Auxilium adventumque DEI.

12. Pleurreus, *Aeneis Sacra* (Paris, 1618), ll. 7–11:

> Ille ego qui quondam gracili modulatus avena
> Carmen, & egressus sylvis per florea rura
> Hactenus arvorum cultus pecorumque canebam
> Bellaque iam fama totum vulgata per orbem
> Aenees magni: (series longissima rerum
> Per tot ducta viros antique ab origine gentis.)
> Maius opus moveo.

13. Ross, *Virgilii Evangelisantis Christiados Libri XIII* (London, 1638), ll. 1–5:

> Ille ego qui quondam gracili modulatus avena
> Carmen, & *Aegypto* egrestius per inhospita saxa
> Perque domus *Arabum* vacuas & inania regna
> Deduxi *Abramidas,* at nunc horrentia *Christi*
> Acta, Deumque cano.

14. Jacobus Strasburgus, *Oratio Prima* (Leipzig, 1565), sig. A8ᵛ:

> Ecce sacro flatu celeres agitante per auras
> Tollitur, & longum per iter circum aera vectus
> In saltus nemorum vacuos ac lustra ferarum
> Fertur, ut incultae juga vasta frequentet Eremi,
> Et quondam exuto stygium victurus Averno
> Praedonem, levibus primum experiatur in armis
> Tyro rudimentum, & magnis se praeparet ausis.

15. Sanguinet, *La Dodécade de l'Evangile,* Book III (Bergerac, 1614), p. 131: "Là dóc Christ est porté pour par armes r'abbattre/ Les armes de Satan, & pour sa corne abbattre/ Corps à corps en duel."

16. Fletcher, "Christs Victorie on Earth," in *Christs Victorie, and Triumph* II.16, 20 (Cambridge, Eng., 1610), pp. 30–31. Of course both Fletcher and Milton may be following, independently, Spenser's *Faerie Queene* I.i.29–35, in which Archimago presents himself as a simple hermit.

17. Antoine La Pujade, *La Christiade,* Book III, in *Les Oeuvres Chrestiennes,* Part I (Paris, 1604), fol. 49ᵛ:

> J'ay pitié de te voir en danger de perir,
> Et personne ne peut icy te secourir:
> C'est un desert horrible où maintenant nous sommes,
> Bien loin & hors des lieux habités par les hommes.

18. Sedulius, *Carmen Paschale* II.177–78, ed. Joannes Huemer (CSEL, Vol. X [Vienna, 1885]), p. 56: "Insidiis temptator adit doctusque per artem/ Fallaces offerre dapes."

19. John Bale, *A Brefe Comedy or Enterlude concernynge the Temptacyon of Our Lorde and Saver Jesus Christ, by Sathan in the Desart* [1538] (Tudor Facsimile Texts [London, 1909]), sig. E2.

20. Fletcher, "Christs Victorie on Earth," sts. 50–52, pp. 40–41.

21. Beaumont, *Psyche: Or Loves Mysterie in XX Cantos, Displaying the Intercourse betwixt Christ and the Soule* IX.149–81 (London, 1648), pp. 148–50.

22. *Aeneid* III.209 35.

23. *Tempest* III.iii.53–59.

24. Beaumont, *Psyche* IX.241, p. 154.

25. Fletcher, "Christs Victorie on Earth," st. 55, p. 41.

26. Quarles, "Meditation 13," *Job Militant,* sigs. K4ᵛ–L.

27. Jacobus Bonus, *De Vita & Gestis Christi* (Rome, 1526), sigs. L–Li.

28. Girolamo Fracastoro, *Joseph* (Frankfurt, 1578), in *Du Bartas His Divine Weekes and Workes,* trans. Sylvester (London, 1621), p. 818:

> Iámque pererratis Judaeae finibus, altae
> Incipiunt turres & moenia Osiridis urbis
> Apparere procul, campis ubi fusa iuventus
> Munera militiae exercent: hi vincere cursu
> Contendunt pedibus, hi fulvo in pulvere sudant
> Luctantes, alii duro sub pondere cestus,
> Pars volucres exercet equos, cursúque fatigat,
> Aut inferre hosti versas post terga sagittas
> Discit equo currente, aut hastam tollere campo,
> Ergo Arabes postquam accessere, & pulcher Joseph,
> Mirati pugnas, placidi & praeludia Martis

Consistunt, oculísque intenti & pectore toto
Vix satis expleri possunt.

29. Philippe Le Noir, *Emanuel,* Book III (4th ed.; Paris, 1664), p. 50: "Vois-tu bien, luy dit-il, l'empire des Romains?/ Sçache que j'en dispose & qu'il est en mes mains./ Je te pourray donner ce Sceptre & cét Empire,/ Sous lequel l'Univers presentement soûpire."

30. Beaumont, *Psyche* IX.225–26, 229, pp. 153–54.

31. Mantuan, *Parthenice Mariana,* Book I (Bologna, 1488), sigs. D5^V–D6:

Carmina discebat: sanctique poemata regis:
Qui tetricis olim fidibus cantabat ad aras
Sacraque fatidico psallebat ad orgia cantu.
Quicquid habent sacrae divina volumina legis:
Quicquid inest arabum libris lustrarat: et omnis
Graiorum annales: romanorumque triumphos:
Et quantum latii fudissent arma cruoris
Punica: quot bellis rubuit navalibus aequor:
Qui troiam petiere duces: quo milite persas
Rex macedum parthosque truces superarit et indos.
Monstra quot Alcides domuit: quo remige cretam
Dedalus ad gelidas fugiens annaverit arctos
Et quibus adiutus pennis equus aliger auras
Presserit et dulcem plantis excusserit undam.

. . . .

Quicquid in his tumidum: quicquid crudele percaxque
Et quaecunque pios non attestantia mores
Offendit damnabat: apes imitata legendo.

32. *Judit,* trans. Thomas Hudson, in Sylvester's *Du Bartas* (1621), pp. 724–26.

33. More [Morus], in *Poëmata* (Paris, 1669), pp. 37, 45:

Plus hortis, Epicure, tuis, & tristibus altae
Porticibus sectae, plus toto parva Lycaeo
Villa sapit, caeloque semel dignata magistro
Iam nihil ignorat: Bethlemi cedite pago,
Cedite Palladiae, memorabile nomen, Athenae:
Ignotum ecce Deum, vacuam cui ponitis aram

. . . .

In quo mira lego veteri ignorata Platoni,
Docta Stagira, tuus quae numquam olfecit alumnus,
Nec tuus ille, Samos: at nec vicinus Hymetto,
Quanquam unum se scire, nihil sescire professus
Princeps è coelo Sophiam deduxit ab astris.

34. Quarles, "Meditation 11," *Job Militant,* sigs. I2^V–I3.

35. Nicolas Frénicle, *Jésus Crucifié* (Paris, 1636), fol. 76: "Tout l'Ocean mugit, & le vent plein d'horreur/ Accompagne en grondant son aveugle fureur,/ Mais le rocher tient ferme, & repousse en arriere/ Les effroyables monts de l'onde mariniere."

36. Fletcher, "Christs Triumph after Death," in *Christs Victorie, and Triumph* IV.1–3, pp. 67–68.

37. Sedulius, *Carmen Paschale* II.199–200, CSEL X, 57: "Ter sese adtollens animo perstare superbo,/ Terque volutus humo fragili confidere bello."

38. Bonus, *De Vita,* sig. L: "Infoelix Daemon ut Cerberus ore trilingui/ Ingemuit magni percussus ab Herculis ictu,/ Callida nec triplici versutia defuit ori."

39. Jean D'Escorbiac, *La Christiade,* Book V (Paris, 1613), pp. 7, 29–30.

CHAPTER VI

1. Allan H. Gilbert, "The Temptation in *Paradise Regained,*" *JEGP,* XV (1916), 606; Douglas Bush, *English Literature in the Earlier Seventeenth Century, 1600–1660* (Oxford, 1962), p. 412.

2. Elizabeth M. Pope, *Paradise Regained: The Tradition and the Poem* (Baltimore, 1947), pp. 34–41.

3. E. M. W. Tillyard, *Milton* (London, 1930), p. 305; Merritt Y. Hughes, "The Christ of *Paradise Regained* and the Renaissance Heroic Tradition," *SP,* XXXV (1938), 277; Arnold Stein, *Heroic Knowledge* (Minneapolis, 1947), pp. 14–16.

4. M. M. Mahood, *Poetry and Humanism* (New Haven, 1950), p. 211; Northrop Frye, "The Typology of *Paradise Regained,*" *MP,* LIII (1955–56), 237.

5. A. S. P. Woodhouse, "Theme and Pattern in *Paradise Regained,*" *UTQ,* XXV (1955–56), 173.

6. Don Cameron Allen, *The Harmonious Vision* (Baltimore, 1954), p. 118.

7. Maurice Kelley, *This Great Argument* (Princeton, 1941).

8. *CE* XIV, 195, 221. William B. Hunter, Jr., in a recent article, "Some Problems in John Milton's Theological Vocabulary," *HTR,* LVII (1964), 354–65, has demonstrated that Milton consistently equates essence with hypostasis (individual being or existence), rather than with substance (*ousia*).

9. *CE* XV, 269, 271.

10. *CE* XIV, 253.

11. *CE* XIV, 178: "EXTERNA [efficientia] est decretorum executio, qua aliquid apud se decretum, extra se efficit." The translation is mine.

12. *CE* XIV, 189.

13. Harry F. Robins, *If This Be Heresy* (*Illinois Studies in Language and Literature,* Vol. LI [Urbana, Ill., 1963]), pp. 95–98, has recently argued that the Son thus "produces himself" in accordance with God's decree since God could not act in terms of external efficiency except through the agency

of the Son. But in the passage cited in note 11, above, "extra se efficit" seems more adequately rendered "outside of himself" than "by external agency," as Summers' translation, cited by Robins, gives it. In any case, Milton himself explicitly refuses to speculate as to just how the Son was produced, though his phraseology leaves no doubt that the Father is the active agent in bringing forth, or generating, the Son. The fact that Milton cites as theories of generation by *external* efficiency the "emanation, procession, spiration" of the Son from the Father (*CE* XIV, 181) though he does not himself accept those theories, indicates that he sees the generation as the Father's own act, and that an external agency is not predicated. Though Milton conceives of God as invisible, inaudible, and unmanifested, he does not appear to understand by this that God cannot act except through the Logos: if Milton's God creates through the Logos it is because he chooses to do so, not because he must, just as his production of the Son is declared to be a matter of will, not of necessity.

14. *CE* XV, 21–27.

15. Denis Saurat, *Milton, Man and Thinker* (New York, 1925); Maurice Kelley, *This Great Argument;* Walter C. Curry, *Milton's Ontology, Cosmogony, and Physics* (Lexington, Ky., 1957).

16. See Harry A. Wolfson, *The Philosophy of the Church Fathers* (Cambridge, Mass., 1956), pp. 332, 359–61; J. N. D. Kelly, *Early Christian Doctrines* (New York, 1958), pp. 223–79.

17. In *Documents of the Christian Church,* ed. Henry Bettenson (New York, 1947), p. 36.

18. *Ibid.*

19. See David Masson, *The Life of John Milton* (7 vols.; London, 1859–94), VI, 823–24; Francis E. Mineka, "The Critical Reception of Milton's *De Doctrina Christiana*," *University of Texas Studies in English* (1943), pp. 115–47; Maurice Kelley, *This Great Argument,* pp. 84–106.

20. Arius, "The Confession of the Arians, Addressed to Alexander of Alexandria," in *Christology of the Later Fathers,* ed. E. R. Hardy and Cyril R. Richardson (LCC, Vol. III [Philadelphia, 1954]), pp. 333–34.

21. Athanasius, "Four Discourses against the Arians," ed. A. Robertson (Library of Nicene and Post-Nicene Fathers, 2d ser., Vol. IV [Oxford, 1892]), p. 309.

22. Louis A. Wood, *The Form and Origin of Milton's Antitrinitarian Conception* (London, Ontario, 1911), pp. 24–25.

23. William B. Hunter, Jr., "Milton's Arianism Reconsidered," *HTR*, LII (1959), 9–35; J. H. Adamson, "Milton's Arianism," *HTR*, LIII (1960), 269–76.

24. Tertullian, "Adversus Praxeas," trans. Peter Holmes (ANCL, Vol. XV [Edinburgh, 1870]), pp. 342–50. Cf. Justin Martyr, *Dialogue with Trypho,* trans. Marcus Dods *et al.* (ANCL, Vol. II [Edinburgh, 1867]), pp. 260–63; and Philo, *De Opificio Mundi,* trans. F. H. Colson and G. H. Whitaker [*Works*] (Loeb [10 vols.; London, 1929–62]), I, 1–21.

25. Origen, *De Principiis* I.ii, trans. Frederick Crombie (ANCL, Vol. X [Edinburgh, 1869]), pp. 19, 22. See also Adolf Harnack, *History of Dogma,* trans. E. B. Speirs and James Miller (7 vols.; London, 1894–99), II, 332–60; Wolfson, *Philosophy of Church Fathers,* pp. 183–363; Plotinus, *The Divine Mind, Being the Treatises of the Fifth Ennead* [*Works*], trans. Stephen MacKenna (5 vols.; London, 1926), IV, 1–15.

26. CE XIV, 193.

27. See Hunter, "Milton's Theological Vocabulary," pp. 359–64; J. N. D. Kelly, *Doctrines,* pp. 231–37.

28. Hunter, "Milton's Theological Vocabulary," p. 364.

29. J. N. D. Kelly, *Doctrines,* pp. 235–36.

30. *Ibid.,* pp. 239–40.

31. CE XIV, 311–13.

32. CE XIV, 313, 337–39.

33. CE XIV, 209.

34. J. N. D. Kelly, *Doctrines,* p. 230.

35. CE XIV, 179–91.

36. CE XIV, 193.

37. Hunter, "Milton's Arianism Reconsidered," pp. 33–35, assumes a two-stage Logos theory in Milton, according to which the Son exists from eternity as the unmanifested Logos. But there is no convincing evidence for such a theory, and passages such as the following tell against it: "As to the eighth chapter of Proverbs, it appears to me that it is not the Son of God who is there introduced as the speaker, but a poetical personification of wisdom" (CE XV, 13).

38. CE XIV, 309, 359.

39. CE XIV, 181, 183, 253. Elaborating further upon John i, Milton declares (CE XIV, 253–55) that the statement "The Word was with God, and was God" means only that he resided in the bosom of the Father, not as sharing his essence but reclining there as John did upon Christ's bosom; further he declares that the Son "was God" only "by proximity and love, not in essence."

40. CE XIV, 189, italics mine. Maurice Kelley, "Milton's Arianism Again Considered," HTR, LIV (1961), 197, cites this passage in proof that Milton denies the eternity of the Son, and Hunter counters, "Theological Vocabulary," pp. 364–65n, by asserting that this passage discusses not the literal but the metaphorical generation of the Son [his exaltation and unction to his mediatorial office] on the strength of Milton's comment, "Hitherto only the metaphorical generation of Christ has been considered" (CE XIV, 191). But a careful reading of the entire section indicates that the passage in question must refer to the literal production of the Son, as it follows upon and concludes a discussion of whether propagation and generation from physical necessity can pertain to the nature of God (CE XIV, 187–89). The discussion of the metaphorical generation begins just after this passage, as Milton takes up the term "only begotten" (CE XIV, 189).

41. *CE* XIV, 187.

42. Adamson, "Milton's Arianism," pp. 269–76, argues that Milton makes impressive poetical use of these metaphors in *Paradise Lost,* but the first example cited, the "Invocation to Light" (*PL* III.1–12), has not been proved to be a reference to the Son (see Merritt Y. Hughes, "Milton and the Symbol of Light," *SEL,* IV, 1964, 1–33), and the other cases (*PL* III.372–86; VI.719–21) seem rather to portray a particular donation of powers from the Father to his Image on specific occasions than the natural participation in God's nature which these metaphors usually suggest.

43. *CE* XIV, 219.

44. *CE* XIV, 317–21.

45. *CE* XIV, 343.

46. In *Documents of the Christian Church,* ed. Bettenson, pp. 66–68.

47. In *Christology,* LCC III, 373.

48. See Friedrich Loofs, "Kenosis," in James Hastings, *The Encyclopedia of Religion and Ethics* (12 vols.; New York, 1908–22).

49. "The Tome of Leo," in *Christology,* LCC III, 363–65.

50. Nestorius himself may not have been a Nestorian in the classic sense of the word. See J. N. D. Kelly, *Doctrines,* pp. 314–17.

51. See "The Chalcedonian Decree," and "The Anathemas of the Second Council of Constantinople," in *Christology,* LCC III, 371–81; articles on "Docetism," "Nestorianism," "Monophysitism," in Hastings, *Encyclopedia of Religion and Ethics;* Harnack, *History of Dogma* IV, 1–267; Wolfson, *Philosophy of Church Fathers,* pp. 372–457; J. N. D. Kelly, *Doctrines,* pp. 138–61, 280–342; John Henry Newman, *The Arians of the Fourth Century* (London, 1883); Friedrich Loofs, *Nestorius* (Cambridge, Eng., 1914).

52. "Monotheletism," in Hastings, *Encyclopedia of Religion and Ethics.*

53. "The Statement of Faith of the Third Council of Constantinople" (Sixth Ecumenical Council), in *Christology,* LCC III, 383–84.

54. *CE* XV, 263.

55. [John Biddle], *The Apostolical and True Opinion concerning the Holy Trinity* (London, 1653); [John Biddle], *The Testimonies of Irenaeus, Justin Martyr . . . concerning That One God, and the Persons of the Holy Trinity* (London [1649?]); *The Racovian Catechisme* (Amsterdam, 1652), pp. 27–164. See also H. John McLachlan, *Socinianism in Seventeenth-Century England* (Oxford, 1951).

56. *CE* XV, 267.

57. *CE* XV, 267–71.

58. William B. Hunter, "Milton on the Incarnation: Some More Heresies," *JHI,* XXI (1960), 349–69.

59. *CE* XV, 273.

60. *CE* XV, 279–81.

61. *CE* XIV, 229.

62. See Augustine, *City of God* IX.15, trans. Marcus Dods (New York,

1950), p. 294: "I do not say that He is Mediator because He is the Word, for as the Word He is supremely blessed and supremely immortal...but He is Mediator as He is man."

63. *CE* XV, 303–9.

64. *The Summe of Christian Religion, Delivered by Zacharias Ursinus,* trans. D. Henry Parry (Oxford, 1601), p. 517: "Christ suffered not according to both natures, neither according to his godhead, but *according to his humane nature onely, both in body & soule.* For his divine nature is immutable, impassible, immortal...And the divinity susteined and upheld the humanity in the griefes and paines thereof, and raised it againe unto life." Cf. Calvin, *The Institution of the Christian Religion* II.xvi, trans. T[homas] N[orton] (London, 1561), fols. 100–100^V.

65. *CE* XIV, 329–31.

66. *CE* XV, 309.

67. *CE* XV, 275–77.

68. Cf. "Kenosis," in Hastings, *Encyclopedia of Religion and Ethics.*

69. *CE* XIV, 343. Hunter, "Milton on the Incarnation," denies that kenosis is an important concept for Milton, but in my view it is of central importance.

70. *CE* XIV, 275.

71. *CE* XV, 275.

CHAPTER VII

1. In an exploratory essay, "Theme and Structure in *Paradise Regained,*" *SP,* LVII (1960), 186–220, I suggested the significance of Christ's three offices for *Paradise Regained.*

2. Michael Fixler's important book, *Milton and the Kingdoms of God* (London, 1964), has appeared too late for me to make use of it, but I am pleased to note that we agree on the importance of the typological perspective in the poem. It will be evident from what follows that we are in essential agreement about the use of many of the Hebraic allusions, but that I find the typological symbolism to be more pervasive than he does, to have a wider range of functions, and to incorporate classical as well as Hebraic types.

3. See above, p. 110.

4. Auerbach, *Mimesis,* trans. W. Trask (New York, 1957), p. 171. See also Auerbach, "Figura," trans. Ralph Manheim, in *Scenes from the Drama of European Literature* (New York, 1959), pp. 11–76. Other treatments of patristic and medieval attitudes to allegorical interpretation include Jean Daniélou, *Origen,* trans. Walter Mitchell (New York, 1955); Robert M. Grant, *The Letter and the Spirit* (New York, 1957); R. P. C. Hanson, *Allegory and Event* (Richmond, Va., 1959); G. W. H. Lampe and K. J. Woollcombe, *Essays on Typology* (Naperville, Ill., 1957).

5. Irenaeus, "Against Heresies," in *Documents of the Christian Church,* ed. Henry Bettenson (New York, 1947), p. 42.

6. Harry A. Wolfson, *The Philosophy of the Church Fathers* (Cambridge, Mass., 1956), p. 43; Jean Daniélou, *Origen*, p. 162.

7. Origen, *De Principiis* IV.i, trans. Frederick Crombie (ANCL, Vol. X [Edinburgh, 1869]), pp. 274–356; Daniélou, *Origen*, pp. 166–67. Origen's relation to the tradition of figural realism is blurred somewhat by his denial of the literal sense of certain difficult parts of Scripture, and by his reading of Scripture in terms of numerological symbolism and Philonic moral allegory as well as typology.

8. Aquinas, *Summa Theologica*, Pt. I, Q. I, Art. 10, in *Basic Writings of Saint Thomas Aquinas*, ed. Anton C. Pegis (2 vols.; New York, 1945), I, 16–17. Hugo of St. Victor, *De Sacramentis*, trans. Roy J. Deferrari (Cambridge, Mass., 1951), p. 5, uses the same categories but defines the second or allegorical level more broadly, as signifying through the event described "something else... done either in the past or in the present or in the future."

9. Cassian, *Conlations* xiv.8, cited in Beryl Smalley, *The Study of the Bible in the Middle Ages* (New York, 1952), p. 85; Dante, "Letter to the Can Grande della Scala," in *A Translation of Dante's Eleven Letters*, trans. C. S. Latham (London, 1918), p. 193.

10. Douay Bible II, 449 (argument to Propheticall Books).

11. Lapide, *Commentaria in Pentateuchum Mosis* (London, 1659); Blaise Pascal, *Pensées* 642, 647, trans. W. F. Trotter (New York, 1941), pp. 216–17.

12. Luther, *Colloquia Mensalia*, trans. Henrie Bell (London, 1652), pp. 482, 480; Luther, "Old Testament Prefaces," trans. C. M. Jacobs, *Works* (6 vols.; Philadelphia, 1915), VI, 367, 379; *The Prefaces to the Early Editions of Martin Luther's Bible*, ed. T. A. Readwin (London, 1863), pp. 6, 67.

13. Calvin, *The Institution of the Christian Religion* II.xvi, trans. T[homas] N[orton] (London, 1561), fol. 97; Calvin, *A Commentarie upon the Booke of Josue*, trans. W[illiam] F[ulke] (London, 1578), preface.

14. Weemse, *The Christian Synagogue, Workes* (3 vols.; London, 1636), I, 233–34.

15. Wither, *A Preparation to the Psalter* (London, 1619), p. 103.

16. H. R. MacCallum, "Milton and Figurative Interpretation of the Bible," *UTQ*, XXXI (1962), 397–415.

17. *CE* XVI, 263. Cf. Joannes Wollebius, *Compendium Theologiae Christianae* (Cambridge, Eng., 1642), p. 8, for an almost identical statement, using the same scriptural references.

18. *CE* XIV, 19, 201; XVI, 111.

19. F. Michael Krouse, *Milton's Samson and the Christian Tradition* (Princeton, 1949).

20. Lewalski, "Structure and the Symbolism of Vision in Michael's Prophecy, *Paradise Lost* XI–XII," *PQ*, XLII (1963), 25–35. See also W. G. Madsen, "Earth the Shadow of Heaven: Typological Symbolism in *Paradise Lost*," *PMLA*, LXX (1960), 519–26, for a convincing argument that the activities

in Eden and the battle in heaven foreshadow events forthcoming in history.

21. Eusebius, *Evangelicae Praeparationis* X, XI (esp. XI.x.527a), trans. E. H. Gifford (Oxford, 1903), p. 567; E. R. Curtius, *European Literature and the Latin Middle Ages,* trans. W. R. Trask (New York, 1953), pp. 219–20; Tertullian, *Apology* xxi.14–15, trans. T. R. Glover (Loeb [London, 1931]), p. 109; Lactantius, *Divine Institutes* I.ix, xviii, trans. William Fletcher (ANCL, Vol. XXI [Edinburgh, 1871]), pp. 11–17; Justin Martyr, *First Apology* xxi, and *Dialogue with Trypho* lxix, trans. Marcus Dods *et al.* (ANCL, Vol. II [Edinburgh, 1867]), pp. 25–26, 184–86.

22. Augustine, *City of God* XVIII.39, trans. Marcus Dods (New York, 1950), p. 646; Lactantius, *Epitome of the Divine Institutes,* trans. William Fletcher (ANCL, Vol. XXII [Edinburgh, 1871]), pp. 94–95; Origen, *Contra Celsum* IV.21; VII.30, trans. Henry Chadwick (Cambridge, Eng., 1953), pp. 197–98, 418–19; Clement, *Stromata* IV.v, viii, trans. William Wilson (ANCL, Vol. XII [Edinburgh, 1869]), pp. 327–28, 339–42; Tertullian, *Apology* xix.2–4, Loeb, pp. 97–99.

23. Justin, *First Apology* liv, ANCL II, 53.

24. Clement, *Stromata* VI.v, ANCL XII, 327–28.

25. Mussato, "Epistola Fratris Joannini," *Historia Augusta Henrici VII ... Opera* (Venice, 1636), pp. 70–75; Boccaccio, *Genealogia Deorum Gentilium* XIV.viii, xiii; XV.vii–viii (Venice, 1547), fols. 252, 257^V–259^V, 275, 276^V.

26. E. Mâle, *The Gothic Image: Religious Art in France of the XIII Century,* trans. Dora Nussey (New York, 1958), pp. 339–40.

27. Nicolas Richelet, Preface to Pierre de Ronsard's *L'Hymne de l'Hercule Chrestien* (Paris, 1617), sig. A2^V; *The XV Bookes of P. Ovidius Naso,* trans. A[rthur] G[olding] (London, 1587), verse epis.

28. More, *An Explanation of the Grand Mystery of Godliness* (London, 1660), pp. 96, 148; Stillingfleet, *Origenes Sacrae, or a Rational Account of the Grounds of Christian Faith* (London, 1663), p. 598.

29. Harding, "Milton and the Renaissance Ovid," *Illinois Studies in Language and Literature,* XXX, No. 4 (1946), 98–99.

30. Ambrose, *In Expositionem ... Lucam,* Pat. Lat. XV, 1614: "Convenit recordari quemadmodum de paradiso in desertum Adam primus ejectus sit (Gen. iii.24); ut advertas quemadmodum de deserto ad paradisum Adam secundus reverterit."

31. Cowper, *Three Heavenly Treatises, concerning Christ* (London, 1612), pp. 122–23.

32. Vertue, *Christ and the Church: Or, Parallels* (London, 1659), pp. 4–5.

33. For discussion of the poem in terms of the triple equation see Elizabeth Pope's study, *Paradise Regained: The Tradition and the Poem* (Baltimore, 1947).

34. Jerome?, *Commentarius in Novum Testamentum,* Pat. Lat. XXX, 558–59; "Evangelium Secundum Matthaeum," *Glossa Ordinaria,* Pat. Lat. CXIV, 85–86; Peter Comestor, *Historia Scholastica,* Pat. Lat. CXCVIII, 1556;

Biblia Pauperum, ed. Jean Philibert Berjeau (facsimile; London, 1859), fig. x; Erasmus, *Paraphrase upon the Newe Testament,* trans. Nicholas Udall *et al.* (2 vols.; London, 1548), fol. xxxii^v; Bonaventure, *In Sacrosanctum Jesu Christi Evangelium Secundum Lucam* (Venice, 1574), pp. 71–72; Quistorpius, "In Matthaeum," *Annotationes in Omnes Libros Biblicos* (Frankfurt, 1648), p. 15; Zwingli, *Annotationes in Evangelium Matthai,* in *Opera* (4 vols.; Zurich, 1545), IV, fol. 9; Lapide, *Commentarius in Quatuor Evangelia* (Augsburg, 1767), I, 106; H[enry] A[insworth], *Annotations upon the First Book of Moses, Called Genesis* ([London], 1616), note to Gen. iii:6.

35. Hall, *Contemplations upon the History of the New Testament, Works* (3 vols.; London, 1628–62), III, 318.

36. Calvin, *A Harmonie upon the Three Evangelistes Matthewe, Marke, and Luke,* trans. E[usebius] P[agit] (London, 1610), p. 128.

37. Calvin, *Harmonie,* p. 129; Lancelot Andrewes, *The Wonderfull Combate (for Gods Glorie and Mans Salvation) betweene Christ and Satan* (London, 1592), pp. 21–41; Luther, *The Creation; a Commentary on the First Five Chapters of ... Genesis,* trans. Henry Cole (Edinburgh, 1858), pp. 196–99; Thomas Taylor, *Christs Combate and Conquest* ([Cambridge, Eng.], 1618), pp. 80–83; Christopher Blackwood, *Expositions and Sermons upon the Ten First Chapters of ... Matthew* (London, 1659 [1658]), p. 94; Geneva Bible, notes to Luke iv:3 ff.; William Perkins, *The Combate betweene Christ and the Devill Expounded, Workes* (3 vols.; Cambridge, Eng., 1616–18), III, 380–84; David Pareus, *In S. Matthaei Evangelium, Commentarius,* in *Operum Theologicorum* (2 vols.; Geneva, 1642), I, 620.

38. Blackwood, *Expositions,* p. 94.

39. Origen?, *Enarrationes in Job,* Pat. Graec. XVII, 62–63; [Jerome], "Excerpta ex Commentarii in Jobum," Pat. Lat. XXIII, 1539–42; Gregory, *Moralia in Job* (LF, Vol. XVIII [Oxford, 1844]), pp. 19–21, 137–39; Victorinus Strigelius, *Liber Job* (Leipzig [1571]), pp. 13–14; John Trapp, *Annotations upon the Old and New Testament* (5 vols.; London, 1654–62), II, 24; Joseph Caryl, *An Exposition upon ... Job* (12 vols.; London, 1643–70), I, 10.

40. Origen?, *In Job Commentarius, Opera Omnia,* ed. Charles Delarue (4 vols.; Paris, 1733–59), II, 878–79: "Non enim venit sicut pridem ab Adam cum victoria, sed sicut post à Job cum confusione. Adam enim olim seduxisti, sed Job post hoc non supplantasti. Adam de paradiso eradicasti, sed Job à sanctitate non avertisti." Gregory, *Moralia,* LF XVIII, 138.

41. Ambrose, *In Expositionem ... Lucam,* Pat. Lat. XV, 1624; Zeno, "De Job," Pat. Lat. XI, 442–43; *Glossa Ordinaria,* Pat. Lat. CXIII, 749–51; Helie Le Cordier, *L'Illustre Souffrant* (Paris, 1667), preface; Gregory, *Moralia in Job* (LF, Vol. XXXI [Oxford, 1850]), pp. 571–72; Jeremy Taylor, *The Great Exemplar of Sanctity and Holy Life* (London, 1653), p. 144.

42. Gregory, *Moralia in Job* (LF, Vol. XXIII [Oxford, 1847]), pp. 3–4.

43. Douay Bible I, 1060 (argument to Job).

44. Philippus Presbyterius, *In Historiam Job* (Basle, 1527), pp. 3–4, 211; Didymus, "Fragmenta in Job," Pat. Graec. XXXIX, 1122; George Hutcheson,

Exposition of the Book of Job (London, 1669), p. 49; Calvin, *Sermons ...upon...Job,* trans. Arthur Golding (London, 1574), pp. 746–47; Arthur Jackson, *Annotations upon...the Five Doctrinall, or Poeticall Books,* Part III (London, 1658), p. 298; Franciscus Titelmann, *Elucidatio Paraphrastica in Librum Job,* ed. J.-P. Migne (SSCC, Vol. XIII [Paris, 1861]), pp. 258–61; Joannes de Pineda, *Commentariorum in Job* (3 vols.; Venice, 1608), I, 1–4, 14, 40 (preface); Gasparus Sanctius, *In Librum Job* (London, 1625), pp. 8–12; Caryl, *Exposition...upon...Job* I, 63; XII, 885.

45. Zeno, "De Job," Pat. Lat. XI, 441–43: "Job justus dictus a Deo est. Ipse justitia, de cujus fonte omnes, qui beati sunt, gustant...Job verax est appellatus. At est vera veritas Dominus...Job dives fuit. Et quid ditius Domino? cujus sunt omnes divites servi: cujus est orbis totus, omnisque natura...Job diabolus ter tentavit. Similiter Evangelista perhibente (*Matth.* iv, *Luc.* iv), et Dominum ter est tentare conatus. Job facultates, quas habuit, amisit. Et Dominus coelestia sua bona amore nostro neglexit, pauperemque se fecit, ut nos divites faceret. Job filios furens diabolus interemit. Et Domini filios prophetas insanus populus Pharisaeus occidit. Job ulceribus maculatus est. Et Dominus sumendo carnem totius humani generis peccatorum est sordibus obsoletatus. Job uxor sua hortatur, ut peccet. Et Dominum, ut corruptelam seniorum sequatur, synagoga compellit. Job amici sui insultasse perhibentur. Et Domino sui sacerdotes, sui insultavere cultores. Job in sterquilinio pleno vermibus sedet. Dominus quoque in vero sterquilinio, id est, in hujus mundi coeno versatus est inter ebullientes diversis sceleribus ac libidinibus homines, qui veri sunt vermes. Job et sanitatem recepit, et facultatem. At Dominus resurgens non sanitatem tantum, sed immortalitatem in se credentibus praestitet, dominiumque totius naturae recuperavit...Job vicarios filios genuit. Dominus quoque post prophetas filios sanctos Apostolos procreavit. Job beatus quievit in pace. Dominus autem manet benedictus in aeternum ante saecula et a saeculis et in cuncta saecula saeculorum."

46. Gregory, *Moralia,* LF XVIII, 26–27.

47. *Ibid.,* 26, 27–29; Jerome, *In Librum Job,* Pat. Lat. XXVI, 655–56; Hugo of St. Victor, "De Scripturis," Pat. Lat. CLXXV, 12; Rabanus Maurus, *De Universo,* Pat. Lat. CXI, 50; Isidore, *Allegoriae Quaedam Sacrae Scripturae,* Pat. Lat. LXXXIII, 108.

48. Augustine, *The Harmony of the Evangelists,* trans. W. Findlay, in *Works,* ed. Marcus Dods (15 vols.; Edinburgh, 1871–76), VIII, 143–44; Rupertus Abbas, *In Evangelium S. Joannis Commentariorum,* Pat. Lat. CLXIX, 487–88; Hildebertus, "Sermones de Sanctis, LXXII," Pat. Lat. CLXXI, 690; Bullinger, *Fiftie Godlie and Learned Sermons,* trans. H. I. (London, 1587), p. 698.

49. Augustine, *Harmony, Works* VIII, 142, 144.

50. Calvin, *Institutes* II.xv, fol. 91^v.

51. Luther, *Colloquia Mensalia,* p. 103.

52. Calvin, *Institutes* II.xv, fols. 91^v–92.

53. Ames, *The Marrow of Sacred Divinity* (London, 1642), p. 86; Wol-

lebius, *The Abridgement of Christian Divinity,* trans. Alexander Ross (London, 1650), p. 107.

54. Luther, *Colloquia Mensalia,* p. 109.

55. Calvin, *Institutes* II.xv, fols. 94–94ᵛ.

56. Ames, *Marrow,* p. 87; Wollebius, *Abridgement,* p. 107.

57. Luther, *Colloquia Mensalia,* pp. 109–10; Calvin, *Institutes* II.xv, fol. 92ᵛ. Fixler's study of the various conceptions of the kingdom of God or Christ prevalent in the seventeenth century greatly illuminates such statements.

58. Ames, *Marrow,* p. [88]; Wollebius, *Abridgement,* p. 107.

59. For similar views of Christ's threefold office and the two modes of its exercise, see William Perkins, *The Foundation of Christian Religion* (Cambridge, Eng., 1608), p. 190; Richard Baxter, *The Life of Faith* (London, 1660), p. 3; Trapp, *Annotations* I, 282 (introduction to Exodus).

60. *CE* XV, 287–89, 291, 297, 299–301.

61. *CE* XV, 301.

62. Ames, *Marrow,* pp. 97–98.

63. Udall, *The Combate betwixt Christ and the Devill* (London [1590?]), sig. [A6]; Andrewes, *The Wonderfull Combate,* pp. 14–15.

64. Calvin, *Harmonie,* p. 125.

65. H[enry] More, *Grand Mystery of Godliness,* p. 106; John Knox, *An Exposition upon Matthew IV, concerning the Temptation of Christ in the Wilderness* (1556), *Works,* ed. David Laing (6 vols.; Edinburgh, 1846–64), IV, 100; John Lightfoot, *The Harmony of the Foure Evangelists* (2 vols.; London, 1644–47), I, 172–82; II, 9–10; Henry Hammond, *A Paraphrase, and Annotations upon All the Books of the New Testament* (London, 1659), p. 19; William Perkins, *Combate, Workes* III, 371; John Diodati, *Pious and Learned Annotations upon the Holy Bible* (London, 1648), pp. 2–3 (argument to Matthew).

66. Aquinas, *Summa Theologica,* Pt. III, Q. 41, Art. 4, trans. Dominican Fathers (3 vols.; New York, 1947–48), II, 2243.

67. Perkins, *Combate, Workes* III, 372; Baxter, *A Paraphrase of the New Testament* (London, 1685), note to Matt. iv:2; Diodati, *Annotations,* pp. 2–3 (argument to Matthew); Blackwood, *Expositions,* p. 89.

68. Perkins, *Combate, Workes* III, 399, 380–99.

69. Taylor, *Christs Combate,* p. 83. See also pp. 80–122, 161–92, 350–91.

CHAPTER VIII

1. Udall, *The Combate betwixt Christ and the Devill* (London [1590?]), sig. C8ᵛ.

2. Daniel Brenius (D. Van Breen), *Breves in Vetus & Novum Testamentum Annotationes,* in *Opera Theologica,* Part II (Amsterdam, 1666), fol. 5: "Erat & Joannes praedicans in deserto cap.3.1, sed Christus ab eo loco in vastiorem actus est solitudinem, ubi ferae degebant, Marc. 1.13, ad complementum veteris figurae. Nam & populus Israeliticus typus Christi ejusque ecclesiae, in

desertum ductus est, ibi tentatus sicut Adam in paradiso, promissa terrae haereditate excidit. At Christus victor diaboli paradisum recuperavit."

3. Cyril of Jerusalem, *Catecheticae Orationes Quinque ad Recens Baptizatos,* Pat. Graec. XXXIII, 1067; Ambrose, *De Sacramentis,* trans. T. Thompson (London, 1950), pp. 127–28; Augustine, *Contra Faustum* XII.29–30, *Works,* ed. Marcus Dods (15 vols.; Edinburgh, 1871–76), V, 224–26; *Glossa Ordinaria,* Pat. Lat. XIII, 291, 295; Douay Bible I, 187–90; Calvin, *Commentaries on the Four Last Books of Moses,* trans. Charles W. Bingham (4 vols.; Edinburgh, 1852–55), I, 61, 221, 270; Hall, *Contemplations upon the Principall Passages of the Holy Storie, Works* (3 vols.; London, 1628–62), II, 903–5, 914.

4. H[enry] A[insworth], *Annotations upon the First Book of Moses, Called Genesis* ([London], 1616), preface.

5. Augustine, *Harmony, Works* VIII, 203–4; Bede?, *Quaestionum super Exodum,* Pat. Lat. XCIII, 370–73; Geneva Bible, fols. 48–49 (argument to Numbers); John Diodati, *Pious and Learned Annotations upon the Holy Bible* (London, 1648), p. 34 (argument to Exodus); John Trapp, *Annotations upon the Old and New Testament* (5 vols.; London, 1654–62), I, 264.

6. *Biblia Pauperum,* ed. Jean Philibert Berjeau (London, 1859), fig. ix.1.

7. Calvin, *Four Last Books of Moses* IV, 346.

8. The bases for this interpretation were John vi:51, "I am the living bread, which came downe from heaven," and I Cor. x:4, "they dranke of that spirituall Rock that folowed them: and that Rocke was Christ." See Basil, *Liber de Spiritu Sancto,* Pat. Graec. XXXII, 122–27; Theodoret, *In Exodum,* Pat. Graec. LXXX, 258; Ambrose, *De Sacramentis,* p. 144; Augustine, *Contra Faustum* XII.29, *Works* V, 224–25; [Prosper], *De Promissionibus,* Pat. Lat. LI, 765; Isidore, *In Exodum,* Pat. Lat. LXXXIII, 298–99; Bede?, *Super Exodum,* Pat. Lat. XCIII, 372; *Glossa Ordinaria,* Pat. Lat. CXIII, 461; Douay Bible I, 209–10; Calvin, *Four Last Books of Moses* I, 270; Henry Ainsworth, *Annotations upon . . . Exodus* (London, 1617), notes to Exod. xvi–xvii; Hall, *Contemplations upon . . . the Holy Storie, Works* II, 906–12.

9. [Prosper], *De Promissionibus,* Pat. Lat. LI, 781–82; *Glossa Ordinaria,* Pat. Lat. CXIII, 419–21; Alcuin, *Commentariorum in Apocalypsin,* Pat. Lat. C, 1104–5; Douay Bible I, 370–74 (notes to Numb. xxv:1–2); Geneva Bible, fol. 60 (note to Numb. xxiv:14); Calvin, *Four Last Books of Moses* IV, 199, 223; John Marbecke, *The Lyves of Holy Sainctes, Prophetes, Patriarches, and Others, Contayned in Holye Scripture* (London, 1574), p. 57; Diodati, *Annotations,* p. 105; Ainsworth, *Annotations upon . . . Numbers* (London, 1619), note to Numb. xxv:1.

10. Origen, "Homilia XIV, Item de Balaam," Pat. Graec. XII, 676–83; Rabanus Maurus, *Enarrationum in Librum Numerorum,* Pat. Lat. CVIII, 729–31; Cornelius à Lapide, *In Pentateuchum Mosis Commentaria* (Paris, 1630), p. 841; Isidore, *Allegoriae Quaedam Sacrae Scripturae,* Pat. Lat. LXXXIII, 110; Alcuin, *Commentariorum in Apocalypsin,* Pat. Lat. C, 1104–5.

11. Calvin, *Four Last Books of Moses* IV, 234.

12. *CE* III, Part I, 53–54.

13. Daniel Dyke, *Two Treatises. The One, of Repentence: The Other, of Christ's Temptations* (London, 1616), p. 222.

14. Rupertus Abbas, *De Gloria et Honore Filii Hominis super Matthaeum,* Pat. Lat. CLXVIII, 1375: "Igitur vocatus ex AEgypto puer Israel, Filius Dei, Dominus Jesus, postquam habitavit Nazareth, ubi et nutritus est, postquam aquas baptismi transivit, ductus est in desertum a spiritu, et cum jejunasset quadraginta diebus et quadraginta noctibus, tentatus et ipse, et fidelis inventus est in tribus tentationibus, ut patrum suorum, filiorum Israel, totidem et easdem tentationem vacuaret atque deleret: qui educti de terra AEgypti, postquam aquas maris Rubri transierunt, quadraginta annis per desertum circumducti sunt et tentati sunt, quia tentaverunt et infideles inventi sunt."

15. *Ibid.,* cols. 1375–79.

16. Paschasius Radburtus, *Expositio in Evangelium Matthaei,* Pat. Lat. CXX, 191.

17. Durant, *L'Histoire de la Tentation de Nostre-Seigneur Jesus Christ* (Geneva, 1627), p. 78.

18. Manton, *Christs Temptation and Transfiguration* (London, 1685; pub. posthumously), p. 41.

19. Hall, *Contemplations upon...the New Testament, Works* III, 39.

20. Cyril of Jerusalem, *Catecheticae Orationes Quinque,* Pat. Graec. XXXIII, 1067; Origen, *In Exodum Homilia VI,* Pat. Graec. XII, 337–39; Theodoret, "Interrogatio XXVII," *In Exodum,* Pat. Graec. LXXX, 258; Isidore, *In Exodum,* Pat. Lat. LXXXIII, 290–98; Eusebius of Caesarea, *De Demonstratione Evangelica* III.ii, Pat. Graec. XXII, 170; Rabanus Maurus, *Commentaria in Exodum,* Pat. Lat. CVIII, 17–18; Calvin, *Four Last Books of Moses* I, 61–62, 221–22.

21. Vertue, *Christ and the Church: Or, Parallels* (London, 1659), p. 27.

22. Lapide, *In Pentateuchum,* p. 828: "Mosis legis, Josue Christi figuram gerit. itaque sicut Moses populum eduxit ex AEgypto, Josue verò eundem in Chanaan introduxit: ita lex ab impietate liberat credentes, Evangelica autem gratia introducit eos in regnum caelorum." See also Origen, *Homiliae in Librum Jesu Nave,* Pat. Graec. XII, 825–46; Augustine, *Contra Faustum* XII.30–31, *Works* V, 225–26; Rabanus Maurus, *De Universo,* Pat. Lat. CXI, 52; Douay Bible I, 469; *The Dutch Annotations upon the Whole Bible,* trans. Theodore Haak (London, 1657), argument to Joshua; Trapp, *Annotations* I, 1 (introduction to Joshua).

23. *CE* XVI, 111.

24. *Dutch Annotations,* note to Deut. xviii:15; see also [Prosper], *De Promissionibus,* Pat. Lat. LI, 767; Douay Bible I, 206 (note to Deut. xviii:15); Lapide, *In Pentateuchum,* p. 455; Trapp, *Annotations* I, 279.

25. *CE* XV, 287.

26. Eusebius, *De Demonstratione Evangelica* III.ii, Pat. Graec. XXII, 170; [Prosper], *De Promissionibus,* Pat. Lat. LI, 767.

27. Vertue, *Parallels*, p. 34.

28. Diodati, *Annotations*, p. 48 (notes to Exod. xvii:9–11).

29. Trapp, *Annotations* I, 268–69.

30. Augustine, "Psalmum CXVIII," *Enarrationes in Psalmos*, Pat. Lat. XXXVII, 1560; Gregory the Great, *In Septem Psalmos Poenitentiales Expositio*, Pat. Lat. LXXIX, 551; Rabanus Maurus, *Allegoriae in Universam Sacram Scripturam*, Pat. Lat. CXII, 932; Calvin, *The Institution of the Christian Religion* II.xv, trans. T[homas] N[orton] (London, 1561), fol. 91ᵛ–92.

31. Peter Martyr [Vermigli], *Common Places* (London, 1583), p. 23.

32. Augustine, *Harmony*, *Works* VIII, 204; Isidore, *In Exodum*, Pat. Lat. LXXXIII, 308; Bede?, *Super Exodum*, Pat. Lat. XCIII, 378; *Glossa Ordinaria*, Pat. Lat. CXIII, 291; Lapide, *In Pentateuchum*, p. 901; Robert Boyle, *Some Considerations touching the Style of the H. Scriptures* (London, 1661), pp. 83–84; Thomas Cartwright, *A Confutation of the Rhemists Translation* (Leyden, 1618), p. 17; Calvin, *Four Last Books of Moses* I, 392; Christopher Blackwood, *Expositions and Sermons upon ... Matthew* (London, 1659), p. 91.

33. Hall, *Contemplations upon ... the New Testament*, *Works* III, 175, 185.

34. Ambrose, *Expositio super Septem Visiones Libri Apocalypsis*, Pat. Lat. XVII, 834–36; [Prosper], *De Promissionibus*, Pat. Lat. LI, 802–3; *Glossa Ordinaria*, Pat. Lat. CXIII, 606; Isidore, *Allegoria Quaedam Sacrae Scripturae*, Pat. Lat. LXXXIII, 113; Rabanus Maurus, *Commentaria in Libros Quattuor Regum*, Pat. Lat. CIX, 206–7.

35. Clement, "The Instructor," trans. William Wilson (ANCL, Vol. IV [Edinburgh, 1867]), p. 301; Hall, *Contemplations upon ... the Holy Storie*, *Works* II, 1264–69; Geneva Bible, fol. 129ᵛ (notes to I Kings xvii:6–10).

36. Hall, *Contemplations upon ... the Holy Storie*, *Works* II, 1267.

37. Manton, *Christs Temptation and Transfiguration*, p. 9; Ambrose, *Expositio super ... Libri Apocalypsis*, Pat. Lat. XVII, 834–36; Gregory the Great, *XL Homiliarum in Evangelia*, Pat. Lat. LXXVI, 1217; Isidore, *Allegoriae Quaedam Sacrae Scripturae*, Pat. Lat. LXXXIII, 113; Rabanus Maurus, *Commentaria in Libros Quattuor Regum*, Pat. Lat. CIX, 206–7.

38. Augustine, *City of God* XX.29, trans. Marcus Dods (New York, 1950), p. 757.

39. *Ibid.*, X.27, p. 333; Rabanus Maurus, *De Universo*, Pat. Lat. CXI, 420–22; Vincent of Beauvais, *Speculum Historiale* (Douai, 1624), pp. 79–80; Sebastiano Castalione, *Sibyllina Oracula* (Basle, 1546), pp. 129–43.

40. Augustine, *Contra Faustum* XIII.14, *Works* V, 251; Lactantius, *Divine Institutes* I.vi, trans. William Fletcher (ANCL, Vol. XXI [Edinburgh, 1871]), pp. 17–18.

41. Peter Martyr, *Common Places*, pp. 19, 92.

42. [Prosper], *De Promissionibus*, Pat. Lat. LI, 781–82; Ainsworth, *Annotations upon ... Numbers*, note to Numb. xxiv:17; Douay Bible I, 373 (note to Numb. xxiv:17); Calvin, *Four Last Books of Moses* IV, 219–22; Diodati, *Anno-*

tations, p. 104; Trapp, *Annotations* I, 381; *Dutch Annotations*, note to Numb. xxiv:17.

43. Calvin, *Four Last Books of Moses* IV, 187; Ainsworth, *Annotations upon ...Numbers*, note to Numb. xxii:12; Diodati, *Annotations*, pp. 102–3; Hall, *Contemplations upon...the Holy Storie, Works* II, 951–56.

44. Calvin, *Four Last Books of Moses* IV, 199, 185, 203.

45. *CE* III, Part I, 363.

46. Schultz, *Milton and Forbidden Knowledge* (New York, 1955), p. 235.

47. See above, p. 185.

48. Don Cameron Allen, *The Harmonious Vision* (Baltimore, 1954), pp. 119–20.

49. Michael Fixler, "The Unclean Meats of the Mosaic Law and the Banquet Scene in *Paradise Regained*," *MLN*, LXX (1955), 573–77.

50. *The Prefaces to...Luther's Bible*, ed. T. A. Readwin (London, 1863), p. 6.

CHAPTER IX

1. See above pp. 177–78, and notes 33–38 to chap. vii.

2. Hughes, ed., *Paradise Regained, the Minor Poems, and Samson Agonistes* (New York, 1937), p. 482n.

3. Torquato Tasso, *Godfrey of Bulloigne; or the Recoverie of Jerusalem* X.64, trans. Edward Fairfax (London, 1600), p. 192.

4. Sir Thomas Malory, *Le Morte D'Arthur* XI.ii–iii, viii; IV.xxi; XIV.ix–x, in *Works*, ed. Eugène Vinaver (3 vols.; Oxford, 1947), II, 793–97, 804–6; I, 164–66; II, 917–20.

5. Cf. *PL* IX.735–43, which describes the appeal of the apple to all the five senses.

6. Cf. *PL* IX.532–38.

7. Jerome, *Expositio Quatuor Evangeliorum*, Pat. Lat. XXX, 559: "ut qui primum hominem per gulam vicit, a secundo per abstinentiam vincatur."

8. Gregory the Great, *XL Homiliarum in Evangelia*, Pat. Lat. LXXVI, 1136: "Avaritia enim non solum pecuniae est, sed etiam altitudinis. Recte enim avaritia dicitur cum supra modum sublimitas ambitur." Cf. Rabanus Maurus, *Commentariorum in Matthaeum*, Pat. Lat. CVII, 784–85.

9. Elizabeth M. Pope, *Paradise Regained: The Tradition and the Poem* (Baltimore, 1947), pp. 67–69.

10. Samuel, *Plato and Milton* (Ithaca, N.Y., 1947), pp. 70–71.

11. Plato, *The Republic* IX.573*b*, 575, 577*c*; VIII.561*a–c*, 553*c*, 548*c*–549*a*, in *The Dialogues*, trans. Benjamin Jowett (4 vols.; Oxford, 1953), II, 443, 445, 448, 429–30, 420, 413–14.

12. Dio Chrysostom, "The Fourth Discourse, on Kingship," trans. J. W. Cohoon [*Works*] (Loeb [5 vols.; London, 1932–51]), I, 207.

13. Spenser, in *The Faerie Queene* II.vii, presented Guyon in the Cave

of Mammon tempted by wealth, then by ambition, then by pleasure; Giles Fletcher in *Christs Victorie, and Triumph* II.41–58 (Cambridge, Eng., (1610) pp. 38–42, portrayed Christ tempted first by a sensuous garden, then by Avarice, then by Ambition, and finally by Pangloretta; Sir Richard Barckley in *A Discourse of the Felicitie of Man* (London, 1598) arranged according to an ascending scale of value the lives devoted, respectively, to pleasure, wealth, ambitious glory, virtuous action, and contemplation.

14. Cicero, *De Officiis* I.xxvii–xxxiii, trans. Walter Miller (Loeb [London, 1913]), pp. 95–121.

15. *CE* XVII, 213.

16. *De Officiis* I.xxxiii.18, Loeb, p. 121.

17. Xenophon, *Memorabilia* II.i.21–26, trans. E. C. Marchant (Loeb [London, 1923]), pp. 95–97.

18. *Memorabilia* II.i.27–33, Loeb, pp. 97–103.

19. "De Diis Gentium et Illorum Allegoris," *Scriptores Rerum Mythicarum Latini Tres,* ed. G. H. Bode (2 vols. [Celles, 1834]), I, 247; Boccaccio, *Genealogia Deorum Gentilium* (Venice, 1547), fols. 16–16ᵛ; Albricus, *De Deorum Imaginibus* (Basle, 1570), p. 169. Milton has cited Hercules as a type of Christ before: In the hymn *On the Morning of Christ's Nativity* (st. 25) Hercules strangling snakes in his cradle foreshadows Christ's control over Satan in his infancy; and in *The Passion* Christ's redemptive mission is spoken of in terms of Hercules' labors—"Most perfect *Hero,* tried in heaviest plight/ Of labors huge and hard, too hard for human wight" (ll. 13–14).

20. An engraving by Cristoff Murer represents Pleasure as a nude woman sitting beside a table laden with grapes and liquor and surrounded by musical instruments; another by Jan Wierx after Crispen Van der Broeck shows the path of Virtue leading up a steep mountain and that of Pleasure leading down to a banquet table where many people are feasting, drinking, dancing, and playing instruments; still another copied after J. Saenredam shows Virtue holding a picture of people laboriously climbing a mountain, and Pleasure pointing to a picture of a banquet scene complete with wine-pouring, drinking, gourmandizing, and love-making. See Erwin Panofsky, *Hercules am Scheidewege und Andere Antike Bildstoffe in der Neueren Kunst* (Berlin, 1930), pl. xxv, fig. 46; pl. xl, fig. 61; pl. xxxix, fig. 60.

21. Andrew Runni Anderson, "Heracles and His Successors," *Harvard Studies in Classical Philology,* XXXIX (1928), pp. 7–58.

22. Dante, *De Monarchia* II.x, in *Latin Works* (London, 1904), p. 213, equates Hercules and Antaeus with David and Goliath; George Sandys, ed., *Ovid's Metamorphosis Englished, Mythologiz'd, and Represented in Figures* (Oxford, 1632), p. 336, records that Samson and Hercules are thought by some to be the same man; Cyril of Alexandria, *In Jonam Prophetam Commentarius,* Pat. Graec. LXXI, 615, points to the story of Hercules and Cacus as an analogue to that of Jonah and the whale. See Arnold J. Toynbee,

A Study of History VI (London, 1951), Annex II to V.C. ii (a), pp. 465–76, for a modern study of the Hercules-Christ analogues, listing some twenty-four.

23. Pierre de Ronsard, *L'Hymne de l'Hercule Chrestien* (Paris, 1617), preface and commentary. See Jacobus Bonus, *De Raptu Cerberi* (Basle [1538]); John Trapp, *Annotations upon the Old and New Testament* (5 vols.; London, 1654–62), I, 25; Alexander Ross, *Mystagogus Poeticus, or the Muses Interpreter* (London, 1647), pp. 119–20.

24. Augustine, *City of God* XVIII.12, trans. Marcus Dods (New York, 1950), p. 619; Lactantius, *Divine Institutes* I.ix, trans. William Fletcher (ANCL, Vol. XXI [Edinburgh, 1871]), p. 22.

25. Seneca, "De Constantia Sapientis," *Moral Essays,* trans. John W. Basore (Loeb [3 vols.; London, 1958]), I, 51.

26. Epictetus, *The Discourses as Reported by Arrian, the Manual, and Fragments* III.xxvi.30–32, trans. W. A. Oldfather (Loeb [2 vols.; London, 1928]), II, 237.

27. Dio Chrysostom, "The First Discourse, on Kingship," Loeb, I, 31–47.

28. Sandys, *Ovid,* p. 326; Georg Pictor, *Theologia Mythologica* (Fribourg, 1532), p. 37; Jean Baudoin, *Iconologie, ou, Explication Nouvelle de Plusiers Images, Emblemes ... de C. Ripa,* Part II (Paris, 1644), p. 85; Ross, *Mystagogus,* p. 116.

29. Thomas Lodge, trans., *The Famous and Memorable Workes of Josephus* (London, 1609), p. 350.

30. *Speculum Humanae Salvationis* (MS Lat. 9584, Bibliothèque Nationale, Paris), chap. xxxix; A. H. Huth, ed., *The Mirroure of Mans Salvacionne* xxxix (London, 1888), pp. 134–37 (a fifteenth-century English translation of the *Speculum*).

31. Cicero, *De Officiis* III.iii–iv, Loeb, pp. 283–85, distinguishes between the perfection of the Stoic "wise men" such as Hercules and Odysseus and the "constant observance of mean duties" by reason of which Fabricius, Cato, the two Decii, the two Scipios, and others were said to bear "a certain semblance and likeness to wise men."

32. Augustine, *City of God* V.18, pp. 169–70. Q. Curtius for the sake of his country threw himself into a ravine and committed suicide, obeying an oracle which proclaimed that the Romans should cast there the best thing they possessed, if they would avoid destruction. Cf. Tasso, *Della Virtù Heroica* (Venice, 1582), fols. 9–9^V.

33. Thomas Elyot, *The Boke Named the Governour* (London, 1534 [1537]), fols. 200–200^V. Milton had cited Curius to similar effect in a letter to Thomas Young, 21 July 1628, commending Young's country retirement, "where you, with moderate means but regal spirit, like some Serranus or Curius, placidly reign in your little farm, and, contemning fortune, hold as it were a triumph over riches, ambition, pomp, luxury, and whatever the herd of men admire" (*CE* XII, 15).

34. Seneca, "Epistle CXX," *Epistulae Morales,* trans. Richard M. Gummere (Loeb [3 vols.; London, 1925]), III, 383. See also Aulus Gellius, *The Attic Nights* I.xiv, trans. John C. Rolfe (Loeb [3 vols.; London, 1927]), I, 71–73.

35. Seneca, "De Providentia" iii.6, Loeb, *Moral Essays* I, 19.

36. Livy, *History of Rome* III.xxvi.7, trans. B. O. Foster *et al.* (Loeb [14 vols.; London, 1922–]), II, 89; Augustine, *City of God* V.18, pp. 169–70.

37. Augustine, *City of God* I.24, pp. 29–30.

38. Seneca, "Ad Helviam . . . de Consolatione" xii.5–6, Loeb, *Moral Essays* II, 461; Silius Italicus, *Punica* VI.304–550, trans. J. D. Duff (Loeb [2 vols.; London, 1934]), I, 304–20; Seneca, "De Providentia" iii.9, Loeb, *Moral Essays* I, 21; Cicero, *De Officiis* III.xxvi–xxx, Loeb, pp. 377–91; J. D. M. [Jean Desmarets de Saint-Sorlin?], *Regulus, ou le Vray Généreux* (Paris, 1671).

39. Theocritus, "Idyll XVII," *The Greek Bucolic Poets,* trans. J. M. Edmonds, (Loeb [London, 1912]), p. 213; Plutarch, *The Lives of the Noble Grecians and Romaines,* trans. Thomas North (London, 1603), pp. 673–74, 687. E. A. Wallis Budge, trans., *The History of Alexander the Great, Being the Syriac Version of the Pseudo-Callisthenes* (Cambridge, Eng., 1889), and Budge, *The Alexander Book in Ethiopia* (London, 1933), present Alexander as a Christian convert in anticipation, a prophet of Christ, and the conqueror of Gog and Magog.

40. Plutarch, *Lives,* pp. 683–84.

41. Plutarch, *The Philosophie, Commonlie Called, the Morals,* trans. Philemon Holland (London, 1603), p. 1270.

42. Seneca, *De Beneficiis* I.xiii.1–3, Loeb, *Moral Essays* III, 41–43.

43. Dio Chrysostom, "The Fourth Discourse, on Kingship," Loeb, I, 195–201. See also pp. 171–73.

44. Clarke, *The Life & Death of Alexander the Great* (London, 1665), p. 64; cf. Seneca, "De Ira" III.xvii.1, Loeb, *Moral Essays* I, 299; Livy, *History* IX.xviii.1–7, Loeb, IV, 231–33; Clement, *Protreptikos, or Exhortation to the Heathen,* trans. William Wilson (ANCL, Vol. IV [Edinburgh, 1867]), p. 90; George Sandys, *Ovid,* p. 328.

45. Plutarch, *Lives,* pp. 717, 714. Cf. Anderson, "Heracles and His Successors," pp. 19–41.

46. Cicero, "Epistulae ad Atticum," cited in *On the Commonwealth,* trans. G. H. Sabine and S. B. Smith (Columbus, Ohio, 1929), p. 220; Cicero, *De Officiis* III.xxi.83, Loeb, p. 357; Samuel Clarke, *The Life & Death of Julius Caesar* (London, 1665), p. 40.

47. Sandys, *Ovid,* p. 319; Silius Italicus, *Punica* XV.1–137, Loeb, II, 325–35.

48. Cicero, *De Re Publica* VI.xxiii–xxiv, trans. Clinton W. Keyes, (Loeb [London, 1928]), p. 279.

49. Lactantius, *Divine Institutes* I.xviii, ANCL XXI, 50–51.

50. Justin Martyr, *First Apology* v, trans. Marcus Dods *et al.* (ANCL, Vol. II [Edinburgh, 1867]), p. 10; *Second Apology* x, ANCL II, 80.

51. Plato, *The Apology* 22a, *Dialogues* I, 346; Seneca, *De Beneficiis*

VII.xxiv.1–2, Loeb, *Moral Essays* III, 511; Gellius, *Attic Nights* II.i.1–5, Loeb, I, 123.

52. Lucian, "Heracles," trans. A. M. Harmon [*Works*] (Loeb [7 vols.; London, 1921–61]), I, 67.

53. L. Gregorius Gyraldus, *De Deis Gentium* (London, 1565), p. 281; Vincenzo Cartari, *The Fountaine of Ancient Fiction,* trans. Richard Linche (London, 1599), sigs. R4^V–S; Gerardus Joannes Vossius, *De Theologia Gentili* (4 vols.; Amsterdam, 1641), II, 384.

54. Grierson, "John Milton," *The Criterion,* VIII (1928), 254; Tillyard, *Milton* (London, 1930), pp. 305–6; Hughes, "The Christ of *Paradise Regained* and the Renaissance Heroic Tradition," *SP,* XXXV (1938), 254–77. Samuel, *Plato and Milton,* pp. 69–95.

55. Cicero, *De Finibus Bonorum et Malorum* II.viii, trans. H. Rackham (Loeb [London, 1914]), pp. 107–9.

56. The writer of Proverbs stated the same commonplace, "hee that ruleth his spirit [is better] than he that taketh a city" (xvi:32).

57. Aristotle, *Nicomachean Ethics* I.vii.1098*a*, in *The Basic Works of Aristotle,* ed. Richard McKeon (New York, 1941), p. 943.

58. *Ibid.,* IV.ii.1123*b*–1124*b*, pp. 991–93.

59. *CE* XVII, 241.

60. Aristotle, *Ethics* I.viii.1099*b*, *Basic Works,* p. 945; X.viii.1178*a*–1179*a*, p. 1107.

61. See Bruno, *De gl'Heroici Furori,* Part I (Paris [London], 1585), sigs. D2–D2^V, G6–G7^V; Tasso, *Della Vertù Heroica;* Baldassare Castiglione, *The Courtier,* Book IV, trans. Thomas Hobys (London, 1588), sigs. Mm8^V–Pp4. See Hughes, "Christ...and the Renaissance Heroic Tradition," pp. 254–77.

62. Cicero, *De Finibus* III.xxii.75, Loeb, p. 295.

63. Dio Chrysostom, "The Eighth Discourse, on Virtue," Loeb, I, 385, 391.

64. Seneca, "Epistle CXVI," *Epistulae Morales,* Loeb, III, 333; "Epistle CXXIII," *Epistulae Morales,* Loeb, III, 435; "Epistle CX," *Epistulae Morales,* Loeb, III, 275–77; "Epistle LXXIII," *Epistulae Morales,* Loeb, II, 111–13.

65. Plato, *Republic* IX.580*c*, *Dialogues* II, 452.

66. *Republic* IX.591–92, *Dialogues* II, 466–67.

67. *Republic* X.613*a*, *Dialogues* II, 490.

68. Augustine, *De Urbis Excido,* Pat. Lat. XL, 717; Isidore, *Allegoriae Quaedem Sacrae Scripturae,* Pat. Lat. LXXXIII, 114; Godefridus Abbas, *Homiliae in Diversos Scripturae Lacos,* Pat. Lat CLXXIV, 1116–21.

69. John Diodati, *Pious and Learned Annotations upon the Holy Bible* (London, 1648), p. 600 (note to Dan. i:8). Henry More, *An Illustration of Those Two Abstreuse Books in Holy Scripture, the Book of Daniel, and the Revelation of S. John* (London, 1685), ascribes the fast to the fact that the food was offered to idols (p. 4). John Trapp, *Annotations* III, 522, identifies the food as forbidden by law, as offered to idols, as a source of scandal to others if eaten, and as evidence of the King's inimical intention

to wean the Israelites from their religion. *The Dutch Annotations upon the Whole Bible,* trans. Theodore Haak (London, 1657), note to Dan. i:8, explains that the food was forbidden both by the Old Law, and because it had been offered to idols.

70. Calvin, *Commentaries...upon the Prophet Daniell,* trans. A[rthur] G[olding] (London, 1570), p. 3; Geneva Bible, fol. 104 (note to Dan. i:8).

71. Augustine, *City of God* XVIII.34, p. 641; Cornelius à Lapide, *Commentaria in Quatuor Prophetas Maiores* (Paris, 1622), pp. ii–iii (argument to Daniel); John Calvin, *Commentaries...upon...Daniell,* sig. C3^V (preface).

72. *Mirroure of Mans Salvacionne* xiii, p. 51; Godefridus Tilmannus, *Allegoriae Simul et Tropologiae* (Paris, 1551).

73. Vertue, *Christ and the Church: Or, Parallels* (London, 1659), p. 56.

74. Geneva Bible, fol. 104 (note to I Sam. xvi:18).

75. *Mirroure* xiii, pp. 52–53; cf. Ambrose, *Expositio super Septem Visiones Libri Apocalypsis,* Pat. Lat. XVII, 833–34; *Glossa Ordinaria,* Pat. Lat. CXIV, 85–86; Venerable Bede, *Quaestiones super Regum Libros,* Pat. Lat. XCIII, 452.

76. Isidore, *Allegoriae Quaedam Sacrae Scripturae,* Pat. Lat. LXXXIII, 112; Hugo of St. Victor, "Sermo LIX," Pat. Lat. CLXXVII, 1077–78; Tilmannus, *Allegoriae Simul et Tropologiae,* p. 146.

77. Cornelius à Lapide, *Commentarius in Josue, Judicum, Ruth* (Antwerp, 1718), pp. 91–92 (argument to Judges).

78. Hall, *Contemplations upon...the Holy Storie, Works* (3 vols.; London, 1628–62), II, 999; Rabanus Maurus, *Commentaria in...Judicum,* Pat. Lat. CVIII, 1155–61; Hugo, "Sermo LXIII," Pat. Lat. CLXXVII, 1095–96; Bede, *Quaestiones super Librum Judicum,* Pat. Lat. XCIII, 424–26; Augustine, *Quaestiones in Heptateucheum,* Pat. Lat. XXXIV, 803–5; Peter Damian, *Collectanea in Vetus Testamentum,* Pat. Lat. CXLV, 1081–82.

79. Peter Martyr, *Most Fruitfull and Learned Commentarie upon... Judges* (London, 1564), p. 147.

80. Peter Martyr, *ibid.,* p. 141; Peter Damian, *Collectanea in Vetus Testamentum,* Pat. Lat. CXLV, 1082–83; Diodati, *Annotations,* p. 150 (note to Judges vii:16); Douay Bible I, 531n (note to Judges vii:9).

81. Vertue, *Parallels,* pp. 43–44; cf. Hugo of St. Victor, "De Filia Jephthe," Pat. Lat. CLXXVII, 323–34.

82. [Prosper], *De Promissionibus,* Pat. Lat. LI, 789: "Haec itaque figurata mysteria ad Judicem Ducemque nostrum Jesum Dominum ita referunt... unicam virginem carnem suam, tanquam filiam immolasse."

83. The allusion is to Job xviii:12, when Bildad says of the wicked man, "His strength shalbe hunger-bitten, and destruction shalbe ready at his side."

84. See above, pp. 20–26.

85. Hieremias Drexelius, *Jobus Divinae Providentiae Theatrum* (Antwerp, 1655), pp. 193–94, 216: "Historia tam sacra quàm profana omni aevo eximios quosdam homines in exemplum aemulandae virtutis proposuit.

Homerus regem Agamemnonem producit, ut principem oppidò prudentem, in qui alii, quid se deceat, velut in speculo contemplentur. Sic Achillem ob oculos ponit. Ita Maro AEneam sapientem & pium regem praedicat. Ita suum poëtae Herculem canunt, ubique invictum, omnibus terrarum monstris imperio novercali objectum, qui labore ac patientiâ domuisset omnia. Ita summ Xenophon Cyrum extollit, in quo reges & monarchae omnes, heroicae virtutis specimen spectarent. Sed multa sane finuerunt hi boni scriptores de iis, quos imitandos in alto statuerunt. . . . Non majorem Regulus in suo ad hostem reditu fidem praestitit, quam in perferendo supplicio patientiam exhibuit & constantiam. Unde triplex hodie laus memoriam hominis comitatur; justitiae una, altera fortitudinis, tertia patientiae admirandae. Sed vale, mi Regule, exemplis grandioribus triumphat Jobus noster."

86. Gregory, *Moralia in Job* (LF, Vol. XVIII [Oxford, 1844]), p. 26 (preface); Corderius, *In Librum Job* (SSCC, Vol. XIII [Paris, 1861]), preface; Joannes de Pineda, *Commentariorum in Job* (3 vols.; Venice, 1608), I, 10 (preface).

CHAPTER X

1. See above, pp. 185–86. It ought to be noted that in Milton's view the Kingdom of Grace, the church, is the invisible church, that is, the whole community of the saved rather than any particular sect or national church. See *De Doctrina, CE* XVI, 57–65; XV, 297–303.

2. Michael Fixler, *Milton and the Kingdoms of God* (London, 1964), pp. 265–66.

3. Arnold Stein, *Heroic Knowledge* (Minneapolis, 1957), pp. 83–88.

4. I and II Maccabees; "Maccabaeus," *Encyclopaedia Britannica*, 14th ed., Vol. XIV; Milton, *Defensio, CE* VII, 239–45.

5. See for example: *Biblia Pauperum*, ed. Jean Philibert Berjeau (London, 1859), fig. xv; cf. Louis Reau, *Iconographie de l'Art Chrétien* (3 vols.; Paris, 1956), II, 304–5; *Bible, Moralized* I (Harley MSS, 1526–27, British Museum), fol. 5; Luther, Preface to I Maccabees (1530), in "Luther's Prefaces to the Old Testament Apocryphal Books," trans. George F. Hall, *Augustana Quarterly* (July, 1934), p. 205; Henry More, *An Illustration of Those Two Abstreuse Books in Holy Scripture . . . Daniel, and . . . Revelation* (London, 1685), p. 96 (notes to Dan. viii:9–12); Jerome, *Commentariorum in Danielem,* Pat. Lat. XXV, 569; Geneva Bible, fol. 100 (notes to Dan. viii:9–12); Douay Bible II, 793–94 (note to Dan. viii:9).

6. John Diodati, *Pious and Learned Annotations upon the Holy Bible* (London, 1648), p. 592 (argument to Daniel).

7. John Calvin, *Commentaries . . . upon . . . Daniell,* trans. A[rthur] G[olding] (London, 1570), sig. B3ᵛ (preface); Milton, *Defensio, CE* VII, 239.

8. Luther, Preface to I Maccabees, in "Luther's Prefaces to . . . Apocryphal Books," p. 205.

9. Calvin, *A Commentarie...upon the Booke of Josue,* trans. W. F. [William Fulke?] (London, 1587), fol. 29ᵛ.

10. Geneva Bible, fol. 104 (note to I Sam. xvi:18); Milton, *Eikonoklastes, CE* V, 278.

11. Lightfoot, *The Harmony of the Foure Evangelists* (2 vols.; London, 1644, 1647), II, 29.

12. Matteo Maria Boiardo, *Orlando Innamorato* I.x (Venice, 1538), sigs. N7–O3.

13. Geneva Bible, fols. 104ᵛ–105 (notes to Dan. ii:31 ff.); Calvin, *Commentaries...upon...Daniell,* fols. 13ᵛ–14ᵛ; Douay Bible II, 772–76 (notes to Dan. ii:29–33); Daniel Brenius, "De Regno Ecclesiae Glorioso," *Opera Theologica* (Amsterdam, 1666), fol. 6.

14. Jerome, *Commentariorum in Danielem,* Pat. Lat. XXV, 528; Jerome commenting on Dan. vii:4, identified the first beast with wings of an eagle as Assyria and in the stage with his wings plucked as Chaldaea (Babylon); he also identified the first beast with the golden head of the Image. Cf. Augustine, *City of God* XX.23, trans. Marcus Dods (New York, 1950), p. 748.

15. Schultz, "Christ and Antichrist in *Paradise Regained,*" *PMLA,* LXVII (1952), 804–5.

16. *CE* VI, 22.

17. Augustine, *Enarrationes in Psalmos,* Pat. Lat. XXXVI, 302; *Glossa Ordinaria,* Pat. Lat. CXIII, 556; Isidore, *Allegoriae Quaedam Sacrae Scripturae,* Pat. Lat. LXXXIII, 112; Ambrose, *Expositio super Septem Visiones Libri Apocalypsis,* Pat. Lat. XVII, 833–34; Bede, *Quaestiones super Regum Libros,* Pat. Lat. XCIII, 451–52; [Prosper], *De Promissionibus,* Pat. Lat. LI, 799–801.

18. Augustine, "Psalm CXXVI," *Enarrationes in Psalmos,* Pat. Lat. XXXVII, 1668: "Quia et iste Salomon aedificaverat templum Domino (*Id.* vi), in typo quidem et in figura futurae Ecclesiae et corporis Domini...quia ergo ipse aedificaverat illud templum, aedificavit sibi templum verus Salomon Dominus noster Jesus Christus, verus pacificus."

19. E. M. W. Tillyard, *Milton* (London, 1930), p. 306.

20. Augustine, "On the Catechising of the Uninstructed" XX.36; XXI.38, trans. S. D. Salmond, *Works,* ed. Marcus Dods (15 vols.; [Edinburgh, 1871–76]), IX, 315, 317–18.

21. Augustine, *City of God* XV.5, p. 482.

22. *CE* III, Part I, 54–55.

23. William Perkins, *The Combate betweene Christ and the Devill Expounded, Workes* (3 vols.; Cambridge, Eng., 1616–18), III, 399.

24. Lightfoot, *Harmony of...Evangelists* II, 30–32.

25. *Ibid.,* I, 130

26. *The Dutch Annotations upon the Whole Bible,* trans. Theodore Haak (London, 1657), notes to Dan. ii:44–45.

27. Geneva Bible, fol. 104^V (notes to Dan. ii:44–45).

28. Cyprian, "Testimonies against the Jews," *The Genuine Works of St. Cyprian,* trans. Nath. Marshall (London, 1707), pp. 39–40; cf. Cassiodorus, *Expositio in Psalterium,* Pat. Lat. LXX, 1015.

CHAPTER XI

1. On the basis of Acts vii:22, Moses was declared to be "learned in all the wisdom of the Egyptians," for example by Clement, in *Stromata* I.xxiii, trans. William Wilson (ANCL, Vol. IV [Edinburgh, 1867]), p. 451. On the basis of Dan. i:4, Daniel was declared to be knowledgeable in the "learning and the tongues" of the Babylonians, for example by Robert Boyle, in *Some Considerations touching the Style of the H. Scriptures* (London, 1661), pp. 162–63. For the traditions regarding Job's learning see above, p. 26.

2. Adams, *IKON: John Milton and the Modern Critics* (Ithaca, N.Y., 1955), p. 127; Watkins, *An Anatomy of Milton's Verse* (Baton Rouge, La., 1955), p. 124; Bush, *The Renaissance and English Humanism* (Toronto, 1939), p. 125; Sensabaugh, "Milton on Learning," *SP,* XLIII (1946), 258–72; Tillyard, *Milton* (London, 1930), p. 309.

3. Schultz, *Milton and Forbidden Knowledge* (New York, 1955), p. 233.

4. Schultz himself notes that the passages on wealth, ambition, and glory "make sense as ethics," and he does not fit them very successfully into the ecclesiastical framework, "Christ and Antichrist in *Paradise Regained,*" *PMLA,* LXVII (1952), 802. Also, Milton's theological treatise *De Doctrina* repudiates the sharp distinction Schultz posits between ministers and laity in the church (*CE* XVI, 245–49).

5. *CE* VI, 93.

6. *CE* VI, 75.

7. *CE* XVI, 263–65.

8. Lewalski, "Milton on Learning and the Learned-Ministry Controversy," *Huntington Library Quarterly,* XXIV (1961), 267–81. It must always be remembered that for Milton the illumination of the Spirit is not an extraordinary private revelation, but the normal accompaniment of the careful, attentive study of Scripture. As he indicates in *De Doctrina:* "I entered upon an assiduous course of study in my youth, beginning with the books of the Old and New Testament in their original languages, and going diligently through a few of the shorter systems of divines ... It was ... evident to me, that, in religion as in other things, the offers of God were all directed, not to an indolent credulity, but to constant diligence, and to an unwearied search after truth" (*CE* XIV, 5–9).

9. Ulrich Zwingli, *A Short Pathwaye to the Ryghte and True Understanding of the Holye and Sacred Scriptures,* trans. Jhon Veron (Worcester, Eng., 1550), sigs. F6^V–F7, H6^V–L8^V.

10. [Joshua Sprigge], *The Ancient Bounds, or Liberty of Conscience Tenderly Stated, Modestly Asserted, and Mildly Vindicated* (London, 1645), p. 41. For attribution see Barbara Kiefer (Lewalski), "The Authorship of *Ancient Bounds*," *Church History*, XXII (1953), 192–96.

11. How, *The Sufficiencie of the Spirits Teaching without Humane Learning* ([London], 1640), sig. C4^v. In his tract *Of Education* Milton gave precisely the same definition as How gives here of the function of learning in the natural order: "The end then of Learning is to repair the ruines of our first Parents by regaining to know God aright" (*CE* IV, 277). These similar statements ought to demonstrate that for Milton also the repudiation of the doctrines of human learning in the area of spiritual revelation does not extend to a repudiation of learning in the natural order.

12. For this range of opinion see the Presbyterian tract by Edward Reynolds, *A Sermon touching the Use of Humane Learning* (London, 1658 [1657]), pp. 15–22, and the Fifth Monarchist tract of John Canne, *The Time of Finding* (London, 1658).

13. Augustine, *City of God* VIII.4, trans. Marcus Dods (New York, 1950), p. 247.

14. Cicero, *De Natura Deorum; Academica* I.iv.15, trans. II. Rackham (Loeb [London, 1933]), p. 425.

15. Eugene R. Rice, Jr., *The Renaissance Idea of Wisdom* (Cambridge, Mass., 1958), pp. 1–92.

16. *Ibid.*, pp. 1–3.

17. Augustine, *De Trinitate* XII.xiv.22, Pat. Lat. XLII, 1010. The Septuagint version, *Septuaginta*, ed. Alfred Rahlfs (2 vols.; Stuttgart, 1935), II, 317, has the following:
'Ιδοὺ ἡ θεοσέβειά ἐστιν σοφία,/ τὸ δὲ ἀπέχεσθαι ἀπὸ κακῶν ἐστιν ἐπιστήμη. The Junius-Tremellius Latin Bible (Biblia Sacra, London, 1585, p. 27, Job) reads: "En reverentia domini est sapientia: & recedere à malo, intelligentia."

18. Augustine, *De Trinitate* XII.xiv.22–23, trans. A. W. Haddan, in *Works*, ed. Marcus Dods (Edinburgh, 1877), VII, 302–3.

19. Rice, *Renaissance Idea of Wisdom*, pp. 1–23, 58–68, 128–29.

20. Vives, *Introduction to Wisedome*, trans. [Sir R. Morison] (London [1575?]), sigs. G6^v, N7–N7^v.

21. Francisco Filelfo, *De Morali Disciplina*, Book II (Venice, 1552), pp. 26–27: "Atqué illa quidem sapientiae est, qua aeterna, & incommutabilia contemplamur. Inferior verò scientiae, qua in rerum temporalium, ac mutabilium actione versamur. Scientia enim, non parum differt à sapientia, ut à contemplatione actio. Id quod etiam eruditissimus ille vir, sanctissimusque; Apostolus Paulus non obscuré ostendit, cum ait; Alii quidem per Spiritum datur sermo sapientiae, alii sermo scientiae secundum eundem spiritum. Idem quóque manifesto docet innocentissimus ille Job, inquiens; Ecce pietas est sapientia, abstinere autem malis scientia est. Qua certè distinctione liquidò

declaratur, & sapientiam esse contemplationis, & scientiam actionis. Pietas enim hoc loco ea est virtus, qua DEUM colimus.... Scientia, enim, quae in huius exercendae temporalis vitae praeceptis est posita."

22. John Calvin, *Sermons ... upon ... Job,* trans. Arthur Golding (London, 1574), p. 479.

23. Trapp, *Annotations upon the Old and New Testament* (5 vols.; London, 1654–62), II, 239; Caryl, *Exposition ... upon Job* (12 vols.; London, 1643–70), VIII, 359, 362.

24. See above, pp. 172–74.

25. Schultz argues (*Forbidden Knowledge,* p. 95) that it is largely because of the angry tone that the learning passage in *Paradise Regained* cannot be read as mere commonplace, and that it must therefore be either a manifestation of Milton's greatly changed ideas about learning, or else simply an argument addressed to the learned-ministry question.

26. Lactantius, "A Treatise on the Anger of God," trans. William Fletcher (ANCL, Vol. XXII [Edinburgh, 1871]), pp. 1–2.

27. Luther, *Colloquia Mensalia,* trans. Henrie Bell (London, 1652), p. 501.

28. Peter Martyr [Vermigli], *Common Places,* Part II (London, 1583), p. 302.

29. Culverwel, *An Elegant and Learned Discourse of the Light of Nature* (London, 1652), pp. 128, 203–4.

30. Anon., *An Exposition touching Al the Bokes of Holie Scripture, and Their Excellencie* (London, 1553), sigs. D4–D4^V.

31. Edna Newmeyer, "Beza and Milton," *Bulletin of the New York Public Library,* LXVI (1962), 485–97.

32. Beza, *Job Expounded,* trans. ? (London [1589?]), sigs. B6–B6^V, C7, B2 (preface).

33. Quarles, *Job Militant* (London, 1624), sigs. I2^V–I3.

34. See above, pp. 40–101.

35. *CE* III, Part I, 238.

36. *CE* VII, 75–103, 267. Henry Bullinger, *Fiftie Godlie and Learned Sermons,* trans. H. I. (London, 1587), p. 10, offers an interesting analogue for this comparison.

37. Smith, "Discourse ... of Prophesie," *Select Discourses* (London, 1660), p. 179.

38. Plato, *Apology* 23*a*–*b,* in *The Dialogues,* trans. Benjamin Jowett (5 vols.; Oxford, 1953), I, 347.

CHAPTER XII

1. *CE* XVII, 247–53.

2. Eusebius of Caesarea, *The Proof of the Gospel, Being the Demonstratio Evangelica,* trans. W. J. Ferrar (2 vols.; London, 1920), II, 165–69; see Jerome, *Commentariorum in Matthaeum, Opera* (5 vols.; Paris, 1693-1706), II, 12; John Mayer, *A Commentary upon the Holy Writings of Job, David, and Solomon* (London, 1653), p. 418.

3. See above, pp. 177–78. See also Geneva Bible, fol. 3ᵛ (note to Matt. iv:5); John Udall, *The Combate betwixt Christ and the Devill* (London [1590?]), sig. F8ᵛ; Thomas Taylor, *Christs Combate and Conquest* (London, 1618), pp. 188–90, 218.

4. Taylor, *Christs Combate*, pp. 154, 190.

5. Trapp, *Annotations upon the Old and New Testament* (5 vols.; London, 1654–62), V, 35. Cf. Matthew Poole, *Annotations* II (London, 1685), notes to Matt. iv; Christopher Blackwood, *Expositions and Sermons upon . . . Matthew* (London, 1659), pp. 97–98; Thomas White, ΠΑΝΘΕΟΛΟΓΙΑ (London, 1654), p. 15.

6. See for example: Geneva Bible, fol. 3ᵛ (note to Matt. iv:5); William Perkins, *The Combate betweene Christ and the Devill Expounded, Workes* (3 vols.; Cambridge, Eng., 1616–18), III, 390; Cornelius à Lapide, *Commentarius in Quatuor Evanglia* (Antwerp, 1732), p. 104.

7. See J. F. Senault, *The Pattern of Patience, in the Example of Holy Job* (London, 1657), sig. A4; Theodore Beza, *Job Expounded,* trans.? (London [1589?]), sig. A2ᵛ (epis. ded.).

8. Chrysostom, "Homily VIII. Philippians ii:12–16," ed. Philip Schaff (Nicene and Post-Nicene Fathers, 1st ser., Vol. XIII [New York, 1889]), p. 222.

9. See above, pp. 18–20, for Protestant interpretations of these laments as evidences of weakness and sin.

10. John Diodati, *Pious and Learned Annotations upon the Holy Bible* (London, 1648), pp. 2–3 (argument to Matthew).

11. See above, pp. 178–80. See especially Origen?, *In Job Commentarius, Opera,* ed. Charles Delarue (4 vols.; Paris, 1733–59), II, 870; Gregory the Great, *Moralia in Job* (LF, Vol. XVIII [Oxford, 1844]), p. 26; Hieremias Drexelius, *Jobus Divinae* (Antwerp, 1655), p. 67; Calvin, *Sermons . . . upon . . . Job,* trans. Arthur Golding (London, 1574), pp. 9–10, 746–47; George Hutcheson, *An Exposition of the Book of Job* (London, 1669), p. 449; Trapp, *Annotations* II, 360.

12. Perkins, *Combate, Workes* III, 388; Diodati, *Annotations,* p. 7 (note to Matt iv·5)

13. Taylor, *Christs Combate*, pp. 161–62.

14. Hall, *Contemplations upon . . . the New Testament, Works* (3 vols.; London, 1628–62), III, 40.

15. Knox, *An Exposition upon Matthew IV, Works,* ed. David Laing (6 vols.; Edinburgh, 1846–64), IV, 110.

16. Aquinas, *Summa Theologica,* Pt. III, Q. 41, Art. 4, trans. Dominican Fathers (3 vols.; New York, 1947–48), II, 2243; cf. Perkins, *Combate, Workes* III, 407; Diodati, *Annotations,* p. 59 (note to Luke iv:13).

17. Diodati, *Annotations,* p. 75 (note to Luke xxii:53); Taylor, *Christs Combate,* p. 190.

18. Diodati, *Annotations,* p. 103 (note to John xiv:30); the biblical passage reads: "the prince of this world commeth, and hath nothing in me."

19. See above, p. 128.

20. Lancelot Andrewes, *The Wonderfull Combate betweene Christ and Satan* (London, 1592); E. Cleveland, "On the Identity Motive in *Paradise Regained*," *MLQ*, XVI (1955), pp. 235–36, has also noted adumbrations of the Crucifixion in the tower episode.

21. Howard Schultz, "Christ and Antichrist in *Paradise Regained*," *PMLA*, LXVII (1952), 806–7.

22. *Be Domes Daege*, ll. 98–101, in Charles W. Kennedy, ed., *Early English Christian Poetry* (London, 1952), p. 261.

23. Taylor, "The Storm Scene in *Paradise Regained*: A Reinterpretation," *UTQ*, XXIV (1954–55), pp. 359–76, argues that belief in false portents is the essence of this temptation, but it seems rather that this aspect is subordinate to Satan's general strategy of terror.

24. See above, pp. 225–41.

25. Lucan, *The Civil War* IV.633–45, trans. J. D. Duff (Loeb [London, 1928]), pp. 219–23. Cf. George Sandys, ed., *Ovid's Metamorphosis Englished, Mythologiz'd, and Represented in Figures* (Oxford, 1632), pp. 321–22; Albricus, *De Deorum Imaginibus* (Basle, 1570), p. 169; G. H. Bode, ed., *Scriptores Rerum Mythicarum Latini Tres* (2 vols.; Celles, 1834), p. 247.

26. See Natale Comes (Conti), *Mythologiae: Sive Explicationis Fabularum* (London, 1605), p. 1007; Palaephatus, *De Fabulis* (Basle, 1536), pp. 96–97.

27. John Lightfoot, *The Harmony of the Foure Evangelists* (2 vols.; London, 1644, 1647), II, 41.

28. I have italicized adverbs and verbs denoting time.

29. I have italicized adverbs and verbs denoting time.

CHAPTER XIII

1. Anne D. Ferry, *Milton's Epic Voice* (Cambridge, Mass., 1963), has recently re-emphasized this point with reference to *Paradise Lost* and has analyzed the epic narrator of that poem.

2. *PL* I.29; IV.492, 495, 659; IX.644; X.1097.

3. See especially *PL* III.13–26.

4. See for example, A. J. A. Waldock, *Paradise Lost and Its Critics* (Cambridge, Eng., 1959), pp. 77–92.

5. E. M. W. Tillyard, *Milton* (London, 1930), p. 306.

6. Louis L. Martz, "*Paradise Regained*: The Meditative Combat," *ELH*, XXVII (1960), 246–47.

7. Daniells, *Milton, Mannerism and Baroque* (Toronto, 1963), pp. 194–208.

8. See above, pp. 256–57, for discussion of this point.

9. Muir, *John Milton* (London, 1955), p. 167; Martz, "Meditative Combat," pp. 223–28.

10. *PR* II.19–24, 183–91, 351–61; III.269–93, 316–21; IV.67–79.

11. For analysis of the epic simile in *Paradise Lost* see especially James

Whaler, "The Miltonic Simile," *PMLA,* XLVI (1931), 1034–74; Whaler, "Compounding and Distribution of Similes in *Paradise Lost,*" *MP,* XXVIII (1930–31), 313–27; Whaler, "Grammatical *Nexus* of the Miltonic Simile," *JEPG,* XXX (1931), 327–34; L. D. Lerner, "The Miltonic Simile," *Essays in Criticism,* IV (1954), 297–308. See also Roberts B. French, "Verbal Irony in *Paradise Lost,*" (Ph.D. dissertation, Brown University, 1964).

12. See above, pp. 318–19.

13. It is perhaps not oversubtle to see the image of the bird soaring above his ground nest as a symbol of Christ in the forthcoming temptations dissociating himself from all earthly restraints and finally realizing his divine nature fully when he himself "towers" in air.

14. Italics mine.

15. Lee S. Cox, "Food-Word Imagery in *Paradise Regained,*" *ELH,* XXVIII (1961), 225–43.

16. Ricks, *Milton's Grand Style* (Oxford, 1963). See also F. T. Prince, *The Italian Element in Milton's Verse* (Oxford, 1954).

17. Here and subsequently in quoting from the poem I have italicized words under discussion for clarity of reference.

18. Definitions here and subsequently are taken from the *OED.*

19. See John E. Parish, "An Unrecognized Pun in *Paradise Regained,*" *N&Q,* CCIX (1964), 337.

20. Tillyard, *Milton,* p. 316; Eliot, "Milton" (1947), *Milton Criticism,* ed. James Thorpe (London, 1956), p. 324. See also Donald Davie, "Syntax and Music in *Paradise Lost,*" *The Living Milton,* ed. Frank Kermode (London, 1960), pp. 70–84.

21. Martz, "Meditative Combat," p. 227.

22. J. B. Broadbent, "Milton's Rhetoric," *MP,* LVI (1958–59), 228.

23. Ricks, *Grand Style,* pp. 78–109.

24. [Puttenham?], *The Arte of English Poesie* (1589), III.xix, ed. G. D. Willcock and Alice Walker (Cambridge, Eng., 1936), pp. 196–97. Subsequent definitions of rhetorical schemes are drawn chiefly from Puttenham and from Henry Peacham, *The Garden of Eloquence* (1593), ed. William G. Crane (facsimile; Gainesville, Fla., 1954).

25. Broadbent, "Milton's Rhetoric," p. 229.

26. Puttenham's definition; Peacham defines it more narrowly.

27. See for example: Arnold Stein, *Heroic Knowledge* (Minneapolis, 1957), pp. 83–84; Cleanth Brooks and J. E. Hardy, *Poems of Mr. John Milton* (New York, 1951), p. 280.

28. S. T. Coleridge, *Lectures and Notes on Shakespeare and Other English Poets,* ed. T. Ashe (London, 1914), p. 527.

INDEX

INDEX TO AUTHORS AND TITLES

Most works are indexed under their authors or probable authors; short titles are used for many works. Anonymous works are indexed under their titles. Cross references are made from the names of certain editors and translators to authors or, in the case of anonymous works, to titles. References to notes (in parentheses following the text page number) are given only when the title and/or author does not appear on the text page.